RELIGION AND SOCIETY
IN
LATIN AMERICA

RELIGION AND SOCIETY IN LATIN AMERICA

*Interpretative Essays
from Conquest to Present*

Lee M. Penyak and Walter J. Petry, editors

ORBIS BOOKS

Maryknoll, New York 10545

Founded in 1970, Orbis Books endeavors to publish works that enlighten the mind, nourish the spirit, and challenge the conscience. The publishing arm of the Maryknoll Fathers and Brothers, Orbis seeks to explore the global dimensions of the Christian faith and mission, to invite dialogue with diverse cultures, and religious traditions, and to serve the cause of reconciliation and peace. The books published reflect the views of their authors and do not represent the official position of the Maryknoll Society. To learn more about Maryknoll and Orbis Books, please visit our website at www.maryknollsociety.org.

Library of Congress Cataloging-in-Publication Data

Religion and society in Latin America : interpretive essays from conquest to present /
by Lee M. Penyak & Walter J. Petry, editors.
     p. cm.
    Includes index.
    ISBN 978-1-57075-850-8 (pbk.)
      1. Latin America – Church history. 2. Latin America – Religion. 3. Christianity and culture –
Latin America. 4. Latin America – Religious life and customs. I. Penyak, Lee M. II. Petry,
Walter J.
BR600.R385 2009
200.98 – dc22

                              2009008809

Dedicated to the sisters of the Daughters of Charity
at Santa Luisa School in San Salvador
for their vocation of service to
"the poorest of the poor"

Contents

Maps and Tables

Maps

Tables

Acknowledgments

Robert Mahony's superb line-editing skills immeasurably improved the entire book. Susan Perry and Catherine Costello at Orbis Books made excellent editorial suggestions. William M. Abbott, Richard Boyer, Ralph Coury, and Chris Lowney provided helpful comments on earlier drafts of chapter 1. Paul Lakeland proffered insightful recommendations on liberation theology that the editors relayed to contributors. Robert A. Parsons translated select phrases in Spanish. Robert Ball eased author-editor revisions to chapter 14. Aileen McHale of Scranton's Center for Teaching and Learning Excellence facilitated document imaging, an activity carried out by Jeffrey M. Nunes and Derek Gelormini. Betsey Moylan, Kevin Norris, Magdalene Restuccia, and Sheila Ferraro at Scranton's Harry and Jeanette Weinberg Memorial Library secured secondary documents. Hillel Arnold and Germán A. Zárate-Sández gave technical assistance. We especially thank the authors who contributed to this collection for their patience and understanding with our heavy-handed editing style.

Lee M. Penyak   Walter J. Petry
South Abington Township, Pa.   New York, N.Y.

About the Contributors

R. ANDREW CHESNUT is the Bishop Sullivan Chair of Catholic Studies at Virginia Commonwealth University. His research focuses on religion in twentieth-century Latin American history. His first book, *Born in Brazil: The Pentecostal Boom and the Pathogens of Poverty* (2007), examines the meteoric growth of Pentecostalism among the popular classes of Brazil. His second book, *Competitive Spirits: Latin America's New Religious Economy* (2003), considers the three religious groups that have prospered the most in the region's new pluralist landscape. His current research focuses on the Virgin of Guadalupe in Spain, Mexico, and the United States.

JOHN F. CHUCHIAK is Associate Professor of Colonial Latin American History, the holder of the Young Honors College endowed professorship, and the Director of the Latin American, Caribbean, and Hispanic Studies program at Missouri State University. His research interests include the history of the Catholic Church, the Inquisition, ecclesiastical courts in colonial Mexico, and the colonial ethnohistory of Maya culture and religion. His articles have appeared in the *Journal of Early Modern History*, the *Journal of Ethnohistory*, and *The Americas*, among others. He is the author of *The Holy Office of the Inquisition in New Spain: A Documentary History* (Forthcoming, 2010).

GROVER ANTONIO ESPINOZA is Assistant Professor of Latin American History at Virginia Commonwealth University. He earned his Ph.D. at Columbia University in 2007 with a dissertation on primary education and state-building in Peru from the early nineteenth to the early twentieth centuries. His research so far has focused on the intersection of politics and society in the educational realm, having published several articles in both compilations and specialized journals. He is currently beginning to study the influence of U.S. foreign policy and aid on peasant education in the Andes during the twentieth century.

VIRGINIA GARRARD-BURNETT is Associate Professor of History, Religious Studies, and Latin American Studies at the University of Texas, Austin. She earned an M.A. in Latin American Studies and a Ph.D. in history from Tulane University. She is the author of three books and more than two dozen articles on religion in Latin America. Her most recent book is *Terror in the Land of the Holy Spirit: Guatemala under General Efraín Ríos Montt, 1982–83* (Oxford, 2009).

LINDSAY HALE teaches anthropology at the University of Texas at Austin, where he earned his Ph.D. in 1994. His research explores the contested fields of race, class, gender, and power in the Umbanda religion in Rio de Janeiro, focusing especially on the aesthetic, sensual, and autobiographical dimensions of ritual performance and narrative. His work has appeared in *American Ethnologist* and several edited volumes. He is the author of *Hearing the Mermaid's Song: The Umbanda Religion in Rio de Janeiro* (2009).

JACQUELINE HOLLER is Associate Professor of History/Women's Studies and Coordinator of Women's and Gender Studies Programs at the University of Northern British Columbia in Prince George, British Columbia. She is the author of *Escogidas Plantas: Nuns and Beatas in Mexico City* (Columbia University Press, 2005), which won the American Historical Association's Gutenberg-e Prize in 1999, and of articles on sixteenth-century New Spain. Her current projects include a study of women's mental and physical health, sexuality, and embodiment in early colonial New Spain, and a book project on the Cortés conspiracy of 1566.

JENNIFER S. HUGHES is Assistant Professor in the Department of Religious Studies at the University of California, Riverside, where she teaches courses on Latin American religion, religion and art, and global Christianities. Her book *The Biography of a Mexican Crucifix: Lived Religion and Local Faith from the Conquest to the Present* is forthcoming with Oxford University Press. Beyond her life as a scholar, she has worked as an advocate for homeless Latinos with HIV/AIDS, as a translator for Angolan refugees in South Africa, with the liberation theology movement in Brazil, and as a parish priest in the inner city United States.

JEFFREY KLAIBER is a Jesuit priest, Full Professor of History at the Catholic University of Peru and Antonio Ruiz de Montoya (Jesuit) University in Lima. His specialty is religion and politics in Latin America. He is the author of *Religion and Revolution in Peru* (1977), *The Catholic Church in Peru* (1992), and *The Church, Dictatorships, and Democracy in Latin America* (1998). He has also written on related subjects such as Protestantism and politics, the Jesuits, and human rights in Latin America.

KAREN MELVIN is Assistant Professor of History at Bates College in Lewiston, Maine. She received her Ph.D. from the University of California, Berkeley, in 2005 and is working on a book manuscript, "Building Colonial Cities of God," about mendicant orders and the creation of urban culture in New Spain between 1570 and 1800. She is a contributing editor to the *Handbook of Latin American Studies,* and her article "A Potential Saint Thwarted: The Politics of Religion and Sanctity in Late Eighteenth-Century New Spain" recently appeared in *Studies in Eighteenth Century Culture* (2006).

MONICA I. OROZCO is presently a visiting scholar at Westmont College in Santa Barbara, California. She received her Ph.D. in history from the University of California, Santa Barbara. Her research explores political and social aspects of U.S. Protestant evangelization in Mexico within the political milieu of Mexican liberalism and nationalism. Her current project focuses on the roles of women's missionary boards and Mexican women converts in the Protestant missionary movement in Mexico, 1870–1900.

REV. ROBERT S. PELTON, C.S.C, Ph.D. is Concurrent Professor of Theology, Fellow of the Helen Kellogg Institute for International Studies, and Director of Latin American/North American Church Concerns at the University of Notre Dame. One of the nation's foremost Latin American specialists, Father Pelton's major areas of expertise include the Catholic Church of the Americas, Small Christian Communities (CEBs), liberation theology, and the Cuban church.

LEE M. PENYAK is Associate Professor of History, Director of Latin American Studies, and a member of Women's Studies at the University of Scranton. He received his Ph.D. from the University of Connecticut. He is co-editor (with Walter J. Petry) of *Religion in Latin America: A Documentary History* (2006) and editor of *Vida y muerte de una cultura regional* (2007), which examines haciendas in San Luis Potosí. His articles have appeared in *Hispanic American Historical Review, The Americas,* and *The Historian,* among other journals. He is currently working on a book concerning the regulation of sexual behavior in Mexico from 1750 to 1850.

WALTER J. PETRY, Fairfield University emeritus, served in the history department and taught courses in European Thought and Culture with emphasis on the Enlightenment and Romanticism. He later taught Latin American history specializing in the colonial era and Mesoamerica and was sometime director of the Latin American and Caribbean studies and of the Black Studies programs. He has donated to the DiMenna-Nyselius Library at Fairfield his extensive collection of documents, journals, newspapers, propaganda, posters, and photos emanating from the revolutionary Sandinista years in Nicaragua. He is co-editor (with Lee M. Penyak) of *Religion in Latin America: A Documentary History* (2006).

JOHN F. SCHWALLER is currently Professor of History and President of the State University of New York at Potsdam. His first two books focused on the secular clergy in sixteenth-century Mexico and the financial underpinnings of the church. In more recent years he has studied the use of Nahuatl, the Aztec language, in the evangelization of Mexico. Along with Barry Sell, he translated and edited Bartolomé de Alva's *Guide to Confession* (1999). At present he is concluding a one-volume history of the Catholic Church in Latin America.

DAVID TAVÁREZ, Assistant Professor of Anthropology at Vassar College, is an ethnohistorian and linguistic anthropologist. His publications on colonial evangelization projects and Nahua and Zapotec religious practices include seven journal articles and ten book chapters; his forthcoming book on these topics is entitled *Invisible Wars: Clandestine Indigenous Devotions in Central Mexico*. He also co-authored a critical edition of *Chimalpahin's Conquest*, a Nahua historian's rewriting of the canonical conquest chronicle by López de Gómara. His research has been supported by the National Endowment for the Humanities, the Foundation for the Advancement of Mesoamerican Studies, and the National Science Foundation.

JAVIER VILLA-FLORES is Associate Professor at the University of Illinois at Chicago. He received his doctorate in Latin American history from the University of California, San Diego. His first book, *Carlo Ginzburg: The Historian as Theoretician* (University of Guadalajara, 1995), offered an epistemological discussion of the historian's craft focusing on Carlo Ginzburg's work. His second book, *Dangerous Speech: A Social History of Blasphemy in Colonial Mexico* (University of Arizona Press, 2006), analyzes the representation, prosecution, and punishment of blasphemous speech in New Spain from 1520 to 1700. He is also the author of several articles, book chapters, and encyclopedia articles.

NICOLE VON GERMETEN has a Ph.D. in history from Berkeley and teaches at Oregon State University. Her first book, *Black Blood Brothers: Confraternities and Social Mobility for Afromexicans* (2006), argues that Catholic brotherhoods helped preserve African identity and community for slaves in New Spain but also contributed to their improved status as free workers. Her second book is an annotated translation of Alonso de Sandoval's 1627 *De Instauranda Aethiopum Salute* (2008). This edition raises unusual questions about the history of slavery in Latin America and the role of Christianity in the formation of the Spanish empire, and also provides insights into early modern concepts of race.

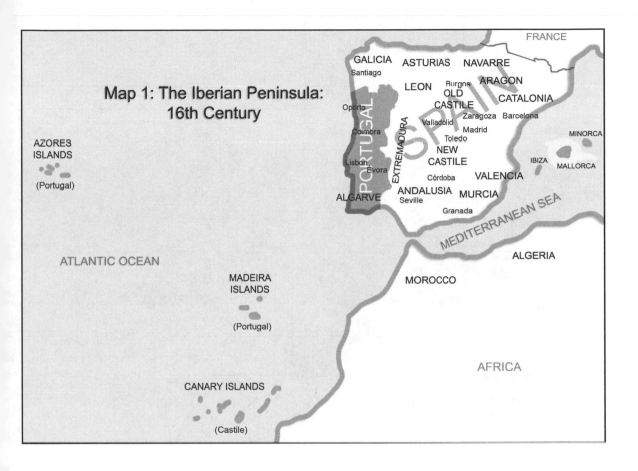

Map 1: The Iberian Peninsula: 16th Century

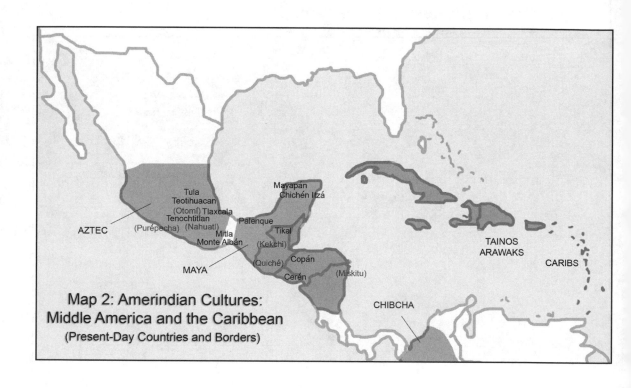

AZTEC

Tula
Teotihuacan
(Otomí) Tlaxcala
Tenochtitlan
(Purépecha) (Nahuatl)
Mitla
Monte Albán

MAYA

Palenque

Mayapan
Chichén Itzá

Tikal

(Kekchi)

(Quiché) Copán
Cerén (Miskitu)

TAINOS
ARAWAKS

CARIBS

CHIBCHA

Map 2: Amerindian Cultures:
Middle America and the Caribbean
(Present-Day Countries and Borders)

Map 3: Amerindian Cultures:
South America
(Present-Day Countries and Borders)

Caribs

Chibchas

Arawaks

MUISCA

Muras

Shuar

Chavin de Huantar

Huari

(Quechua)

Cuzco

Tiahuanaco

INCA

(Aymara)

(Guaraní)

Guaranies

TUPÍ-SPEAKING
INDIANS

Pampas

Mapuches
(Araucanians)

Patagones

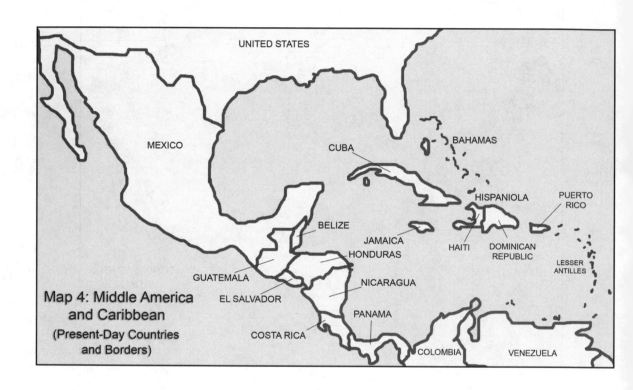

Map 4: Middle America and Caribbean (Present-Day Countries and Borders)

Map 5: South America
(Present-Day Countries and Borders)

Table 1: Religious Affiliation by Country: CIA Factbook, 2008 (1990)

Country	Catholic	Protestant	Other	None	Additional Information
Argentina	92* (90)	2	4		*Less than 20% practicing; Jewish 2%
Belize	50 (60)	27	14	9	Pentecostal 7%; Seventh-Day Adventist 5%; Jehovah's Witness, 2%
Bolivia	95 (95)	5*			*Evangelical Methodist
Brazil	76* (90)	15	2	7	*Nominal; Spiritualist 1%
Chile	70 (89)	16*	5	8	*Evangelical=15%; Jehovah's Witness, 1%
Colombia	90 (90)		10		
Costa Rica	76 (95)	14*	5	3	*Evangelical=14%; Jehovah's Witness, 1%
Cuba	85* (85)				*Nominal; Protestants, Jehovah's Witness, Jews, and Santería also exist
Dominican Republic	95 (95)		5		
Ecuador	95 (95)		5		
El Salvador	83 (97)		17		
Guatemala					Roman Catholic, Protestant, and indigenous Mayan beliefs
Haiti	80	16*	3	1	*Baptist 10%; Pentecostal 4%; about half of the population practices voodoo
Honduras	97 (97)	3			
Mexico	77 (97)	6	6	3	
Nicaragua	73 (95)	15*	2	8	*Evangelical; Moravian 2%
Panama	85 (93)	15			
Paraguay	90 (90)	6	3	1	
Peru	81		1	16*	*Unspecified or other; Seventh-Day Adventist 1%
Puerto Rico	85 (85)	15			
Uruguay	66* (66)	2	31		*Nominal; Jewish 1%
Venezuela	96 (96)	2	2		

Numbers in Table 1 are listed as percentages and have been rounded off. Statistics on religious affiliation are notoriously unreliable. Countries employ different methods to acquire information and devise different religious categories. Churches sometimes inflate membership statistics. Affiliation does not indicate active participation. Pentecostals may or may not be included in the category of Protestant. Percentages without parentheses are derived from *The World Factbook 2008* (Washington, D.C.: Central Intelligence Agency, 2008), *www.cia.gov/library/publications/the-world-factbook/fields/2122.html,* and percentages with parentheses are derived from *The World Factbook 1990* (Washington, D.C.: Central Intelligence Agency, 1990).

Table 2: Percentage of Catholics in Select Archdioceses: *Annuario Pontificio,* 1979, 2008

	1979	*2008*
Asunción, Paraguay	90.0	90.6
Bogotá, Colombia	96.8	85.7
Brasília, Brazil	91.7	68.6
Buenos Aires, Argentina	90.0	91.5
Caracas, Venezuela	88.0	85.0
Guadalajara, Mexico	94.0	91.0
Guatemala City, Guatemala	99.4	80.0
La Paz, Bolivia	92.0	86.5
Lima, Peru	96.0	89.9
Managua, Nicaragua	99.0	75.0
Medellín, Colombia	95.3	86.8
Mexico City, Mexico	95.0	87.1
Montevideo, Uruguay	75.8	49.8
Panama City, Panama	90.0	85.0
Port-au-Prince, Haiti	93.5	71.9
Quito, Ecuador	90.3	90.0
San Cristóbal de la Habana, Cuba	48.3	71.7*
San José, Costa Rica	97.5	73.2
San Juan, Puerto Rico	80.2	75.1
San Salvador, El Salvador	84.4	70.0
Santiago, Chile	81.8	69.4
Santiago, Cuba	–	23.9
Santo Domingo, Dominican Republic	93.9	94.4
São Paulo, Brazil	87.0	73.0
São Salvador da Bahia, Brazil	94.8	70.9
São Sebastião do Rio de Janeiro, Brazil	88.0	60.7
Tegucigalpa, Honduras	95.0	86.1

The percentages of Catholics in the twenty-seven archdioceses in Latin America, which include all the capitals of Latin American nations and a few other large cities, have been calculated from statistics printed in the official yearbook of the Roman Catholic Church, the *Annuario Pontificio.* Each year this Vatican publication gives a statistical profile of every diocese and archdiocese in the world, which includes the total population of the diocese or archdiocese and the number of baptized Catholics therein. Source: *Annuario Pontificio* (Città del Vaticano: Libreria Editrice Vaticana, 1979, 2008).

*Statistics for the Habana archdiocese vary wildly (from a likely figure of 47.3 percent in 1980 to an unlikely 96.4 percent in 2002) and inconsistently over the past thirty years, but since 2003 the average Catholic population is recorded at 72 percent.

Introduction

Five Hundred Years
of Evangelizing Latin America

LEE M. PENYAK AND WALTER J. PETRY

Faith in God has animated the life and culture of these nations for more than five centuries. From the encounter between that faith and the indigenous peoples, there has emerged the rich Christian culture of this Continent.... At present, this same faith has some serious challenges to address, because the harmonious development of society and the Catholic identity of these peoples are in jeopardy....

Yet what did the acceptance of the Christian faith mean for the nations of Latin America and the Caribbean? For them, it meant knowing and welcoming Christ, the unknown God whom their ancestors were seeking, without realizing it, in their rich religious traditions. Christ is the Saviour for whom they were silently longing.... In effect, the proclamation of Jesus and of his Gospel did not at any point involve an alienation of the pre-Columbian cultures, nor was it the imposition of a foreign culture. Authentic cultures are not closed in upon themselves, nor are they set in stone at a particular point in history, but they are open, or better still, they are seeking an encounter with other cultures, hoping to reach universality through encounter and dialogue with other ways of life and with elements that can lead to a new synthesis, in which the diversity of expressions is always respected as well as the diversity of their particular cultural embodiment....

The Utopia of going back to breathe life into the pre-Columbian religions, separating them from Christ and from the universal Church, would not be a step forward: indeed, it would be a step back. In reality, it would be a retreat toward a stage in history anchored in the past.

The wisdom of the indigenous peoples fortunately led them to form a synthesis between their cultures and the Christian faith which the missionaries were offering them. Hence the rich and profound popular religiosity, in which we see the soul of the Latin American peoples.[1]

Benedict XVI
Aparecida, Brazil
May 13, 2007

The contributors to this anthology seek to address many of the themes included in Pope Benedict's startling statement. What did the "acceptance" of the Christian faith mean for the peoples whom the Spanish and Portuguese colonizers confronted in what we now term "Latin America and the Caribbean"? In what ways did the beliefs of the indigenous and African peoples affect the Christian religion so many of them adopted? Is it accurate to assert that "the proclamation of Jesus and of his Gospel did not at any point involve an alienation of the pre-Columbian cultures, nor was it the imposition of a foreign culture"? If it may be sustained that indigenous (and African) peoples hope "to reach universality through encounter and dialogue with other ways of life and with elements that can lead to a new synthesis," is it because the Catholic Church has promoted dialogue and welcomed a diversity of religious expression in the region? What are current examples of the "profound popular religiosity" of the Latin American peoples and how have the pope and Catholic bishops of Latin America responded to it?

Several excellent collections on religious experience in Latin America have been published during the past ten years. John F. Schwaller's edited work, *The Church in Colonial Latin America* (2000), contains nine scholarly articles organized into three units on issues related to policy, parish, and culture, and concentrates on Mexico and the Andes from the conquest to independence. In examining "the dynamics of the Christian evangelization of the New World by the Spanish missionaries," these essays are particularly well suited to graduate students and others who already possess considerable knowledge of the political, economic, and social realities of Spanish imperial policy and missionary activities.[2] The nine chapters of Virginia Garrard-Burnett's *On Earth as It Is in Heaven: Religion in Modern Latin America* (2000) include sections on liberation theology, church-state relations in the nineteenth century, popular religion, Protestantism, and later twentieth-century developments in the Catholic Church. Subjects of individual chapters range from an old Jewish community in Mexico to the church in Nova Iguaçu, Brazil.[3]

Three recent collections consider such issues as religion and nation, Christianity and globalization, and contemporary conversion. Henry Goldschmidt and Elizabeth McAlister include twelve interdisciplinary studies in *Race, Nation, and Religion in the Americas* (2004). Topics such as "The Jews in Haitian Imagination" and "The Race of the Hindu in *United States v. Bhagat Singh Thind*" help the reader develop "a theoretical and methodological understanding of the complex ways such strategies [of race, nation, and religion] intersect in the construction of collective identity, difference, and hierarchy."[4] Post-1960 expressions of Christianity and the dynamic of globalization are emphasized in *Christianity, Social Change, and Globalization in the Americas* (2001), edited by Anna L. Peterson, Manuel A. Vásquez, and Philip J. Williams. Catholic (charismatic and liberationist) and Protestant (mainline and Pentecostal) Christianity are presented in case studies of El Salvador, Peru, and Washington, D.C., with a focus on social change "exacerbated by globalization . . . economic adjustments, transitions to democracy, and the resurgence of religion in the public sphere."[5] "Contemporary religious change" is the focus of *Conversion of a Continent* (2007), edited by Timothy J. Steigenga and Edward L. Cleary. The rise in influence of Pentecostalism, African-based religions, and charismatic Catholicism prompted these editors to include thirteen chapters that evaluate religious expression so that the reasons for conversion during the previous two decades could be better understood.[6]

Faced with the annual conundrum of selecting required books for students in courses that consider religion and society in Latin America, we have assigned the abovementioned works in whole or in part to students and have used them to formulate our own understanding of religious developments in Latin America. But undergraduate students frequently lamented that, while they had learned interesting details about select communities and new scholarly approaches to understanding religion, they were left asking basic questions about the subject matter itself: Why did the Spaniards assume they had the right to appropriation? What were the daily activities of priests and nuns? How did the Inquisition operate? Why did nineteenth-century liberals attack the Catholic Church with such vehemence? Why has Pentecostalism grown at an increasingly rapid rate in Latin America? What is the state of the Catholic Church today in the region? The success of our *Religion in Latin America: A Documentary History* (Orbis Books, 2006) further convinced us of the need to publish a companion book that provided detailed explanations of the same general themes as in our anthology. While we have our own interests and strengths in the field, we knew that we would have to call upon experts to help us provide answers to the aforementioned questions as well as discussions of other basic aspects of religion in Latin America. Assembling a team of contributors with recognized expertise who could write clear prose, devoid of jargon, was our goal. We hope this edited work stands as a testament to the efforts of these contributors and their commitment as educators.

The Right to Appropriate

Penyak and Petry coauthored the first chapter on Spanish Christendom and the Conquest. Our goal was to provide the core assumptions the Iberians brought with them to the New World and to place the "spiritual conquests" of Spanish and Portuguese America into proper historical context. We believe that quoting frequently from documents of the era strongly contributes to these ends. The essay begins with an explanation of the marriage of state and church on the Iberian peninsula, the reasons for this alliance, and the ways in which it proved mutually beneficial. We posit, clearly but nonjudgmentally, that late medieval Spain and Portugal, like the "West" as a whole, were authoritarian, hierarchical, classist, intolerant, materialist, warlike, *and* religious. Further, conquistadores and colonizers carried these attitudes to the New World and purposely constructed societies that privileged white Spaniards and their creole progeny and permanently disadvantaged Amerindians and people of color. We describe "the patriotic myth" that grew out of the Christian symbols dear to the emerging nation of Castile and the epic literature that exemplified the Iberian values of bravery, skill, and honor. We record the use of the Holy Office of the Inquisition as a political and religious tool of empire. We examine the conquest of the Canary Islands and view the enslavement of its populations for labor on sugar plantations on land taken from the natives as a precursor to later developments in the New World. We continue with the institution of African slavery and the slave trade, sanctioned by the church and distinct from its medieval variant because of its new identification with the color black. The essay ends with a discussion of the Spaniards' preoccupation with law and their need to rationalize Spain's imperialist ventures via philosophical and ethical disquisitions. We contend that these historical events and cultural beliefs culminated in a dual vision shared by most Iberians: the right of appropriation and the duty to evangelize.

Friars' Accounts

Chapter 2, by John F. Schwaller, affords the reader the opportunity to appreciate the extraordinarily difficult task missionaries faced as they attempted to learn Nahuatl, Maya, Quechua, and other native languages and thus communicate Christian tenets to indigenous peoples. Not focusing on the nature of conversion per se (treated in the following essay by Tavárez and Chuchiak), Schwaller's essay illuminates the process and stages by which missionaries "acquired knowledge of the natives." To that end, he sheds light on their production and development of grammars and bilingual dictionaries, catechisms in native languages, and finally their ethnographic and anthropological studies on pre-Columbian native religious practices and beliefs. The reader quickly recognizes the supreme efforts of Franciscans such as Toribio de Benavente, Andrés de Olmos, Alonso de Molina, and Bernardino de Sahagún. Their writings remain definitive sources even today; Molina's dictionary of Nahuatl and Sahagún's *Florentine Codex* are cornucopias of the culture and history of the Nahua. As Schwaller underscores, however, other missionaries in different regions of Spanish America did not demonstrate the same interest in producing detailed ethnographic studies. The author, for example, skillfully explores the complex history of Franciscan Diego de Landa, long maligned by scholars for his role in the torturing of Maya for apostasy and ordering the destruction of their books and artifacts. He argues forcefully that Landa's *Relación de las cosas de Yucatan* provides a thorough account of Maya culture prior to contact and during the sixteenth century and is now appreciated for its accurate insights into Maya language. We hope this essay prompts students (1) to consider the difficulties inherent in teaching Catholicism to peoples who followed radically different belief systems prior to contact and (2) to explore the various motives of select friars for compiling dictionaries. The missionaries, of course, were convinced that Spain had been given the providential mission to bring Christianity and European civilization to the heathen Amerindians. How much value, if any, according to Schwaller's account, did they attach to Amerindian cultures?

The Spiritual Conquest

Like Schwaller, David Tavárez and John F. Chuchiak elaborate on language obstacles to evangelization. They provide critical insight on the use of pictograms, the coupling of Latin and Nahuatl words to convey religious concepts, and efforts by missionaries to learn indigenous languages in order to teach Catholic doctrine. In the process they expand the scholarly discourse on conversion and the spiritual conquest. As one of their subheadings ("From Utopia to Debates on Rationality") suggests, moreover, they emphasize competing missionary mentalities concerning "proper" and "effective" religious instruction and conclude that optimistic assessments by Spaniards for rapid evangelization were largely spent by the end of the sixteenth century. Their essay reminds us that most Spanish conquistadores, including Hernán Cortés, considered the spread of Christianity an integral component of the conquest. While the crown initially charged the regular clergy with the task of converting Amerindians to Christianity, conversion strategies varied among and within the orders. The authors expertly assess the conundrums faced by the clergy: Should Indians be persuaded or forced to convert? Should they be baptized prior to comprehending the intricacies of their new religion or baptized en masse? Should friars deal with apostasy harshly or benignly? Should Indians be permitted to take holy orders? How should the clergy deal with "hybrid" Christian devotions and the pairing of Christian saints with indigenous deities? The reader should be prepared to weigh the various motives for acceptance, rejection, or accommodation of Catholicism by indigenous peoples. Given the brutality of the conquests, the reader may desire to speculate upon the authors' contention that, ultimately, "indigenous communities developed strong and often intimate links with the Catholic Church and its many agents."

Afro-Latin Americans

Following chapters 2 and 3, which consider the extraordinary efforts made by early missionaries to proselytize Amerindians, Nicole von Germeten and Javier Villa-Flores's assertion that Iberian colonizers maintained no "sustained attempt to convert Africans" may come as a surprise. The ignominy ascribed to Africans and African slavery in the New World has been touched upon in chapter 1. It may also be explained in part as resulting from the colonizers' belief that Africans brought to the Americas had been originally defeated in the African tribal wars and sold to Europeans by their captors, thus rendering them without dignity or rights. This clearly placed them beneath the status of the Amerindian whose freedom, independence, and legitimate governments before the conquest were officially recognized by crown and church. Evangelization of the innocent but spiritually deprived indigenous peoples thus became a priority. Perhaps the apparent adoption of Catholicism, or at least its outward manifestations, by large numbers of slaves eliminated the urgency to evangelize them. The essay by von Germeten and Villa-Flores identifies the complex and perhaps conflicted nature of priests such as Antonio Vieira, Alonso de Sandoval, and Pedro Claver, all Jesuits, who devotedly ministered to Africans while accepting their society's institution of slavery. The authors explain the importance of confraternities to Africans and their descendants, offer examples of slave resistance and rebellion and the formation of runaway communities that "tended to synchretize Christian and African indigenous elements in their worship," and emphasize the ways in which the cultural traditions of African peoples thrived in the diaspora and affected the religious outlook of future generations of Latin Americans. The reader will want to compare the views expressed by von Germeten and Villa-Flores concerning the blending of religious traditions with those expressed by Tavárez and Chuchiak. The reader may also note the ways by which slaves and their progeny became "fervent Catholics" — a theme already broached by Tavárez and Chuchiak, who had noted the strong links forged by many indigenous peoples with the Catholic Church. This evidence in turn should give important insight about coping strategies of the colonized and even suggest something about the human need for religion.

Priests and Nuns

Karen Melvin explores the lives of men and women who took holy orders or assumed other church-sponsored roles in Spanish and Portuguese America. She offers detailed discussions of the daily activities of secular and regular clergy and explores the background of the women who lived and labored in convents. Of particular importance is the stress she places on the racial, social, and educational composition of religious and her succinct and lucid analysis of their concept of duty. Melvin describes the racial impediments to ordination faced by *mestizos* and Indians, though restrictions lessened by the end of the colonial period. Some priests served their flocks dutifully whereas others sought easy and lucrative assignments, living at the expense of their parishioners. She also details the manner by which the crown favored the secular over the regular clergy by the 1570s. The author recounts the existence of the women who "spent their lives enclosed in convents, never setting foot outside convent walls from the day they entered to the day they died." Each convent was connected to a religious order and operated as a separate institution with its own covenants and bylaws. Spanish and creole nuns typically had servants and slaves to tend to their needs, run errands, and sell goods produced by the convent to the greater community (some convents even acting as banks for local merchants). The social arrangement was designed to reinforce feminine virtues — obedience, chastity, and humility — for wealthy colonial women while protecting the honor of their male relatives. The remarkable achievements of Sor Juana Inés de la Cruz, though unique, may show the reader why convents proved attractive places of refuge for some colonial women. The reader should have no problem substantiating Melvin's claim that "internally, convents reproduced many of the social hierarchies of the colonial world."

The Inquisition and Women

Jacqueline Holler's substantial and cogent essay provides essential background on the founding, development, and flowering of the Spanish and Portuguese Inquisitions and pays special attention to women who were called as suspects, accusers, and witnesses before the Holy Office. Drawing from both primary and secondary documentation, Holler closely examines cases dealing with the persecution of *conversos*, Protestants, and those accused of violating Christian morality. Female Judaizers, suspected heretics, illuminist holy women, and witches all came under the purview of the Inquisition. The author also considers changes in inquisitorial activity over time. Holler's essay requires readers to ponder several key issues: the author's view of the Inquisition as "an instrument of nationalism and state power"; how her account contributes to a better understanding of the close working relationship between church and state; which of those two entities held the upper hand; and the kind of piety encouraged by the institutional church during the colonial period.

Church-Sponsored Education

Grover Antonio Espinoza's chapter traces the different types of education and their evolution during the colonial period and the reasons leaders in the new republics reluctantly relied on churchmen as educators after independence and during the long nineteenth century. Espinoza begins by explaining the church's responsibility for providing education to all members of colonial society, albeit of different qualities depending on the race, class, and gender of pupils. Upper-class males of European descent could matriculate in *colegios* and state- and church-run universities where they trained to become bureaucrats, priests, lawyers, and physicians. Indigenous boys could attend the equivalent of primary schools where they were given rudimentary instruction in reading, writing, and Christian doctrine. A few Amerindian elite attended the famous but short-lived Colegio of Santa Cruz of Tlatelolco. Espinoza gives particular emphasis to the Society of Jesus as the educators of creole and gifted *mestizo* youth in cities and of indigenous youth in the far-flung missions of the empire. He also describes the ideological and institutional changes that occurred during the second half of the colonial period as the still controversial theories of Copernicus and Descartes were introduced into the curriculum. Although Aristotle could then be criticized more freely, Thomas Aquinas remained off limits to intellectual reassessment. Espinoza provides ample support for the argument that "political elites expected the educational institutions run by the church to continue to support the local, political, social, and cultural objectives of the state." In the second half of the essay the author considers the quandary of forward-thinking liberals having to succumb to continued clerical predominance in education. He makes careful distinctions regarding church-state relations in Mexico, Colombia, Peru, Brazil, Argentina, and Chile in order to gauge the relative degrees of seriousness in church-state conflicts. Readers will have to grapple with Espinoza's surprising suggestion that whatever their own views about the church, most elite families wanted their children to receive what might be called "a Catholic education."

Anticlericalism

Jeffrey Klaiber, S.J.'s detailed examination of anticlericalism further explores the deepening rift between liberal elites and the Catholic Church during the nineteenth and early twentieth centuries. His main goal is to communicate how the Catholic Church adjusted to postcolonial rule and the results of the different arrangements between the church and the new republics. He agrees with Espinoza that the state's initiatives to strip the church of its sweep and power began during the final century of colonial rule, but emphasizes that the first generation of post-independence liberals were not necessarily anticlerical. In fact, many members of the lower clergy were respected for having supported independence, fought in its wars, and served in the constituent assemblies of the new sovereign states. Many second-generation liberals, however, influenced by the ideas emanating from their Masonic lodges, became strongly anticlerical, their ire centering upon the religious orders, especially the Jesuits. Forecasting a theme developed by Monica I. Orozco (in the next essay), Klaiber argues forcefully that liberals "looked with envy at the progress of Protestant England and North America, [and] saw toleration as a way of attracting non-Catholic European immigrants from advanced industrial nations." Liberals in the later nineteenth century, adopting the positivist ideology, viewed religion as "merely a social necessity providing a moral framework for lesser educated members of society, Indians, blacks, peasants, workers, and children."

Klaiber takes pains, however, to emphasize that church-state relations differed by country, and chooses Mexico, Uruguay, Chile, Ecuador, and Brazil to illustrate wide divergences in policy. He agrees with the idiosyncratic Peruvian political thinker José Carlos Mariátegui (d. 1930) that "liberal anticlericalism had run its course" by the 1920s and suggests that the church may have actually benefited from the ultimate separation of church and state. The reader might evaluate the astute observation by Mariátegui that liberals had actually missed their opportunity to promote significant social change and why Klaiber suggests that "anticlericalism played a positive role by forcing the church to shift its focus from defense of its own narrow interest to…other priorities [liberty, social justice, and respect for human rights]." One suspects that Hughes and Pelton, the authors of chapters 13 and 14 respectively, might agree with this assessment. Nonetheless, the reader should also try to identify those church officials and social groups who would have preferred postindependence governments to have promoted religious orthodoxy and the church to have remained a bulwark against revolutionary change.

Protestant Perceptions of Catholicism

As the contributions by Espinoza and Klaiber demonstrate, battles between liberals and conservatives dominated much of the political landscape in the 1800s. While Klaiber cautions us to remember that church-state relations varied dramatically by country, he also acknowledges the general trend toward political compromise that allowed key aspects of the liberal agenda, such as freedom of worship, to be incorporated by society. One important consequence of this religious toleration was the arrival of mainline Protestant groups, mostly from the United States, who began proselytizing during the second half of the nineteenth century. Monica I. Orozco outlines some of the key factors that contributed to their successes and failures. She stresses the preconceived ideas held by most North American missionaries concerning the nature and state of Catholicism and the "quality" of the Latin American populace. These missionaries viewed Catholicism as wracked with superstition and idolatry, corrupted by indigenous and African elements, and essentially moribund. Orozco offers a clear description of the racist, elitist, and imperialist objectives of many Protestant missionaries and looks closely at the reasons mid-century Mexican liberals were anxious for Protestantism to gain a foothold, although by the end of the century they became apprehensive of creeping "Americanism." The second half of Orozco's essay centers on the strategies employed by missionaries to gain converts, the hostility from certain sectors of society to Protestant advance, and the impact of Protestant missionary activity by 1900. The reader should identify the assumptions of those liberals who favored the influx of Protestantism as well as those of other members of society who opposed foreign penetration: the way conservatives might have responded to those late nineteenth-century liberals who finally awakened to the jingoism of "Manifest Destiny"; and the social and economic factors more likely to suggest abandoning Catholicism and embracing Protestantism.

Growth of Protestantism

Virginia Garrard-Burnett's insightful chapter outlines the ways in which Protestantism grew and developed in Latin America during the twentieth century. She commences with an impressive array of statistics to suggest that the slow start of Protestantism evidenced by Orozco in the previous chapter was followed by a storm of activity "like a mighty rushing wind," especially in Brazil, Guatemala, Chile, and El Salvador. As a result she focuses on British and American missionaries, the initial push by the historic, mainline denominations such as the Methodists, Presbyterians, Baptists, and Episcopalians, and the emphasis on the Bible as the ultimate authority. She argues forcefully against the notion that Latin American Protestant churches operated "under the strict paternalistic control of North American missions." She turns to Pentecostalism, as practiced in the Brazilian Igreja Universal do Reino de Deus (IURD), for example, and explains its accounting for the recent explosion of Protestant churches in Latin America. The influence of this form of veneration of the Holy Spirit is so appealing to Latin Americans that mainline denominations have recently " 'Pentecostalized' their worship and liturgy to some extent." The author addresses several issues that will be raised by subsequent contributors to this anthology and that merit consideration here, such as the political, economic, and social motivations for conversion, the meaning of conversion, and the more recent phenomenon of changing religious affiliation to fit "changing circumstances and perceptions of need." Readers, of course, can also consider those ways in which religion has always been tied to the social and economic realities that determine politics. Perhaps most provocatively, Garrard-Burnett suggests that Pentecostalism represents "arguably the single most important social movement to sweep though the region in the late twentieth and early twenty-first centuries." Readers will want to consider the validity and implications of that statement while scrutinizing the essays by Chesnut, Hughes, and Pelton. Would those authors agree with Garrard-Burnett's bold assessment?

Charismatic Competitors

Andrew Chesnut brings the discussion of Pentecostalism into sharp focus in his astute and jarring treatment of charismatic competitors in Latin America. Garrard-Burnett introduced readers to Chesnut's methodological approach to the study of religion in her chapter when she cited his "religious supermarket" theory. Nonetheless, readers unfamiliar with Chesnut's books and articles may be disconcerted by his use of liberal economic discourse to explore personal religious choice. For instance, he refers to congregants as "consumers," religious tenets as "practical products," proselytizing as "packaging," and conversion experience as "free market salvation." Those readers who initially find Chesnut irreverent will soon discover that he is both a lively and a fair analyst. This chapter on Protestant and Catholic Pentecostalism thoroughly details the rapid growth and personal expectations of those people who choose to emphasize the power of the Holy Spirit, faith healing, and pneumacentric spirituality. Chesnut compares these constituencies and distinguishes between the generally middle-class membership in Catholic charismatic renewal and the overwhelmingly poor and female followers of the Universal Church of the Kingdom of God (IURD), Assemblies of God, Foursquare Gospel, and International Church of the Grace of God. But Chesnut is careful to avoid an overly rigid categorization of those for whom "Jesus and the Holy Spirit have the power to cure." There is no denying, however, that the distinguishing feature between these two groups is the emphatic role of the Virgin Mary for Catholic charismatics. Chesnut ends his essay by reiterating that the current trend is toward Pentecostalized churches. He asserts that "over the past four decades popular religious consumers in Latin America have exhibited a strong preference for pneumacentric spirituality in both its Christian [Protestant Pentecostal and Catholic charismatic] and non-Christian [Umbanda, Candomblé, among others] forms. In contrast," he continues, "organizations such as the [Catholic] CEBs [Christian base communities] and mainline Protestantism, which offer neither supernatural healing nor direct contact with the Holy Spirit, have failed to thrive in the popular religious marketplace." Readers might consider whether Hale, the author of the next chapter on Umbanda, would agree that pneumacentric spirituality captures the essence of followers of African-based religions and whether Hughes, who celebrates the role of CEBs in chapter 13, or Pelton, who examines current movements in Catholicism in chapter 14, would acknowledge the relevancy of Chesnut's religious supermarket theory.

Umbanda

One of the principal findings of von Germeten and Villa-Flores in their essay on enslaved Africans and Christianity (chapter 4) was that African peoples shared a set of cultural understandings that influenced religious practice in Latin America during the colonial period. Lindsay Hale's chapter on Umbanda with ancillary information on Candomblé clarifies the importance of African-based religion today for many individuals both with and without African ancestry. Hale's strong personal relationship with Dona Luciana and his own observations and experiences at Afro-Brazilian centers of worship inform this sensitive treatment of

Umbanda. Hale's training as an anthropologist has determined his methodological approach of utilizing the "stories" behind the history of Umbanda. First, the author notes that, in many ways, people who attend worship centers grapple with typical problems: "Financial troubles, loss of a job, friction with a spouse or lover, fits of irrational anger or bouts of depression, drinking, a rebellious child or a string of bad luck." But the reader quickly learns not to expect "typical" religious solutions to those problems when Hale asserts "and the caboclos stand ready to help." The end result is a fascinating and deft examination of the underlying doctrines of Umbanda. Hale introduces readers to Caboclo Seven Crossroads, numerous *orixás*, the old slaves, and Exu the trickster. Neophytes in the study of Umbanda will be excused if they find its doctrine baffling. The difficulty of incorporating new religious concepts can give the reader a greater appreciation for both the Amerindians (chapters 2 and 3) and Africans (chapter 4) who were expected to assimilate the intricacies of Christianity as well as for those missionaries who had to explain religious doctrine and practices in diverse Amerindian and even African languages. As Hale might aver: Make a wish!

The Catholic Church and Social Revolutionaries

The final two chapters in this anthology return the discussion of religion to Catholicism, the faith still practiced by the vast majority of Latin Americans. Previous readings by Garrard-Burnett, Chesnut, and Hale outlined many of the social ills that prompt people to seek answers in a church, solace from its pastors, and change in their personal conduct. Jennifer Hughes focuses on those individuals and groups who during the past fifty years have sought structural change in order to address the massive injustices and poverty of the masses and to end brutal political-military regimes. She tackles the challenging topic of social revolutionaries in twentieth-century Latin America who were inspired by what may be termed "liberation theology." Throughout her essay she stresses three major developments that occurred in the 1960s: the renewed emphasis that Vatican II (1962–65) placed on the duty of Christians to love, meaning specifically the commitment of Christians to do justice in this world; the solicitude of Latin American bishops in Medellín (1968) for the church's poorest parishioners; and the determined efforts by many clergy and lay women and men to implement the principles coming out of these two great conferences and end gross violations of human rights. She describes the counterrevolutionary efforts by those who have attempted to return the church to that mythical time when it eschewed politics. Hughes proves particularly adept at placing the contributions of key personages such as Hélder Pessoa Câmara, Samuel Ruiz García, Sergio Méndez Arceo, Gustavo Gutiérrez, and Oscar Romero in historical perspective. Drawing from her own experiences in Pernambuco in 1989, Hughes also offers an excellent example of how liberation theology and popular religiosity prove complementary. In this specific case, people in a shantytown in the Brazilian *sertão* proved enthusiastically receptive to the penitential message of mystic Frei Damião and the liberationist message of Padre Andres. Hughes concludes with a section on "the undoing of liberation theology," in which she suggests that Popes John Paul II and Benedict XVI, convinced of the "errors and excesses of liberation theology," dismantled the infrastructure of the movement, silenced its prominent spokespeople, and replaced liberationist bishops "with conservative traditionalists and members of Opus Dei." Readers should pay particular attention to Hughes's final sentence, in which she provides a penetrating critique of the historic role of the Catholic Church: "What may be unique about the liberation theology movement is that, for a moment in this cyclical history, the institutional Church stood close to that struggle [on behalf of the poor]."

From Medellín to Aparecida

Robert Pelton, C.S.C. attended Vatican II and the four Latin American Bishops Conferences from Medellín in 1968 to Aparecida in 2007. His vast experience, deep knowledge of the region, and pastoral work make him an ideal person to assess the current state of the Catholic Church in Latin America. The editors of this anthology asked Pelton to shed light on the following topics:

1. the image of the Catholic Church in Latin America;
2. the Vatican's stance on centralization and subsidiarity;
3. the "preferential option for the poor" as guiding principle today for parish priests and religious orders;
4. the vitality of Christian base communities;
5. the church and social issues such as reproductive rights, homosexuality, and the role of women;
6. the role of deacons and lay ministers;
7. trends in vocations;
8. the impact of charismatic movements;
9. religious pluralism; and
10. Pope Benedict's episcopal appointments.

Pelton responded with a thoughtful portrayal of a church that remains, in sum, "committed to a full and creative expression of the Second Vatican Council...faces very different but no less daunting challenges in the twenty-first century than it did in the final decades of the twentieth...has retained its own distinctive identity, and...has much to share with the world." The reader will appreciate several of the author's candid statements: "Pope John Paul II's episcopal appointments rarely challenged the status quo maintained by the national security states"; "the current Vatican position is closer to centralization than to the principle of subsidiarity"; "younger priests, who increasingly come from wealthier families and who grew up under conditions quite different from those experienced by most of their parishioners, often leave the seminaries with more conservative viewpoints"; and "the Vatican-approved document [of Aparecida] presents a decidedly minimal vision for the CEBs." Pelton notes that the famous "preferential option for the poor" has been modified to become "a preferential *and evangelizing* option for the poor." The reader might ask what would be the social and religious implications of this new phrase and whether Pelton would agree with Hughes that liberation theology represented a unique period in the history of the Catholic Church in Latin America when the official church championed the cause of the poor.

In sum, the reader should ask how contributors to this anthology grapple with Pope Benedict's forthright assessment of the historical role of the Catholic Church in Latin America and his understanding of the meaning and potential of the religious impulse of its peoples.

Notes

1. Excerpt taken from section 1: "The Christian Faith in Latin America," inaugural session of the Fifth General Conference of the Bishops of Latin America and the Caribbean: Address of His Holiness Benedict XVI (May 13, 2007). This extraordinary (6,223 word) document contains five additional subtitles: (1) "continuity with other conferences"; (2) "disciples and missionaries"; (3) "so that in him they may have light"; (4) "other priority areas"; (5) "stay with us"; and a conclusion. See *www.vatican.va/holy_father/benedict_xvi/speeches/*.

2. John F. Schwaller, "Introduction," in *The Church in Colonial Latin America,* ed. John F. Schwaller (Wilmington, Del.: Scholarly Resources, 2000), xi.

3. Virginia Garrard-Burnett, ed., *On Earth as It Is in Heaven: Religion in Modern Latin America* (Wilmington, Del.: Scholarly Resources, 2000).

4. Henry Goldschmidt, "Introduction: Race, Nation, and Religion," in *Race, Nation, and Religion in the Americas,* ed. Henry Goldschmidt and Elizabeth McAlister (New York: Oxford University Press, 2004), 5.

5. Anna L. Peterson, Manuel A. Vásquez and Philip J. Williams, eds., *Christianity, Social Change, and Globalization in the Americas* (New Brunswick, N.J.: Rutgers University Press, 2001), x.

6. Timothy J. Steigenga and Edward L. Cleary, eds., *Conversion of a Continent: Contemporary Religious Change in Latin America* (New Brunswick, N.J.: Rutgers University Press, 2007). Instructors who desire to assign books specifically on religion in Mexico have three new options. Editor Martin Austin Nesvig includes ten scholarly articles related to religious practices in colonial Mexico in *Local Religion in Colonial Mexico* (Albuquerque: University of New Mexico, Press, 2006). Another book on religion in colonial Mexico by the same press is Susan Schroeder and Stafford Poole's edited collection of sixteen articles in *Religion in New Spain* (2007). Ten themes related to the postindependence period in Mexico are treated in Martin Austin Nesvig, ed., *Religious Culture in Modern Mexico* (Lanham, Md.: Rowman & Littlefield Publishers, 2007).

1

The Right to Appropriate, the Duty to Evangelize

Spain and the Conquest of the New World

Lee M. Penyak and Walter J. Petry

Christendom

"... to unite the world and give to those strange lands the form of our own...."
— Hernán Pérez de Oliva (1528)[1]

Since the Middle Ages the European world has frequently been referred to as "Christendom," a loose geocultural construct employed largely by Western thinkers to locate that area of the world believed to be operating according to values propagated by Christian institutions (in contrast to such equally medieval phenomena as feudal social formations). Thus Peter Beyer speaks of Christendom as "the notion and effective reality of a society characterized by Christian institutions, world view, and self conceptions."[2] Pablo Richard describes it, more analytically and critically, as a "peculiar kind of relationship between the *church* and *civil society*, a relationship in which the *state* is the primary mediation. Where Christendom is in place, the church seeks to safeguard its presence and expand its power in civil society, particularly by making use of the state."[3] Other theologians and historians have continued to study the concept of Christendom, analyzing the interplay of the "Christian" institutions that have historically comprised it. As in the case of Richard, some have concluded that Christendom was actually a kind of internal imperialism. They locate its origins in the early fourth-century religious policies of Constantine, policies that became definitive with the edict promulgated by the jointly ruling Emperors Gratian, Valentinian II, and Theodosius I, on February 27, 380. The edict's last sentence reads:

> They ["mad and raving" Arian* "heretics"] are to be punished not only by Divine retribution but also by our own measures, which we have decided in accordance with Divine inspiration.[4]

---

*Arianism is the "heretical" belief that, in the Trinity, the Son is inferior to the Father.

The institutional church of Christendom, derived from the communities of congregants dispersed throughout the empire during the first three Christian centuries, had forged an alliance with the political state that was mutually beneficial and that helped to maintain and increase the power and influence of both.[5]

After the collapse of the western portion of the Roman Empire in 476, its successors, the Merovingian and Carolingian kingdoms in "France," the Germanic kingdoms, and the Visigothic kingdom in "Spain" continued the arrangement of close collaboration between state and church. The state was clearly the dominant entity although the monarchs (especially the Visigothic) were usually respectful of the moral authority of the church. The church unhesitatingly accepted the legitimacy and independence of secular authority even when the monarchs, as was the case in Spain, were heretical Arians. Thus the Christendom of early medieval Europe, now broken into an assemblage of different-sized kingdoms, retained the essentials of the edict proclaimed in the fourth century by the three emperors.

In the far north of Iberia, in an area untouched by Muslim power, the small passionately Christian kingdom of Asturias initiated the reconquest of the peninsula as early as the mid-eighth century, only a few years after the Muslim conquest. Stanley Payne, a noted historian of modern Spain and also the author of the broader survey, *The History of Spain and Portugal,* elucidates the nature of state-church relations within a kingdom that was highly committed to restoring to Spain its allegedly Christian identity:

> Relations between the monarchy and Church in Asturias were extremely close, with the crown predominating to an even greater extent than in the preceding Visigothic kingdom.... As in contemporary Christian France, it was accepted that the role of the Christian king was active leadership and reform in the affairs of the Church whenever that was needed. *Thus early was established a practice that with varying degrees of zeal would be followed by the Spanish crown for a full millennium.*[6]

By the high Middle Ages (c. 1150–1350) the Roman popes, armed with the arguments of their learned canonists, had developed the startling doctrine of *plentitudo potestatis,* which gave unmediated supremacy to the papacy over secular affairs. Pope Boniface VIII's *Unam sanctam* of 1302 is perhaps the most famous formulation of that doctrine.[7] In spite of the royal repudiation of the doctrine, a forthright and exact summary of it is provided by a document that was drafted some two hundred years later in response to a royal order by King Ferdinand. The famous document, the *requerimiento* (requirement, 1513), discussed later in this chapter, was designed to "calm the conscience of Christians" and explain the

16

righteousness of the Spanish conquest to New World indigenous people.* The crown, in effect, based its own legitimacy and authority in the New World on a papal doctrine that it had itself repudiated.

> Of all these nations [the "many kingdoms and provinces" of earth] God our Lord gave to one man, called St. Peter, that he should be Lord and Superior of all the men in the world, that all should obey him, and that he should be the head of the whole human race, wherever men should live, and under whatever law, sect or belief.... [H]e permitted him... to judge and govern all Christians, Moors, Jews, Gentiles, and all other sects. This man was called Pope... [and]... the men who lived in that time obeyed [him] and took him for Lord, King, and Superior of the universe... also... others who after him have been elected to the pontificate.... One of these Pontiffs... made donation of these isles and Tierra-firme to the aforesaid King and Queen and to their successors....[8]

What may be termed the medieval marriage of church to state was actually incorporated into Castilian law during the reign of Alfonso X, *El Sabio* (1252–85) whose *Siete Partidas* — seven books of law representative of Spain's sophisticated legal tradition — regulated the interdependence of crown and papacy. Book 2, dedicated in part to royal rights and prerogatives, discusses why this alliance must exist and how it must work:

> Imperium is a great dignity, noble and honored above all other temporal offices which men can hold in this world. For the lord on whom God confers such an honor is both king and emperor... All persons of the empire obey his commands, and he is not bound to obey anyone except the Pope, and that only in spiritual matters.... Moreover, wise men declared that the emperor is the Vicar of God in the empire, in order to dispense justice in temporal matters, just as the Pope does in those which are spiritual.[9]

Note that the above excerpt makes clear that royal legitimacy comes directly from God, thereby rendering null and void the doctrine of *plentitudo potestatis*. So the Spain of Isabella and Ferdinand** (*Los Reyes Católicos*) can be regarded as a maturation of the Catholic Christendom of the Middle Ages, resulting from the inauguration of a new entity, the "nation," similar to the nations later created by Henry VIII (*Defender of the Faith*) in England and Francis I (*le roi très Chrétien*) in France. When Spain expanded into the New World and initiated the "conversion"

---

*The words "indigenous" and "Amerindian" are used interchangeably in this essay to denote people native to the New World at the time of Spanish and Portuguese contact.

**The reversal of the usual ordering of the monarchs' names is used when Isabella is the initiator of an action or the main protagonist.

of its "heathen" indigenous populations, its extension of the borders of Christendom involved a great deal of violence and it imposed a form of Christianity that was far removed from its biblical origins.

Although medieval Christendom had achieved a high degree of intellectual and artistic sophistication, it was at the same time authoritarian, paternalistic, warlike, intolerant, materialist, and accepting of a socioeconomic system based on class exploitation. The "first estate" of the European elite, the clergy, still believed that they were unique in possessing a definitive understanding of God and the workings of his universe, based on their readings of the Old and New Testaments and the Graeco-Roman heritage. Although the lay thinkers of the Italian renaissance had begun to make inroads into the clerical monopoly and Spain herself was engaged in its own humanist renaissance, it is inconceivable that any European of 1500 would have been able to approach the New World's indigenous peoples in the spirit of modern anthropologists who seek to transcend their own worldview in a quest for nonjudgmental understandings.

The attitudes, behavior, and actions of Spaniards — from the crown to the lowest level invader in the Indies — have traditionally been perceived as vicious, hypocritical, wanton, and un-Christian, and as having contributed to inexcusable violations of human rights.[10] When considered from the perspective of sixteenth-century European Christendom, however, they can be regarded as normal, typical, reasonable, and even Christian, or as no more un-Christian than the attitudes, actions, and institutions of the post-Christian "civilized" citizens of our contemporary West.

This essay will explore the beliefs and assumptions of Spanish Christendom on the eve of the establishment of an empire whose expanse was greater than that of Rome. It will also examine institutions and actions that subsequently created and sustained that empire.

The Notion of a "Spain"

"Spain," wrote Isidore, *"is the most beautiful of all the lands extending from the West to India....She is the Mother of many peoples and rightfully the Queen of all the provinces, for through her East and West receive light...."* The glorification of Spain, *"the most illustrious part of the globe,"* was also to serve as a foundation for empire, when that time came and Spain became, in its turn, the greatest world power since Rome. St. Isidore was one of the founders of the Spanish empire.
— Carlos Fuentes (1992), acknowledging St. Isidore of Seville
(c. 560–636) as a founding father of the Spanish nation.[11]

"Spain," of course, did not exist as an entity during the medieval period (fifth through fifteenth centuries). Five separate Christian kingdoms occupied the

Iberian peninsula: Castile, León, Navarre, Aragón, and Portugal. Portugal secured recognition by Castile as an autonomous realm by virtue of the 1143 Treaty of Zamora arranged by Pope Celestine II. Until the thirteenth century, Muslim kingdoms operated independently in the southern part of Castile. Even so, the peninsula's rulers and inhabitants shared a common historical background. Iberia, known as Hispania, had been a province of the Roman Empire from the third century B.C. until the Visigoth conquest in the fifth century A.D. Muslim areas (from the eighth century forward) were subsequently referred to as al-Andalus (the Arabic expression for Spain). Iberia's geographical characteristics — a peninsula separated from its northern neighbors by the formidable Pyrenees mountain range — also fostered a sense of common identity, as did the fact that Arabic became a lingua franca for Christian, Jewish, and Muslim inhabitants of the peninsula following the Arab conquests.* Three hundred years of Visigothic control over much of the peninsula further inspired some medieval Christian Spaniards to try to reestablish Christian unity throughout Iberia.[12]

The Visigoths, one of the many barbarian tribes to invade Europe during the disintegration of the Roman Empire, conquered northern Iberia in the fifth century and controlled the entire peninsula within two hundred years. The approximately 4 million Hispano-Roman, Christian-pagan Iberians fell under the domination of a force of perhaps 250,000 Visigoths. Plagued, however, by continuous internal strife between two competing factions within the ruling family, the Visigoths never established an effective system of hereditary monarchy, and this failure allowed the Catholic bishops to become the real governors of Spain. According to Stanley Payne, "The Christian church became the only cohesive institution in Visigothic Hispania," a development that perhaps would not be forgotten.[13] Ultimately, therefore, Spain was vulnerable. Invasions by North African Muslims (Moors) from 710–714 led to the defeat of King Roderic. The fall of the Visigoth capital of Toledo to Tariq ibn Ziyad's army of seven thousand soldiers initiated the nearly eight hundred years of Muslim presence in much of southern and central Iberia.[14]

Iberian Christians under Muslim (Moorish) rule received treatment similar to that given to other non-Muslim communities in the Mediterranean world. Some Christian warriors were enslaved following military confrontations, while Christian communities after the conquest enjoyed significant degrees of tolerance. Although they were usually prevented from building new churches or proselytizing, and, in more repressed areas such as Córdoba, from holding religious processions and ringing church bells, and although they had to pay an annual tribute to their overlords, they were largely self-governing and allowed to continue to practice their religion. Nevertheless, Islam, a missionary religion, eventually made

---

*By the eleventh century, e.g., it is estimated that perhaps half of the Andalusian Jews had adopted Arabic.

inroads and approximately 80 percent of all Christians in Muslim areas came to adopt both the religion and culture of their conquerors.[15]

Al-Andalus shone in cultural achievements. Muslim patrons of the arts and sciences encouraged Muslim scholars such as Ibn Rushd (1126–98), known as Averroës in the West, and these scholars drew upon, and sometimes superseded, the Greek legacy that had been influential in Arab/Islamic culture since the ninth century. Muslim libraries were the largest and most impressive in western Europe and contained thousands of volumes on astronomy, mathematics, agronomy, architecture, and medicine, and ultimately contributed to the development of medieval Christian culture.[16]

The origin of Spain's Jews, the Sephardim, is obscure. They certainly predate both the Arian Christian Visigoths and the Muslims, and they had lived and worshiped in Spain since the third century or earlier. While never more than 2 percent of Iberia's population during the Middle Ages, the Sephardim represented Europe's largest Jewish community. Most lived in small villages sprinkled throughout the peninsula. But there were larger settlements in the south and east. Most Jews pursued occupations common to the medieval era. They were farmers, shepherds, shopkeepers, blacksmiths, weavers, or carpenters. Some highly educated Sephardim in urban areas served as influential political and military advisers, or secured positions as administrators, court physicians, and tax collectors. Jews had little difficulty existing alongside Christians and Muslims as long as Christians did not become strong enough to enforce a national policy of religious uniformity.[17] Muslim leaders generally granted Jews the same tolerance as they did Christians, and the flourishing of Jewish culture under Muslim rule in Spain has prompted many scholars to refer to this period of Jewish history as a "golden age."

The coexistence and widespread commingling of peoples of the three monotheistic religions have led some scholars to regard the period from about 800 to 1300 as a time of *convivencia* (accommodation for coexistence), inasmuch as Christians, Muslims, and Jews shared aspects of their cultures and found ways to live productively alongside one another. Ferdinand III, *El Santo,* of Castile (1230–52), even proclaimed himself "King of the Three Religions," and central and southern Spain in particular became more culturally heterogeneous than anywhere else in Europe. As we have already indicated, positive relations between Jews and Muslims were especially strong. Interfaith marriages and cooperation in business ventures were not unheard of. Intellectuals such as the Jewish Maimonides (1135–1204) were inspired by Muslim philosophers like Averroës. Ties among adherents of all three religions were sufficiently strong for Christian and Muslim rulers to occasionally issue edicts forbidding such close contact, but to little avail. Nevertheless, while Iberians of different faiths consorted and became friends and associates, mutual tolerance was not guaranteed. For many, coexistence seems to have been a pragmatic way for large groups to share the same social space while avoiding constant friction. Moreover, Christians in the far north seldom had contact with Iberians of other faiths. The story of the rise of Catholic Spain in the fifteenth century is, in spite of the frailties to which we have just referred, the story of the destruction of the multiculturalism and the interpenetration of cultures that had been characteristic of Iberia for centuries. As Chris Lowney explains, "Tolerance seemed less necessary and less useful. Spain no longer needed to balance the needs and interests of its religious minorities to secure peace, prosperity, or borders."[18] Spain should surely be taken here to mean Christian Spain, whose leaders and populations were, overall, less open than the Muslims to religious toleration.

Militant Christian Patriotism

For a whole month he [the Infante, son and heir of James I of Aragon] remained in the said kingdom [Moorish Murcia] with his hosts, burning and sacking; and all who were with him became wealthy men.... The Lord Infante sent to the Lord King his father, full a thousand head of big cattle and full twenty thousand of small cattle, and full a thousand male Saracen [Muslim] captives ... the said Lord King ... gave ... of the males, some to the Pope, some to the cardinals and to the Emperor Frederick ... so that he left none for himself ... of which the Holy Father and the cardinals and other powers of the Christian world were very joyous and content, and made processions in honor of Our Lord the true God Who had given this victory to the Lord Infante.
— Ramón Muntaner (c. 1270–1336)[19]

It is unlikely that St. James the Greater, traditionally the first apostle to be martyred for the faith (c. 42), actually visited Spain, but by the ninth century a legend had developed that he proselytized in Iberia after Jesus' death and that his body was buried in Galicia. King Alfonso II of Asturias (791–842) purportedly ordered the construction of a church over James's tomb, thus founding Santiago de Compostela, which became one of Christian Europe's holiest shrines. Pilgrims from the farthest reaches of western Europe traveled to this site to atone for sins, solicit miracles and cures, and mingle with fellow believers. Asturian kings (who initiated the *reconquista*) were crowned there. Over time St. James the Pilgrim, disciple of Jesus and evangelizer of Spain, metamorphosed into St. James Matamoros, the Moor slayer, patron and protector of Christian Asturias and spiritual leader of the Christian reconquest of Spain. The battle cry of St. James — *Santiago y cierra España* (St. James and close ranks for Spain) — would also later be employed by Spaniards against Spain's "pagan" Amerindian enemies in the New World.[20]

Epic poems such as the *Song of Roland* and *El Cid* contributed to a crusading zeal that swept through Christian Iberia in the later Middle Ages. In the *Song of Roland*, the great French epic finally set down about 1100, Charlemagne and his nephew Roland attempt to rid Iberia of all Muslims and create a homogeneous Christian peninsula. In the epic, St. James appears to Charlemagne in a vision and implores him to free his tomb and the Gallegans from Muslim control. Its message was clear: good Christians and evil Muslims can never live together peacefully. Chaos and warfare will reign until all Spaniards are Christians. *El Cid,* based on the real-life exploits of Rodrigo Díaz de Vivar and written in the Castilian vernacular c. 1201–7, became, like the *Song of Roland,* popular entertainment. This captor of Muslim Valencia, warrior against North African Berbers, and occasional fighter against dishonorable Christian princes on behalf of honorable Muslim lords, always proved invincible. His exploits suggested that fame and fortune belonged to those who demonstrated courage, faith, and loyalty. The legends of Roland's religious fervor and the Cid's honor and bravery helped to forge what was regarded as the ideal Spanish male personality of the fifteenth century.[21]

Ian Michael, a specialist in medieval Spanish literature, places the poem of *El Cid* in the context of developments in late twelfth-century Spain:

> The basic aim of the poem of *El Cid* is to present the Cid as a hero, that is, as a man who proves himself in action to be superior to his fellow men. This superiority is not only shown to be physical and combative, it is also seen to include excellence in generalship, religious devotion, family obligation, vassalage, knowledge and observance of legal procedure, generosity, courtesy, wiliness and discretion....
>
> The Cid also represents and idealizes the restless, hardy ethos of Castile in an outward-looking moment, when there were lands to conquer and fortunes to be made.... It may not be too fanciful to see a poem which exalted the Cid as a man who succeeds by his own efforts in Moorish territory being used in part as a recruiting drive in a lull before the new and unstoppable Christian advance that began in 1212.[22]

Christian devotion, bravery, skill and, by no means least, honor: Iberian adventurers in the New World would assert these as their own exemplary values.

Spanish nobles and ambitious commoners were attentive to crusader rhetoric, first in the form of a response to Pope Urban II's call (1095) for Christian princes to recapture Jerusalem from the infidel, and later in the form of an attempt to make up for the ignominy of the Christian defeat by the Muslims at Alarcos, New Castile, in 1195. Popes provided funding and readily promised indulgences (in some cases total remission of sins) for those who fought on behalf of Christianity. Participants in the Crusades were equally anxious to acquire booty, land, honor, and status. These rewards were also available to those who fought against Muslims in Iberia. During the thirteenth and fourteenth centuries, the military religious orders, especially the powerful and wealthy orders of Calatrava, Santiago, and Alcántara, exemplified the infusion of militant Christianity into the Spanish ethos.[23]

Seven centuries of this internal crusade against Muslims gave Spain's diverse Christian populace a common cause, an emblem of what it meant to be a Spaniard, or in George Young's phrase, the "patriotic myth," wherein "each individual must be attracted by some commonly shared ideal which can move him to contribute his efforts to the collective enterprise."[24] Columbus's opportune "discovery" of the Indies enabled Spain's military and religious machine to continue its mission. All levels of Spain's Catholic populace were convinced of their God-given responsibility to purify and extend Catholicism for the good of their souls, their nation, and humanity.[25] And such a project by the adventurers to the New World, as Ramón Muntaner wrote about the Aragonese above, would make them "wealthy men."

Isabella and Ferdinand End the Reconquista

> *O rey Don Hernando y Doña Isabel*
> *En vos comenzaron los siglos dorados;*
> *Serán todos tiempos nombrados*
> *Que fueron regidos por vuestro nivel.*

> *O King Don Fernando and Doña Isabel*
> *With you the golden years began;*
> *They will be for all time renowned*
> *As having been governed under your standard.*
>   — Juan del Encina (1495)[26]

In the traditions of European Christendom since Constantine, the secular and religious authorities worked to develop a power structure wherein each entity — state and church — saw its interests enhanced by the other. This structure was to reach a unique climax in Spain in the thirty-year era following the 1469 dynastic marriage of eighteen-year-old Isabella of Castile-León and her seventeen-year-old distant cousin Ferdinand of Aragón, both members of the same Trastámara family. Isabella became queen of Castile in 1474 and Ferdinand king of Aragon in 1479, his troops conquering the remaining Christian kingdom of Navarre in 1511. Since Castile contained 73 percent of Spain's Christian population and 65 percent of its land, Isabella had the upper hand in this union until her death in 1504.[27]

In 1482, in their first joint venture, Isabella and Ferdinand resumed military activities against the Muslims. Nearly 80 percent of Muslim territories had already come under Christian control following the fall of Toledo (1085), Córdoba (1236), and Seville (1248). Much later, in 1487, Muslim Málaga suffered a crushing defeat at the hands of Spain's Christian army, and internal unrest inside Granada's ruling Nasrid dynasty gave Isabella and Ferdinand the opportunity to launch a final offensive against this last Muslim kingdom in Iberia. King Abu Abdullah (Boabdil) was forced to sign capitulations (agreements) with the two monarchs and surrender the magnificent Alhambra palace on January 2, 1492. Under the liberal terms of the agreement, Granada's populace became tribute-paying vassals but received guarantees that they could practice Islam "forever more." The monarchs quickly displayed the royal standard and a crucifix on Alhambra's tallest tower.[28]

Despite their promises, Spain's two monarchs and its ecclesiastical hierarchy were uneasy about the sincerity of the defeated Muslim populace's acceptance of their new lords, and encouraged — even assisted — their migration to North Africa. Clerics set about converting Muslims to Christianity, a process initiated peacefully by Hernando de Talavera, the saintly first archbishop of Granada (1492–1507), who forbade any coercion and encouraged the use of Arabic in the Catholic Mass. Francisco Jiménez de Cisneros, archbishop of Toledo and primate of Spain (1495–1517), named cardinal in 1506, was far less tolerant. After a minor uprising by Muslims in the Albaicín in Granada, he promoted forcible conversion. This, in turn, provoked a larger though ultimately unsuccessful uprising.* Then, in 1502, Isabella and Ferdinand ordered Muslims either to accept Christian baptism or leave the realm. Most feigned conversion and remained on their ancestral lands. These *moriscos* ("little Moors") were thereafter harassed continually until 1609 when Phillip III expelled all those remaining.[29]

This identification of the Spanish nation with the Catholic religion would bode ill for the indigenous "heathen" of the New World, who, in the eyes of the invaders, perversely maintained their "idolatrous" religious traditions, in the manner of the *moriscos* and Jews.

Ethnic Cleansing?

If you know or have heard of anyone who keeps the Sabbath according to the law of Moses, putting on clean sheets and other new garments, and putting clean cloths on the table and clean sheets on the bed in feast-days in honour of the Sabbath, and using no lights from Friday evening onwards; or if they have purified the meat they are to eat by bleeding it in water; or have cut the throats of cattle or birds they are eating, uttering certain words and covering the blood with earth; or have eaten meat in Lent and on other days forbidden by Holy Mother Church; or have fasted the great fast, going barefooted that day; or if they say Jewish prayers, at night begging forgiveness of each other, the parents

---

*Jiménez de Cisneros (1436–1517), inquisitor general, Franciscan ascetic, militant reformer of the church and the religious orders, patron of learning and of the arts, protector of humanists, scourge of Jews and Muslims, and later (at the age of seventy-one), commander-in-chief of an expedition against the Muslims in North Africa, personifies the colonizers in their varied incarnations.

placing their hands on the heads of their children without making the sign of the cross or saying anything but, "Be blessed by God and by me"; or if they bless the table in the Jewish way; or if they recite the psalms without the Gloria Patri; *or if any woman keeps forty days after childbirth without entering a church; or if they circumcise their children or give them Jewish names; or if after baptism they wash the place where the oil and chrism was put; or if anyone on his deathbed turns to the wall to die, and when he is dead they wash him with hot water, shaving the hair off all parts of his body.* . . .

— Typical instruction of Spanish inquisitors
upon their entry into a district in the sixteenth century.[30]

The fourteenth century also saw growing antipathy toward another alien "nation," the Jews, even though they had resided in Spain since the third century and despite the fact that the Jewish elite had long played major roles in both Muslim and Christian kingdoms. This antipathy culminated in bloody riots in 1391, especially in Seville, Madrid, and Córdoba. Many Jews left an increasingly intolerant Spain, while others converted to Catholicism (and were called *conversos* or New Christians). Although some of these achieved high office in Castile and especially in Aragón, the preeminence and success of even third- and fourth-generation *conversos* made them objects of envy and subject to accusations of perpetuating atrocities against Christians, of "Judaizing," and of heresy.[31]

Even before Ferdinand succeeded to the throne of Aragón, he and Isabella persuaded Pope Sixtus IV in 1478 to grant them the right to establish a Holy Office of the Inquisition under royal control, and they appointed the Dominican friar Tomás de Torquemada to serve as its first grand inquisitor. The Holy Office's primary goal was to root out "secret" Jews from the suspect *converso* community. During the first few decades of its operation, more than 99 percent of cases in the Barcelona tribunal and 91 percent of those in Valencia concerned members of this group. Under Torquemada's stewardship (1483–98) more than two thousand *conversos* were executed and another fifteen thousand, ruined economically and socially, were "reconciled" to the church. The Holy Office was popular with the Old Christian population and elites in Castile, though despised in traditionally autonomous areas such as Catalonia. Most Old Christians concurred that *marranos* ("swine," a pejorative term for Jews/*conversos*) had to be eliminated for the benefit of Spanish Catholic civilization. In March 1492, Ferdinand and Isabella gave Spain's remaining Jews an ultimatum: convert to Christianity or leave within four months. Most left with nothing more than the clothing they wore, being forced to sell all their possessions at well beneath their value, and at times for no remuneration at all.[32]

As a result of this relentless campaign to denounce and chastise *conversos*, those Christians with "pure" blood, whatever their class, could claim superior honor and increased stature. Christians with even a distant Jewish or Muslim ancestor were theoretically excluded from a large number of occupations:

> The children and grandchildren of those condemned [by the Inquisition] may not hold or possess public offices, or posts, or honours, or be promoted to holy orders, or be judges, mayors, constables, magistrates, jurors, stewards, officials of weights and measures, merchants, notaries, public scriveners, lawyers, attorneys, secretaries, accountants, treasurers, physicians, surgeons, shopkeepers, brokers, changers, weight inspectors, collectors, tax-farmers, or holder of any other similar public office.
>
> — Torquemada's Instruction, Seville (1484)[33]

Well-established families whose members had married into prominent and wealthy *converso* families during previous generations ran great risk of exposure, inasmuch as loss of position or further preferment could result from subsequent genealogical inquiries. Though commoners could not acquire social status, they proudly equated their exclusive Catholic pedigree with "honor." The idea of *limpieza de sangre* (purity of blood, "a mixture of religious fanaticism, race prejudice, social ambition, exclusivism, and political monopoly") and the elaboration of racial hierarchies would be broadened by the Spanish overlords in the New World to create a pyramid with the most pure and the most white at the apex.[34] Perhaps a caveat is in order here. Ruth MacKay, in her extraordinary *Lazy, Improvident People,* states, "divisions between Old and New Christians may appear more stark than they really were" and that "Limpieza frequently served as a placeholder for power and status, not race or religion. Accusations of having Jewish heritage, indeed, could and did take place even when there was not the remotest possibility that the subject or anyone whom he knew was a Jew. 'Proving' one's cleanliness was not cheap; it required money and contacts. It was proof of one's economic resources and connections, not one's bloodline."[35] As happened so frequently in Spain, when it was not convenient to the parties' concerns, the law was not always observed.

The Holy Office's edicts of faith, posted in churches and read in public, encouraged parishioners, emboldened by promises of anonymity, to denounce heretics. A cadre of "consulters," "qualificators," and "familiars" helped inquisitors in Spain's fifteen tribunals to convict errant Catholics and secret Jews. The masses lined the streets and shouted insults at transgressors as they were marched in solemn procession behind drums, trumpets, and dignitaries of the Holy Office. "Heretics" in the *auto de fe* (an extravagant public ritual for punishment of heretics) wore the *sanbenito,* a yellow penitential garment emblazoned with the cross of St. Andrew, their family name, and sometimes their crime. They also wore the *coroza,* or dunce cap. These unrepentant heretics and "Judaizers" marched in their own funeral processions, inasmuch as they had been "relaxed" to the secular authorities for punishment upon completion of the *auto*, i.e., for the confiscation of their property and execution. Lesser offenders faced imprisonment and fines. All were publicly ridiculed and their families humiliated. Scholars of the Holy Office emphasize that the secular authorities punished heretics and "Judaizers" in the same way they did other criminals. There was nevertheless a special ignominy attached to those exposed as inferior and alien and therefore beneath contempt. The influences of such prejudices, brought by the colonizing Spanish overlords to the "alien" inhabitants of the New World, should be apparent.[36]

The Impulse to Empire

Behind any material factors there lay a set of attitudes and responses which gave the Spaniards an edge in many of the situations in which they found themselves: an instinctive belief in the natural superiority of Christians over mere "barbarians"; a sense of the providential nature of their enterprise, which made every success against apparently overwhelming odds a further proof of God's favor; and a feeling that the ultimate reward made up for every sacrifice along the route. The prospect of gold made every hardship tolerable.... They sensed, too, that they were engaged in a historical adventure and that victory would mean the inscribing of their names on a roll-call of the immortals, alongside the heroes of classical antiquity. — J. H. Elliott (1987)[37]

Castile's territorial expansion (the *reconquista*) within the Iberian peninsula during the Middle Ages was externalized with its incursion (1478–93) into the Canary Islands. Indigenous, non-Christian inhabitants lived in virtual isolation on these islands located from ninety to three hundred miles west of the southern coast of today's Morocco. Italian and Portuguese adventurer-traders began enslaving the inhabitants as early as the 1340s. A 1479 treaty between Spain and Portugal gave Spain the "ownership" of the islands, and Spaniards quickly imposed an exploitative *encomienda* system (the grant of the use of land and the indigenous inhabitants thereof in return for "protection" and religious instruction of those inhabitants) that they would duplicate in the New World. They met strong resistance from the natives, but subdued them militarily by supporting shifting alliances to encourage indigenous groups to fight one another. Spaniards initially sought gold, but later turned to sugar production, a sequence soon duplicated in the West Indies. Brutal treatment of the natives (Canarians, Gomerans, and Guanches) and diseases such as plague reduced the indigenous population by nearly 90 percent by the early sixteenth century, again a phenomenon to be repeated shortly in the West Indies. When the supply of indigenous laborers was depleted on the larger sugar-producing islands, such as Grand Canary, Palma, and

Tenerife, the Spaniards raided nearby smaller islands and redistributed their inhabitants as needed. The Spaniards later resorted to purchasing enslaved Africans to sustain production. Spain thus gained significant experience dealing with non-Christian, less technically sophisticated indigenous peoples prior to Columbus's landing in the Caribbean. The Canary Islands became "the perfect laboratory for Castile's colonial experiments, serving as a natural link between the *reconquista* in Spain and the conquest of America."[38]

Beginning in the year 1477, when Spain was endeavoring to end Portuguese incursions into the smaller Canary Islands, and continuing for the next eleven years, the Genoese navigator and explorer Christopher Columbus (1451–1506) found himself passing wearily back and forth between the Portuguese court of John II (1481–95) and the Spanish court of Isabella and Ferdinand. Columbus was seeking support for what he claimed would be a relatively short sail to the west, which would terminate in islands off the coast of Cipangu (Japan) and thus allow Europeans to reach the Far East by sea without having to circumnavigate the south African coast and cross the Indian Ocean. Isabella finally agreed to support Columbus's scheme. The conquest of Granada freed Spain's resources for needs other than war, and she realized that Portugal would benefit from Bartholomew Dias's success in rounding the newly named Cape of Good Hope, and that this country would reap the benefits of a soon-to-be-mapped full sea route to India (achieved ten years later in 1498 by Vasco da Gama).

Isabella and Ferdinand's capitulations of April 17 and 30, 1492, defined Columbus's mission, status, and responsibilities (copied into his *Diario* of 1492–93). These contractual documents contain fully developed theological and philosophical formulations and a synopsis of Spanish cosmology involving the nature of God and his creation, the divine origin of monarchy, the monarch's role in governing, dispensing, and exploiting God's creation, and the absolute right of monarchs to appropriate any part of that creation (land or wealth) without regard to already existing sovereign jurisdictions. While the capitulations do not include any mention of evangelization — despite their profoundly religious rhetoric — Columbus's acknowledgement of the capitulations emphasizes proselytism as the chief aim of his journey.[39]

There can be little doubt about the depth of Columbus's desire to spread the Christian faith in East Asia (where he expected to land) and to defeat the Muslims in western Asian Holy Land. Often wearing the Franciscan habit during the last years of his life, he referred to himself in his 1501 *Book of the Prophesies* as "the messenger of the new heaven and the new earth of which [God] spoke in the Apocalypse." His discovery of the West Indies convinced him that the second coming of Christ was near, an event that he calculated would occur in 155 years. The wealth generated in the Indies, he maintained, would be used to capture Jerusalem from the Muslims in preparation for Christ's return.[40]

He was simultaneously ready to acknowledge his secular interests when he thanked the Catholic monarchs for recognizing him and his heirs as "General Admiral of the Ocean Sea and Viceroy and perpetual Governor of all the islands and lands that I might discover."[41]

The right of appropriation and the zeal to evangelize professed by Columbus became the official and legitimizing mission of all the subsequent adventurers, explorers, colonizers, and missionaries, whatever their rank or status. This dual vision was probably the most significant set of assumptions that the Spanish brought with them to the New World. Before we return to the spiritual half of this vision, i.e., how the Spanish people understood Catholicism on the eve of the great migrations to the Americas, we should consider the state of the institutional church at that time.

New Life in an Old Institution: Catholicism on the Eve of Empire

El oro es excelentíssimo; del oro se hace tesoro, i con él, quien lo tiene, hace quanto quiere en el mundo, i llega á que echa las ánimas al Paraíso.

Gold is most excellent, from it treasure is made and with it, he who has it does whatever he wants in the world, and even to the extent of sending souls to Paradise. — Christopher Columbus, 1503[42]

The last decades of the fifteenth century witnessed a vigorous spiritual, moral, and intellectual reform movement in the church, encouraged by the Catholic monarchs and vigorously championed by highly educated, deeply spiritual prelates such as Talavera, Cisneros, Juan Tavera (1472–1545), Alonso Fonseca (1475–1534) and Alonso Manrique, an inquisitor general (d. 1538), the latter two enthusiastic Erasmians (church reformers and Christian humanists). New stipulations for proper clerical conduct simultaneously painted a dismal picture of the condition of the clergy* and the lack of spiritual care provided for parishioners: clergy were now instructed to reside in their parishes and end their high rates of absenteeism, to hear confession and say Mass regularly, and to refrain from flaunting [*n.b.*] their concubinage, attending their children's marriages, or leaving lands and property to their mistresses.[43]

Efforts to educate clerics were part of a larger initiative directed at improving university education for elite members of society. The great University of Salamanca, founded c. 1230, included faculties of theology, law, and medicine. Some

---

*An idea of the laxity, corruption, and arrogance of the clergy with whom the reformers had to contend is exemplified (c. 1500) by the four hundred Franciscan friars in Andalusia who converted to Islam and emigrated to Morocco in order to maintain their female concubines rather than follow the newly enforced rules of their order.

eleven other universities were established by 1500. Cisneros founded the University of Alcalá in 1508 and presided over its publication of the famous "Polyglot Bible" (1517) with the Hebrew, Chaldean, and Greek originals in columns parallel to the Latin vulgate.[44] Many of the beneficiaries of these reforms were members of the religious orders whose deep Christian convictions and solid learning would allow them to play enlightened roles in the New World.

Intellectual and ecclesiastical reforms were closely associated with the rise in Spain of humanism, i.e., the critical study of classical and biblical texts in Latin and Greek. Many scholars avidly pursued the works, as they came off the press, of the classical and biblical scholar Desiderius Erasmus (1466–1536). Erasmus authored the *Handbook of the Christian Soldier* (1503), which stressed the importance of inward Christian piety and charity rather than the public display of formal rituals, as well as the *Praise of Folly* (1509), a witty but scathing indictment of superstition and corruption within the church. Subsequent writings of Erasmus were popular with clerical and lay scholars through the middle of the century, at which time the advance of Protestantism in Europe ironically made the Spanish church suspicious of this Dutch Christian humanist who had debated Martin Luther and remained loyal to Rome.[45]

The continued pursuit of reform in the broadest sense was always necessary for such a privileged and sacrosanct institution as the church, and in the early decades of the sixteenth century the reform pursued by a large number of Spanish clergy — diocesan and religious, university professors, mystics, prelates, and lowly clerics — testifies to a degree of institutional well-being.

The congregants who made up that church ranged from the elite nobility and the higher clergy to unlettered, poor, rural day laborers and urban vagabonds, with *hidalgos, caballeros,* professionals, merchants, artisans, peasants, and unskilled workers in between. Individuals from the middle and lower groups — excluding the nobility or members of the military/religious orders — constituted the vast majority of colonizers in the New World, and the level of religious instruction that they received determined the quality of their Catholicism.

All but the isolated and unchurched rural poor would know the Catechism, be able to recite, in Latin, the Credo, Paternoster, and Ave María, perform their annual Easter duty, venerate the Virgin Mary and their local patron saint, and call upon them in time of need. Some would join the local religious brotherhood and go on pilgrimages to Santiago de Compostela or other shrines.[46]

European Christians (medieval and, later, Catholics and Protestants through 1800 and beyond) shared a belief in the literal presence of Satan, who sought to seduce them into straying from orthodox beliefs or righteous conduct. In his masterpiece of ascetic theology with its deep insight into human psychology, *Spiritual Exercises* (1541), the Basque soldier, mystic, missionary, and founder of the Society of Jesus, Iñigo de Loyola (1491–1556), devotes twenty-four of the book's three hundred seventy exercises to "some rules toward discerning various spirits ['good spirits' or 'the enemy,' and 'evil spirits'] moving the soul." It was a new and analytical treatment of a concern — the problem of Satan — that has been shared by pastors and theologians throughout Christian history.[47]

This belief in the reality of Satan in the everyday lives of humans (see Matt. 13:38–39; 1 John 3:8; and New Testament passim) played an important role in shaping the Spaniards' understanding or, rather, misunderstanding, of the New World indigenous peoples. Three men from contemporary but very different early colonizers provide telling examples.

Fray Francisco de los Angelos Quiñones, minister general (1523–27) of the Order of Friars Minor, gave orders to "the Twelve," the first friars sent to New Spain (1523). His long letter of instruction describes their mission as "liberating and snatching away from the maw of the dragon the souls...deceived by satanic wiles, dwelling in the shadow of death, held in the vain cult of idol."[48]

Gonzalo Fernández de Oviedo y Valdés (1478–1557) was a noble educated at the court of Ferdinand and Isabella and secretary to the *Gran Capitán*, Gonzalo Fernández de Córdoba, during his brilliant campaigns in Italy. He spent some fifteen years in the Caribbean colonies, during which he gathered information for the *General and Natural History of the Indies,* his major work as humanist and royal chronicler. "Now Satan is expelled from this island [Hispaniola]," Fernández exalted, "all his influence has vanished now that the majority of Indians are dead....Who will deny that to use gunpowder against pagans is to offer incense to the Lord?"[49]

Pedro Cieza de León (1520–54) was a highly unusual soldier-scholar who also spent fifteen years in the Caribbean and Andes as soldier, government official, historian, and ethnographer. Although he was curious about the Indians and sympathetic to their plight, he too could nevertheless write:

> We and all these Indians, have our origins in our ancient parents Adam and Eve, and the Son of God came down to earth from heaven on behalf of all men, and clothed in our humanity he met a cruel death on the cross to redeem us and to free us from the power of the devil, *the devil who possessed these peoples,* with permission from God, [and] kept them *oppressed and captive* for such a long time.[50]

Acknowledgement of the power of Satan is the only point the three writers have in common. The effect of this identification of Satan with the Amerindians and their culture would give even the most educated and pious colonizers license to regard them scornfully and treat them harshly.*[51] An excerpt from Michele

---

*An example of the colonizers' callousness toward the Amerindians in one small corner of the West Indies can be seen in David R. Radell's calculation that 448,000 Amerindians in Nicaragua were captured and exported as slaves to Panama and other provinces between 1523 and 1530. "The Indian Slave Trade and Population of

Cuneo's account of Columbus's second voyage to the New World, in which Cuneo participated, demonstrates the degree to which the Spanish were oblivious to the sufferings of the indigenous peoples from the earliest conquests:

> Obliged to depart for Spain our caravels...had collected into the town six-teen hundred men and women of the said Indians, of whom, male and female, we loaded the said caravels with five hundred fifty of the best....As to the remainder there was given an order that whoever [of the Spaniards] wished might take whatever he liked, and it was thus done....Among the captured persons there was taken also one of their kings with two subalterns, whom it had been resolved to kill the next day....When we got into Span-ish waters there died on our hands about two hundred of the said Indians, whom we threw into the sea, the cause I believe to be the unaccustomed cold....We landed all the slaves at Cádiz, half of them sick. They are not people suited to hard work, they suffer from the cold, and they do not have a long life.　　　　　　　　　　— Michele Cuneo (February 1495)[52]

Because of the unique history of medieval Spain, adherence to the doctrines of the church and respect for its magistrates were probably stronger in that land than anywhere else in Europe. The following reflection on the uniqueness of Spanish history and culture by the scholar Ramón Menéndez Pidal (1869–1968), who combined expertise in Spanish philology, literature, and history, is still worth considering. Despite being the editor of the monumental multivolume *Historia de España* (begun in 1935), he sometimes writes more as a philosopher/psychologist of history than as a historian proper, as the excerpt may indicate. It may be interpreted as suggesting that being "Spanish" was, in its origins, synonymous with being "Catholic."

> The pure unfettered religious spirit which had been preserved in the north gave impetus and national aims to the Reconquest. Without its strength of purpose Spain would have given up in despair all resistance and would have become denationalized. In the end it would have become Islamized as did all the other provinces of the Roman Empire in the east and south of the Mediterranean. In the period from the eighth to the tenth centuries Islam appeared so immensely superior in power and culture to the West that it was amazing that Spain did not succumb as did Syria and Egypt when they were Arabized, in spite of their more advanced Hellenistic culture; and as did Libya, Africa and Mauritania, likewise Arabized. What gave Spain her exceptional strength of collective resistance and enabled her to last through

---

Nicaragua during the Sixteenth Century," in *The Native Population of the Americas in 1492*, ed. William M. Denevan (Madison: University of Wisconsin Press, 1976), 67–76.

three long centuries of great peril was her policy of fusing into one single ideal the recovery of the Gothic states for the fatherland and the Redemption of the enslaved churches for the glory of Christianity.[53]

On the other hand, in her astute comment on the origins of Spanish self-awareness, Ruth MacKay perceives the Spanish experience in the colonies as the catalyst for promoting a national consciousness: "The development of the notion of what it meant to be Spanish was an intrinsic part of the process by which Spain ruled its colonies, and imagining what it meant to be Spanish ran parallel to imagining what it meant to be Indian (or *mestizo* or Creole)."[54]

The Cohort of Invaders

E yo, como so ome como otro pecador....

And I, since I'm a man like any other sinner....
— Juan Ruiz, archpriest of Hita (c. 1330)[55]

The majority of Spaniards who come here are of low quality, violent and vicious.... — Hernán Cortés to Charles V (October 15, 1524)[56]

Crusading zeal and even fervent adherence to the tenets and rituals of the church did not of course translate into exemplary behavior even by the standards of the times. Antonio Domínguez Ortiz (1909–2003), a Spanish historian of early modern Spain, succinctly describes the gap between social behavior and religious convictions:

Crimes of bloodshed were common, owing to the concept of honor, which extended to the lowest classes, to the general practice of bearing arms, and to the inefficiency of the forces of public order. Sexual license was common, increased by the very prohibitions against it.... Abandoned infants were plentiful, though it is not possible in this instance to distinguish reasons of poverty from those of sexual misconduct.... In this frequent contradiction between belief and practice there was no hypocrisy, but instead a humble or unthinking acceptance of the gap between the ideal and the real worlds.[57]

Perhaps Spaniards both at home and abroad would attribute the "shocking ...moral discrepancies" in their behavior to Satan's power over them. Perhaps Fernando de Rojas had such satanic influence in mind when he wrote *La Celestina* (1499), the most popular work of fiction of this turbulent era, which went through eighty editions in Spain by 1600 and which celebrates the life of an amoral, pleasure-seeking protagonist. Though few of the intruders into the New

World would have read this racy work, nevertheless it undoubtedly reflected their license and their wanton behavior there.[58]

Those intruders, conquistadors, and adventurers who strove to subject the New World to Spain and to themselves — first by the conquest of the Caribbean Isles (1492ff.), then of New Spain (1519ff.),* and then of Peru (1532ff.) — were of "an intermediate class of *hidalgos* — second sons, soldiers and officials," frequently literate, with some degree of education and familiarity with the law.[59] The generation that followed them, according to Lyle McAlister, were "by and large, practical, hardheaded, and ruthless men."

> Most came from unprivileged and impoverished families...a few recognized hidalgos, rather more *caballeros* who enjoyed no formal noble status, a few men of urban middle-class origins, a sprinkling of sailors, and a very substantial number of artisans and rural laborers....In short, most of the first immigrants to the Indies were have-nots, spectators at the feast of life rather than participants.[60]

Robert Ricard's portrait of Hernán Cortés in his *Spiritual Conquest of Mexico*, still definitive some seventy-five years after its publication in French, remains the most compelling brief portrait not only of Cortés himself but of the "Eternal Conquistador," whose traits mimic those of Cortés:

> One cannot study the history of the evangelization of Mexico without giving emphasis to the religious preoccupations of the Conqueror Cortés. He was greedy, debauched, a politician without scruples, but he had his quixotic moments, for, despite his weakness, of which he later humbly repented, he had deep Christian convictions. He always carried on his person an image of the Virgin Mary, to whom he was strongly devoted; he prayed and heard Mass daily; and his standard bore these words: *Amici, sequamur crucem, et si nos fidem habemus, vere in hoc signo vincemus* (Friends, let us follow the cross, and if we have faith, truly in this sign we shall conquer). He had another standard, on the side of which were the arms of Castile and León, on the other an image of the Holy Virgin. His main ambition seems to have been to carve out a kind of autonomous fief for himself, theoretically subject to the King of Spain, but he could not admit the thought of ruling over pagans, and he always strove to pursue the religious conquest at the same time he pursued the political and military conquest.[61]

---

*Note the "ff.," which indicates that "conquest" was long and arduous, met with many setbacks, and has never actually been completed.

34

As with Cortés so with the thousands of Spaniards who emigrated and took possession — *ir a valer más en las Indias*.[62] They brought with them the attitudes and the economic and social institutions that would advance their goal of "counting for more" — "the thirst for command, for acquiring nobility and renown, for leaving an honored name…ideals of the renaissance Spaniard."[63] Matthew Restall's brilliant *Seven Myths of the Spanish Conquest* modifies McAlister's two-decades-old generalizations concerning the degree of literacy — Restall thinks, rather low — possessed by most of the invaders. He also derides the concept of the "typical conquistador":

> But if we were to create such a figure, constructed from the averages and patterns from conquistador biographies, he would be a young man in his late twenties, semiliterate, from southwestern Spain, trained in a particular trade or profession, seeking opportunity through patronage networks based on family and hometown ties. Armed as well as he could afford and with some experience already of exploration and conquest in the Americas, he would be ready to invest what he had and risk his life if absolutely necessary in order to be a member of the first company to conquer somewhere wealthy and well populated.[64]

Iberian women represented another group of Spanish "invaders," though the characteristics outlined above do not accurately describe their status, burdened as they were with the constraints imposed upon them by the sexist ideology of Iberian males. Thirty such women accompanied Columbus in 1498 on his third voyage to the New World. By 1520 the number of Spanish immigrant women was numbered at only about 10 percent of the Spanish population and at only 17 percent by 1560, thus laying the foundation for a significant demographic gender imbalance among Spaniards.[65] The nature of women had already been defined and their roles codified in the *Siete Partidas*, a product of Roman, Visigothic, and canon law. A husband, by virtue of *patria potestas*, was master in his household and controlled "all those who live under him." The institution of marriage was understood in patriarchal terms that regulated sexual practices and insured harmonious relations between the sexes; otherwise, reasoned "learned men" and "ancient sages," it would be impossible "to avoid quarrels, homicides, insolence, violence, and many other wrongful acts which would take place on account of women."[66] In general, male Spaniards in America (like their European counterparts) believed that women lacked intelligence and judgment, needed supervision, were emotional and gossipy, and inclined to moral laxity and treachery. These conditions were exacerbated in America by the disproportionally low number of "decent" and respectable women, i.e., white women of legitimate birth, to serve as appropriate marriage partners for the conquerors, and by the abundance of "shameless" women, i.e. Indian, African, and mixed-blood women, who would fill the invaders' sexual needs. Whether or not a woman was decent or shameless, she was barred from becoming a government official, lawyer, doctor, or, of course, cleric. She could not "preach," "bless" or "sit in judgment": Jesus had conferred these powers on his disciples "because they were men."[67] All positions of power and prestige were reserved for men.

Slavery Old and New

We permit you [Francisco Pizarro] to transport from these our kingdoms... to the said land of your governorship [Peru], fifty negro slaves, of which number at least one third must be females. These slaves are to pass free of all duties.
       — I, The Queen [Doña Juana], Toledo (July 26, 1529)[68]

The institutions of slavery and the slave trade were well known in the Iberian world. Iberians who lived during the interminable conflicts between Christians and Muslims, and who resided in Portugal, Andalusia, Catalonia, or the environs of Toledo-Madrid, had probably seen slaves at some time: enslavement of enemy captives by each side after a skirmish was a longstanding practice. After the final defeat of the last Muslim kingdom in Iberia in 1492, Christians and Muslims continued enslaving captives taken in battles in the Mediterranean, many of the Muslims being sold at slave markets in Spain.

While slavery itself was common in Iberia during the Middle Ages, it also existed, though to a lesser degree, in the rest of Europe. There, however, especially in the Mediterranean world, we see the slave *trade* flourishing, carried on largely by Venetians and Genoese. So commonplace and profitable was it that the traders eventually even included Christians (Greeks and Christian Slavs) in their merchandise, which of course was contrary to Christian teaching and longstanding custom.

By the middle of the fifteenth century, another source of slaves had been inadvertently discovered by the Portuguese who, under the visionary Infante Henry of Portugal, the "Navigator" (1394–1460), began exploring, subduing, and colonizing the Atlantic islands off the coast of Africa — the Madeiras, Canaries, and Cape Verdes, and who ultimately established contact with the African coastal mainland and its peoples.[69]

Henry, the initiator, administrator, and sustainer of the venture down the coast of Africa, may be regarded as an exemplar of the ideals of the Portuguese aristocracy: pious, intelligent, brave (he fought valiantly in four engagements against the Muslims, the last when he was sixty-four), and visionary. His long-term goal was to discover a passage to India, which he hoped would add to the greatness and wealth of the Portuguese nation. Like his Spanish cousins he was ever resentful of past Muslim control of much of the peninsula and the continued Muslim presence in North Africa and the Levant. He dreamed of finding Prester John, "the fabulous priest-king of the dim Orient and Ethiopia," and of forging a military alliance with him to create a Christian pincer movement that would finally cripple Muslim power.[70] The Iberians — Portuguese and Spanish — shared the same mantra: God, Gold, Glory.

By 1450 the Portuguese had established a lucrative trade along the Guinea coast and had named each of its divisions for the product provided: Grain coast, Ivory coast, Gold coast and Slave coast. Thus, Prince Henry had created a direct sea route for transporting enslaved black Africans to Iberia.

The purchase of black Africans by the Portuguese from native black African slavers did not pose a major ethical problem because, as we have seen, the sale of men captured in war (in this case intra-African conflicts) was a time-honored custom. In addition, if the men sold were Muslim (as many actually were in the early years of the trade) their enslavement was eminently justified because all Muslims were considered enemies of the Christian world, even if they did not know such a world existed. As Payne states:

> The justice of Negro slavery was debated in the first years when slaves were brought back from the Guinea coast, and children of the first African slaves in Portugal were set free, but by the end of the fifteenth century the ethics of perpetual slavery for Negroes were rarely questioned.[71]

Further, the blanket papal declaration from which we excerpt the following passage would have helped to erase any lingering doubts about the morality of enslaving people who had no previous history of hostility to Christendom:

> We grant to you [Alfonso V, King of Portugal] by these present documents, with our apostolic authority, full and free permission to invade, search out, capture and subjugate the Saracens and pagans and any other nonbelievers and enemies of Christ wherever they may be as well as their kingdoms, duchies, counties, principalities, and any other property...and to reduce their persons into perpetual slavery, and to apply and appropriate and convert to the use and profit of yourself and your successors, the Kings of Portugal in perpetuity.
>   — Pope Nicholas V, *Dum diversas* (June 14, 1452)[72]

Later, when it had finally caught up with the fifty years of Portuguese supremacy in exploration and "discovery," Spain itself was to receive her own mission charge, which was identical to that of the Portuguese:

> We...as a gift of special favor, grant to you [Ferdinand and Isabella] and your aforesaid heirs and successors, all and singular the graces and privileges,

37

exemptions, liberties, faculties, immunities, letters, and inducts that have been thus granted to the king of Portugal, the terms whereof we wish to be understood…as if they had been inserted word for word in these presents.
— Pope Alexander VI, *Eximiae devotionis* (May 3, 1493)[73]

Almost none of the colonizers, with the probable exception of the zealous, well-read, and strongly motivated Columbus, would have been aware of the existence of these bulls, but they would know that war and enslavement were sanctioned by the church and that indulgences were granted for battling the infidel. While they therefore brought with them an institution, i.e., slavery, that had long been prevalent in Europe, Asia, and Africa, they added to it a significant new element, *color prejudice.* Earliest evidence of this bias may be seen in the writing of the Portuguese historian Gomes Eannes de Azurara (d. 1474), *Chronicle of the Discovery and Conquest of Guinea:*

And the [captives from Africa], placed together in [a field], were a marvelous thing to behold, because among them there were some who were reasonably white, handsome, and genteel; others not so white, who were like mulattos; others as black as Ethiopians, so deformed both in their faces and bodies, that it seemed to those who guarded them that they were gazing upon images of the lowest hemisphere.[74]

Whatever the reason — the symbolism attached to the colors white and black in European Christian culture, the rarity of dark-skinned peoples in Europe, the color prejudice inherited from the Spanish and Arabs, or the seeming primitiveness of some of the enslaved sub-Saharan Africans ("dog-faced, dog-toothed people, satyrs, wildmen, and cannibals") — black was abhorrent, and, with the decrease by the early sixteenth century of the number of white slaves brought from the Slavic east and from North Africa, slavery became exclusively identified with the color black for the first time in history.[75]

Scholars agree that enslaved blacks in Iberia, a small number amid a sea of whites, were perceived as sincere Christians since they readily accepted baptism. They were not regarded as an alien presence, as were the *moriscos, conversos,* and the despised gypsies. They were usually forced to accept the most menial occupations,* and were not considered a threat despite their concentrations in

---

*There are, of course, always exceptions: Alonso Valiente gave his *mulato* slave, Juan, permission to join Pedro de Alvarado's army as it was moving from Guatemala to Peru in 1534. So valiant was Juan, "despite his skin" (McAlister, *Spain and Portugal in the New World,* 127), that the great *adelantado* (crown-appointed commander of a conquering expedition) Pedro de Valdivia granted him an *encomienda* with tribute-paying Amerindians. Juan was posthumously cheated out of his attempt to purchase his freedom from his master who, unaware of his death in battle, commenced legal proceedings to reclaim his slave and whatever property he had, a cautionary tale of the permanence of the stigma of origin. For further information on black conquistadors, see Restall, *Seven Myths of the Spanish Conquest,* 54–63.

cities such as Lisbon and Seville.[76] A 1475 entry from the chronicle *Anales* by Galíndez de Carvajal, the Spanish royal counselor and historian, brings out three points: the ordinariness of the presence of blacks even in a small town in northern Spain, the practice of manumission, and the existence of an environment in which freedmen with abilities could be given positions of responsibility. Some of the main features of the institution of slavery in the Spanish and Portuguese colonies are prefigured in this brief entry:

> 8 of November 1475 at Dueñas [in Old Castile] they liberated Juan de Valladolid, *negro*, lord and mayoral *of negros y negras, loros y loras* [brown people, i.e., *guanches* from Canaries] who, by that time, by contract had already delivered a great quantity of such from Guinea to Seville.[77]

Manumission of slaves in their masters' wills and their liberation through self-purchase in the later colonial era became noticeable features of the slave systems in Portuguese and Spanish America. The same practices were not as frequent in French and even less so in British and Dutch possessions.[78]

The Spanish Conscience

The strange mixture of anarchical feuds, disputes, rebellions and petty civil wars which mark the Conquest, along with the strongly legalistic turn of mind in the conquerors, proves to be but the outcome of the struggle between those two forces latent in the Spain of those days: on the one hand, the cohesive force of the law, the norm, which was the essence of the Nation, born of, and still attached to, the Roman Empire... and on the other hand, the fierce individualism of men whose powers of endurance and achievement have never been equaled... men, moreover, who suddenly found themselves in a political, as well as a physical, wilderness.   — Salvador de Madariaga (1947)[79]

The best example of the extent of Spanish preoccupation with law is the *requerimiento*, the 1513 document described previously. It was to be proclaimed in the Castilian language to New World peoples facing invading Spaniards. These people were to give up their religion, autonomy, and sovereignty, and embrace the Christian God and lordship of the Spanish monarch who would preside over their evangelization and exploitation. Refusal to accept this plan would mean conquest and subjection to Spanish rule as opposed to becoming loyal vassals.

Over the centuries, historians and commentators have treated this document with disbelief, condescension, and ridicule. Phrases such as "notorious legalism and religiosity" and a "rubbish heap of documents" have been used by reputable historians. The culture that produced the *requerimiento* has been labeled legalistic and its jurists accused of casuistry and hypocrisy. Even Lewis Hanke (1905–93), the historian whose scholarship compelled a reevaluation of the "Black Legend" that had made Spain the villain of New World colonialism, alludes to some pretentiousness within the Spanish rhetorical tradition:

> Sixteenth century Spaniards were thoroughly saturated also with the spirit of legal formalism, and the New World offered many opportunities for the exercise of juridical formalities....Spaniards were so accustomed to certifying every action they took that notaries were as indispensable to their expeditions as friars and gunpowder. The extraordinary concern for legality [was characteristic] of even the Spanish soldier of the period.[80]

In order to evaluate the above-cited interpretations by Madariaga and Hanke, it is necessary to comprehend the Spanish legal tradition that valued both Roman law and local, regional, and corporate *fueros* (privileges). The *Siete Partidas*, for example, provided detailed descriptions of moral, civil, and criminal codes of conduct for all members of society while carefully determining rights and responsibilities according to sex, lineage, religion, ecclesiastical and military rank, and free versus slave status. This diversified aggregation of legal precedents produced a longstanding tension between theory and reality. The *requerimiento* may be understood in this larger context as well as in the particular context of the new theological, philosophical, and political currents of the time: theology required the colonizers to evangelize the pagan, philosophy presumed that the pagan corresponded to Aristotle's "natural slave," and the politics of Cisneros and Ferdinand called for the continued expansion of Spanish and Christian imperialism. None of the humanists, jurists, churchmen, counselors to the crown, or missionaries, questioned the absolute right and duty of Spain to preach the Gospel and establish Christianity in the New World. However, those engaged in discussing the morality and legality of the "encounter" differed about the legitimacy of the existing institutions of the indigenous peoples, the extent to which Spaniards should modify their mores and practices, and, ultimately, the *type* of empire that Spain should impose and maintain. Even Bartolomé de Las Casas (1484–1566), the adamant "Protector of the Indians," acknowledged the theoretical legitimacy of Spanish sovereignty, though he instantly repudiated its actuality:[81]

> without prejudice to the title and royal sovereignty which the monarchs of Castile exercise over the new world of the Indies, everything which has been done there — both by unjust and tyrannical conquest and by the *repartimiento* [irregular conscription of indigenous to serve Spaniards] and *encomienda* — is null and void and without value or sanction of any right.[82]

The scholar charged with formulating the actual document known as the *requerimiento* was Juan López de Palacios Rubios (1450–1525), a distinguished university professor, a humanist, and one of Spain's foremost jurists, who had already tackled the problem of determining whether the invasion of the New World qualified as a "just war" — a philosophical and ethical inquiry apparently unique to Spain among the European colonial nations. In his *De las islas del mar* Palacios Rubios portrayed the Amerindians as embodying Aristotle's concept of "natural slaves" whose "barbarity" could be diminished under the tutelage of civilized and Christian Spaniards. This argument was common to one of the two schools of sixteenth-century thought that were disputing the institutions and practices of the overlords and other colonizers within the growing Spanish empire.[83] Juan Ginés de Sepúlveda (1490–1574), a humanist and major spokesman of this school, writes, characteristically, in 1544:

> Those who surpass the rest in prudence and talent, although not in physical strength, are by nature the masters. Those, on the other hand, who are retarded or slow to understand, although they have the physical strength necessary for the fulfillment of all their necessary obligations, are by nature slaves, and it is proper and useful that they be so, for we even see it sanctioned in divine law itself, because it is written in the Book of Proverbs that he who is a fool shall serve the wise.... If they reject such rule, then it can be imposed upon them by means of arms, and such a war will be just according to the laws of nature.[84]

The other school accepted the dominance of the adventurer/colonizer but was critical of the methods used in the actual conquest as well as of the subsequent treatment of the indigenous peoples and the institutions created to maintain Spanish control. Fray Antonio de Montesinos, whose famous sermon in Santo Domingo in 1511 sounded the moral alarm, was followed by Matías de Paz, a professor of theology at Salamanca, whose treatise "Concerning the Rule of the King of Spain over the Indies" was the first to lay out a full critique of the larger enterprise. Francisco de Vitoria (1486–1546) was the most thorough and nuanced critic within this school while his famous Dominican colleague, Las Casas, was the most caustic critic of the methods of the various cohorts of invaders, whom he perceived as destroying a potentially righteous Christian empire. In his *De Indiis* (1537/38), after expressing substantial agreement with the suppositions of the first school concerning Indian inferiority, Vitoria concluded with this admonishment:

> Let this, however, as I have already said, be put forward without dogmatism and subject also to the limitation that any such interposition be for the welfare and in the interests of the Indians and not merely for the profit of the Spaniards. For this is the respect in which all the danger to soul and salvation lies.[85]

Menéndez Pidal points out that "Spanish literature in its most popular and representative types has always betrayed an interest in juridical questions," and that

"Here [the debate on the legitimacy of the Spanish empire] we had the unusual occurrence of a State undertaking to discuss with itself the legality of its own dominion."[86]

Chroniclers write of hearing the laughter of the Spanish raiders when the *requerimiento* was shouted or mumbled to the uncomprehending indigenous peoples. Palacios Rubios, perhaps the most prestigious of the Christian humanist jurists of the era, also laughed when he heard of the misuse of his succinct summation of this Spanish theory of empire. Las Casas, who respected Palacios, wrote that he did not know if the *cosa es de reir o de llorar* (the thing is to laugh or cry).

Perhaps that is still the question: when Spaniards theorized about their imperial project and called on notaries to scrupulously verify events, were these just cultural mannerisms that rightly evoke amusement, or were they national traits that should arouse wonder and respect for a people who honestly grappled with an unsolvable conundrum — can empire ever be legitimate?

The Reality of Empire

I command you, our said Governor, that beginning from the day you receive my letter you will compel and force the said Indians to associate with the Christians of the island and to work on their buildings, and to gather and mine the gold and other metals, and to till the fields and produce food for the Christian inhabitants. . . . This the Indians shall perform as free people, which they are, and not as slaves. — I, The Queen (December 20, 1503)[87]

This chapter has so far demonstrated that, like many modern people, the sixteenth-century Spaniards who sought to enslave, dispossess, and exploit, were conflicted. The fixed moral beliefs of those who ventured to the New World were at variance with how they would have to behave in order to realize the promise of fame and fortune. Isabella's famous instruction to Governor Ovando of Hispaniola, which we quote above, provides a subtle reflection of the contradictions: she demands forced labor of the indigenous peoples even though she is simultaneously aware of the consensus articulated by her jurists, theologians, and philosophers of the basic right of every human to be free.

Was Isabella aware of the sophistry of her command? Was the inherent contradiction in the conquest apparent, i.e., that subjugated people, even those treated benignly, are not free? Did the lackluster evangelization of the recently acquired (1479) Canary Islands that accompanied the rapid disappearance of their indigenous population due to forced labor become the model for Spanish imperialism, i.e., to work a population to death for quick profit while seeking new territories and peoples to exploit?

Under that policy the once numerous Amerindians of Hispaniola had virtually disappeared by 1550. The 1512 "Laws of Burgos," which laid down rules for more humane treatment of the Amerindians, came too late and were palpably irrelevant. The strong support of the crown for evangelization and pacification developed only when it became clear that the huge labor force on the mainlands of the "Americas" should be preserved. Most members of the religious orders sought to evangelize and maintain the labor force, but some defended the Amerindians aggressively, a position strongly embraced by the crown. Others, such as the Franciscan Diego de Landa (1524–79), imposed brutal punishments upon indigenous peoples whom they judged deficient in their commitment to their new Christian faith.

Perhaps King Charles I (1516–56) and his son Philip II (1556–98) believed that the efforts of the good friars balanced the deeds of savage aggressors such as Nuño Beltrán de Guzmán (c. 1485–1558), Pedro Arias de Avila (c. 1440–1531), Francisco Pizarro (c. 1478–1541), Pedro de Alvarado (c. 1485–c. 1541), and Lope de Aguirre (1518–61), all of whom, possibly excepting Aguirre, probably died professing their Catholic faith and confessing their sins of wanton brutality. "Gentler" invaders such as Juan Vázquez de Coronado (1523–65), Pedro Cieza de León (c. 1520–54), and the extraordinary Álvar Nuñez Cabeza de Vaca (c. 1490–1564) were far outnumbered by their cruel colleagues.

In his demolition of "the Myth of Exceptional Men" and of "the White Conquistador" Restall does not address the question of the conquistadors' brutality in their warfare against the Amerindians. He only writes: "Both Spaniards and natives engaged at times in the killing of non-combatants, in mass slaughter, in killing from a distance (natives used arrows most effectively), and in ritual displays of public violence and ritualized executions...."[88] Surely he does not intend to downplay the relentlessly bloodthirsty careers of such ruthless invaders as those listed above. While the consensus of historians today points to disease as the major factor in what may be the greatest demographic catastrophe in human history, the violent careers of these conquistadors must be recognized.[89] But their actions must also be laid side by side with those that accompanied other wars of either aggression or defense. The reader might ask whether the Hebrews behaved any differently when they destroyed Jericho c. 1200 B.C., the Athenians Melos in 416 B.C., the Romans Carthage in 146 B.C., or the crusaders Jerusalem in 1099. Pope Innocent III ordered the massacre of the Albigensian heretics in 1208–13 and the French nobility violently suppressed the Jacquerie in 1358. The term "sack of Rome" given to the actions of the German and Spanish troops of Holy Roman Emperor Charles V (Charles I of Spain) in 1527 disguises the wantonness and ferocity of the event. Readers may add their own examples of military excess, which are legion, before or after the Spanish conquest.

Conclusion: Balance Sheet of Empire

Veníamos a desagraviar y quitar tiranías....

We had come to right wrongs and abolish tyrannies....

¿Qué hombres habido en el Universo que tal atrevimiento tuviesen?

What men in the entire world have shown such daring?

Nuestros muchos y buenos e nobles servicios que hemos hecho a Dios y a Su Majestad y a toda la Cristiandad.

Our good and many noble services have been done for God and His Majesty and for all of Christianity.

Pues murieron (más de quinientos y cincuenta conquistadores) aquella crudelísima muerte por servir a Dios y a su Majestad, e dar luz a los questaban en tinieblas, y también por haber riquezas, que todos los hombres comúnmente venimos a buscar.

The (more than five hundred and fifty conquerors) died a particularly cruel death to serve God and the King, to give light to those who lived in darkness, and also to get rich, which all men commonly came in search of.

— Bernal Díaz del Castillo (1560s)[90]

This essay has examined the emergence of a military, orthodox, Catholic, Spanish nation under the aegis and tutelage of the shrewd Catholic monarchs who reigned individually and collectively from 1474 to 1516. Their remarkable achievement moved the kingdoms in Spain from European medieval centrifugalism to renaissance centripetalism. The twelfth- and thirteenth-century reconquest, i.e., the internal expansion of Christian Spain into Muslim Al-Andalus led by the nobility and warrior priests, did not see the breakdown of feudal traditions: local lords remained powerful and independent. Isabella and Ferdinand were the ones to initiate the processes of centralizing national power and of creating a uniform Christian identity. Isabella also strongly supported overseas expansion led by *hidalgos* and missionaries to create a global Spanish empire. By the time Antonio de Mendoza, the inspired choice as first viceroy in the New World, completed his tenure in 1550, the fifty-year-old empire rested on solid cultural and religious foundations and had achieved, with some difficulty, political stability and economic success.

This overseas extension of European Christendom was, like the original, hierarchical, authoritarian, repressive, sexist, and religiously orthodox. Its wealth was produced by enslaving and exploiting indigenous and African populations. The Spanish crown, through its missionaries, sought to restrain the violence and shortsighted opportunism of the colonizers so that the *república de indios* could survive.[91] However, a "race" of *mestizos* and *mulatos,* spawned at first mostly by rape and later by both forced and constructed consensual sexual encounters between Spaniards and Amerindians or Spaniards and Africans, was an unforeseen result of the conquest. These "castes," as they were termed, were politically illegitimate since they belonged neither to the *república de indios* nor to the *república de españoles,* the two theoretical political entities posited by Spanish juridical thinkers of the time. They were marginalized and "dangerous," with neither vested interests nor standing, becoming, inevitably, the underclass of the *república de españoles.*

Thus the conquistadors, missionaries, and colonizers, with the necessary if ironic help of their sometime indigenous allies, created an extension of the imperfect and morally inferior institutions and mores of European Christendom in the New World. There was one major addition — a new, unwanted and reviled populace, i.e., the *mestizos* and *mulatos,* the majority of that world's contemporary inhabitants — and the elaboration of a racist ideology to justify their ongoing suppression. Latin American reformers, progressives, and radicals have been striving for the nearly two hundred years since independence to overcome that "imperfection," that "inferiority."

Notes

1. Quoted in J. H. Elliott, *The Old World and the New 1492–1650* (Cambridge: Cambridge University Press, 1970), 15.

2. Peter Beyer, review of Hugh McLeod and Werner Ustorf, eds., *The Decline of Christendom in Western Europe, 1750–2000* (Cambridge: Cambridge University Press, 2003), in the *Canadian Journal of Sociology Online* (March–April 2004).

3. Pablo Richard is licentiate in sacred scriptures from the Pontifical Biblical Institute and doctor in sociology of religion from the Sorbonne. See his *Death of Christendoms, Birth of the Church: Historical Analysis and Theological Interpretation of the Church in Latin America,* trans. Phillip Berryman (Maryknoll, N.Y: Orbis Books, 1987), 1. Luigi Sturzo sees the ninth century as the birth and exemplar of a Christendom that would be recognizable to Richard but one wherein the church seems less calculating. See his *Church and State* (Notre Dame, Ind.: University of Notre Dame Press, 1962), especially 65–69, 168–70, 185–86.

4. Sidney Ehler and John Morall, eds., *Church and State through the Centuries* (Westminster, Md: Newman Press, 1954), 6–7. For additional sources on Christendom, see Francis Urquhart, "Christendom," in *The Catholic Encyclopedia: An International Work...,* vol. 3, ed. Charles G. Herbermann et al. (New York: Robert Appleton Company, 1908), 699–704; Friedrich Heer, *The Medieval World: Europe, 1100–1350* (New York: New American Library, 1962), 20–27, 326, 365–66; and Gustavo Gutiérrez, *A Theology of Liberation: History, Politics and Salvation,* trans. and ed. Sister Caridad Inda and John Eagleson (Maryknoll, N.Y.: Orbis Books, 1973), especially 53–61.

5. Richard, *Death of Christendoms,* ix; Leonardo Boff, "Quaestio Disputata I: Did the Historical Jesus Will Only One Institutional Form for the Church?" in *Ecclesiogenesis* (Maryknoll, N.Y.: Orbis Books, 1986), especially 45–60; Mary Anne Perkins, *Christendom and European Identity: The Legacy of a Grand Narrative since 1789* (Berlin: Walter De Gruyter, 2004).

6. Stanley G. Payne, *Spanish Catholicism: An Historical Overview* (Madison: University of Wisconsin Press, 1984), 8 (emphasis added).

7. Ewart Lewis, *Medieval Political Ideas* (New York: Alfred A. Knopf, 1954), especially 2:357–69.

8. Juan López de Palacios Rubios, "The Requerimiento [1513]," in *Religion in Latin America: A Documentary History,* ed. Lee M. Penyak and Walter J. Petry (Maryknoll, N.Y.: Orbis Books, 2006), 26.

9. *Siete Partidas,* Part II, Title I, Law I, in *Las Siete Partidas,* trans. Samuel Parsons Scott (Chicago: The Comparative Law Bureau of The American Bar Association; Commerce Clearing House, 1931), 1:269.

10. Spain has been the victim of the "Black Legend" (*leyenda negra*) since it was devised in the late sixteenth century by its Dutch and English enemies and expanded in the succeeding centuries by those and others. Designed to make Spain a pariah in the Western world, it suggests that Spain's culture was intolerant, repressive, and retrograde and its colonial policies inexpressibly cruel and inhumane: in our contemporary terms, without any notion of or respect for human rights. The United States used the myth to justify its takeover of Cuba, Puerto Rico, and the Philippines in 1898. Murdo J. MacLeod best expresses today's consensus among historians on the major cause of the demographic catastrophe of the indigenous in sixteenth- and seventeenth-century Spanish America: "For the moment, with many caveats, pandemics are the villains, brought on by the introduction of Eurasian and African diseases to a population that had no acquired immunities to them." See his "Mesoamerica since the Spanish Invasion: An Overview" in *The Cambridge History of the Native Peoples of the Americas,* vol. 2: *Mesoamerica, Part 2,* ed. Richard E. W. Adams and Murdo J. MacLeod (Cambridge: Cambridge University Press, 2000), 11. For a similar interpretation, see Matthew Restall, *Seven Myths of the Spanish Conquest* (New York: Oxford University Press, 2003), 140–41. Classic treatments of Spain's colonial record can be found in Charles Gibson, ed. *The Black Legend: Anti-Spanish Attitudes in the Old World and the New* (New York: Alfred A. Knopf, 1971); Benjamin Keen, "The Black Legend Revisited: Assumptions and Realities," *Hispanic American Historical Review* 49, no. 4 (November 1969): 703–19; Lewis Hanke, "A Modest Proposal for a Moratorium on Grand Generalizations: Some Thoughts on the Black Legend," *Hispanic American Historical Review* 51, no. 1 (February 1971): 112–27; Benjamin Keen, "The White Legend Revisited: Reply to Professor Hanke's 'Modest Proposal,'" *Hispanic American Historical Review* 51, no. 2 (May 1971): 336–55.

11. Carlos Fuentes, *The Buried Mirror: Reflections on Spain and the New World* (Boston: Houghton Mifflin, 1992), 45.

12. Erika Rummel, *Jiménez de Cisneros: On the Threshold of Spain's Golden Age* (Tempe: Arizona Center for Medieval and Renaissance Studies, 1999), 1; J. H. Elliott, *Imperial Spain, 1469–1716* (London: Penguin Books, 1990), 19, 43.

13. Stanley G. Payne, *A History of Spain and Portugal* (Madison: University of Wisconsin Press, 1973), 11.

14. Joseph F. O'Callaghan, *A History of Medieval Spain* (Ithaca, N.Y.: Cornell University Press, 1975), 37–38; Chris Lowney, *A Vanished World: Muslims, Christians, and Jews in Medieval Spain* (Oxford: Oxford University Press, 2005), 29.

15. Derek W. Lomax, *The Reconquest of Spain* (New York: Longman, 1978), 19, 105; Lowney, *A Vanished World,* 60, 63, 69.

16. Jan Carew, "The End of Moorish Enlightenment and the Beginning of the Columbian Era," *Race & Class* 33 (1992): 5, 14; Lowney, *A Vanished World,* 256.

17. Henry Kamen, *The Spanish Inquisition: An Historical Revision* (London: Weidenfeld & Nicolson, 1997), 8; Payne, *Spanish Catholicism,* 32; Lowney, *A Vanished World,* 95, 101.

18. Lowney, *A Vanished World,* 225.

19. Ramón Muntaner, a soldier who fought in the wars of Aragonese expansion, quoted in James Muldoon, ed., *The Expansion of Europe: The First Phase* (Philadelphia: University of Pennsylvania Press, 1977), 81.

20. Lowney, *A Vanished World,* 43, 46, 255; Payne, *Spanish Catholicism,* 9.

21. Lomax, *The Reconquest of Spain,* 62, 73–74; Lowney, *A Vanished World,* 120, 132, 135.

22. Ian Michael, "Introduction," *The Poem of The Cid* (New York: Penguin Books, 1975), 4.

23. Lowney, *A Vanished World,* 107–11; Lomax, *The Reconquest of Spain,* 62.

24. George F. W. Young, "The Trajectory of Castile: 1492–1700," *Historical Reflections* 6 (1979): 356, 365.

25. Henry Kamen, *Empire: How Spain Became a World Power, 1492–1763* (New York: Harper Collins Publishers, 2003), 16.

26. Hugh Thomas, *Conquest: Moctezuma, Cortés, and the Fall of Old Mexico* (New York: Simon and Schuster, 1993), 55. Translation by the authors.

27. Kamen, *Empire,* 7; Elliott, *Imperial Spain,* 24–25.

28. Payne, *Spanish Catholicism,* 14; Lomax, *The Reconquest of Spain,* 162–63; Kamen, *Empire,* 19; Elliott, *Imperial Spain,* 49.

29. Roger Boase, "The Muslim Expulsion from Spain," *History Today* (Great Britain) 52, no. 4 (2002): 22–23; Elliott, *Imperial Spain,* 51–52; Rummel, *Jiménez de Cisneros,* 33; Kamen, *The Spanish Inquisition,* 214–29 passim.

30. Kamen, *The Spanish Inquisition,* 286.

31. Kamen, *The Spanish Inquisition,* 21–23; E. Gutwirth, "Hispano-Jewish Attitudes to the Moors in the Fifteenth Century," *Sefarad* 49 (1989): 251; Kamen, *Empire,* 22.

32. Lowney, *A Vanished World,* 232–34; Kamen, *The Spanish Inquisition,* 40, 48, 57, 81; Payne, *Spanish Catholicism,* 34–35.

33. Kamen, *The Spanish Inquisition,* 234.

34. John Lynch, "Spain after the Expulsion," in *Spain and the Jews: The Sephardi Experience 1492 and After,* ed. Elie Kedourie (London: Thomas & Hudson, 1992), 144.

35. Ruth MacKay, *"Lazy, Improvident People": Myth and Reality in the Writing of Spanish History* (Ithaca, N.Y.: Cornell University Press, 2006), 185.

36. Elliott, *Imperial Spain,* 219; Marcelin Defourneaux, *Daily Life in Spain in the Golden Age,* trans. Newton Branch (New York: Praeger Publishers, 1971), 38, 123–27; Kamen, *The Spanish Inquisition,* 243–44.

37. J. H. Elliott, "The Spanish Conquest," in *Colonial Spanish America,* ed. Leslie Bethell (Cambridge: Cambridge University Press, 1987), 31–32.

38. Elliott, *Imperial Spain,* 58; John E. Kicza, "Patterns in Early Spanish Overseas Expansion," *William and Mary Quarterly* 49, no. 2 (1992): 229–33; Felipe Fernández-Armesto, *The Canary Islands after the Conquest: The Making of a Colonial Society in the Early Sixteenth Century* (Oxford: Clarendon Press, and New York: Oxford University Press, 1982), 2, 9–11, 38–40.

39. Charles Gibson, ed., *The Spanish Tradition in America* (New York: Harper & Row, 1968), 27–34.

40. Christopher Columbus quoted in Lowney, *A Vanished World,* 251, 249; Kamen, *Empire,* 45; Kicza, "Patterns in Early Spanish Overseas Expansion," 238.

41. Oliver Dunn and James E. Kelley, Jr., eds., *The Diario of Christopher Columbus's First Voyage to America, 1492–1493* (Norman: University of Oklahoma Press, 1988), 19.

42. Christopher Columbus cited in John Leddy Phelan, *The Millennial Kingdom of the Franciscans in the New World,* 2nd ed. (Berkeley: University of California Press, 1970), 134 n. 21.

43. See Elliott, *Imperial Spain,* 104.

44. John C. Olin, *Catholic Reform: From Cardinal Ximénes to the Council of Trent* (New York: Fordham University Press, 1990), 6; Payne, *Spanish Catholicism,* 39; Elliott, *Imperial Spain,* 103–5; Kamen, *The Spanish Inquisition,* 83–84.

45. Elliott, *Imperial Spain,* 128; Olin, *Catholic Reform,* 5, 12; Kamen, *Empire,* 3; O'Callaghan, *History of Medieval Spain,* 640–41.

46. Antonio Domínguez Ortiz, *The Golden Age of Spain: 1516–1659* (New York: Basic Books, 1971), 206.

47. George E. Ganss, *Ignatius of Loyola: The Spiritual Exercises and Selected Works* (New York: Paulist Press, 1991), 201–7; 423 n. 129; 424 n. 132.

48. Francisco de los Angeles quoted in Kenneth Mills and William B. Taylor, eds., *Colonial Spanish America: A Documentary History* (Wilmington, Del.: Scholarly Resources, 1998), 48.

49. Gonzalo Fernández de Oviedo y Valdés (1478–1557) quoted in Juan Friede and Benjamin Keen, eds., *Bartolomé de Las Casas in History: Toward an Understanding of the Man and His Work* (DeKalb: Northern Illinois University Press, 1971), 517.

50. Pedro Cieza de León quoted in Luis N. Rivera, *A Violent Evangelism* (Louisville: Westminster/ John Knox, 1992), 157–58.

51. David R. Radell, "The Indian Slave Trade and Population of Nicaragua during the Sixteenth Century," in *The Native Population of the Americas in 1492,* ed. William M. Denevan (Madison: University of Wisconsin Press, 1976), 67–69.

52. Carl Ortwin Sauer, *The Early Spanish Main* (Berkeley: University of California Press, 1969), 88.

53. Ramón Menéndez Pidal, *The Spaniards in Their History* (New York: W. W. Norton, 1950), 41–42.

54. MacKay, *"Lazy, Improvident People,"* 209.

55. Juan Ruiz, *The Book of Good Love,* trans. Rigo Mignani and Mario A. DiCesare (Albany: State University of New York Press, 1970), 20.

56. Lesley Byrd Simpson, *The Encomienda in New Spain* (Berkeley: University of California Press, 1950), 61.

57. Domínguez Ortiz, *Golden Age of Spain,* 206–8.

58. For additional information on this popular work, see *La Celestina: A Novel in Dialogue,* trans. Leslie Byrd Simpson (Berkeley: University of California Press, 1971), 101, and Gerald Brenan, *The Literature of the Spanish People: From Roman Times to the Present* (Cleveland and New York: Meridian Books; World Publishing Company, 1957), 133–34. For comments concerning the conquistadors' hostility to reading literature, see J. H. Elliott, "Cortés, Velázquez and Charles V," in A. R. Pagden, ed. *Hernán Cortés: Letters from Mexico* (New York: Grossman Publishers, 1971), xlvi.

59. Domínguez Ortiz, *Golden Age of Spain,* 288; Elliott, "The Spanish Conquest," xlvii.

60. Lyle N. McAlister, *Spain and Portugal in the New World, 1492–1700* (Minneapolis: University of Minnesota Press, 1984), 79–80.

61. Robert Ricard, *The Spiritual Conquest of Mexico* (Berkeley: University of California Press, 1966), 15–16.

62. McAlister, *Spain and Portugal in the New World,* 80.

63. Domínguez Ortiz, *Golden Age of Spain,* 289.

64. Restall, *Seven Myths of the Spanish Conquest,* 43.

65. Susan Migden Socolow, *The Women of Colonial Latin America* (Cambridge: Cambridge University Press, 2000), 53–54.

66. *Siete Partidas,* Part VII, Title XXXIII, Law VI and *Siete Partidas,* Part IV, Title II, "Introduction," in Scott, *Las Siete Partidas,* 1473, 866.

67. *Siete Partidas,* Part I, Title VI, Law XXVI, in ibid, 94. Women's experiences in Latin America were also shaped by indigenous and African normative traditions of gender. See Socolow, *Women of Colonial Latin America,* especially 16–31.

68. Gibson, *Spanish Tradition in America,* 96.

69. Charles Verlinden, *The Beginnings of Modern Colonization: Eleven Essays with an Introduction,* trans. Yvonne Freccero (Ithaca, N.Y.: Cornell University Press, 1970), 26–29; Payne, *History of Spain and Portugal,* 192, 161.

70. Boies Penrose, *Travel and Discovery in the Renaissance 1420–1620* (New York: Atheneum, 1962), 45.

71. Payne, *History of Spain and Portugal,* 195.

72. John Francis Maxwell, *Slavery and the Catholic Church: The History of Catholic Teaching Concerning the Moral Legitimacy of the Institution of Slavery* (Chichester: Rose [for] the Anti-Slavery Society for the Protection of Human Rights, 1975), 53.

73. Quoted in "The Bull *Eximiae devotionis,* May 3, 1493," *www.kwabs.com/spanish_claim_.html.*

74. Gomes Eannes de Azurara quoted in Robert E. Conrad, *Children of God's Fire: A Documentary History of Black Slavery in Brazil* (University Park: Pennsylvania State University Press, 1994), 9.

75. "Duarte Pacheco, 1505, a well-travelled Portuguese Gentleman," quoted in McAlister, *Spain and Portugal in the New World,* 534–55.

76. See Leslie Rout, *The African Experience in Spanish America, 1502 to the Present Day* (Cambridge: Cambridge University Press, 1976), 76–77.

77. Thomas, *Conquest,* 667 n. 34.

78. Rout, *The African Experience in Spanish America,* 21–22; Domínguez Ortiz, *Golden Age of Spain,* 162–65; McAlister, *Spain and Portugal in the New World,* 53–55; Frank Tannenbaum, *Slave and Citizen: The Negro in the Americas* (New York: Vintage, 1946), 65, 65 (n. 153); Herbert S. Klein, *African Slavery in Latin America and the Caribbean* (New York: Oxford University Press, 1986), especially 195–96.

79. Salvador de Madariaga (1886–1978), engineer, linguist, and diplomat, was a highly accomplished twentieth-century polymath whose well-researched accounts of Spanish colonial America offer valuable insight to the historian. See Salvador de Madariaga, *The Rise of the Spanish American Empire* (London: Hollis and Carter, 1947), 6–7.

80. Lewis Hanke, *The Spanish Struggle for Justice in the Conquest of America* (Philadelphia: University of Pennsylvania Press, 1949), 6. Murdo J. MacLeod, no doubt alluding to the plethora of treatises justifying the "civilizing" nature of aggressive European empire building in the nineteenth century, somewhat off-handedly acknowledges the uniqueness of Spain's — Castile's — early sensitivity: "To the extent that European monarchs and their court thinkers felt obliged to justify their invasions and conquests — and only the Castilians made much of a fuss over this early on...." See MacLeod, "Mesoamerica since the Spanish Invasion: An Overview," 5. See also note 10 in this chapter.

81. Luis N. Rivera, *A Violent Evangelism: The Political and Religious Conquest of the Americas* (Louisville: Westminster John Knox Press, 1992), 71, 64–79.

82. Bartolomé de Las Casas, "Proposition XXX: Thirty Very Juridical Propositions (1552)," in *Columbia College Staff: Introduction to Contemporary Civilization in the West,* 2nd ed. (New York: Columbia University Press, 1954), 1:512. Amerindians and their lands were apportioned to conquistadores on *encomiendas* for the purpose of securing forced labor and tribute payments to their Spanish overlords. *Repartimientos* were forced labor-drafts of Amerindians.

83. Hanke, *The Spanish Struggle for Justice in the Conquest of America,* 31–36; McAlister, *Spain and Portugal in the New World,* 90; Mario Góngora, *Studies in the Colonial History of Spanish America* (Cambridge: Cambridge University Press, 1975), 36–41; Thomas, *Conquest,* 71–72.

84. Juan Ginés de Sepúlveda, "Democrates Alter; or, On the Just Causes for War against the Indians (1547)," in *Columbia College Staff,* 494.

85. Vitoria quoted in Marvin Lunenfeld, *1492 — Discovery, Invasion, Encounter: Sources and Interpretations* (Lexington, Mass.: D.C. Heath, 1991), 198.

86. Menéndez Pidal, *Spaniards in Their History,* 44, 48.

87. Kal Wagenheim with Olga Jiménez de Wagenheim, eds., *The Puerto Ricans: A Documentary History* (Garden City, N.Y.: Doubleday, 1973), 22–23.

88. Restall, *Seven Myths of the Spanish Conquest,* 144.

89. Ibid., 128, 187 (n. 80); Noble David Cook, *Born to Die: Disease and New World Conquest* (Cambridge: Cambridge University Press, 1998); Thomas, *Conquest,* 72.

90. Bernal Díaz del Castillo, *Historia Verdadera de la Conquista de la Nueva España,* 2nd ed. (Mexico City: Editores Mexicanos Unidos, 1992), 115, 203, 719, 720.

91. Spanish authorities never succeeded in creating "two strongly separated worlds [or republics]." See Teresa C. Vergara, "Growing Up Indian: Migration, Labor, and Life in Lima (1570–1640)," in *Raising an Empire: Children in Early Modern Iberia and Colonial Latin America,* ed. Ondina E. González and Bianca Premo (Albuquerque: University of New Mexico Press, 2007), 78.

2

Friars' Accounts of the Native Peoples of the Americas

John F. Schwaller

When the Spanish reached the New World, they had effectively discovered two vast continents inhabited by tens of millions of natives whose languages, customs, cultures, and cosmologies were completely unknown to them. The Spanish had to confront the problem of communication with such peoples quickly. Initially, the Spanish captured natives on the Caribbean islands, taught them Castilian Spanish so that they could serve as interpreters, and schooled them in the European, Christian worldview. A few Spaniards began the long process of acquiring some understanding of and facility with the native languages. On the mainland, intercultural exchanges were made easier by the accidental discovery of a shipwrecked Spaniard who had learned Maya in captivity. Eventually the company of Hernán Cortés acquired a native bilingual woman who spoke Maya and Nahuatl, the Aztec language.[1] Using the two interpreters, Cortés could communicate with many indigenous in what is today central and southeastern Mexico. Later, Francisco Pizarro captured two native boys along the Peruvian coast, who were taught Spanish and served as interpreters of Quechua, the Inca language.[2]

Once the major hostilities of the conquest ended in the centers of colonization, scores of missionaries descended upon Mexico and Peru, eager to convert Spain's new "subjects" to the Christian faith. The spread of Christianity was a major feature of Spanish imperial policy for legitimizing its empire. The missionaries confronted the same issue as the conquerors: how to communicate with the natives. It was clearly more feasible for missionaries to learn Nahuatl, Maya, Quechua, or other native languages than for millions of natives to learn Spanish. This decision meant that the missionaries had to both learn the native languages and understand native culture sufficiently to explain Christianity in terms the natives could grasp at least minimally.

The evangelization of Mexico officially began with the arrival of "The Twelve," the first company of Franciscan missionaries in 1524, barely three years after the fall of Mexico-Tenochtitlan. The conversion of the natives of Mexico was principally the responsibility of the regular clergy: Franciscans, Dominicans, and

Augustinians. They were assisted in their efforts by members of the secular clergy. Later in the century, once initial attempts at conversion were complete, members of the Society of Jesus, established only in 1540, joined the evangelization effort and eventually gained a prominent reputation for their work in frontier areas. Evangelization in Peru followed a very similar pattern — only the order of arrival and the exact mix of religious orders differed. In Peru the Mercedarians gained primacy, followed by the Franciscans, Dominicans, and Augustinians.

Of course, the approach of the missionaries changed over time. Procedures and practices that suited the initial conversion were of less use in an already nominally Christian society. Likewise, over time the missionaries sought to gain a better understanding of the language, customs, and culture of the natives. The evangelization has traditionally been divided into three phases based on the Mexican model. The first phase began with the arrival of the twelve Franciscans and lasted until the erection of the diocese of Mexico in 1536. The second phase continued until the arrival of the Jesuits in 1571 and the pestilence of 1576, while the third phase began in the last quarter of the sixteenth century. The timetable for Peru was similar although all phases occurred fifteen to twenty years later.[3]

In order to better understand the process of Christianization, it is helpful to look at a similar process for which we have better documentation. At the same time that the Spanish were converting the natives to Christianity, Spaniards were learning their languages and natives were learning Spanish. As these cultures continued to develop in proximity aspects of each were incorporated into the other.

James Lockhart and Frances Karttunen have studied the linguistic implications of this interpenetration, scouring thousands of documents written in Nahuatl using European characters, during the period following the initial invasions. In particular, Lockhart and Karttunen studied the degree to which the Nahua adopted Spanish words as their own.[4] Lockhart then extrapolated those findings to develop three periods of cultural exchange. In considering the language exchange between the Nahua and the Spanish, they also identified three major periods or stages. The first stage encompassed the conquest and its immediate aftermath. In this period the Nahua borrowed no Spanish words. The Nahua, however, did use neologisms, modifications of existing Nahuatl words, to describe new things introduced by the Spaniards. Having never seen a horse, the Nahua described it as if it were a deer, *mazatl*. Similarly they called sheep "cotton," *ichcatl*. Anything made of metal received the Nahua name for copper, *tepoztli*. Thus a chain was called a "copper rope," *tepozmecatl*. This first stage lasted until approximately 1545.

The second stage (approx. 1545–1600) witnessed the adoption of Spanish nouns into Nahuatl, but they functioned according to the rules of Nahuatl. Thus, a Spanish noun received a plural using the Nahuatl rule for pluralization. For example, the Spanish word for angels, *ángeles*, in Nahuatl is *angelesme*, where the plural marker of -*me* was added to the already plural Spanish word. Similarly a

Spanish word used in Nahuatl might become part of a compound word, using Nahuatl rules. A horse stable in Stage 2 would be a *cahuallocalli*. Here the Spanish word for horse, *caballo*, was compounded with the Nahuatl word for house or structure, *calli*. The second stage lasted until the end of the sixteenth century in central Mexico, but continued for a longer time in outlying areas.

The third stage of Spanish borrowing by the Nahuas occurred in the seventeenth century when they began to borrow Spanish verbs and other parts of speech, but again guided by rules internal to Nahuatl. This stage also saw the breakdown of some of the older rules regarding nouns. For example, nouns appeared with a Spanish plural. Even Spanish numbers began to predominate, displacing the elegant, yet complex, number system of the Nahua. The Spanish verb *notificar*, for example, became the Nahuatl verb *notificaroa*, as in *nicnotificaroa*: "I notify him."

In keeping with the schema proposed by Lockhart, one can study the process whereby the Spanish, in general, and the missionary priests and friars, in particular, acquired knowledge of the natives in the New World. The first phase, as noted above, was characterized by simple language acquisition. The first generation of missionaries attempted to learn the rudiments of native languages. Their goal was to develop grammars and bilingual dictionaries. Considering the actual number of books printed, they seem to have been quite successful. The printing press was brought to Mexico in 1536 and the first book was printed in Spanish and Nahuatl. Since the press was not brought to Peru until 1582, language books for that province were printed elsewhere prior to that date. Scores of early books printed in the Americas were grammars of native languages and bilingual dictionaries. In fact one can document the initial contact between the missionaries and new groups of natives by tracing the publication of grammars and dictionaries. During the 1540–50s in Mexico one finds such publications for Nahuatl, Matlazinga, Huasteca, Tarascan (now known as Purépecha), Mixteca, Cachiquel, and Totonac. Since the conquest of Peru occurred later than that of Mexico, a Quechua grammar was not printed until 1560 and in Spain. Guides were later printed for other languages such as Timucua (Florida) and Aymara (Bolivia).

Once Spaniards had learned the rudiments of native languages they attempted to translate Christian doctrine into the new tongues. In fact the first book printed in the New World was a Christian doctrine written in Nahuatl. Usually, however, the published catechisms and other missionary texts were printed after the initial grammars and dictionaries. The printed doctrine introduced a wide range of problems into the missionary process, despite their original intent, because most native languages had no appropriate terms for Christian concepts such as sin, redemption, and especially the word for one God. While the missionaries could use terms from the native languages that approximated Christian concepts, they would risk confusing Christian doctrines and practices with native ones. The missionaries could also develop neologisms in the native languages to represent the Christian concept. For example they developed the word *tlacatecolotl* (owl man) to describe the Christian devil to the Nahua. Lastly, they could simply use the appropriate Spanish term and thus not risk one kind of confusion while introducing another.

The third phase of missionary activity consisted of studying and describing native practices and beliefs. Once a territory was conquered, native languages learned, and Christian doctrines translated, the missionaries could spend more time studying native cultures. As contact with the natives increased and the Spaniards gained additional insights into native cultures, the missionaries wrote more analytical, sophisticated, and virtually anthropological studies. The passage of time, however, may have worked to compromise the accuracy of natives' memories of their culture as it had been at the moment of invasion.

Father Toribio de Benavente (c. 1487–1569) was a member of the original expedition of twelve Franciscans to Mexico in 1524. After acquiring familiarity with the sound of Nahuatl, he noticed that the natives could be heard using the word *motolinia* whenever the friars passed. Benavente questioned one of the interpreters and learned that the word meant "he goes around being poor." Benavente adopted this phrase as his own name, reflecting one of the missionary goals of the first Franciscans, to teach apostolic poverty by example.[5] Motolinía became a keen observer of native culture. Between 1536 and 1541 he composed a long treatise on the history and culture of the natives and the evangelization process. He also made a shorter version. Parts of both of these and additional notes and drafts have been preserved. One, *Historia de los indios de la Nueva España,* is the shorter but better organized. The other, *Memoriales o Libro de las cosas de la Nueva España,* while much longer and containing more information on most topics, is less well organized and may have actually been the drafts and notes for a lost work. Motolinía's observations are generally accepted as more accurate and less biased than the works of other missionaries.[6]

Andrés de Olmos, O.F.M., who arrived in New Spain in 1528 and quickly learned Nahuatl, was another astute student of native culture who collected information about the native past, though his major works have been lost. We know about them only through commentaries written by his contemporaries. The one work that has survived is a collection of Nahua metaphorical speech. The Nahua were fond of complicated poetic descriptions of virtues and vices. Both the complexity and poetry of these sayings stand out. One describes a child as follows:

> The beloved child is as precious as the plumes of
> Flamingos, the quetzal,
> The egret, the heron.[7]

This metaphor shows a common rhetorical device of the Nahua: the use of birds to symbolize precious objects. The quetzal, a turquoise blue feathered bird from the tropical lowlands, was especially prized. While most of Olmos's work has been lost, his Franciscan brethren drew upon his research and manuscripts to fashion their own anthropological studies.

Two Franciscans became the leading scholars of Nahuatl in the sixteenth century. Alonso de Molina (c. 1513–79) developed the most comprehensive dictionary of the language. He was born in Spain, but moved to Mexico as a small child with his parents soon after the conquest. Molina learned Nahuatl as a child, probably entered the Franciscan convent as a youth, and served as an interpreter before formally joining the order.[8] He continued to work in native villages where he perfected his Nahuatl. Early in his career he wrote several works in Nahuatl, including sets of ordinances for religious sodalities and hospitals in native communities. Based on his own research, and that of fellow Franciscans, in 1555 Molina published his famous *Vocabulario en lengua castellana y mexicana*, a Spanish to Nahuatl dictionary. In this work Molina provided Nahuatl glosses for some thirteen thousand Spanish words. He drew heavily on his predecessors, Olmos and Motolinía, and others such as the native Hernando de Ribas, who had been trained by the Franciscans in their Colegio de Santa Cruz Tlatelolco (Holy Cross College) in Mexico City.

Following the publication of the dictionary, Molina turned his attention to more traditional projects. In 1565 he published two widely used confessional guides, one long, one short. These consisted of questions asked by the confessor in Nahuatl, with common responses also in Nahuatl. Using these books, priests who had only a superficial acquaintance with Nahuatl could at least work through the basics of confession in that language. Molina's successful guides were subsequently reprinted.

Molina's ongoing project, however, was the revision of his dictionary. The original work had included only Spanish to Nahuatl translations. In 1571 he published the larger and more comprehensive Spanish to Nahuatl and Nahuatl to Spanish dictionary. This thorough work became the standard dictionary of the Nahua language and remains so today. It expanded the number of Spanish words for which he provided Nahuatl glosses. Further, a unique factor in the new dictionary was his addition of neologisms, i.e., new Nahuatl words developed to accommodate European plants, animals, and products. Some of these were true neologisms while others were Spanish words absorbed into Nahuatl according to Nahuatl grammatical conventions.

The other towering figure in the study of native peoples of Mesoamerica is Bernardino de Sahagún, O.F.M. (1499–1590), who first came to prominence in his role as translator in the Don Carlos affair. Don Carlos, the native ruler of Texcoco and one of the Spaniards' first allies, was arrested in 1536, charged with idolatry and apostasy, and tried before an inquisitorial court convened by the bishop of Mexico, Juan de Zumárraga. Although Don Carlos had been baptized and overtly embraced Christianity, he had not abandoned his traditional beliefs and apparently worshiped a large collection of pre-Hispanic images. His arrest, conviction, and execution sent shock waves through the colony.[9] The Franciscans had put considerable effort into the conversion of native leaders like Don Carlos, based upon their belief that if a native leader converted to Christianity, as the Roman Emperor Constantine had done, then others would follow. For this same reason they established schools for the sons of the native nobility, first in Texcoco and later in Mexico City.[10] Don Carlos, upon whom much energy was expended, had not been what he seemed.

The Don Carlos affair produced major changes in the colony. The friars were forced to reconcile themselves to the inevitability of a lengthy conversion process. They also realized it was impractical to hold Indians to the same standards of orthodoxy as Spaniards, especially when Indian nobles who were in close contact with the friars apparently maintained allegiance to their gods. And, as was stated earlier, the trial also signaled the entrance of the friar who would significantly contribute to future conversion strategies: Bernardino de Sahagún.

Sahagún had been in New Spain since 1529 and had learned Nahuatl well.[11] Although Sahagún was an active missionary throughout his career, he occasionally taught the sons of the Nahua nobility at the Holy Cross College. In about 1547 Sahagún began collecting data about the life, culture, and history of the Nahua. His technique of conducting extensive interviews of native elders has led some modern scholars to consider him the first ethnographer. Sahagún's investigations ultimately resulted in his writing many different types of work, each with a specific purpose. The unifying vision behind his multifaceted productions was the creation of a *corpus* of materials to assist missionaries and parish priests in the conversion of the natives.[12] Sahagún believed that well-trained missionaries would be better able to deal with alien cultures and languages. His experience at the trial of Don Carlos of Texcoco and service in the evangelization of rural areas of New Spain had demonstrated to him the incomplete nature of Indian conversion during the first twenty years after the conquest of Tenochtitlan. Sahagún wished to go beyond producing grammars, dictionaries, and confessional guides to more fully equipping and arming the missionaries with works outlining the pre-Columbian belief systems. This information, he believed, would assist the parish priest in identifying and thus eliminating vestiges of traditional Indian religion. As part of this program, Sahagún produced several works put to immediate use by his fellow missionaries, including collections of sermons, the "Psalmodia christiana," a collection of native hymns recast to celebrate the saints and feasts of the Christian calendar; the translation of the Epistle and Gospel readings for the Sunday Mass into Nahuatl; as well as the commentary on these readings. These works, taken as a whole, have been characterized as a "doctrinal encyclopedia."[13] As with his doctrinal works, he wrote his ethnographic works in Nahuatl with additional Spanish glosses. The most famous of these latter works is the *Historia universal de las cosas de la Nueva España,* also known as the *Florentine Codex.*

The *Florentine Codex* is a twelve-volume encyclopedia of Nahua history and customs. The original work was written in a two-column format, with Nahuatl in one and a Spanish gloss in the other, and was extensively illustrated. Because Sahagún attempted to preserve so many aspects of Nahua culture, he aroused opposition from some of his fellow friars and from quarters of the royal government. Both of these groups believed his efforts would preserve native customs and thus undermine evangelization. In fact the work was confiscated by colonial officials and forwarded to officials in Spain. Within a few years it appeared in the library of the dukes of Tuscany, in Florence, hence the modern name *Florentine Codex.*

Sahagún's work described the origins of and ceremonies for the ancient gods, the duties of soothsayers, the nature of omens, Nahua rhetoric, and moral philosophy. It detailed the religious and cultural significance of sacred and ordinary objects such as the sun, moon, and stars, kings, merchants, and common people, and flora and fauna. He concluded with an account of the Spanish invasion from the native perspective. Under Sahagún's direction, several students from the Holy Cross College collaborated in writing this work, including Antonio Valeriano from Atzcapotzalco, Alonso Vegerano and Pedro de San Buenaventura from Cuauhtitlan, and Martín Jacobita from Tlatelolco. These young men were multilingual, having been trained in Spanish, Latin, and Greek, as well as being familiar with native Nahuatl. Sahagún also used the students to draft and polish his works in Nahuatl.

In considering the three periods of cultural encounter, one can place Sahagún firmly in the third. While the Nahuatl in which he wrote was only slightly influenced by Spanish, his European view of the world differed significantly from that of his clerical peers. While he shared the goal of extirpating the native religion in favor of Christianity, he believed true conversions could be achieved only by thoroughly understanding native cultures. With that understanding the missionary friars could better identify and correct traditional behaviors inimical to Christianity.

Compared with that of other friars working in Mexico at the time, Sahagún's approach was unquestionably the most nuanced and attuned to the native cultures. One sees his deep sympathy for the natives, for example, in the words he uses to describe the arrival of the first Franciscan friars into Tenochtitlan after its destruction, which are almost identical to Nahua descriptions of the ancient gods convening to create the present world.[14] Similarly, in his collection of songs, Sahagún places Christian themes within images and structures of pre-Columbian Nahua poetics.[15] For example, Sahagún imitates an ancient song composed by Nezahualcoyotl, the fifteenth-century ruler of the city of Texcoco, who had written the phrase "There! The turquoise swan, the trogon, the roseate swan is singing, warbling, happy with these flowers."[16] Sahagún, in a song celebrating Easter, echoed this: "You divine orioles, you grosbeaks, you mockingbirds, you humming birds, all you sons of God, you angels; come, circle around the courtyard of our church."[17]

While there is evolution in the care and sophistication with which some missionary friars approached the native language and culture in central Mexico among the Nahua, the same does not hold true for other regions of Latin America. In both the Yucatan Peninsula, home to the Maya culture, and in Peru and Bolivia, home to the Inca, one simply does not find the same degree of interest on the part of most friars. Nevertheless, some missionaries did seek to acquire a deeper knowledge of native cultures in a manner similar to Motolinía, Molina, and Sahagún.

In the Yucatan, as in Central Mexico, the Franciscans were the leading missionaries. While there was some early ethnographic interest, it did not compare with the intensity of the work of Olmos or Motolinía among the Nahua, although several grammars, dictionaries, and confessional guides written by and for the use of the friars appeared. The large number of dialects within Maya complicated missionary activity in Yucatan, Chiapas, and Guatemala. Within a few decades, however, works were written in Yucatec Maya, Quiché, Cachiquel, Tzeltal, Tzotzil, and Lacandón, among others. Diego de Landa, O.F.M. (1524–79), was the leading figure in the missionary efforts among the Yucatec Maya. His career is a model for developing an understanding of the value of native languages and traditions.

Landa, born in Spain, entered the Franciscan order there and was assigned to the missions in Yucatan. He arrived sometime before 1549 and quickly set about learning Maya. For many years he served as a missionary in several parishes, notably Itzamal. In 1561 he was elected provincial of the newly formed Franciscan Province of San José de Yucatán. His leadership of the order brought him into conflict with both the local royal authorities and the local bishop. The conflict concerned Landa's use of an Inquisition against various native leaders for apostasy. The bishop complained that Landa had overstepped his powers by launching an Inquisition, a power strictly limited to bishops. Moreover, local royal authorities complained that Landa had dealt too harshly with the natives. As part of these dealings, Landa collected as many native books and artifacts as he could and destroyed them, thus permanently doing away with significant religious and cultural information on the pre-Hispanic Maya peoples. By 1563 Landa was forced to return to Spain to answer for his actions. There he wrote his most famous work, *Relación de las cosas de Yucatán,* a treasure trove of information on the Maya. He was eventually acquitted of all charges and even appointed bishop of Yucatan in 1573. His service as bishop contrasted significantly with his time as provincial. Rather than repeating the violence of his inquisitorial period, Bishop Landa manifested a greater appreciation for native culture.

Landa's *Relación* existed only in manuscript form until the nineteenth century. As a result his work did not inform scholars until quite recently. They questioned the credibility of the work, largely because of Landa's reputation for cruelty while a provincial and as a result of one section in the work wherein he presented an equivalency between Maya glyphs and European letters. It was not until the 1980s that scholars realized that the glyphs reported by Landa had the sound value of European letters. Maya writing was not truly phonetic but constituted a transitional phase between representational, wherein each glyph actually represents what it depicts, and phonetic, wherein the glyph has a sound value but little representational value.[18] As a result, Landa has been somewhat vindicated. His "alphabet" was a true and faithful representation of sounds, but not letters. Scholars have increasingly given more credence to other sections in his *Relación* now that his linguistic analyses have proven accurate.

In modern editions the *Relación* consists of some fifty chapters. While not as extensive as Sahagún's work, it represents a rich and detailed account of native culture both before and after the conquest. The account is written in Spanish, not Maya, and is clearly intended for a European audience. Importantly for modern scholars, Landa observed Maya society as it existed shortly after the conquest. Unlike the Aztec civilization, which was at its high point at the time of the arrival of the Spanish, Maya civilization was much older. It had reached its peak in the tenth century and had then declined. In the two hundred years prior to the arrival of the Spanish the Maya culture had begun to regain something approaching its earlier glory. It was this later Maya culture that the friars observed and that Landa described in his book.

In South America the explorers and conquerors found the massive Inca empire stretching down the Andean region from what is now southern Colombia into modern-day Chile and Argentina. The conquest of this immense area had similarities to and differences from the conquest of the Maya and Aztecs. The conquerors of the Inca had learned lessons from earlier invasions and gained an advantage by immediately capturing the reigning sovereign of the empire, Atahualpa. The Spaniards were not aware that the empire had just emerged from a debilitating civil war between two claimants to the throne, and that Atahualpa, while victorious, ruled a weakened empire. So, although actual conquest occurred in a fairly brief manner, Peru continued to be wracked by civil war among the Spaniards. Repeating a trend begun in the Caribbean islands and then spread to the mainland, many conquistadors in Peru felt that they had not been sufficiently rewarded for their military services. Protracted resistance by indigenous peoples and political intrigue by Spanish conquistadors continued well into the 1540s. The unsettled political environment discouraged missionaries from entering the territory.

While the Franciscans had been among the vanguard of missionaries in North America, in the Andean region they arrived later than the Mercedarians and Dominicans. Following the well-known pattern, the missionary orders first established houses and convents in the major Spanish cities, such as Lima and Cuzco, and then in smaller provincial cities, like Arequipa or Trujillo, and used those outposts as launching pads for conversion of the natives. While the friars learned the local language, especially Quechua, the number of missionary materials in that language never equaled that of publications in Nahuatl or even Maya.

The lack of missionary materials in Quechua has puzzled scholars for decades. Some have noted that the Inca, unlike the Maya and the Aztec, did not employ a writing system using paper. The Inca used knotted and colored strings for record keeping. The size, frequency, pattern of knots, colors of string, and other features allowed the Inca to record and maintain vast quantities of data. The knotted strings were called *quipu*, and Inca officials charged with maintaining the records were *quipucamayoc*. Some scholars believe that *quipu* were in fact mnemonic devices: that the patterns, knots, and colors allowed the *quipucamayoc* to recall the information he had memorized. As such, each person's records would be unique and probably unintelligible to others. Thus, the *quipu* was not a universal record keeping system, but many different systems.

The political instability that contributed to the late arrival of the missionaries and later the lack of the printing press made it difficult to obtain accurate information about Inca culture prior to the invasion. Mexico benefited from a quick introduction of the printing press barely a dozen years after the conquest. In sharp contrast Lima did not have a press until 1582, fully forty years after the conquest. In Mexico dozens of works in native languages had been printed during the first fifty years of the press. As with Quechua, many of these languages had no indigenous form of writing. In Peru the absence of the press thus discouraged the use of the printed word as a medium for evangelization. Therefore, the fact that Quechua was not recorded in a manner intelligible to the Spaniards probably did not contribute significantly to the lack of written materials in that language among the missionaries. It seems more likely that missionaries in Inca areas simply did not take as active a role in the accumulation of information about the native society as their brethren in Mexico. In fact, of the major works written within a century of the conquest, only three came from the pens of religious. Royal officials who arrived in the Andes shortly after the conquest authored the earliest accounts. Perhaps the millennial spirit of the first generation of missionary friars in the Americas was largely spent by the time missionary orders became fully established in Peru in the 1550s.

Pedro Cieza de León (1520–54) arrived in the Indies shortly after the major conquests. He had served as a conqueror and in various official positions in what is now Colombia before joining the entourage of Pedro de la Gasca, the newly appointed viceroy of Peru in 1547. Although he spent only three years in Peru before returning to Spain, while in the Andean region he collected vast amounts of information about the native past. Once in Spain he wrote and published the first part of his *Chronicle of Peru,* which dealt extensively with the native cultures as they existed at the time of contact. Cieza wrote two additional parts, one on the conquest of the Inca and the other on ensuing civil war among the conquerors.[19]

The other government official to write about the Inca civilization was Juan Polo de Ondegardo (d. 1575). Polo also arrived in Peru in the entourage of La Gasca and participated in the final assault on the region. He served in a number of government positions, mostly as local magistrate, or *corregidor,* and governor of various provinces. From that vantage point he wrote three works on the native culture and history of the Inca, the most famous being "Of the Lineage of the Incas and How They Extended Their Conquests."[20] Although this work remained unpublished until the late nineteenth century, it did influence early missionary activity in Peru. Two of the leading religious involved in missionary activity, José de Acosta and Bernabé Cobo, drew heavily from Polo's work in their own studies of Inca customs and history. Polo's work also provided background material for the bishops of the ecclesiastical province of Peru when they met in 1583 during the Third Provincial Council. The prelates ordered an abstract of his work published for the use by local parish priests.[21]

Two major works written by persons of indigenous heritage detailing native culture and history appeared at the beginning of the seventeenth century. The best-known work, entitled *Royal Commentaries of the Inca,* was written by Garcilaso de la Vega, "el Inca" (1539–1616). His father was a Spanish conqueror and his mother a member of the Inca royal family. Shortly after his father's death Garcilaso traveled to Spain in 1560, where he spent the remainder of his life, living in the southern city of Córdoba. During the late sixteenth and early seventeenth centuries he composed his *Royal Commentaries* based upon the information he had gathered as a child and young adult in Peru.[22] Though this work did not receive acclaim during the colonial period because of its critical portrayal of Spanish colonizers, Garcilaso's first-hand knowledge, quite literally at his mother's knee, is now regarded as one of the most authentic accounts of pre-Hispanic Inca society and a key source of information for scholars.

The other and more recently discovered work, *First New Chronicle and Good Government,* was written by Felipe Guaman Poma de Ayala (c. 1535–1615). Guaman Poma was the son of a noble Inca mother and a Spanish father who learned to read and write Spanish. He was a *kuraka* (local Indian leader) working under the authority of the Spaniards. His work is an extensive narrative of the history and customs of the Inca and contains large sections that detail the abuses of the Indians at the hands of priests and Spanish officials. Guaman Poma seasoned his narrative with words in Quechua and included his own illustrations in the manuscript, which have become as famous as the text itself. The work was not discovered until the mid-twentieth century.[23] As a result, although it aids modern scholars and provides another point of view into the Andean world, its impact on missionaries and others at the time was indirect.

Recent scholarship has demonstrated that Poma de Ayala worked as an assistant to another missionary friar, Father Martín de Murúa, a Mercedarian friar who composed three works between 1590 and 1610. The earliest was the *Historia y genealogía real de los Reyes Incas del Perú.* It was written as a report and dedicated to Philip II. The second work was a treatise written in 1613 on the history of the natives and their culture, the *Historia general del Perú.* Murúa was unable to secure permission to publish the work, but it circulated in manuscript. The work is heavily illustrated, and scholars have recently concluded that the drawings were made by Guaman Poma, his contemporary. His other manuscript probably dates from around the same period, and exists only in a nineteenth-century copy. The content of these works demonstrates that Murúa was a keen observer of native customs and history. His impact was great, insofar as he might have inspired Poma de Ayala to compose his *Corónica.* The works of both of these individuals circulated in manuscript form, especially among the Mercedarians, and thus impacted their missionary activities.[24]

Another missionary, José de Acosta (1540–1600), a Jesuit sent to Peru in 1569, spent considerable time in the Andean highlands and a briefer period in Mesoamerica. He served in various positions until 1585, when he was called back to Europe. He reported his findings on the New World in his *Natural and Moral History of the Indies,* published in Seville in 1590. Acosta's book is unique in many ways. A talented observer and highly educated, he was able to appreciate events that sometimes challenged and contradicted his own traditional learning. While Aristotelian science indicated that climates near the equator were hot and dry and moderate the further north one traveled, Acosta observed snow-capped peaks in the Andes and concluded that altitude shaped climate as much as latitude. Acosta drew heavily upon the work of others who had also visited these same regions in the Americas, such as Polo de Ondegardo. Acosta can be considered at the pinnacle of clerical writers who described the cultures of the peoples of Peru.

Luis Jerónimo de Oré (c. 1554–1630), born in Huamanga, Peru, to a Spanish family, became a Franciscan friar and active missionary and also wrote works describing the native cultures of the Andes. His didactic works assisted in the conversion of the natives. Unlike so many other works that appeared only in manuscript, Oré's work was published in Lima in 1598 as the *Símbolo católico indiano.*[25] It contained theological discussions designed to assist missionaries in converting the natives. Oré also composed statements of Christian doctrine in both Quechua and Aymara, the leading native languages of modern-day Peru and Bolivia. Later in his career he served as an ecclesiastical judge in the Franciscan province of Florida and wrote yet another book on the conquest of that region and the evangelization of its peoples.[26] The works of Oré became widespread during the colonial period among missionaries, and served as useful tools in the evangelization, due to the accuracy of his observations.

Taken as a whole, the missionary friars in the New World contributed significantly to our understanding of the native peoples whom they encountered. Frequently the missionary is envisioned as determined to eradicate the culture of the natives as part of the Christianizing mission. While this is true, it fails to adequately take into account both the vocation of the missionary and the perspective of the native. In general, the writings of the missionaries demonstrate that many had a great appreciation of native cultures despite the priority of their divine calling, a vocation to spread the Gospel.

The three periods of cultural contact outlined by Lockhart help explain missionary activity. The first period was the most difficult. Missionaries sometimes felt driven not only to spread the Gospel but also to eliminate all vestiges of pre-Hispanic cultures. They assumed that religion could exist only as part of a larger culture. By the second period most missionaries had developed a more nuanced perspective. The friars better understood that certain aspects of native culture were not inimical to Christianity but were, in fact, strongly supportive of it. The traditions of mutuality and sharing that pervaded native cultures, for example, were seen as highly supportive of Christian charity. In this middle period, missionaries then began to focus on those specific features of native culture that did not fit well into Christianity. Clearly, the Aztec rites of human sacrifice had to give way to the Christian notion of sacrifice embodied in the Eucharist. As a result, works from this period focused more specifically on similarities and differences between the cultures. Some of the great confessional guides, such as that of Alonso de Molina, date from this middle period. Landa, an iconic figure in evangelization, might be perceived as straddling the first and second periods. As provincial he supervised the destruction of native texts, yet later as bishop he recognized the need to learn as much as possible about indigenous cultures. By the later period friars such as Sahagún in Mexico and Oré, Murúa, and Acosta in Peru fully understood the need to immerse themselves in those cultures. They produced detailed and complex accounts drawn from a deep and intimate understanding of both Christian and indigenous worlds.

Thus, in looking at the three phases of cultural contact from the perspective of the evangelization of the Americas, one can see that the Spanish moved from an approach based on their own assumptions and misconceptions of the native cultures to a deeper understanding and appreciation of cultural difference. While in even the third phase both the Spaniards and the natives fell victim to the "double mistaken identity," each side had become far more skilled in interpreting the actions and intention of the other. This process of cultural change and increasing cultural awareness would form the basis upon which colonial relations developed for nearly three centuries.

Notes

1. The shipwrecked Spaniard was Diego de Aguilar. The native woman given to Cortés by a local native ruler was called Marina, a variant of María, her baptismal name.

2. James Lockhart, *Men of Cajamarca* (Austin: University of Texas Press, 1972), 448–53. The exact manner whereby they joined the Spanish is unclear. They might have been kidnapped, or they might have been purchased as slaves from local natives.

3. This general chronology was first proposed by John L. Phelan in his analysis of the works of Gerónimo de Mendieta, an early Franciscan missionary. Phelan proposes only two periods, a golden age from the conquest until 1564, and a silver age that followed, marking the reign of Phillip II, until 1598, and then decline thereafter. John L. Phelan, *The Millennial Kingdom of the Franciscans in the New World,* 2nd rev. ed. (Berkeley: University of California Press, 1970), 81–83.

4. All of the examples cited below come from James Lockhart, *The Nahuas after the Conquest* (Stanford, Calif.: Stanford University Press, 1992), 63–318. Lockhart drew from research that he and Karttunen had conducted on language change; Frances Karttunen and James Lockhart, *Nahuatl in the Middle Years: Language Contact Phenomena in Texts of the Colonial Period* (Berkeley: University of California Press, 1976).

5. Bernal Díaz del Castillo, *Historia Verdadera de la Conquista de la Nueva España* (Mexico City: Editorial Porrúa, 1942), 2:176–177.

6. Ernest J. Burrus, "Religious Chroniclers and Historians: A Summary and Annotated Bibliography," in *Handbook of Middle American Indians,* vol. 13, *Guide to Ethnohistorical Sources, Part Two,* ed. Robert Wauchope (Austin: University of Texas Press, 1973), 144–45.

7. Judith M. Maxwell and Craig A. Hanson, *Of the Manners of Speaking that the Old Ones Had* (Salt Lake City: University of Utah Press, 1992), 172.

8. Miguel León-Portilla, "Estudio Preliminar," in Alonso de Molina, *Vocabulario en lengua castellana y mexicana y mexicana y castellana* (Mexico City: Editorial Porrúa, 1970), xxi–xxvi.

9. Documents related to the trial are printed in Luis González Obregón, ed. *Proceso inquisitorial del Cacique de Texcoco* (Mexico City: Archivo General de la Nación, 1910); the best modern study of the trial is Richard Greenleaf, *Zumárraga and the Mexican Inquisition, 1536–1543* (Washington, D.C.: Academy of American Franciscan History, 1961), 68–74.

10. José María Kobayashi, *La educación como conquista: Empresa franciscana en México* (Mexico City: El Colegio de México, 1974), 232–59 and 292–357, passim.

11. Luis Nicolau d'Olwer, *Fray Bernardino de Sahagún, 1499–1590,* trans. Mauricio Mixco (Salt Lake City: University of Utah Press, 1987), 17–18.

12. Ibid., 6–7.

13. Ibid., 41.

14. John F. Schwaller, "'Centlalia' and 'Nonotza' in the Writings of Sahagún: A New Interpretation of his Messiological Vision," *Estudios de Cultura Nahuatl* 33 (2002): 295–314.

15. John F. Schwaller, "Pre-Hispanic Poetics of Sahagún's *Psalmodia christiana,*" *Estudios de Cultura Nahuatl* 36 (2005): 67–86.

16. John Bierhorst, trans., *Cantares Mexicanos, Songs of the Aztecs* (Stanford, Calif.: Stanford University Press, 1985), 190–91.

17. Sahagún, *Psalmodia christiana,* 112–13.

18. Michael Coe, *Breaking the Maya Code* (London: Thames and Hudson, 1999).

19. Pedro Cieza de León, *The Discovery and Conquest of Peru,* ed. and trans. Alexandra Parma Cook and Noble David Cook (Durham, N.C.: Duke University Press, 1998).

20. Clements R. Markham, *Narratives of the Rites and Laws of the Yncas* (London: Hakluyt Society, 1873), 151–73.

21. Ana María Presta and Catherine Julien, "Polo de Ondegardo (ca. 1520–1575)," *Guide to Documentary Sources for Andean Studies, 1530–1900,* ed. Joanne Pilsbury (Norman: University of Oklahoma Press, 2008), 3:531.

22. Garcilaso de la Vega, *Royal Commentaries of the Inca,* 2 vols., trans. Harold Livermore (Austin: University of Texas Press, 1966).

23. *www.kb.dk/permalink/2006/poma/info/en/frontpage.htm.*

24. Juan M. Ossio, "Murúa, Martín de (?–ca. 1620)," *Guide to Documentary Sources for Andean Studies, 1530–1900,* ed. Joanne Pilsbury (Norman: University of Oklahoma Press, 2008), 3:436–41.

25. Luis Jerónimo de Oré, *Símbolo católico indiano* (Lima: Australis, 1992).

26. Luis Jerónimo de Oré, *The Martyrs of Florida (1513–1616),* ed. and trans. Maynard Geiger (New York: Joseph F. Wagner, 1939).

3

Conversion and the Spiritual Conquest

David Tavárez and John F. Chuchiak

Introduction

In the early morning of May 13, 1524, a ship docked at the port of Veracruz. Among its many passengers and crew were twelve Franciscan friars, wearing old, torn garments. Their goal was to create a Christian humanist utopia in the New World. The conversion campaign they would soon initiate, under the leadership of Friar Martín de Valencia, has been called the "Spiritual Conquest" by scholars who have attempted to describe the phenomena of Christian evangelism and mass conversion of native peoples in the sixteenth century.[1]

The conversion of the indigenous peoples of Latin America to Catholicism and the eradication of their ancient beliefs and religious rituals were as important to most Spaniards as the military conquest. Thus, although Hernán Cortés is well known for his political prowess and military achievements, he also evangelized throughout the conquest and after the destruction of Tenochtitlan he was always an advocate for the immediate conversion of the Amerindian.[2]

Mendicant Franciscan, Dominican, and Augustinian friars employed different methods to convert indigenous peoples to Spanish Catholicism. Some of the earliest missionaries believed that their goals could be achieved simply by destroying the natives' temples, prohibiting their ancient rites, and punishing natives who continued to maintain allegiance to their ancient beliefs. Other missionaries believed it was imperative to convince the natives of the righteousness of conversion through pious sermons and moral example. Many missionaries learned indigenous languages, compiled dictionaries, and gathered information on indigenous cultures as a means of facilitating Christian evangelism.

Early Evangelization Efforts: From Utopia to Debates on Rationality

Pope Alexander VI, in his bull *Inter Caetera* (1493), divided the world into two spheres of influence, Spanish and Portuguese, and charged Iberia's Catholic monarchs with the responsibility for evangelizing newly discovered lands. Although

Spanish evangelization began on the island of Hispaniola in 1500 with the establishment of the first Franciscan mission, the most ambitious push for conversion of large numbers of indigenous peoples came to New Spain in 1524. Other regions of the Americas would witness similar attempts at conversion, but seldom with the same intensity of missionary activity visited upon New Spain in the sixteenth century.[3] Early evangelization efforts in Peru, which began shortly after a Spanish force led by Francisco Pizarro took over the Inca capital of Cuzco in 1532, provide a measure of contrast. While the Dominican order sent missionaries into the mountain villages north of Lima and presided over evangelization efforts in central Peru during the 1530s and 1540s, a series of military and political confrontations between rival factions of Spanish conquerors did not provide a favorable climate for the development of doctrinal methods and approaches targeting Andean communities.[4]

Mendicants held divergent beliefs concerning the inherent abilities of the natives to understand, receive, and accept the fundamental doctrines of Christianity. Although not initially convinced of the rational abilities of the natives, most Franciscans and a smaller number of other religious remained steadfast in their commitment to working with them. They maintained respect for certain aspects of native culture and considered Indians *gente de razón* (rational people). Their opponents, which included a number of Dominicans, Augustinians, and ecclesiastical authorities, decried the mass-conversion methods favored by the Franciscans, denied Indian rationality, and classified the Indian in a lower category of peoples, namely, *gente sin razón* (irrational people), incapable of conversion. Pope Paul III sided with the former and issued two bulls that embodied the church's position on Indian conversion.[5] The first, *Veritas ipsa* (1537), officially condemned Indian slavery and outlawed its continuance by Christians, while the second, *Sublimis Deus* (1537), unequivocally stated that Indians were truly rational human beings who had the aptitude for becoming fully Christian.[6] The crown, however, prohibited these bulls from being published in Spain and the colonies because of fear that their proclamation would interfere with Indian policy.[7] Nevertheless, the crown sponsored the "Great Debate" at Valladolid, Spain, in 1550–51 in order to reach its own conclusions regarding Indian rationality.[8]

The Dominicans Bartolomé de las Casas (1484–1566) and Juan Ginés de Sepúlveda (1494–1573) represented the two divergent categorizations expressed above in that debate in Valladolid. Ginés de Sepúlveda, royal historian and theologian, presented the Aristotelian argument that Amerindians and other human populations were predisposed to being enslaved by nature, due to their limited capacity for reason and barbarous customs. Las Casas, named the "Protector of the Indians," argued that Amerindians were rational beings, and as such could not be reduced to slavery or forced to accept the Christian faith. In the end, the crown's indigenous policies did not express a clear preference for either argument, featuring instead an array of contradictory provisions that both favored the use of nonviolent methods for teaching Christianity and European customs and at the same time treated indigenous peoples as childlike legal subjects.[9]

The admittance of indigenous converts to the priesthood became an even more divisive issue for missionaries. The Augustinian order, first represented in New Spain in 1532, was generally receptive to the idea of Indian clergy. Augustinians insisted on the high moral capacity of the Indians and encouraged them to receive the third sacrament of Christian initiation, the Eucharist.[10] Most Franciscans believed that indigenous people had the ability to learn basic Christian tenets but disagreed on whether they possessed sufficient mental capacity for ordination. Zealous friars such as Jerónimo de Mendieta (1525–1604) and Bernardino de Sahagún (1499–1590), for example, treated converts like children, forever unfitted for ordination. Further, they noted that indigenous peoples were also incapable of celibacy, whereas Juan de Zumárraga, the first bishop and archbishop of New Spain, held that the Indians were rational and capable of performing priestly duties. Dominicans — excepting the extraordinary Las Casas — were more conservative than their Augustinian and Franciscan counterparts. Most believed that Indians were childlike and should never be ordained,[11] and this view was influenced by a generally negative position regarding indigenous people's capacity for true conversion held by their intellectual leader in New Spain, Domingo de Betanzos (c. 1480–1549).[12] The debate over the advisability of ordaining indigenous people went through a complex and protracted exchange involving theologians, doctrinal authors, and advisors to the Spanish monarchy that lasted to the end of the sixteenth century. The papacy and the Jesuit order tended to favor ordination, and they encountered steadfast opposition from prominent Franciscans, Dominicans, and episcopal authorities. In the end, only a handful of men of indigenous descent were ordained or even admitted to the mendicant orders in colonial Spanish America. In New Spain, this select group included the *mestizo* Diego Valadés, who became the Franciscan general procurator in Rome (1575–77); Pedro Ponce de León, a parish priest of Nahua origin who investigated native religious practices in central Mexico in the early seventeenth century; and Nicolás del Puerto, a priest of Zapotec origin who eventually served as bishop of Oaxaca (1679–81).

The Controversy over Early Mass Baptisms

The Franciscan drive to baptize the largest possible number of indigenous converts in the Americas has been attributed to the influence of millenarist theories about world history, which were inspired in part by the writings of the twelfth-century mystic Joachim de Fiore. By the early sixteenth century, some influential Franciscans had come to believe that, after human history had gone through the ages of the Father (epitomized by the Old Testament) and the Son (which had begun with the teachings of Jesus Christ), they were now living in the age of the Holy Spirit.

The main task for this new epoch was, in their view, the conversion of millions of nonbelievers who lived in recently discovered territories all over the Americas and Asia. Some Franciscan millenarists also believed that the second coming of Christ would occur once all nonbelievers in distant lands had embraced Christianity.[13]

The general practice of the early missionaries was to baptize Indians immediately upon basic indoctrination, which was cursory at best. Mass baptisms were common: some early Franciscans claimed to have baptized a hundred thousand yearly. Pedro de Gante (1490–1572), a Flemish Franciscan and relative of Emperor Charles V (Charles I of Spain) (r. 1516–56), even claimed to have baptized fourteen thousand in a single day. Toribio de Benavente, known as Motolinía (d. 1568), wrote, "Neophytes preparing for baptism would line up with children in front, and then the ceremony of baptism was done and then some adults were questioned about their instruction, and in many instances the friars…could barely lift their arms due to exhaustion."[14] But scholars doubt that so few priests could have baptized so many Amerindians.[15] Motolinía's contention that 4 million natives had been baptized by 1530 is questionable since that number is more than 40 percent of the total population of central Mexico.[16] Whatever the accuracy of those figures, the Franciscans felt that they had made great strides in their conversion efforts, leading Mendieta to remark that no other group of missionaries since the days of the primitive church had come close to converting and baptizing so many pagans.[17] Not surprisingly, many friars questioned the efficacy of mass baptisms. Whereas the Franciscans argued that detailed knowledge of Christian doctrine was less important than baptism, most Dominicans and Las Casas in particular attacked the Franciscan policy, suggesting that baptizing natives who had no knowledge of Christian tenets was sinful. Franciscans labeled such criticism "diabolically inspired."[18]

Missionary Methods and Linguistic Barriers

Except for a few instances of corporal punishment and judicial torture, which will be discussed below, along with idolatry extirpation methods, most mendicants worked to inculcate doctrine peacefully.[19] Early methods of evangelization remained experimental and centered on training the friars to first teach the concept of monotheism in native languages.[20] Basic tenets of the Christian faith included:

Major Theological Concepts	Prayers and Pious Practices
1. Monotheism	1. Pater Noster (Our Father)
2. Trinity	2. Salve Regina (Hail Holy Queen)
3. Incarnation	3. Ave María (Hail Mary)
4. Virgin Birth	4. Reverence for the Cross
5. Sacraments	5. Respect for the Clergy
6. Special Emphasis on Sacrament of Marriage	6. Punctual Attendance at Mass

A major obstacle faced by the friars was the translation of these concepts into the various indigenous languages. Imitating the pre-Hispanic device of pictograms to communicate names, words, and concepts, Franciscans and other mendicants used pictographic catechisms to evangelize the Indians.[21] The French Franciscan Jacobo de Testera is reputed to have invented this teaching device, now known as the "Testerian catechism." The frequency of its use is unknown, but examples found as late as the seventeenth century suggest, if not pragmatic usage, at least an abiding interest in this pedagogical tool. Soon after the arrival of the colonizers, some indigenous peoples learned Castilian, the language of empire, and Latin, the language of the church. Spanish teachers and Nahua pupils also associated the sounds of select Latin words with Nahuatl words that shared phonetic similarities. For instance, since *pater* resembled *pantli* (banner) and *noster* resembled *nochtli* (prickly pear cactus), a Nahua with proficiency in the pre-Hispanic pictographic system could render these two words as

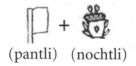

(pantli)   (nochtli)

Hence, without a precise knowledge of Castilian or the Christian doctrine, neophytes could recite the opening of "Our Father." Friars in central Mexico sometimes taught prayers in Latin by using pebbles; in the case of the Pater Noster, one pebble signified the initial utterance "Our Father," followed by other pebbles that stood for subsequent phrases in this prayer.

Missionaries also memorized key Catholic prayers and devotions in native languages, which enabled them to convey basic teachings of the church. As Louise Burkhart notes, however, a large part of Christian doctrine was simply "lost in translation."[22] Once missionaries learned to speak indigenous languages and to produce dictionaries, more accurate formulations of Christian concepts became possible.[23] Perhaps the most emblematic dispute about the use of native languages to convey Christian doctrine concerned rendering the Trinity into Nahuatl. A sixteenth-century Nahuatl translation rendered the Trinity as *ey personas, çan ce huel nelli Dios teotl* (three persons, but only one true God), but was later criticized by Franciscans and Dominicans in the early seventeenth century because Nahua speakers might mistakenly believe that only one of those three persons was the true deity.[24] Because of the difficulty of relaying Christian tenets in indigenous languages some missionaries insisted that only Castilian and Latin should be used.

Missionary concern for an accurate transmission of the Catholic faith by suitable translations into native tongues proved especially difficult when basic Christian concepts had no indigenous semantic counterparts. How could the word *Dios* ("God") be translated into indigenous languages whose terms for native deities bore few similarities to a monotheistic being? One solution was to keep this and other terms (such as those for soul, person, and Eucharist) in the original Spanish or to use them in tandem with the closest possible indigenous words or phrases. In order to convey the Christian concept of Satan and simultaneously chide pre-Hispanic religions, the friars occasionally substituted the names of indigenous deities for Satan. Thus, "devil" was conveyed in Nahuatl by the term *tlacatecolotl,* which referred to a sorcerer god who took the shape of an owl, and in Zapotec by Becelao, the name of the deity who presided over the Zapotec underworld. Among the Maya, the Franciscans used *cizin* ("devil") to refer to all pre-Hispanic images and idols.[25] The result was an uneven understanding of the basic concepts of Spanish Catholic Christianity.[26]

The Catholic Church and Local Indigenous Institutions

By the end of the sixteenth century, in spite of the challenges posed by conversion, indigenous communities developed strong and often intimate links with the Catholic Church and its many agents. From an administrative standpoint, these indigenous communities most often complied with church directives regarding public Christian observances. Crown officials collected tributes and supervised the local governance of Amerindian peoples, who were required to live in exclusively indigenous communities called *pueblos de indios,* and priests supervised the local parish and charitable organizations. Both authorities worked in tandem to insure that Indians complied with their labor obligations to state and church. These Indian pueblos were known either as *cabeceras de doctrina* (the main town in a parish) or as *sujetos* (a smaller town within the same parish). The preconquest political geography was rearranged during the late sixteenth and early seventeenth centuries by *congregaciones,* which were resettlement projects for Indians carried out by civil authorities. While hierarchical standing and political relations between important native settlements and their subjects were often confirmed through *congregaciones,* this process also resulted in the emergence of new population centers.

Cabeceras de doctrina customarily had at least one resident priest who visited the *sujetos* periodically, imparted or managed doctrinal education within the parish, and was responsible for keeping baptismal, marriage, and burial records. In order to carry out their duties, resident ministers had to establish a cooperative rapport with local native authorities. Every year or every other year, indigenous people elected several officials to positions in the town's *cabildo,* or city council. Native *fiscales,* charged with monitoring their townspeople's religious compliance, aided priests in the religious sphere. Local confraternities, which had a system of offices and responsibilities that was often kept separate from *cabildo* offices, organized religious celebrations such as the veneration of a town's patron saint. The top posts in these confraternities were often rotated among local males with kinship ties to traditional elite native groups, since the amount of personal resources required to hold such offices proved prohibitive for most commoners.[27] Members raised money throughout the year in order to sponsor collective celebrations that featured public feasting, processions, and short religious plays — the latter sometimes written by missionaries or highly educated and respected members of the community.[28] Many confraternities also functioned as productive and money-lending enterprises. One Nahua confraternity in eighteenth-century central Mexico used funds generated from the veneration of local saints to lend money to members and nonmembers at steep interest rates.[29]

Hybrid Christian Devotions: The Cult of Guadalupe

The idea of employing rough equivalences between Spanish and Indian religious concepts allowed missionaries to promote, in a selective manner and with highly variable results, the identification of specific Christian saints with indigenous deities or deity complexes. The Yucatec Maya interpreted Spain's Virgin of the Assumption, with her lunar imagery, as a Christian correlate of both the traditional moon goddess and the goddess of childbirth, Ix Chel.[30] Similarly, St. John the Baptist became associated with water deities by Mesoamerican peoples who struggled to make sense of the new Christian saints and intercessors they had learned about during catechism.[31]

Indigenous veneration of Christian saints should not be conceived in terms of strict structural correspondences between deities and saints, since many saints were transformed into novel hybrid forms inspired by the natives' comprehension of Christianity through their own cultural and linguistic categories. For instance, a series of songs composed by Amerindians under the supervision of Sahagún depicted St. James "Matamoros," the patron saint of Spain and slayer of infidels, in the guise of a Nahua military leader of supernatural appearance.[32] St. James also became a victorious figure on a white horse who assisted indigenous ritual specialists.[33]

The most influential, prominent, and best known example of the transformation of the cult of a Christian saint into a hybrid colonial cult is that of the Virgin of Guadalupe. According to this narrative, in 1531 a Nahua native named Juan Diego had several encounters with the Virgin Mary, who eventually prevailed upon him to request that Bishop Zumárraga build a shrine in her honor at the hilltop site of Tepeyacac. While it might be possible that this site had once housed a temple devoted to the cult of Toci (Our Grandmother), a Nahua deity who had given birth to several gods, almost no details about this cult survive.[34] While in the twentieth and twenty-first centuries the cult of Guadalupe came to symbolize an "indigenous" form of Christian worship, the available historical evidence indicates that this was an early local cult appropriated by Spanish civil and ecclesiastical elites and then popularized as an apparition unique to New Spain that served as an historical metaphor for indigenous conversion to Christianity. Excluding a few terse references to the Marian cult in the mid-sixteenth century by both indigenous and Spanish observers, there exist few details about the development of this devotion before the 1640s.[35] Moreover, the existence of various inspired examples of Marian literature in Nahuatl prior to the early seventeenth century demonstrates that the cult of the Virgin Mary among indigenous peoples predates the Guadalupan tradition.[36] The Guadalupan cult, however, was favored by a few influential mendicants (but not by Sahagún), as well as by elite Spaniards and creoles from the 1560s. Its increased popularity may explain the sudden appearance of two accounts of the apparitions — one in Spanish and the other in Nahuatl — in the late 1640s. Even during the later colonial period there existed a dispute in New Spain concerning the initial date of the apparition. The controversy about the historicity of the apparition and the actual existence of Juan Diego has continued into the present.[37]

Guadalupe is one of many influential cults that emerged in hundreds of native communities, promoted by rival mendicant orders. For instance, another Nahua, a servant in a Franciscan monastery known also as Juan Diego, was reputed to have seen a miraculous apparition of the Virgin in Ocotlan, Tlaxcala, in 1541. Not to be left out of the series of Franciscan apparitions, the Augustinian order promoted the apparition of a miraculous crucified Christ in a shrine located in their monastery in Chalma. In 1533, several natives who had been conducting indigenous rituals in nearby Ocuilan claimed to have seen a miraculous crucifix.[38] In Oaxaca, the Dominicans embraced and promoted the cult of the Virgin of Solitude, an effigy of which was said to have been found by a muleteer in the mid-seventeenth century. In Upper Peru, the appearance by the Virgin of Cochabamba near an Inca *huaca* (generally a cult object, often a geographical feature) serves as a further example of the plethora of apparitions during the early period of evangelization of the New World.[39]

A Second Spiritual Conquest:
Campaigns to Extirpate Idolatry in New Spain and Peru

In principle, the legal category of idolatry established by ecclesiastical and civil judges in colonial Spanish America was patterned after an ancient proposition in Judeo-Christian thought: only God may receive rightful worship (*latria*), and the misguided or rebellious worship directed toward an entity other than God could be regarded, depending on the intentions of the worshiper and the harshness of the judge, as *idolatría*.[40] However, the application of this seemingly simple formula to indigenous religious understanding was intimately fused with social and cultural practices and produced a paradoxical result. Every single religious practice could be regarded with suspicion from the standpoint of orthodox Catholicism. If one adopted the perspective of the great Dominican theologian Bartolomé de Las Casas and argued that many indigenous religious practices were parallel to but inverted reflections of Christian beliefs, institutions, and ritual actions, one could end up with a "Lascasian net" of sorts.[41] In other words, "idolatry" was reduced to a self-evident juridical category requiring minimal explicit elucidation and maximal procedural clarity. Many clergy believed that they could recognize idolatry when faced with it even though they were actually unable to comprehend what they were seeing.

In the first half of the sixteenth century, Spanish law treated Indians as jurisdictional subjects who were tried and punished for idolatry, sorcery, and apostasy by apostolic inquisitors. During this period, several mendicants selectively used physical violence to try or punish indigenous defendants. Bishop Zumárraga of Mexico employed juridical torture and sentenced those convicted of idolatry to public lashing as he investigated traditional native religious practices in central Mexico between 1537 and 1540. His decision to allow the Nahua nobleman Don Carlos Chichimecateuctli of Texcoco to be publicly executed for heresy in 1539 was decried by many, and contributed to the exclusion of natives from inquisitorial jurisdiction. In 1562, the Franciscan friar Diego de Landa and his associates confiscated and destroyed a large number of idols in several Yucatec Maya towns, submitting Indian ritual specialists to the water and rack tortures that even Zumárraga had used only twice. A civil colonial official commissioned to investigate these abuses reported in 1565 that 157 natives had died as a result of the tortures; many Indians were left sick, physically handicapped, even armless, while others committed suicide to avoid questioning and torture.[42] When a separate Inquisition tribunal was established in Mexico in 1571, Indians were excluded from its jurisdiction, but ritual specialists continued to be investigated and punished by priests at the local level and in ecclesiastical courts. As neophytes to Christianity, Indians were required to keep only a partial fast during Lent and only ten of forty-one official holidays, in keeping with the widespread notion that they were weak and childlike in matters pertaining to the Christian faith.

In both central Mexico and the Andes, activities to extirpate idolatry depended on the particular interests of the ecclesiastical authorities and parish priests, interests which shifted with local political realities. There was, however, an important difference between institutional efforts against native specialists in the two viceroyalties. The idolatry campaigns in the archbishopric of Lima were often conducted via a partnership among seculars, bishops, and Jesuits in a relatively compact and linguistically homogeneous region, and this triad left behind an abundant corpus of trial records. On the other hand, the enemies of idolatry in

New Spain orchestrated their campaigns in an ad hoc manner in isolated communities that encompassed a substantial number of different ethnic and linguistic entities; unfortunately, the records of most of these trials have been lost. The relative peaks in the campaigns against idolatry in the Andes correspond to the 1610s, 1650s, 1660s, 1690s, 1720s, and the mid-eighteenth century.[43] On the other hand, one could divide idolatry extirpation campaigns in central Mexico into four phases: the first, "apostolic," led primarily by Franciscans and Dominicans between 1527 and 1571;[44] the second, by secular ecclesiastical judges between the early 1600s and the 1660s; the third, representative of a more systematic application of extirpation policies and the emergence of unique punitive measures (such as the "perpetual prison of idolaters" in Oaxaca) between the 1660s and the 1720s; finally the fourth phase, began circa the 1720s, was influenced by mid-century Bourbon political reforms and lasted until the early nineteenth century.

Disillusioned by their converts and unsure of the success of their mission, mendicants soon became embroiled in a struggle with the secular clergy for the souls of their parishioners. During the first two decades of the seventeenth century, a number of secular parish priests located in Oaxaca and in central Peru began investigating and punishing indigenous peoples engaged in ritual practices that were, according to Catholic teaching, unorthodox. These parish priests paid particular attention to the worship of local and regional supernaturals ("idolatry"), but they also investigated accusations against ritual specialists ("sorcery"), suspicious medical practices, love magic, and forecasting and divination ("superstition"). Although this was not the first time that secular priests had been given the responsibility of investigating indigenous religious deviance, their newfound emphasis on extirpation of idolatry must be seen within the larger framework of transatlantic Counter-Reformation projects and responses to guidelines that emanated from the Council of Trent (1545–63). During the late sixteenth and early seventeenth centuries, local ecclesiastical authorities and inquisitorial courts collaborated in a number of campaigns against local devotions and agrarian cults throughout Spain, France, and Italy. While there were no direct intellectual exchanges among these extirpators and those in the New World, the two shared a similar Counter-Reformation reforming zeal, constant attempts to survey and police public behavior, and careful attention to specific unorthodox practices.

Two Seventeenth-Century Extirpators:
Francisco de Ávila and Hernando Ruiz de Alarcón

A comparison of the careers of Francisco de Ávila in Peru and Hernando Ruiz de Alarcón, in Mexico, both secular clergy, demonstrates the range of methods and practices employed by secular extirpators. In late 1609, an ambitious and politically shrewd Ávila, who at the time was being investigated for a long list of abuses at the request of his indigenous parishioners, convinced the newly arrived archbishop of Lima of the need to intervene against native idolaters in the province of Huarochirí. Having met with success, on December 20, 1609, Ávila helped orchestrate a punitive spectacle patterned after inquisitorial *autos de fe* in which he delivered an anti-idolatry speech in Quechua moments before Hernando Pauccar, a respected indigenous ritual specialist who had fostered the worship of local Andean deities such as Paria Caca and Chaupi Ñamca, received two hundred lashes in Lima's main square.[45] During the next decade, Ávila not only put an end to his legal troubles, but also gained renown as a dynamic extirpator. Spanish officials rewarded him with a coveted ecclesiastical post in Charcas toward the end of his career. Documentation acquired by Ávila comprises the most detailed account of a local Andean cosmology in an Amerindian language. Over a period of several years, Ávila supervised the work of Cristóbal Choque Casa and other literate natives who wrote the "Huarochirí Manuscript," which provides key ethnohistorical information on pre-Hispanic Andean beliefs and origin narratives.[46]

Ávila's activities contrast with those of Hernando Ruiz de Alarcón, the rather obscure brother of the famous Golden Age playwright Juan Ruiz de Alarcón. Between 1614 and the early 1630s Hernando investigated the ritual and healing practices of dozens of Nahua villagers who lived in or near his home parish of Atenango del Río in present-day Guerrero.[47] Unlike Ávila, Ruiz de Alarcón was unable to advance his career through extirpation of idolatry; in fact, he was investigated by inquisitors in 1614 for punishing natives "in the manner of the Holy Office." Since his intentions were regarded as honorable, despite his lack of inquisitorial credentials, he eventually gained the confidence of Archbishop Juan Pérez de la Serna, who granted him permission to investigate and punish native idolaters.[48] Like Ávila, Ruiz de Alarcón had good command of his parishioners' language — Nahuatl — and employed his linguistic skills to compile a treatise on local divinatory and calendar systems and healing practices. This invaluable work on colonial indigenous religiosity featured transcriptions of some sixty-six different incantations in Nahuatl, most of which Ruiz de Alarcón acquired from local indigenous specialists, although he did copy a few from clandestine manuscripts. None of the legal proceedings conducted by him survives, but his treatise provides unique data regarding the propitiation of specific Nahua deities such as Quetzalcoatl, Tezcatlipoca, and the Macuiltonaleque, and the practical context for the deployment of many of these incantations. Despite Ruiz de Alarcón's inability to parlay his efforts into an ecclesiastical promotion, significant portions of his treatise were copied and used by Jacinto de la Serna in his own manuscript on the extirpation of idolatry. De la Serna ultimately attained high ecclesiastical and academic posts for his efforts.

Visitas de idolatría (periodic visits to the settlements in a particular region to investigate and punish native ritual specialists) were far more common in the Andes than in New Spain. However, if one were to measure the impact of a single *visita* or campaign by the number of communities affected and the amount of information obtained regarding clandestine practices, the campaign conducted by Bishop Angel Maldonado in northern Oaxaca in 1704–5 would qualify as among the most ambitious campaigns against indigenous ritual specialists in colonial Spanish America. In 1704, Maldonado issued amnesty to anyone in the province who denounced indigenous ritual specialists, proffered ritual texts, and included information on ritual practices in their confessions. Authorities from 104 Zapotec, Mixe, and Chinantec communities accepted the offer and journeyed to the province's administrative center to meet with Maldonado and his cohorts.[49] This innovative strategy netted Maldonado an exceptional set of ritual texts: 106 separate booklets containing local versions of the 260-day Zapotec divinatory calendar and four collections of Zapotec ritual songs. Recent scholarly analysis of these calendars shows that local specialists had continued to employ the divinatory calendar to direct collective and individual ritual practices and had kept records of eclipses until Maldonado's *visita*.[50] Moreover, while some ritual songs were performed during the public (but clandestine) worship of Zapotec deities and founding ancestors, other songs were actually adaptations from Dominican-indigenous verses previously used to convey Christian teachings to Zapotec neophytes.[51] This unique set of records, along with the Yucatec Maya books of Chilam Balam — a corpus of texts by unknown authors that feature calendrical observations, predictions, and a set of hermetic riddles that may have been used to test candidates for indigenous offices — form the largest corpus of clandestine ritual texts produced by indigenous specialists in the colonial Americas.

Conclusions

The broad acceptance of Christianity on the part of thousands of indigenous communities certainly cannot be classified as a failure; nevertheless, from the standpoint of missionaries and priests, it did not appear to be an unqualified success, as it was kept in place by a series of compromises with orthodox beliefs.[52] Indigenous peoples, however, did accept, practice, and embrace a wide range of Christian beliefs and observances, and many ecclesiastical and episcopal figures embraced, in turn, the indigenous acceptance of public and formal aspects of Spanish Catholicism. Genuflection, the Pater Noster, Ave María, and other Catholic prayers, remained for many parish clergy the only pragmatic litmus test that could be used to ascertain that their parishioners were truly Christian.[53] Nevertheless, as late as the eighteenth century many clergy bitterly lamented that indigenous knowledge of even these rudimentary prayers and basic Christian concepts remained uneven at best.

The protracted and sometimes conflictive "spiritual encounters" throughout the colonial period were guided, in part, by a fundamental misunderstanding of indigenous religious beliefs and practices. In many cases, the moral dialogue that linked indigenous cosmological beliefs and ways of speaking to Christian beliefs yielded a number of surprising heterogeneous texts and insights. However, such dialogue did not result in novel policies that radically transformed the administration of sacraments and Christian observances in many parishes. Since some of the local indigenous ways of practicing Christianity allowed for the coexistence and continued devotion to pre-Hispanic deities and founding ancestors, such a compromise was aggressively and sometimes violently rejected by those spiritual conquistadores who termed such beliefs idolatrous and directed campaigns against their propagators.

The diversity in local ways of embracing and accommodating Christian practices led to the emergence of a hybrid set of religious practices that could be termed "indigenous Christianities." These allowed many native peoples to regard themselves as sincere Christian believers. Scholars frequently describe these practices as a syncretic "blend" of indigenous and European elements; however, such an interpretation presupposes that hybrid practices can be dissected into a series of discrete and distinct elements. A more tenable explanation is that through moral dialogue, quotidian practice, political negotiation, and occasional violent confrontation, several generations of missionaries and clergy were able to inculcate a core set of Christian beliefs and practices, especially public religiosity, into most indigenous communities. How Amerindians observed Christian tenets, adhered to Christian precepts, and comprehended and transformed the religion of the colonizers varied across the cultural geography of Spanish America.

Notes

1. Robert Ricard, *The Spiritual Conquest of Mexico: An Essay on the Apostolate and the Evangelizing Methods of the Mendicant Orders in New Spain: 1523–1572* (Berkeley: University of California Press, 1966); Pedro Borges, O.F.M., *Métodos misionales en la cristianización de América: Siglo XVI* (Madrid: CSIC, 1960); Stafford Poole, "Some Observations on Mission Methods and Native Reactions in Sixteenth Century New Spain," *The Americas* 50, no. 3 (January 1994): 337–49.

2. The Franciscans recognized their debt to Cortés, and friar Toribio de Benavente (known as "Motolinía," Nahuatl for "he makes himself humble") echoed the early Catholic missionaries' opinion that through Cortés "God had opened the door for us to preach his Holy Gospel, and it was he who caused the Indians to revere the holy Sacraments and respect the ministers of the Church." See Fray Toribio Motolinía, *Historia de los Indios de la Nueva España* (Mexico City: Editorial Porrúa, 2001), 186.

3. See Hugo Nutini, "Native Evangelism in Central Mexico," *Ethnology: An International Journal of Cultural and Social Anthropology* 39, no. 1 (Winter 2000): 39–54.

4. Kenneth Mills, *Idolatry and Its Enemies* (Princeton, N.J.: Princeton University Press, 1997), 17. Mills notes that the most authoritative work on early evangelization in the Andes is still Fernando de Armas Medina's *Cristianización del Perú, 1532–1600* (Seville: Escuela de Estudios Hispanoamericanos, 1953).

5. See Carlos Sempat Assadourian, "Hacia la *sublimis deus:* Las discordias entre los dominicos indianos y el enfrentamiento del franciscano Padre Tastera con el Padre Betanzos," *Historia Mexicana* 47, no. 3 (1998): 465–536.

6. See Lewis Hanke, "Pope Paul III and the American Indians," *Harvard Theological Review* 30, no. 2 (April 1940): 65–102.

7. See Mauricio Beuchot, "Escolástica y humanismo en Fray Julián Garcés," *Novahispania* 3 (1998): 7–43.

8. See Elsa Cecilia Frost, "Indians and Theologians: Sixteenth-Century Spanish Theologians and Their Concept of the Indigenous Soul," in *South and Meso-American Native Spirituality: From the Cult of the Feathered Serpent to the Theology of Liberation,* ed. Gary H. Gossen (New York: Crossroad, 1993), 131.

9. See Lewis Hanke, *All Mankind Is One: A Study of the Disputation between Bartolomé de las Casas and Juan Ginés de Sepúlveda in 1550 on the Intellectual and Religious Capacity of the American Indians* (DeKalb: Northern Illinois University Press, 1974).

10. Antonio Rubial García, *El convento agustino y la sociedad novohispana, 1533–1630,* Serie historia novohispana, vol. 34 (Mexico City: Universidad Nacional Autónoma de México, 1989).

11. For a vindication of the early Dominicans, see Pedro Fernández Rodríguez, *Los dominicos en el contexto de la primera evangelización de México, 1526–1550,* vol. 3 (Salamanca: Editorial San Esteban, Monumenta histórica iberoamericana de la Orden de Predicadores, 1994).

12. See Juan Rodríguez Cabal, *Betanzos: Evangelizador de México y Guatemala* (Pamplona: Editorial OPE, 1968).

13. See John Leddy Phelan, *The Millennial Kingdom of the Franciscans in the New World* (Berkeley: University of California Press, 1970), 1–10, 22–25.

14. Fray Toribio Motolinía, *Historia de los Indios de la Nueva España* (Mexico City: Editorial Porrúa, 2001), 116–18.

15. See Sarah Cline, "The Spiritual Conquest Reexamined: Baptism and Christian Marriage in Early Sixteenth-Century Mexico," *Hispanic American Historical Review* 73, no. 3 (August 1993): 453–80.

16. For the original figure of 4 million natives baptized cited by Motolinía see Fray Toribio Motolinía, *Historia de los Indios de la Nueva España* (Mexico City: Editorial Porrúa, 2001), 116. For more contemporary views of these mass baptisms and central Mexican population see Jerónimo de Mendieta, *Historia Eclesiástica Indiana y descripción de la relación de la Provincia del Santo Evangelio, que es en las Indias Occidentales que llaman la Nueva España, hecha el año de 1585* (Mexico City: Antigua Liberia Portal de los Agustinos No. 3, 1870); see Sherburne F. Cook and Woodrow W. Borah, *Essays in Population History: Mexico and California,* vol. 3 (Berkeley: University of California Press, 1979).

17. Mendieta, *Historia Eclesiástica Indiana,* Capítulo 38, 275.

18. Ibid., Capítulo 36, 267–69.

19. See Inga Clendinnen, "Disciplining the Indians: Franciscan Ideology and Missionary Violence in Sixteenth-Century Yucatan" *Past and Present* 94 (1984): 27–49.

20. Se John F. Schwaller, "The Ilhuica of the Nahua: Is Heaven Just a Place?" *The Americas* 62, no. 3 (2006): 391–412; David Tavárez, "The Passion according to the Wooden Drum: Doctrinal Appropriation of a Colonial Zapotec Ritual Genre," *The Americas* 62, no. 3 (2006): 413–44.

21. See John B. Glass, "A Census of Middle American Testerian Manuscripts," in Howard F. Cline, *Guide to Ethnohistorical Sources* (Austin: University of Texas Press, 1978), 3:281–96; Ann Norman, "Testerian Codices," Ph.D. dissertation, Tulane University, 1985.

22. Louise M. Burkhart, *The Slippery Earth: Nahua-Christian Moral Dialogue in Sixteenth Century Mexico* (Tucson: University of Arizona Press, 1989), 44.

23. Jorge Klor de Alva, "Spiritual Conflict and Accommodation in New Spain: Toward a Typology of Aztec Responses to Christianity," in *The Inca and Aztec States, 1400–1800: Anthropology and History,* ed. George A. Collier, Renato I. Rosaldo, and John D. Wirth (New York: Academic Press, 1982), 345–66.

24. David Tavárez, "Naming the Trinity: From Ideologies of Translation to Dialectics of Reception in Colonial Nahua Texts, 1547–1771," *Colonial Latin American Review* 9, no. 1 (2000): 21–47.

25. See Burkhart, *The Slippery Earth;* John F. Chuchiak, "The Sins of the Fathers: Franciscan Missionaries, Parish Priests and the Sexual Conquest of the Yucatec Maya, 1545–1785," *Ethnohistory* 54, no. 1 (Winter 2007), 71–129; Jorge Klor de Alva, "Sin and Confession among the Colonial Nahuas: The Confessional as a Tool for Domination," in *Ciudad y campo en la historia de México,* 2 vols., ed. Richard Sánchez, Eric Van Young, and Gisela von Wobeser (Mexico City: Instituto de Investigaciones Históricas, Universidad Nacional Autónoma de México, 1990).

26. See José Rabasa, "Writing and Evangelization in Sixteenth-Century Mexico," in *Early Images of the Americas: Transfer and Invention,* ed. Jerry Williams and Robert Lewis (Tucson: University of Arizona Press, 1993), 65–92.

27. Charles Gibson, *The Aztecs under Spanish Rule* (Stanford, Calif.: Stanford University Press, 1964), 175–76.

28. See Burkhart, *The Slippery Earth;* Viviana Díaz Balsera, "A Judeo-Christian Tlaloc or a Nahua Yahweh? Domination, Hybridity and Continuity in the Nahua Evangelization Theater," *Colonial Latin American Review* 10, no. 2 (December 2001): 209–28.

29. Danièle Dehouve, "The 'Money of the Saint': Ceremonial Organization and Monetary Capital in Tlapa, Guerrero, Mexico," in *Manipulating the Saints,* ed. A. Meyers and D. E. Hopkins (Hamburg: WAYASBAH, 1988), 149–74.

30. See Fray Bernardo de Lizana, *Devocionario de nuestra Señora de Izamal y conquista espiritual de Yucatán,* vol. 12, ed. René Acuña (Mexico City: Universidad Nacional Autónoma de México, Fuentes para el estudio de la cultura maya, 1995).

31. See John F. Chuchiak, "Christian Saints and their Interpretations in Mesoamerica" in *Oxford Encyclopedia of Mesoamerican Cultures,* ed. David Carrasco (New York: Oxford University Press, 2001), 3:113–16.

32. Louise Burkhart, "The Amanuenses Have Appropriated the Text: Interpreting a Náhuatl Song of Santiago," in *On the Translation of Native American Literatures,* ed. Brian Swann (Washington, D.C.: Smithsonian Institution Press, 1992), 339–55.

33. William B. Taylor, "Santiago's Horse: Christianity and Colonial Indian Resistance in the Heartland of New Spain," in *Violence, Resistance, and Survival in the Americas: Native Americans and the Legacy of Conquest,* ed. William B. Taylor and Franklin Pease (Washington, D.C.: Smithsonian Institution, 1992), 153–89.

34. See Stafford Poole, *Our Lady of Guadalupe: The Origins and Sources of a Mexican National Symbol, 1531–1797* (Tucson: University of Arizona Press, 1995).

35. For this view, see Poole, *Our Lady of Guadalupe;* Xavier Noguez, *Documentos guadalupanos: Un estudio sobre las fuentes de información tempranas en torno a las mariofanías en el Tepeyac* (Toluca: El Colegio Mexiquense; Mexico City: Fondo de Cultura Económica, 1993); Sylvia Santabella, "*Nican Motecpana:* Nahuatl Miracles of the Virgin of Guadalupe," *Latin American Indian Literatures Journal* 11, no. 1 (Spring 1995): 34–54. For a dissenting view, see David Brading, *Mexican Phoenix: Our Lady*

of Guadalupe: Image and Tradition across Five Centuries (Cambridge: Cambridge University Press, 2001).

36. See Louise M. Burkhart, *Before Guadalupe: The Virgin Mary in Early Colonial Nahuatl Literature* (Albany: Institute for Mesoamerican Studies, State University of New York, 2001).

37. All of the alleged instances of sixteenth- and seventeenth-century documents regarding the existence of a historical Juan Diego are questionable; see Stafford Poole, "History versus Juan Diego," *The Americas* 62, no. 1 (July 2005): 1–16. In late colonial times, the creole patriot friar Servando Teresa de Mier caused a political scandal by stating in a sermon that the Guadalupan cult among the Nahua could be interpreted as proof that St. Thomas or St. Brendan had preached about Christianity in the Americas centuries before the arrival of the Spaniards.

38. Gonzalo Obregón, "El Real Convento y Santuario de San Miguel de Chalma," *Estudios Históricos Americanos, Homenaje a Silvio Zavala* (Mexico City: El Colegio de México, 1953), 109–82.

39. For other examples in the Andes, see David Patrick Cahill, "The Virgin and the Inca: An Incaic Procession in the City of Cuzco in 1692," *Ethnohistory* 49, no. 3 (2002): 611–49.

40. See David Tavárez, "Idolatry as an Ontological Question: Native Consciousness and Juridical Proof in Colonial Mexico," *Journal of Early Modern History* 6, no. 2 (2002): 114–39; John F. Chuchiak "Toward a Regional Definition of Idolatry: Reexamining Idolatry Trials in the *Relaciones de Méritos* and Their Role in Defining the Concept of *Idolatría* in Colonial Yucatán, 1570–1780," *Journal of Early Modern History* 6, no. 2 (2002): 1–29.

41. Carmen Bernand and Serge Gruzinski, *De la idolatría: Una arqueología de las ciencias religiosas* (Mexico City: Fondo de Cultura Económica, 1992), 209–210.

42. France V. Scholes and Eleanore Adams, *Don Diego Quijada, Alcalde Mayor de Yucatán, 1561–1565* (Mexico City: Editorial Porrúa, 1938): lii. In the end, Landa successfully argued that his actions were justified by papal ordinances, and canonical experts decreed that his use of force had not been excessive. By 1572, he was appointed the second bishop of Yucatan, thus replacing his former accuser Toral, who had been the first bishop in the province (ibid.: ci–civ).

43. See Mills, *Idolatry and Its Enemies*, 27–32; Nicholas Griffiths, *The Cross and the Serpent: Religious Repression and Resurgence in Colonial Peru* (Norman: University of Oklahoma Press, 1996).

44. See Richard E. Greenleaf, "The Mexican Inquisition and the Indians: Sources for the Ethnohistorian," *The Americas* 34, no. 2 (1978): 315–44; and Richard E. Greenleaf, "The Persistence of Native Values: The Inquisition and the Indians of Colonial Mexico," *The Americas* 50, no. 3 (1994), 351–75; María Teresa Sepúlveda y Herrera, *Procesos por idolatría al cacique, gobernadores y sacerdotes de Yanhuitlán, 1544–1546* (Mexico City: Instituto Nacional de Antropología e Historia, 1999); France V. Scholes and Ralph L. Roys, *Friar Diego de Landa and the Problem of Idolatry in Yucatán* (Washington, D.C.: Carnegie Institution of Washington, Publication Number 501, 1938), 585–620; John F. Chuchiak "*In Servitio Dei:* Friar Diego de Landa, the Franciscan Order, and the Return of the Extirpation of Idolatry in the Colonial Diocese of Yucatán, 1573–1579," *The Americas* 61, no. 4 (2005): 611–45.

45. Mills, *Idolatry and Its Enemies*, 27–32; see also Pierre Duviols, *Procesos y visitas de idolatrías: Cajatambo, siglo XVII* (Lima: Pontificia Universidad Católica del Perú/Institut français d'études andines, 2003); Griffiths, *The Cross and the Serpent;* Sabine MacCormack, *Religion in the Andes: Vision and Imagination in Early Colonial Peru* (Princeton, N.J.: Princeton University Press, 1991); Luis Millones, "Religion and Power in the Andes: Idolatrous Curacas of the Central Sierra," *Ethnohistory* 26, no. 3 (1979): 143–263.

46. See Frank Salomon and George Urioste, eds., *The Huarochirí Manuscript: A Testament of Ancient and Colonial Andean Religion* (Austin: University of Texas Press, 1991); Karen Spalding, *Huarochirí: An Andean Society under Inca and Spanish Rule* (Stanford, Calif.: Stanford University Press, 1984).

47. J. Richard Andrews and Ross Hassig, *Treatise on the Heathen Institutions That Today Live among the Indians Native to This New Spain, 1629* (Norman: University of Oklahoma Press, 1984).

48. David Tavárez, "La idolatría letrada: Un análisis comparativo de textos clandestinos rituales y devocionales en comunidades nahuas y zapotecas, 1613–1654," *Historia Mexicana* 49, no. 2 (1999): 197–252.

49. José Alcina Franch, *Calendario y religión entre los zapotecos* (Mexico City: Universidad Nacional Autónoma de México, 1993).

50. See David Tavárez and John Justeson, "Eclipse Records in a Corpus of Colonial Zapotec 260-Day Calendars," *Ancient Mesoamerica* 19, no. 1 (2008): 67–81; John Justeson and David Tavárez, "The Correlation of the Colonial Northern Zapotec Calendar with European Chronology," in *Skywatching in the Ancient World: New Perspectives in Cultural Astronomy,* ed. Clive Ruggles and Gary Urton (Niwot: University Press of Colorado, 2007), 19–96.

51. Tavárez, "The Passion according to the Wooden Drum," 440–44.

52. Gibson, *The Aztecs under Spanish Rule,* 134–35.

53. See William B. Taylor, *Magistrates of the Sacred: Priests and Parishioners in Eighteenth-Century Mexico* (Stanford, Calif.: Stanford University Press, 1996).

4

Afro-Latin Americans and Christianity

Nicole von Germeten and Javier Villa-Flores

From the beginning of the Atlantic slave traffic, spreading the Christian faith among the "heathen" and Muslim Africans constituted the main argument advanced by the emerging Iberian powers to justify engagement in the trade. Thus, when in 1444 the first large group of West African slaves arrived at the Portuguese port of Lagos aboard a caravel, chronicler Gomes Eannes de Azurara reported that their enslavement was for the "greater benefit [of the Africans] ... for though their bodies were now brought into some subjection, that was a small matter in comparison with their souls, which would now possess true freedom forever more." Considering the African bodies as mere containers of their souls, Azurara justified their forced migration to Europe in order to set them free from the bonds of sin. Surely it was a horrifying spectacle to see them crying out loudly, throwing themselves to the ground, and clinging one to the other, pleading that their families not be separated and dispersed among different owners; but, he reasoned, they would otherwise have died as heathens in Africa, "without the clearness and the light of the holy faith." Conversion to Christianity was deemed a most laudable goal, and Azurara's arguments were tirelessly repeated throughout the colonial period on both sides of the Atlantic, as more than 4 million enslaved Africans were transported to Brazil and more than 2 million others were sent to Spanish America.[1]

Christian Instruction of Africans

In the 1400s, the Portuguese looked to Africa for several interrelated reasons: to access fabled wealth in gold; to create outposts for attempts to reach the Far East; to continue their centuries' long efforts to fight Islamic expansion and to evangelize more of the known world. In 1452, Pope Nicholas V authorized a Portuguese monopoly on African enslavement and conquest for the stated purpose of saving souls from eternal damnation. In 1508, Pope Julius II gave both Spanish and Portuguese monarchs control over founding churches and sending priests and friars to all parts of their empires. Under Portuguese influence, some African leaders and nobility accepted Christianity, although these conversions were far from definitive or permanent. Catholic missions to Africa were often temporary and ineffective, sometimes even ending in violence and death for the intrusive missionaries.

By the seventeenth century, Jesuits had made efforts to Christianize Africans brought to Brazil as slaves. Perceptive priests, such as the Jesuit Antonio Vieira (1608–97), understood that by building overseas empires and actively engaging in both the indigenous American and African slave trades, the Portuguese acted far more in the interests of greedy masters than for the sake of spreading Christianity. In 1633, Vieira delivered a sermon to a group of Africans and free people of color that may be understood as a Christian "theology of slavery."[2] Vieira stated that slavery only exaggerated the extremes of inequality in this world and incited masters to terrible cruelty. At the same time, he tried to console the slaves by emphasizing the equality of all souls and the certainty that God would hear their cries of pain, assuring them that in the afterlife he would reward the humble slaves and punish the merciless masters. In 1707, the archbishop of Salvador de Bahia, Sebastião Monteiro daVide, included the following "questions" in his "Brief Instruction in the Mysteries of the Faith, Accommodated to the Manner of Speaking of the Slaves of Brazil, So That They May Be Catechized by It":

Who made this world?	God.
Who made us?	God.
Where is God?	In Heaven, on earth, and in the whole world.
Do we have one God, or many?	We have only one God.
How many persons?	Three.
Tell me their names.	The Father, the Son, and the Holy Spirit.
Which of these persons took our flesh?	The Son.
Which of these persons died for us?	The Son.
How is this Son called?	Jesus Christ.
How is His Mother called?	The Virgin Mary.
Where did the Son die?	On the Cross.
After he died where did He go?	He went under the earth in search of the good souls.
And later, where did He go?	To Heaven.
Will He Return?	Yes.
What will He come to search for?	The souls of good heart.
And where will He take them?	To Heaven.
And the souls of bad heart, where will they go?	To hell.
Who is in hell?	The devil is there.
And who else?	The souls of bad heart.
And what are they doing there?	They are in the fire, which never goes out.
Will they ever leave there?	Never.

84

When we die, does the soul die also?	No. Only the body dies.
And the soul, where does it go?	If the soul is good, it goes to Heaven; if the soul is bad it goes to hell.
And the body, where does it go?	It goes to the earth.
Will it leave the earth alive?	Yes.
Where will the body go which had a soul of bad heart?	To hell.
And where will the body go which had a soul of good heart?	To Heaven.
Who is in Heaven with God?	All those who had good souls.
Will they leave Heaven, or will they be there forever?	They will be there forever.[3]

Some slaves probably memorized and others may have even internalized key Catholic tenets. Too frequently, however, slavers did not allow enslaved Africans even to receive much less frequent the sacraments that were ordinarily available to others. Jorge Benci (c. 1650–1708), an Italian Jesuit assigned to Brazil, lamented, "[The Holy Eucharist] is not the only sacrament that masters deny to their slaves; they also prevent them from marrying." Those slaves fortunate enough to marry, continued Benci, often suffered the indignity of separation, "husband from wife...[and] the sale of the other."[4] It is perhaps revealing that the lamentable state of evangelical fervor in the clergy and secular elites is noted by a foreign missionary who could perceive the realities better than the *mazombos* (people of European descent born in Brazil) and Portuguese-born themselves.

Evangelization of enslaved Africans was not a priority for the Catholic Church in Spain and Spanish America. While the Portuguese focused their efforts on Africa and Asia, the Spanish focused theirs on Christianizing indigenous Americans, a project that absorbed the efforts of most Spanish missionaries. Africans played almost no role in the Spanish theory of American empire, although in practice, African labor, religion, and culture shaped both Spanish and Portuguese holdings in the Americas.[5] For the first few centuries of the American slave trade, until the 1785 *Código negro carolino*, no official Spanish royal legal policy ruled on slaves' religious instruction. This new policy was reiterated (but never enforced) in the 1789 *Código negro español*. Neither in Spain nor in the Americas was there a sustained attempt to convert Africans. Evangelization of the enslaved, freed, and creole Africans depended on the rigor of the pastoral vision of the local priests and the interest of their bishops. Slave and free Afro-Latin Americans also adapted to Christian beliefs and practice for personal reasons such as solace or consolation, need for community, or as a way of ingratiating themselves with the authorities.

In 1604 the Jesuits, to combat the absence of evangelization of African slaves, established a *colegio* in Cartagena de Indias (in today's Colombia), the most important port and slave market in Spanish South America. Many of the thousands of slaves entering this port each year were sold to slave dealers for work in Bogotá, the silver mines in the viceroyalty of Peru, or in the gold mines of the Chocó region to the west of Cartagena. One of the first Jesuits to work in Cartagena was Alonso de Sandoval (1577–1652), born in Spain and educated in Lima, the capital of the viceroyalty of Peru. Sandoval decided that the Jesuit mission in Cartagena would be dedicated to instructing newly arrived slaves in Christian catechism and to ensuring their baptism in the proper manner, neither forced nor rushed, in contrast to the baptisms that commonly occurred on the African coast. Sandoval wanted slaves to make an informed, voluntary decision to accept baptism. In 1627 he published a long, detailed book, *Naturaleza, policía sagrada i profana, costumbres i ritos, disciplina i catechismo evangélico de todos etíopes* (The Nature, Sacred and Profane Government, Customs and Rites, Discipline and Evangelical Catechism of All Ethiopians), in an attempt to standardize the Jesuit approach to catechizing the Africans.

This system would require the Jesuits to tend to the emaciated and dehydrated slaves who arrived in horrific physical and psychological condition, in dire need of clothes, food, and medical care. After they were taken from their ships, the missionaries would divide the slaves into their distinct language groups, later slowly instructing the captives in Christian doctrine using African translators. In order to instruct African slaves effectively, the Cartagena Jesuits used at least eighteen African interpreters from the 1620s to the 1650s. Many of the interpreters worked with the Jesuits for years and became skilled independent catechists, speaking in the languages of Angola and Congo, as well as the West African languages of Wolof and Fula. Through these interpreters, the priests would explain the idea of the Christian God, heaven and hell, and the resurrection of Jesus Christ. When the slaves had a basic understanding of these beliefs, they would be baptized. Often baptism was actually followed by last rites, since many of the slaves were dying.

Sandoval developed an enormous passion for propagating this mission. Like Vieira after him, he neither argued for the abolition of slavery nor rejected the powerful racial biases common to seventeenth-century Europeans. A close reading of his book, however, indicates strongly that he believed slavery was an immoral institution that could be justified only by providing the enslaved with the opportunity to voluntarily accept baptism.

While Sandoval is remembered for his passionate writings asserting the slaves' humanity, it was one of his Jesuit colleagues, Peter Claver (1581–1654), who is known for actually engaging in concrete activities to make that humanity palpable. After many years of Jesuit training in Spain and Bogotá, in 1616, in response to Sandoval's many requests for volunteers, Claver went to work in the Jesuit mission in Cartagena. He boarded the slave ships, washed away the filth that had accumulated on the bodies of the enslaved during their two-month ordeal, and then baptized them. Like his fellow missionaries throughout the colonial period, Claver used physical punishment when he perceived that the newly baptized were reverting to "heathen" practices. Legend says Claver converted three hundred thousand Africans during his lifetime (with very little support from his fellow Jesuits) although only a fraction of that number could have passed through Cartagena during that period. After the deaths of Sandoval and Claver, the Jesuits lost most of their enthusiasm for catechizing the African slaves.

Despite the low level of proselyzation, over a period of time a number of slaves and their descendants became fervent Catholics, some even local heroes. The lives of three of these individuals were recorded by their devotees. All three worked as servants in convents and, due to their African heritage, were prohibited from taking official vows. Most convents (male and female) used African slaves who sometimes outnumbered the friars and nuns. Juana Esperanza de San Alberto was a slave in the Carmelite Convent in Puebla, Mexico, during the seventeenth century. Her devotees described her as "raised by the grace of God to spiritual perfection, despite being a poor, black woman, crude, ignorant and rustic, [whom] it seems that the Lord destined…to be exemplary in such a holy community." They considered her saintly because of her habits of fasting, ignoring taunts, remaining silent, and caring for the sick.[6] She modestly refused to take vows to become a nun when the convent offered this option to her (a demonstration of the malleable nature of colonial race-based regulations) and instead chose to return to self-effacing slave status. Another woman who became known for her ardent Catholic mysticism was Ursula de Jesús (1604–66), a slave in the Convent of Santa Clara in Lima.[7] After almost dying by falling into a well, Ursula became a fervent Catholic, experienced visions, and spent her time in prayer and self-mortification. Even after a nun purchased her freedom in 1645, she remained a servant in the convent, taking a special vow that affirmed her dedication to Catholicism. Ursula reported her communication with souls in purgatory to her confessor, including those of slaves who complained that no one prayed for them, and those of deceased priests and nuns in purgatory who expressed guilt for the sins they had committed during their lifetimes.

One Afro-Peruvian, Martín de Porres (1579–1639), the son of an important Spanish official and an African slave, spent his life in a Dominican friary in Lima, where he worked as a lay brother. Although he was part of the community he was not permitted to take official vows. Contemporaries saw Martín as a humble, modest, and self-deprecating individual despite his extraordinary influence over superiors and elites. His success at healing the friars of his convent and important officials of the viceroyalty suggested to contemporaries that God's hand was empowering him. He incongruously and stubbornly cared for stray dogs, despite scornful rebukes and taunts by friars and patients that Porres was himself a *perro mulato*. He declared, "I already know I am a mulato dog," confirming the humility that gave him a saintly reputation. His training of dogs, cats, and mice to eat from the same bowl cloaked him in the aura of St. Francis of Assisi. Some present-day analysts consider Martín's behavior as evidence of criticism, subtle though it may be, of the social order in which privileged elites depended on the support of the despised castes.[8] The same elites who labeled him a "mulatto dog" glossed over the fact that the dog was a symbol of loyalty and devotion, as well as an emblem of the Dominican order itself. And in a modest protest of colonial race hierarchies, the physically unequal animals eating from the same bowl might suggest the moral equality of the races.

Afro-Latin Americans and Confraternities

The major institution that helped Africans and their descendants, free and slave, forge an enduring link to the Catholic Church was the institution of the confraternity or brotherhood. Despite the masculine terminology, many women both joined and led these Catholic organizations. In Spanish, confraternities were called *cofradías, hermandades, congregaciones,* or *cabildos,* a word that also means council. In Portuguese, the term was *irmandade.* In fifteenth century Spain and Portugal, with the encouragement of the clergy, Africans had created confraternities for religious purposes as well as to maintain a sense of community and to address concerns related to dying and death. In Spanish America, Africans and their descendants organized and led brotherhoods, which they established as extensions of convent churches and cathedrals. Typically each confraternity would maintain side altars throughout the edifices and celebrate festivals connected with the Holy Sacrament, Jesus, the Virgin Mary, St. Nicholas Tolentino, or Benedict of Palermo (beatified in 1743; canonized in 1807), a Franciscan friar who was the son of African slaves. The Virgin of the Immaculate Conception and Our Lady of the Rosary were two of the most popular recipients of confraternal devotion. Other confraternities dedicated themselves to honoring an aspect of Catholic doctrine connected to Jesus Christ. Because of the significance of the Eucharist in Catholic doctrine, members of the European elite usually controlled and led confraternities dedicated to the Sacrament. Unfortunately, many records have been lost over the centuries and, for that reason, knowledge of them is restricted to brotherhoods in Cuba, Brazil, and Mexico. These organizations continued to thrive well into the nineteenth century, and some exist in Brazil even today.[9]

Other confraternities reenacted some aspects of the Passion of Christ in Holy Week processions. In New Spain specifically, documents show that at least sixty Afro-Mexican brotherhoods existed in the viceroyalty, and among those, at least eight practiced public flagellation as part of a penitential procession during Holy Week. Members viewed these practices as a way to re-create and experience Christ's suffering and crucifixion and to display their Christian piety. Men, women, and children walked in the penitential processions, although only men participated in the *disciplina* of flagellation. Women carried candles and images of saints — thus the processions were described as *de luz y sangre* (of light and blood). Penitential brotherhoods had names such as the "Exaltation of the True Holy Cross and the Tears of St. Peter" or the "Humility of Christ."[10] An early brotherhood in Mexico City was founded in 1602 in a Dominican church and dedicated to the "Expiration of Christ." Other brotherhoods in seventeenth-century Mexico City included one dedicated to the "Precious Blood of Christ," a common name for penitential brotherhoods. Another founded in 1668 practiced penitential flagellation and chose "St. Nicholas of Mount Calvary" as their advocate.

Confraternities as organizations that brought people together socially also celebrated with yearly fiestas that included music, dancing, food, drinking, and firework displays, all financed by the brotherhood. They also served important charitable functions, including care for sick members. In addition, confraternities provided shrouds and burials for their members, as well as annual Masses for the souls in purgatory, since many feared that their souls would languish there because they lacked adequate family and friends to pray for them after death. Furthermore, members believed that prayers were more effective and more likely to receive saintly intercession when recited by a group. For this reason, if an individual could afford to pay dues, he or she might join many confraternities. Slaves also feared that their bodies would be neglected when they died and treated as debris to be discarded. Confraternity members who failed to attend a member's funeral lost the privilege of having a funeral entourage themselves.

In order for the Catholic Church to grant an organization official approval, members had to submit a list of rules, called a *constitución* in Spanish or a *compromisso* in Portuguese. The brotherhoods elected or appointed their officials, including secretaries, treasurers, and majordomos, the latter being the most important office, ultimately controlling the funds and organizing the *fiestas/festas*. Majordomos, almost always men, often had to make up losses with their own money, which became a vehicle for them to demonstrate community spirit, wealth, and status. Many confraternities were open to all races and classes. Membership fees were often minimal or nonexistent. Some confraternities specified that members had to be from a particular African nation or had to be American-born creoles, or *mulatos*, or *mestizos*. Some Afro-Latin American brotherhoods admitted slaves, though often limiting leadership positions to free people of color. Confraternities replicated colonial social structure and divisions and attempted to be autonomous. A few brotherhoods were comprised of members of the same occupation, thus fulfilling the roles of traditional guilds. Confraternities raised money by charging membership dues, investing in properties and businesses, or publicly begging for contributions on a prescribed day of the week. African confraternities occasionally cooperated with each other in order to buy the freedom of a particular member. Women of African descent played leadership roles in all these activities.

Differences among confraternities in New Spain, Cuba, and Brazil derive from the long-term and profound impact of forced African immigration into the latter two areas, which strengthened their African roots and consciousness. Few Africans arrived in the viceroyalty of New Spain after 1640. Only one example of a brotherhood based on an African ethnic group has been discovered in New Spain: the *Zape* brotherhood in Mexico City, which disappeared by the mid-seventeenth century. Due to the intensification of slave importation into both Cuba and Brazil, African confraternities continued to thrive in those areas.[11]

Afro-Brazilian brotherhoods flourished in ways unmatched in Spanish America, save Cuba. In Minas Gerais, Salvador de Bahia, and elsewhere, Afro-Brazilian *irmandades* were eventually able to control their own church buildings. Many African brotherhoods were distinguished by their ethno-linguistic groups, such as Angolan, Jeje, or Nagô. But despite maintaining strong religious beliefs and ritual from their native lands, these confraternities were located in churches and dedicated to Catholic saints.

Since their early founding in Bahia in the 1600s, the most popular advocation for Afro-Brazilian brotherhoods was the Virgin of the Rosary. Although Africans appreciated the charity and social activities of the brotherhoods, churchmen were there to constantly remind them of their spiritual nature. From the perspective of the former the prime reason for the existence of the brotherhoods was to assist their members in attaining eternal salvation. In 1633, for example, Antonio Vieira preached the following to a Rosary brotherhood in Bahia:

> Your brotherhood of Our Lady of the Rosary promises all of you a Certificate of Freedom, with which you will not only enjoy eternal liberation in the second transmigration of the other life, but with which you will also free yourself in this life from the most terrible captivity of the first transmigration.[12]

In the wake of the late seventeenth-century gold rush that was the impetus for a massive movement of slaves and free people of color to the gold fields of Minas Gerais, Rosary brotherhoods began to flourish. By the early eighteenth century, new residents had formed dozens of brotherhoods. Slaves from the Mina coast as well as from Central Africa enthusiastically organized Rosary brotherhoods in towns throughout the region, which generally lacked a strong presence of the Catholic Church. By the end of the century, many of these organizations had their own lavish official churches. Their processions were lengthy and opulent, and members dressed in white silk, carrying statues encrusted with gold and diamonds.

In late eighteenth-century Salvador de Bahia, Afro-Brazilians challenged the domination of the international charitable brotherhood called the Santa Casa da Misericórdia. This organization, controlled by the sugar-growing elite, had obtained a monopoly on burials, which made it the only legal source of funeral biers and litters.[13] Several black brotherhoods complained that the Misericórdia abused its privileges, overcharging Afro-Brazilians and treating slave cadavers roughly and impiously. The brotherhoods ultimately managed to gain control over their members' funerals and burial locations. Many Afro-Bahians chose burial inside a church under the church floor, or on the grounds of the churches controlled by African and creole black brotherhoods. In the nineteenth century, most Bahians still preferred to be buried near a church building because they perceived it as a physical manifestation of links between this world and the next. Only suicides, paupers, criminals, political rebels, and slaves who died upon arriving in Bahia were buried in the city cemetery, which many equated with a refuse dump since it was controlled by a sanitation official.

Bahians, especially members of the brotherhoods, including the Afro-Bahian brotherhoods, were appalled when, because of sanitary concerns, early nineteenth-century reformers in the government forbade burials within the city limits. At that time, Afro-Brazilians made up over 72 percent of the population of the former colonial capital city.[14] The government proposed a new cemetery, called the Campo Santo, which would be under the control of a private company. These innovations threatened both the spiritual values and the livelihood of brotherhoods, essentially challenging one of their main reasons for existing. Some impoverished Bahians needed work as paid mourners to support their slender existence. Burials in churches in the city made it possible for them to participate in several funeral corteges in one day. Led by a local nobleman and several confraternities, 280 people signed a petition against the new cemetery plan in 1836, beginning the movement called the Cemiterada. The brotherhoods then organized a protest march, in the name of religion, which drew thousands of residents, some of whom raided a government office to assert their demands. Women stoned the offices of the private cemetery company, and other demonstrators marched to the Campo Santo, crying "long live religion," "long live the brotherhoods," and "death to the Cemetery!" Upon arriving at the cemetery, the members, using tools taken from construction sites, proceeded to tear down its pillars, gates, grills, ossuaries, stables, headstones, and walls, ultimately demolishing the entire cemetery. Unlike their reaction to other popular rebellions in Brazilian history, especially those involving Africans, the authorities remained aloof and did not violently suppress or punish the participants, either during the destruction or afterward by pressing charges against those who had damaged the cemetery property. The revolt was unsuccessful. The Misericórdia, which the brotherhoods had previously challenged, ultimately managed the Campo Santo. During a devastating cholera epidemic in 1855, the town government again forbade city burials. This time the brotherhoods did not object, because now they had access to their own permanent cemetery outside the city and under their management.

Resistance and Rebellion

Colonial authorities frequently claimed that the Christianization of African bondsmen would make them more docile and content with their lives under servitude, but Christian slaves became resisters, rebels, and runaways with the same frequency as the nonacculturated ones. Iberian legislation such as the *Siete Partidas* famously gave rights and privileges to slaves (Muslims and Slavs), but the constant fear of rebellion by the growing number of enslaved Africans compelled colonial officials to be ever more tolerant of the masters' excesses. Slaves could theoretically sue their masters for mistreatment (*sevicia*), but few slaves were able to take advantage of this right. Ironically, for many, protection could be obtained only by forcing colonial institutions such as the Holy Office to intervene on their behalf since slaves who blasphemed God because of their master's brutality were sometimes called before inquisitors.[15] Other slaves coped with the harsh slave regime through work slowdowns, but many others opted to escape and engage in banditry, or participate in open rebellions.

The first major slave insurrection took place as early as 1522 on the island of Hispaniola (now Haiti and Dominican Republic), which was governed at the time by Diego Columbus, son of the famous explorer. Eight years later, in what is now Colombia, Santa Marta became the first town to be destroyed by slave rebels.[16] Mexico City suffered its first slave scare in 1537, when a group of slaves sent from the Antilles planned a rebellion that aimed at establishing an African kingdom in the New World. Learning that the Africans had chosen a king and had agreed to kill all Spaniards, Viceroy Antonio de Mendoza led a fierce campaign against the plotters, which culminated in the torture and execution of the leaders. As a preventive measure, Mendoza recommended halting the importation of new slaves, but his advice was not followed because of the colony's growing labor demands. Bands of maroons (runaway slaves) were active on the *camino real* between Puebla and Veracruz and along the Pacific Coast, robbing and killing both Indians and Spaniards. By the turn of the seventeenth century the activity of maroons was so successful that travel between Mexico City and Veracruz was deemed unsafe.[17]

More disturbing to colonial authorities, however, slaves even used Christian institutions such as confraternities to organize their uprisings. In 1611 an angry crowd of fifteen hundred blacks belonging to the confraternity of Nuestra Señora in Mexico City filed past the viceregal and Inquisition palaces carrying the corpse of a female slave who had been flogged to death. The angry rioters threw stones at the home of the master, Luis Moreno de Monroy, obliging him to seek protection from Spanish guards. Later, the Afro-Mexicans selected an Angolan couple, Pablo and María, as their king and queen and planned to launch an ambitious rebellion on Holy Thursday (April 19) of 1612, with the financial support of several of the capital's black confraternities. Portuguese merchants in Mexico learned of these plans by accident and reported them promptly to the Audiencia of Mexico (the colony's high court), which ordered the main leaders arrested and tortured. On May 2, 1612, thirty-five blacks, seven women included, were publicly hanged in the main square of the city. Authorities quartered six of their bodies and scattered them on the roads, while their heads remained on display above the gallows. As a preventive measure, the Audiencia ruled illegal the attendance of more than four black men or women in funerals of blacks, and ordered the disarming of all blacks and the dissolution of all Afro-Mexican confraternities but to no avail.[18] Black confraternities not only survived into the eighteenth century but even grew in number.

Large-scale slave rebellions often led to the creation of maroon communities — *quilombos* in Portuguese, *palenques, manieles,* and *cumbes* in Spanish — in mountains, densely forested zones, and other areas difficult to access. The most famous were Palmares in northeastern Brazil, San Basilio in northern Colombia, and Yanga's settlement in Veracruz. Living in isolation, maroons re-created African traditions, sometimes incorporating elements of Christian worship. Although plantation owners considered such communities a bad example for their slaves and complained about constant raids, colonial authorities hesitated to initiate costly and difficult campaigns against the rebels and many expeditions intended to be punitive ended at the "negotiating table," with the maroons securing for their settlements the status of lawful towns in exchange for loyalty, tribute, and the promise to help authorities capture other fugitives.[19]

In the mountains near Orizaba, in New Spain, a Congolese chief called Yanga or Ñanga established an almost impenetrable *palenque,* raiding the neighboring towns and plantations with impunity for over thirty years. After several unsuccessful attempts to subdue Yanga, Spanish officials sent Franciscan Alonso de Benavides in 1608 to negotiate peace. The priest returned without success after nearly five months among the fugitives. In 1609 Viceroy Luis de Velasco (the younger) commissioned Captain Pedro González de Herrera to pacify the area, but the Spanish forces were impeded by fierce resistance. Eventually the undefeated Yanga negotiated the freedom of his followers and secured the status of a free town for their settlement near Veracruz, which later became San Lorenzo de los Negros.[20]

The *palenque* of San Basilio was established c. 1619 when survivors of an old settlement led by a slave named Domingo Bioho established a new village near Cartagena. Under the leadership of Bioho, later crowned King Benkos, the rebels had routed two punitive military campaigns against them (1612–13), forcing the Spanish governor to offer them amnesty. King Benkos accepted the terms and demanded the right to dress as a Spaniard. Six years later, however, another revolt took place in Cartagena, after which colonial authorities imprisoned and executed the former king. Benkos's followers then retreated into the interior and established the famous *palenque,* which did not receive official recognition from the crown until 1713, when the rebels reached a peace agreement with colonial authorities.[21]

The great *quilombo* of Palmares was a confederation of eleven settlements located in the outlying states of Alagoas and Pernambuco. At its peak, the encampment had as many as twenty thousand inhabitants, though this included many impoverished free men and women who joined the fugitives. Many had escaped from the infamous sugar plantations of the Brazilian Northeast, where slaves endured appalling working conditions. The first settlements were probably established in the late sixteenth or early seventeenth centuries, but their number grew substantially during the Dutch invasion of Pernambuco (1630–54). The first major expeditions against Palmares took place in 1676–77, but it was not until 1694 that Portuguese forces captured the main settlement of Macao. The following year, Palmares's king, Zumbi, was captured and executed and his head taken to Recife for public display.[22]

In these three maroon communities, the rebels tended to synchretize Christian and African indigenous elements in their worship, thus making evident that the acceptance of Christianity by Africans did not necessarily imply acquiescing in a life of forced servitude. At Yanga's *palenque,* for example, the maroons had erected a small church with a bell tower and adorned its altar with lighted candles and arrows planted on the ground in front of it.[23] Similarly, upon entering Palmares, the Portuguese troops found in the abandoned villages several churches with statues and saints.[24] More recently, in the *palenque* of Gracia Real de Santa Teresa de Mose, in present-day Florida, archeologists have found religious items such as rosary beads and a handcrafted medal of St. Christopher, the patron saint of travelers, along with broken coins, pottery, and military artifacts.[25] Although it is difficult to reconstruct patterns of worship from these religious artifacts, the evidence does show that maroons tended to combine African and Christian rituals. In Yanga's *palenque,* Africans married in accordance with Christian religion, but the husband-to-be generally abducted his future wife. As the maroon Francisco Mozambique told Franciscan Alonso de Benavides, "Marriage in the hills isn't the same as marriage in the city."[26]

African Religious Beliefs in the Diaspora

The conversion of Africans to Christianity in the New World did not necessarily mean the rejection of their old beliefs and rituals. In accordance with the first commandment ("Thou shalt have no other gods before me"), Christian dogma demanded religious exclusivity from the faithful, but Africans tended to supplement and combine elements of their own religions with that of the colonizers.

Undoubtedly, their ability to combine different religions stemmed from the "additive" nature of religiosity in Africa, where it was not unusual for people to accept cosmologies and revelations from inhabitants of areas foreign to them. As with Christianity, African religions envisioned a cosmos divided into a world of the dead and a world of the living, with the possibility of transworld communication through revelations. While Christianity had a strong priesthood to define the meaning, legitimacy, and orthodoxy of revelations, African religious leaders did not attempt to impose orthodoxy or discredit revelations advanced by groups other than their own. This religious permeability grew in the diaspora, for the exposure to disparate belief systems in America led Africans to adopt practices from Christians and other African groups with whom they had not had contact in their native land.[27] African slaves belonged to different ethnic groups, spoke an astonishing variety of languages, and followed widely dissimilar traditions, but they also shared a set of cultural understandings or principles regarding the nature of power and the supernatural, and a strong emphasis on ancestor worship that facilitated the merging of religious traditions in the New World.[28]

A common belief in African societies was the conviction that a Supreme Creator ruled the cosmos without being involved in the daily affairs of humans, while a host of lesser gods and ancestral spirits was perpetually present in every aspect of their lives.[29] This hierarchical division of the cosmos into two groups of spirits allowed Africans to worship a distant Christian god associated with the master class, while keeping a loyal reverence to African deities in their daily lives.[30] Catholic authorities frequently reported on the facility and eagerness with which Africans converted to Christianity, and this should be understood as a desire to partake in the religious power of the colonizers' gods and not as a decision to abandon their own beliefs. While religious syncretism cannot be easily accounted for by merely matching cosmologies between different belief systems, it is undeniable that there was a tendency among slaves to endow Christian saints with African attributes. Thus in Brazil, Yoruba slaves from West Africa linked Ogum, the orisha (divinity) of iron and war, to a sword-carrying St. George, while in Cuba Ogún (in Spanish) was linked to St. Peter because Ogún held an iron key. Both in Cuba and Brazil, Changó (or Xangó), the Nigerian macho womanizer and god of thunder, was similarly associated with the courageous St. Barbara, while St. Lazarus was linked to Babalú Ayé, the orisha of illness and disease.[31] Even Jesus, Satan, and the Virgin Mary found "equivalents" in African cosmology. While Jesus was associated with Oxalá (or Obalá), a creator god, Exu, an orisha of vengeance, lust, and greed, was identified with Satan. Finally, Yemajá, the moon goddess, controller of the sea, and mother of all orishas, was linked to the Virgin Mary in Brazil and the Virgin of Charity in Cuba.[32]

Catholic authorities objected to these forms of syncretism, but they found even more disturbing the widespread use of African arts of divination, healing, and witchcraft, practices generally deemed diabolic and superstitious by the church. Following Pope Sixtus V's famous bull *Coeli et terrae* (1585), which commanded priests, prelates, and inquisitors to prosecute those who practiced divination and similar arts like magic and incantations, the Holy Office of the Inquisition prohibited divinatory consultations and punished transgressors. In African societies, divination constituted a legitimate and trusted source of vital knowledge for making difficult decisions in daily life. Through their arts, diviners were instrumental in identifying the causes of misfortune, allocating responsibility for acts of malevolence, and directing afflicted clients to relevant solutions. Many diviners with physical or psychological "abnormalities" that marked them as marginals or outcasts counteracted such disadvantages with their extraordinary ability to communicate with ancestral spirits.[33] In Iberoamerica, diviners were frequently slaves who resorted to mantic arts to offset their social marginality under colonialism. Although the colonial authorities never accepted slave diviners as vehicles of legitimate means for redressing grievances, propitiating the divinities, or working out social tensions, the diviners were sometimes able to secure a measure of prestige and economic independence, and even the protection and promotion by their own masters.

As in Africa, enslaved diviners resorted to a variety of objects, auguries, omens, and ordeals to elicit precious information from the other world, but few forms of divination were as spectacular as those involving spirit mediumship. In seventeenth-century Mexico, slave women practiced an astonishing form of mediumistic divination known as "talking through the chest." Using speech techniques similar to contemporary ventriloquism, the slaves created entities that offered advice, located stolen or lost objects, or helped their clients to make important decisions. The slaves responded to questions in a "thin" muffled voice that some witnesses compared to the reverberations of a soft whistle, or the distant squeak of a rabbit. More impressive than the unearthly voice, however, was that it was produced covertly, for witnesses did not see slave mediums "move their lips." Inquisitorial prosecutors were convinced that it was a demon or Satan himself who spoke through the diviner's chest, but the ventriloquist's arts were closer to the forms of mediumistic divination practiced on the African west coast, particularly in Congo and Angola, to communicate with the ancestral spirits, or *ngoomb*.[34]

More directly related to these forms of mediumistic divination, however, was the healing practice known as *calundú*. A divinatory technique of Angolan origin, the *calundú* took root in Brazil, particularly in Bahia and Minas Gerais, in the seventeenth century and was widely used to identify the causes of illness. As in Central Africa, people consulted their ancestral spirits through mediums who induced possession using animal skins, ribbons, feathers, chicken or cow blood, and white clay. Singing and dancing often accompanied the ceremonies, culminating with the possessed speaking in the voice of the deceased relatives to explain the clients' illnesses and prescribe remedies.[35] Like the masters of African "ventriloquism" in colonial Mexico, owners of *calundú* practitioners offered them special treatment, for they considered the African diviners valuable moneymakers. Slaves also took advantage of crisis situations to gain promotions and protection from their masters and even managed to keep profits obtained from consultations without their owners' awareness.

While diviners strove to contact supernatural beings, African practitioners of sorcery across the Atlantic aspired to control such forces, resorting to a variety of objects including herbs, bones, feathers, heads of selected birds, fingernails, earth from graveyards, and mountains. Practitioners and their clients both used sorcery for a variety of purposes that included securing sexual favors, acquiring certain special qualities, and, most importantly, "taming" the slaveholders.[36] Talismans and amulets were also common among slaves, aimed at gaining protection against their masters and avoiding bodily harm. In colonial Brazil, the most common talismans were the pouches of cloth or leather known as *bolsas de mandinga* or *patúas*. These small bags were particularly popular during the eighteenth century and normally contained a variety of objects that included bones, hairs, powders, animal skin, and even written Christian prayers.[37] By linking elements of African and other religious traditions in rituals and devices, conjurers and healers paved the way for the creation of forms of folk Catholicism with strong African content. Moreover, because religious specialists not only catered to their fellow slaves but also served a larger multiethnic clientele, they played an important role in the gradual acceptance of African ways of knowing, healing, and accessing the supernatural in the New World. African beliefs did not merely survive in the diaspora: they thrived.

Notes

1. Gomes Eannes de Azurara, *The Chronicle of the Discovery of New Guinea,* cited in J. Albert Raboteau, *Slave Religion: The "Invisible Institution" in the Antebellum South* (New York: Oxford University Press, 1978), 96–97.

2. Lee M. Penyak and Walter J. Petry, eds., *Religion in Latin America: A Documentary History* (Maryknoll, N.Y.: Orbis Books, 2006), 121. This was Vieira's first public sermon; he began preaching in 1633. See Thomas Cohen, *The Fire of Tongues: Antonio Vieira and the Missionary Church in Brazil and Portugal* (Stanford, Calif.: Stanford University Press, 1998), 4.

3. Robert Edgar Conrad, *Children of God's Fire: A Documentary History of Black Slavery in Brazil* (University Park: Pennsylvania State University Press, 1984), 157–58.

4. Ibid., 174–75.

5. For an assessment of the evangelization of enslaved Africans in colonial Mexico, see Joan Cameron Bristol, *Christians, Blasphemers, and Witches: Afro-Mexican Ritual Practice in the Seventeenth Century* (Albuquerque: University of New Mexico Press, 2007).

6. Joan Bristol describes Esperanza's life in "Negotiating Authority in New Spain," Ph.D. dissertation, University of Pennsylvania, 2001, 141, 137–49.

7. For Ursula's diary, see Nancy van Deusen, *The Souls of Purgatory: The Spiritual Diary of a Seventeenth-Century Afro-Peruvian Mystic, Ursula de Jesús* (Albuquerque: University of New Mexico Press, 2004).

8. Alex Garcia-Rivera, *St. Martin de Porres: The Little Stories and the Semiotics of Culture* (Maryknoll, N.Y.: Orbis Books, 1995).

9. Elizabeth Kiddy, *Blacks of the Rosary: Memory and History in Minas Gerais, Brazil* (University Park: Pennsylvania State University Press, 2007), 4–5.

10. Nicole von Germeten, *Black Blood Brothers: Confraternities and Social Mobility for Afro-Mexicans* (Gainesville: University Press of Florida, 2006), 227–29.

11. For examples of how newly arrived slaves formed organizations directly connected to indigenous African traditions, see Philip A. Howard, *Changing History: Afro-Cuban Cabildos and Societies of Color in the Nineteenth Century* (Baton Rouge: Louisiana State University Press, 1998), 21–27.

12. Penyak and Petry, *Religion in Latin America*, 121.

13. João José Reis, *Death Is a Festival: Funeral Rites and Rebellion in Nineteenth-Century Brazil* (Chapel Hill: University of North Carolina Press, 2003), 129–32.

14. For additional information on the *cemiterada*, see Reis, *Death Is a Festival*, especially 24.

15. See Javier Villa-Flores, "Voices from a Living Hell: Slavery, Death, and Salvation in a Mexican Obraje," in *Local Religion in Colonial Mexico*, ed. Martin Austin Nesvig (Albuquerque: University of New Mexico, 2006), 235–58; see also Javier Villa-Flores, *Dangerous Speech: A Social History of Blasphemy in Colonial Mexico* (Tucson: University of Arizona Press, 2007), 127–47.

16. Leslie B. Rout, *The African Experience in Spanish America*, with a new introduction and bibliographical update by Miriam Jiménez Román and Juan Flores (Princeton, N.J.: Markus Wiener Publishers, 2003), 104, 109.

17. Jonathan I. Israel, *Race, Class and Politics in Colonial Mexico, 1610–1670* (New York: Oxford University Press, 1975), 67–68.

18. Colin Palmer, *Slaves of the White God, Blacks in Mexico, 1570–1650* (Cambridge, Mass.: Harvard University Press, 1976), 138.

19. On maroon communities in Latin America, see the classic essays collected in Richard Price and Sally Price, *Maroon Societies: Rebel Slave Communities in the Americas*, 3rd ed. (Baltimore: Johns Hopkins University Press, 1996).

20. On Yanga's maroon community, see Jane Landers, "Cimarrón and Citizen: African Ethnicity, Corporate Identity, and the Evolution of Free Black Towns in the Spanish Circum-Caribbean," *in Slaves, Subjects, and Subversives: Blacks in Colonial Latin America*, ed. Jane G. Landers and Barry M. Robinson (Albuquerque: University of New Mexico Press, 2006), 121–32.

21. Rout, *The African Experience in Spanish America*, 110.

22. Mary Karasch, "Zumbi of Palmares: Challenging the Portuguese Colonial Order," in *The Human Tradition in Colonial Latin America*, ed. Kenneth J. Andrien (Wilmington, Del.: Scholarly Resources, 2002), 104–20.

23. Landers, "Cimarrón and Citizen," 126.

24. Roger Bastide, *African Civilisations in the New World*, trans. Peter Green with a foreword by Geoffrey Parrinder (New York: Harper and Row, 1971), 49.

25. Landers, "Cimarrón and Citizen," 115.

26. Bastide, *African Civilisations*, 49. It is possible that in Guerrero, as in contemporary Cuijla, the abduction was just a symbolic act, for the betrothed couple did not elope but simply spent the day together and returned to the village in the evening. See Gonzalo Aguirre Beltrán, *Cuijla: Esbozo etnográfico de un pueblo negro* (Mexico City: Fondo de Cultura Económica, 1958), 148–63.

27. See John Thornton, *Africa and Africans in the Making of the Atlantic World, 1400–1800* (Cambridge: Cambridge University Press, 1998), 246–48; Sidney W. Mintz and Richard Price, *The Birth of African-American Culture: An Anthropological Perspective* (New York: Beacon Press, 1976), 45.

28. Karen Fog Olwig, "African Cultural Principles in Caribbean Slave Societies: A View from the Danish West Indies," in *Slave Cultures and the Cultures of Slavery,* ed. Stephan Palmié (Knoxville: University of Tennessee Press, 1995), 23–39.

29. Rout, *The African Experience in Spanish America,* 8–11.

30. Olwig, "African Cultural Principles," 33.

31. Christine Ayorinde, "Santería in Cuba: Tradition and Transformation," in *The Yoruba Diaspora in the Atlantic World,* ed. Matt D. Childs and Toyin Falola (Bloomington: Indiana University Press, 2005), 219–20.

32. George Reid Andrews, *Afro-Latin America, 1800–2000* (New York: Oxford University Press, 2004), 28.

33. Philip M. Peek, "Introduction: The Study of Divination, Present and Past," in *African Divination Systems: Ways of Knowing,* ed. Philip M. Peek (Bloomington: Indiana University Press, 1991), 196.

34. See Javier Villa-Flores, "Talking through the Chest: Divination and Ventriloquism among African Slave Women in Seventeenth-Century Mexico," *Colonial Latin American Review* 14, no. 2 (December 2005), 299–321.

35. See James Sweet, *Recreating Africa: Culture, Kinship, and Religion in the African-Portuguese World, 1441–1770* (Chapel Hill: University of North Carolina Press, 2003), 144–52.

36. See Palmer, *Slaves of the White God,* 159; Kris Lane, "Taming the Master: Brujería, Slavery, and the Encomienda in Barbacoas at the Turn of the Eighteenth Century," *Ethnohistory* 45, no. 3 (Summer 1998), 505 n. 7.

37. Laura de Mello e Souza, *The Devil and the Land of the Holy Cross: Witchcraft, Slavery, and Popular Religion in Colonial Brazil,* trans. Diane Grosklaus Witty (Austin: University of Texas Press, 2004), 130.

5

Priests and Nuns
in Colonial Ibero-America

Karen Melvin

In 1696 Catarina de Telles Barretto and her family processed to the door of the Destêrro Convent (Bahia, Brazil) accompanied by bells and music, images of saints, and crowds of people. Catarina entered the convent, where she exchanged her regular clothes for a nun's habit and her family name for a new religious name, Catarina de Monte Sinay. In a Carmelite friary in early seventeenth-century Puebla (New Spain), Rodrigo Yáñez, who had previously lived a dissolute life as a soldier, swore vows of poverty, chastity, and obedience and became Rodrigo de Santa Catalina, Discalced Carmelite friar. At a special ritual officiated by the archbishop of Mexico in 1574, Juan González de Urbina had his head shaved into a tonsure (leaving a bald spot on the back of his head) marking the sacrament of ordination by which he became a secular priest.[1]

Such ceremonies signaled the formal separation of those who went through them from the rest of the population. These men and women had entered a divinely ordained profession that set them apart from other members of colonial society. From now on they would wear distinctive garments that marked their special status, and in some cases, they would also change their names, literally taking on new identities. They were to give up marriage and family in order to dedicate their lives to serving God. They enjoyed a distinct legal status, falling under the jurisdiction of church rather than the royal courts. How well those who entered religious life fulfilled their obligations varied considerably, depending not just on whether one was a nun or priest, but also on the type of nun or priest they became. This essay examines three general categories of religious men and women — nuns, regular clergy (members of male religious orders), and diocesan (secular) priests. It looks first at the characteristics of those who entered religious life and then at what sorts of activities they performed or were expected to perform as nuns and priests.

During the first decades of colonization in the sixteenth century, the handful of priests present in the Americas were mostly Europeans who had already embarked on their careers before making the voyage across the Atlantic. These priests came as missionaries, with the purpose of converting Amerindians to Christianity, and most were members of religious orders. These men lived together in communities, followed a common Rule (a canonically approved set of guiding principles adopted by each order), and took vows of poverty, chastity, and obedience. This first wave of missionaries consisted of friars from the mendicant orders, especially Franciscans, Dominicans, Augustinians, and Mercedarians. Because these orders were mobile and dedicated to preaching and because their vows of poverty meant they could live cheaply, the Spanish crown considered them especially well-suited to the enormous missionary project at hand.[2] The crown's close involvement in the project came about after the pope granted the Spanish and Portuguese monarchies the right, known as the *patronato real,* to appoint clerics in the Americas in exchange for overseeing the conversion of Amerindians. Later in the century, members of other orders joined the missionary efforts, notably the Society of Jesus (Jesuits), which became the wealthiest and most powerful order in Brazil and vied for this position in the Spanish Americas.

Most prospective friars joined mendicant orders between the ages of thirteen and fifteen, although it was not unusual for someone to join during his later teens or early twenties. There were rare cases of men entering religious life as late as in their seventies, such as the famous Sebastián de Aparicio, who joined the Franciscan order at age seventy-two after having been twice married and twice left a widower. To become a friar, men were required to be of legitimate birth and pure blood, which meant their background had to be without the taint of Jewish, African, or Indian ancestry. These requirements were not always enforced, however. Illegitimacy was far less an issue in practice than in theory, but even in the more carefully scrutinized issue of racial purity, there were also cases where men entered despite having their applications rejected for failing to prove their purity of blood. Such cases were more likely to occur when men possessed qualities useful to the order, such as language skills or important connections. While uncertainty about someone's background might be overlooked, people officially categorized as Indians, *mestizos,* or *mulatos* most frequently entered orders as servants. Nor were the sons of the very elite or the very poor well represented in the orders. Instead, the majority of friars came from families with moderate resources. For example, many friars' fathers were artisans, landowners, merchants, or government officials who had already provided their sons with basic educations and now sought career paths for them.[3]

The first step to becoming a friar was to undergo a year-long probationary period called a novitiate, during which the entrant was introduced to religious life and had his vocation tested. Could he handle the privations of convent life, fasting, submitting to the commands of his superiors, rising at midnight and again before dawn to join his brethren in communal prayers? One friar referred to his order's novitiate as a forge, melting down men and reshaping them into friars. If this forging process was judged successful, the novice would profess, taking solemn vows of poverty, chastity, and obedience, thereby becoming a full-fledged member of the order. At this point, he would either begin his studies to become a priest or start work as a lay brother. Lay brothers performed or supervised much of a convent's day-to-day functions, including overseeing the kitchen, collecting alms, and ensuring that the church and its sacred objects were properly maintained. Those who intended to become priests studied philosophy and theology for several years. Upon completion of these studies, they were eligible to be ordained as priests. Whereas the ceremonies performed upon the candidate's entry and profession into his order were specific to each order, the sacrament of priestly ordination required the local bishop to anoint the candidates. Ordination ceremonies were typically held once a year and included friars from multiple orders.

The practices of the Jesuits differed in some crucial ways from those of mendicants. The order had only recently been founded in 1540, partly in response to new Protestant threats to the church. Jesuits emphasized their active ministries among the laity, forgoing the daily rounds of communal prayers that mendicants did in combination with their active ministries. The order quickly expanded around the world, so that a century after its founding it comprised several hundred residences spread out over Europe, Asia, Africa, and the Americas. In the Spanish Americas, the Jesuits competed with the mendicant orders for the territories where they established missions, but in Brazil, the order held a virtual monopoly on missions.

Men who sought to become Jesuits undertook a longer spiritual journey than potential mendicants. At the end of a two-year-long novitiate, these men professed the three sacred vows of poverty, chastity, and obedience. The men then began a probationary period that was even more important than the novitiate and that lasted several years. During this time, they completed their studies and were ordained. These "fathers," as they were called, could now begin their true mission as Jesuits: ministering to the laity. They were evaluated in this work and, if judged successful, they would take a fourth vow, which was unique to their order: special obedience to the pope and agreeing to work wherever they were needed. Only now were these Jesuits full members of their order and eligible to hold high-ranking positions. Those not judged successful during the probationary period would remain Jesuits but at the rank of spiritual coadjutors and would generally be limited to low-level positions within the order. At first, some Jesuit officials were willing to accept *mestizos* into the order. According to the Jesuit chronicler José de Acosta, the order accepted them because they were native speakers of indigenous languages and had been brought up to be good Catholics by their European family members.[4]

On the heels of missionaries came members of the secular clergy. These men administered the parishes that made up the church's most basic structure, and their primary duty was to minister to the spiritual needs of the laity. Parish priests were responsible to the local bishop or archbishop who was, in turn, accountable to the pope and crown. The crown therefore viewed secular clergy as more easily controlled than regular clergy and beginning in the 1570s tended to privilege the former over the latter. Unlike friars, secular clergy did not live in communities nor perform daily rounds of prayers collectively. They took vows of chastity and obedience but not poverty, and so they were not expected to renounce material wealth and comforts. Some priests were, in fact, property owners and quite wealthy, such as Gracián de Agüero, a parish priest in eighteenth-century New Spain who owned two haciendas.

As with mendicant friars and Jesuits, the process of becoming a diocesan priest often began when a boy was in his early teens. He entered a seminary where he studied Spanish, Latin, grammar, rhetoric, and philosophy. These courses typically took about eight years to complete. During the process the prospective priest would take minor orders, which allowed the young man to enjoy some of the worldly benefits of a career in the church, since now he could obtain income from church positions and came under the jurisdiction of church rather than state courts. Some men never proceeded beyond minor orders. Those who continued their formal training also completed a four-year course in theology, at which point, if they met all other requirements, they were ordained as priests.

These requirements included legitimate birth and "Old Christian" lineage. As in the case of the regular clergy, a questionable background could be overcome if witnesses testified to an aspirant's legitimate birth and family background. Secular clergy seem to have come from more varied racial backgrounds than regular clergy. Certainly the majority of priests were creoles, but there were a handful described as Indians, *mestizos,* or *mulatos.* After early prohibitions against Indians becoming priests were abandoned, some Indians were ordained, and during the late colonial period, approximately 5 percent of parish priests in the Archdiocese of Mexico were Indians.[5] Candidacy for a *mulato* proved to be an even more difficult proposition. For example, when Rafael Ramírez Becerra first applied to the priesthood, witnesses from his hometown testified that his family was commonly considered *mulato.* As a result and despite testimonials to his good behavior, he was not allowed to take minor orders. According to the diocesan attorney who argued against his entry, men with African blood were prohibited from entering the priesthood "because there has been noted in this kind of person bad and perverse inclinations and because of this they are reputed as contemptible and as base persons."[6]

The secular clergy was also marked by strong social distinctions. Men who came from wealthy families often entered the priesthood with access to an endowed fund that family members established specifically for that priest. In exchange for the income from this fund, the priest would celebrate a certain number of Masses each month or year for souls in purgatory. These sons could hope for appointments to cathedral chapters or at least plum parishes. One of the keys to winning such highly desired appointments was a superior education, which was typically the prerogative of the rich or well-connected. A well-educated priest would have the tools to compete in the written and oral examinations held to decide who would fill vacant parochial benefices.

Priests who came from less privileged families and who lacked a good education could expect more challenges. The lucky few who earned appointments to their own parish typically served in poor, isolated, or otherwise undesirable locations. Pedro de Ubiarco, for example, recalled having endured "an extremely hot climate, the abundance of poisonous animals, and the scarcity of healthy provisions" during his stint in Iscuintla (New Spain).[7] A much more likely career path for someone without the advantages of wealth or connections was a series of appointments as assistants to parish priests, and most struggled to make a living as they moved from one temporary assignment to another. These men often entered the priesthood as *curas de idioma,* or language priests. This path was created to solve a chronic shortage of priests fluent in native languages, allowing humble but bilingual young men with only a rudimentary education and without an endowed fund to become priests. Some of the challenges of a career as a language priest can be seen in the not unusual career of Francisco Antonio de Urueta, who, in the fourteen years after his ordination, served as an assistant in eight different parishes.[8]

Women could also find their vocation, spiritual fulfillment, or career by entering religious life, but these nuns — unlike the friars, Jesuits, or secular priests whose vocations included close work with the laity — spent their lives enclosed in convents, never setting foot outside convent walls from the day they entered to the day they died. The first convents for women in the Americas were established in the 1540s and spread quickly throughout the cities of the Spanish Americas. In Portuguese Brazil, however, the first convent for women was not created until 1677, and even then the number of new convents grew slowly, in part because crown policy sought to keep the relatively small population of elite women available for marriage.

Convents of nuns were connected to religious orders, such as the Carmelites or the Poor Clares (Franciscans) and based many of their practices and standards on their order's traditions. Administratively, however, each convent of nuns operated as a discrete institution with its own constitution and rules. Convents fell into one of two general categories: relaxed or reformed. In the former, a nun might live in her own "cell," which could consist of multiple rooms with luxurious furnishings, her own kitchen, which served sumptuous meals, and a private altar so she could fulfill some spiritual obligations without having to leave her quarters. These nuns might even have several servants or slaves to take care of their personal needs. In reformed convents, nuns were supposed to follow more austere lifestyles, living in tiny, sparsely furnished cells, eating simple meals together in the refectory, and following strict routines centered on religious services and individual prayers. On some occasions, differences in opinion about how reformed or relaxed a particular convent should be created highly charged situations within the convent. For example, a rebellion took place in the convent of La Purísima Concepción in San Miguel, New Spain, during the 1760s when a group of nuns tried to enforce a stricter interpretation of convent rules, such as increasing the number of hours spent in prayer each day and prohibiting personal servants. Another faction of nuns protested, arguing that they would not be able to carry out their spiritual obligations properly if they had to spend so much time doing the chores required to keep the convent running. The conflict was intense enough to burn off and on for more than a decade, force two abbesses to resign, and require the intervention of the local bishop.[9]

Many convents were founded specifically for the daughters and other relatives of those whose funds built and endowed the new foundations. When the Convent of the Most Holy Trinity was founded in Puebla (New Spain), for example, fourteen of the initial seventeen nuns were related to the founding patrons. Not surprisingly, given these close connections to the wealthy and powerful, nearly all convents were created for elite women of European backgrounds. Aspirants had to demonstrate that they were of pure blood — no Jewish, Muslim, or Indian ancestors — and legitimate birth. As in the case of the male religious, there was more emphasis on the former than on the latter. For example, when João Luis Ferreira's illegitimate daughter had to prove her racial purity to enter Bahia's Destêrro convent in 1695, there were no objections to her illegitimacy, only questions as to whether her mother (the unknown parent) might have been a *mulata*.[10] There were a few exceptions to convents that catered to elite women, including those of Santa Clara in Cuzco and Corpus Christi in Mexico City. Santa Clara was founded in 1551 specifically for *mestizas,* the daughters of Spanish conquistadors and noble Indian women, with the goal of ensuring that these women would be culturally Spanish and not lost to what convent founders viewed as the abyss of Indian culture and society. Within two decades, however, Santa Clara had already morphed into a convent for elite creole women, shutting its doors to new *mestizas* and leaving those who had already entered as second-class members. Mexico City's Corpus Christi convent was established in 1724 specifically for the daughters of Indian nobles. Here, aspirants were required to be full-blooded Indians and had to demonstrate that they came from good Christian families whose members had never worked in lowly occupations such as selling *pulque* (an alcoholic drink traditionally consumed by Indians).[11]

Internally, convents reproduced many of the social hierarchies of the colonial world where women from wealthy European and creole families were at the top of the social, economic, and racial pyramid. The key distinction was between nuns who wore black veils and those who wore white veils. Black veil nuns usually came from wealthy or well-connected families who could afford to pay the full dowry (entrance fee). These women held the convent's most important offices and were responsible for its governance. White veil nuns typically paid only half the dowry of a black veil nun. These women were generally not of the same social standing as their full-paying counterparts and might even have entered their convents as charity cases. Despite having completed a novitiate and professed solemn vows, the white-veiled nuns performed much of the convent's day-to-day functions, such as cooking and cleaning, but rarely became part of the convent's power structure.

Beginning in the late sixteenth century, the number of men and women entering religious life in the Spanish Americas increased dramatically, and populations of nuns and friars peaked in the early to mid-eighteenth century. For example, the number of Franciscans in the order's Mexico province grew from 225 friars in 1569 to 556 in 1682 and reached its zenith in the 1730s at 840. Similarly, the population of nuns in Lima's La Concepción convent increased from 80 nuns at the beginning of the seventeenth century to 247 in 1700.[12] In Brazil, convent growth began later than in the Spanish Americas. Not only were convents of nuns founded later, but so too were diocesan structures so that in 1549, when the first diocese in Brazil was established, there were already twenty-two dioceses in the Spanish Americas. Similarly, the number of Jesuits in Brazil did not increase significantly until the second half of the seventeenth century, at the time when the sugar industry, new immigration, and the importation of slaves dramatically transformed Brazil's economy and demographics.[13]

Most growth in populations of nuns and priests resulted from increased numbers of creoles who sought suitable career options for their sons and daughters. The overwhelming majority of nuns and priests were creoles. Nuns born in Europe were rare and usually made the journey across the Atlantic only if already professed nuns were needed to start new convents. Regular clergy, once the initial burst of missionizing in the sixteenth century ended, consisted primarily of creoles. Their numbers were supplemented by European friars and Jesuits who came over to staff missions, especially on the northern frontier (now northern Mexico and the southwestern United States) and southern frontier (now Chile and Argentina) of the Spanish empire. In addition, some mendicant orders needed *peninsulares* (people born in Spain or Portugal) for the crown-mandated rotation of important offices between American- and European-born friars.[14] Although the relative number of creoles and *peninsulares* varied greatly by order and even province (the orders' administrative units), there were often enough *peninsulares* to generate intense rivalries between the two groups. Finally, while the parish priests who made up the bulk of the secular clergy were mostly creoles, bishops and archbishops were almost exclusively *peninsulares,* sent by the crown to help maintain control over distant American possessions.

Overall, the number of nuns and priests continued to grow through the mid-eighteenth century, but the second half of the century produced a range of trends. During this time, reform-minded state officials pushed for smaller populations of regular clergy. Reformist monarchs viewed religious orders, which possessed greater independence from royal authority than diocesan clergy, as obstacles to their goal of restricting church power and authority. Accordingly, they sought to reduce the size of these orders, and royal decrees in the 1730s and 1750s limited the number of novices entering mendicant orders. Some of the most dramatic results took place in the Franciscans' Mexico province, where populations of friars fell from their 1730s high of 840 to 699 in 1780 and 307 in 1801.[15] In addition, the Jesuits' great wealth and close connection to the pope made them especially vulnerable to Portuguese and Spanish monarchies determined to establish greater control over their realms, and the monarchs expelled the Jesuit order from their respective territories in 1759 and 1767. On the other hand, numbers of secular clergy grew during the second half of the eighteenth century. After royal decrees in 1749 and 1753 forced the mendicants to relinquish most of their *doctrinas* (Indian parishes) to secular clergy, additional priests were needed to staff the new parishes. So while there were approximately 465 priests in the Archbishopric of Mexico in 1767, there were about 600 at the beginning of the nineteenth century.[16] Populations of nuns after mid-century seem to have held steady, especially in New Spain. Populations of individual convents sometimes fluctuated, but any declines were usually short term and often in response to ebbs in a convent's financial situation or to state or church reform efforts rather than to waning interest in religious life.[17] At the end of the colonial period the total number of male clerics (regular and secular) was estimated at 6,800 in New Spain alone, and the number of nuns in all Spanish Americas at 6,000.[18]

People's reasons for entering religious life varied from a genuine vocation to careerist ambition to parental choice, but throughout the colonial period, this career path remained a popular option. Even during the second half of the eighteenth century, when state or church reforms made their strongest impact on convents of both men and women, communities that continued to provide career options continued to attract new members.

Men and women religious structured their daily activities according to their affiliation's particular mix of spiritual exercises, active ministries, and mundane tasks. For mendicants and nuns, convent life was ordered according to a cycle of services, prayers, and observances. Depending on the strictness of the order, friars and nuns might rise before dawn to hear Mass and sing or recite common prayers, then return for additional services several times throughout the day until the final service at midnight. Punctual completion of these obligations could be trying.

Histories and hagiographies (works celebrating the lives of spiritually noted religious men and women) lauded men and women religious for their dedication to their order's demands. For example, according to the life story of the Franciscan Alonso de Escalona, who lived in sixteenth-century New Spain, he "was unremitting and persevering in observing choir and community exercises" and when traveling alone in open country would still light a fire at midnight in order to recite his prayers.[19] On the other hand, internal decrees from the seventeenth and eighteenth centuries repeatedly lamented the number of nuns and friars who attended daily offices and encouraged convent leaders to crack down on truancy. Not all of these absences were unexcused, however, and nuns or friars who held certain offices, were engaged in time-consuming activities, or claimed poor health could be exempted from attending services. Some orders were more likely to grant these exemptions. Dominicans, who strongly encouraged intellectual pursuits, were far more generous with dispensations than the Discalced Carmelites, who strongly valued communal prayers.

Although nuns and mendicants placed far more emphasis on schedules of prayers and services than Jesuits and secular clergy, these religious communities shared fundamental beliefs about piety and pious practice that were rooted in broader traditions within the Catholic Church. Hagiographies and spiritual biographies reveal practices that emphasized meditation on or imitation of Christ and Mary as ways of strengthening and purifying the soul. In particular, contemporary authors encouraged men and women religious to focus on Christ's crucifixion and the intense pain he experienced because of his love and devotion to humanity. For example, Franciscan friar Diego de Medellín spent the two years before his death in his convent's infirmary with so many painful ailments that his seventeenth-century hagiographer needed a lengthy paragraph to list them all. The hagiographer then explained how Christ's example helped Friar Diego bear his agony "with such great patience...that he seemed a saint." He gave daily thanks to God for blessing him with such infirmities and "easily overcame it all with the memory of the Lord and his Passion."[20] Religious men and women did not need to wait for illness or infirmity to strike in order to imitate Christ's sufferings, and especially pious men and women commonly engaged in acts of penance that included flagellation, wearing hairshirts or crowns of thorns, and impressing nails into their flesh. Sor Juana Gertrudis was said to have reenacted the Stations of the Cross, a heavy cross bound to her back, while the rest of her fellow nuns slept. The secular priest Juan Antonio Pérez de Espinosa was reported to have slept in a coffin to remind him of death's imminence. He also fasted regularly and three times a week lashed himself with a scourge until he bled. For these men and women, physical suffering was a means of becoming closer to God.

Beyond these shared foundations, there were variations in pious practices, some of which were closely associated with certain orders. For example, Franciscans promoted the Way of the Cross, a series of stations where the faithful meditated on the stages of Christ's Passion. Dominicans had a special devotion to the rosary, and most of their houses sponsored confraternities (lay sodalities) dedicated to Our Lady of the Rosary. Jesuits emphasized an interior spirituality marked by the careful searching of one's conscience and taking frequent communion. Key to this process were the Spiritual Exercises, which Jesuits were required to complete once a year. Written by Ignatius of Loyola, the order's founder, these consisted of a month of prayers, meditations, and contemplative exercises designed to examine one's way of life and to correct deficiencies.

Spiritual biographies of religious men and women also lauded the virtues of poverty, chastity, and obedience. Jesuit chronicler Andrés Pérez de Ribas (1576–1655) used similies to indicate that members of the order were to love poverty "as a mother" and obey one's superiors blindly "like a corpse."[21] Nuns and priests were to adhere to these virtues even in the face of great temptation. One didactic tale told of a voice waking a young Carmelite in his cell. "Do you want a woman?" it asked. The friar then saw the devil in the figure of a "dishonest woman inviting him to sin." Although he experienced great temptation, he repeatedly made the sign of the cross over his heart until she disappeared, thus protecting his chastity.[22]

In addition to cultivating their own interior piety, men and women religious also worked for the good of the wider community, although the nature of their contributions varied considerably. During the first decades of colonization, these services primarily consisted of evangelizing Amerindian populations. In Spanish territories, mendicants initially took charge of this enterprise by establishing hundreds of houses in Indian towns where priests lived in small communities, sometimes with as few as two priests in residence. These houses were part of administrative units known as *doctrinas*, which were temporary parishes that would be turned over to diocesan priests once the inhabitants had been fully Christianized. The missionaries destroyed native temples and altars whenever they could, often building their churches on the ruins, and they sought to root out idolatry. Friars were to teach Indians the basic principles of Christianity and baptize them, making them members of the church. The best way to Christianize Indians provoked heated debate among the orders. Many Franciscans, believing that the discovery of the Americas signaled the Second Coming of Christ, practiced mass baptisms, sprinkling water over crowds so large that in one day hundreds, perhaps thousands, of people were baptized and therefore eligible for salvation should the apocalypse occur. Others, Dominicans in particular, argued that a deeper understanding of Christianity was required prior to baptism. Indians, they argued, should therefore be well instructed and then tested in the basic tenets of the faith beforehand. To teach church precepts, whether before or after baptism, friars established schools, used didactic art, and employed mnemonic devices.

During the late sixteenth century, Jesuits joined mendicant friars in this missionary work. Jesuits had a reputation as passionate evangelizers and efficient businessmen, and they used the profits from agricultural enterprises such as haciendas and sugar plantations to fund their missionary activities. Throughout the colonial period, they, along with the Franciscans, remained most heavily involved in running missions on the frontiers of the Spanish and Portuguese empires, in areas such as the Yucatan peninsula (Franciscans), Paraguay (Jesuits), and northern New Spain (Franciscans and Jesuits).

Missionaries, from whatever order, might spend weeks or months alone in a distant mission or traveling between Indian communities. It could be a lonely and dangerous endeavor, especially if the missionary was working with or near native groups hostile to his presence. Even so, the most dedicated missionaries welcomed the possibility of martyrdom, seeing their work as comparable to that of the Twelve Apostles and their ultimate sacrifice as similar to those made by Christ and various saints. For example, after two Jesuits were martyred on New Spain's northern frontier in the sixteenth century, their brethren recounted their deaths in heroic terms: "they both fell to their knees and asked Our Lord for His favor and grace. They began to be struck by thousands of arrows covered with a poisonous herb. These rained upon their bodies until they became two Saint Sebastians."[23] Aside from the hardships endured by many missionaries, one of the most formidable obstacles to converting Indians to Christianity was language, and most missionaries learned, to varying degrees of proficiency, difficult indigenous languages. As a result, regular clergy became important contacts between native and Spanish populations. Men from these orders realized the value of this connection and often used it to defend their roles as missionaries, or *doctrineros,* against those who sought to replace them with secular clergy, who tended to be less fluent or interested in native languages.

From the late sixteenth century, as the number and size of cities in the Spanish Americas grew, the regular orders shifted their work to these areas. Over the next two centuries the number of friars and urban houses grew dramatically. Priests in these locations focused their ministries on broader sectors of the population than in the rural Indian missions, attending to people of all races and social standings. They provided the usual priestly services, celebrating Mass, dispensing sacraments, preaching sermons, and organizing charitable works. They sponsored lay organizations and elaborate celebrations of feast days in honor of Christ, Mary, and the saints. Jesuits became known for educating the sons of elites in their order's famous schools, and by the early seventeenth century, the majority of Jesuits worked in urban colleges.[24]

Secular clergy could be employed in a wide range of activities from teaching in universities to staffing the Holy Office of the Inquisition. Most, however, worked in parishes where they offered priestly services like the regular clergy but with the additional right to administer the sacraments of baptism and marriage. Parish priests also functioned as agents of the state and so fulfilled more secular functions as well, often serving as judges and reporting on local conditions for state officials.

The relationships of priests to the laity varied. Some served their flocks faithfully and were respected and even beloved by their communities. Others were less attentive to their duties and spent much of their time away from their parishes. Some were praised for providing services to the poor without charge, while others were accused of demanding excessive fees or forced labor. Some were celebrated for their kindheartedness, while others were chided for inflicting excessive beatings or whippings. A 1793 report described Juan de Dios Castro Tobio, a parish priest in New Spain, as excelling "in exemplary virtue, renowned learning, notorious zeal, selflessness and charity, and the fullest performance of his pastoral duties." At the other extreme were priests like Miguel José Losada, who, during the late 1790s, operated an illegal cane alcohol still, carried firearms, and once traveled to Mexico City with three women, throwing wild parties along the way.[25]

The most coveted assignments for secular clergy were those that paid well and allowed the priest to live in an urban area. Since secular clergy did not live in communities as mendicants and Jesuits did, those without trusted assistants or who were posted to Indian villages without social peers might well find themselves without social support or networks. As one priest wrote from his isolated rural parish: "I now have spent four years and four months of purgatory in this parish.... It is not possible to explain...how I have suffered in this terrible solitude, where bitterness has been my bread both day and night."[26]

Despite nuns' lifelong enclosure, they remained closely connected to colonial society and were considered integral to its spiritual health. Cloistered behind convent walls where they were supposed to be protected from the corrupting influences of the world, they served as models of feminine virtues, including chastity, humility, obedience, and modesty. Paradoxically, nuns were also considered models of "the good wife." Upon entering the convent, nuns became "brides of Christ" and were to serve him dutifully and faithfully, the same way married women were to serve their husbands. Nuns' prayers were thought to be especially effective. They could release souls from purgatory (where the dead atoned for their sins before entering heaven) or help assuage divine wrath believed to take the forms of earthquakes, hurricanes, or volcanic eruptions. The female convent was thus considered a valuable local resource, serving as a "fortress standing against moral lapses and worldly perversity" and keeping its community in good stead with the heavenly forces that regularly intervened in the mundane world.[27]

Somewhat ironically, these enclosed nuns also played an active role in the outside world. Because women could not beg for alms nor be paid for performing priestly services like the male religious, convents required substantial wealth to

support their residents. Much of this wealth, which came from dowries and donations, was lent to members of the local community, and nunneries became the
primary source of credit in colonial society.[28] Although convents had syndics to
manage their outside business affairs, nuns, especially the convent abbess and
treasurer, actively took part in management and decision making.

Just as nuns participated in the business of the outside world, so, too, did the
outside world participate in convent life. Besides the servants and slaves who came
and went, buying and selling goods or running errands, family and friends visited
nuns in the convents' *locurios* (visiting rooms with a metal grill to separate nuns
from visitors). Locurios were among the busiest and loudest places in the city,
filled not only with voices of nuns and visitors but sometimes with music as well.
Convents were also home to women who were not nuns. These women included
widows seeking a secure place to live out their days, orphans abandoned at the
convent's doors, and young girls whose parents placed them with the nuns for
safekeeping until they married or took their own vows as nuns. Nuns may have
been separated from the world, but they certainly were not isolated from it.

Nuns also spent much of their time in secondary occupations, such as sewing,
embroidery, and educating the girls who lived with them in feminine virtues and
skills — pious practices, sewing, music, and some reading and writing. In the
eighteenth century, a few convents were even established with the purpose of
running day schools for girls. Some individual nuns moved into less traditional
occupations. For example, it was not uncommon for nuns to make candies and
desserts for sale to the public, either by means of turnstiles in convent doors (to
protect the nuns from direct contact with outsiders) or by dispatching slaves or
servants to sell the goods. These could be small operations that supplied friends
and family or sizable and profitable businesses. For instance, Catarina de Monte
Sinay, at the time of her death in 1758, employed twelve slaves who made and
sold pastries and caramels that became famous throughout Bahia. Finally, there
were also a very few nuns who engaged in intellectual pursuits, most famously
Sor Juana Inés de la Cruz (1651–95). She was an author of lyric poetry and
plays, an avid reader, and a researcher deeply interested in science and religion,
and her renown spread far beyond Mexico City. Although her work was much
celebrated and she enjoyed the patronage of important colonial figures, many of
her seventeenth-century contemporaries were disturbed by her transgressing of
"conventional boundaries for women's lives and spiritual activities."[29]

Men and women who entered religious life may have set themselves apart from
other members of society, but they clearly remained an integral part of that society.
Parish priests were said to be "separate but in the world" because they were to
keep their vows even as they lived among the laity. Regular clergy may have lived
separately, but both mendicants and Jesuits were actively involved in the day-to-
day functioning of local communities and the lives of their residents. Even nuns —

with their businesses, the secular women living in their convents, the comings and goings of servants, and the regular visits of family and friends — had considerable contact with the world. These close connections provide an excellent reminder of the church's overwhelming presence in the laity's daily lives. Cycles of holy days and the hourly tolling of church bells regulated the pace of life. People depended on priests for the sacraments that kept their souls in good spiritual health as well as for counsel on mundane issues such as a troubled marriage. Church members asked nuns and priests to pray for their souls and arranged to be buried in their churches, sometimes paying large sums for these privileges. Visitors flocked to these churches for services and for the images they housed, some of which inspired great devotion. In short, the church was at the center of colonial society, and nuns and priests were vital to its functioning.

Notes

1. Susan A. Soeiro, "Catarina de Monte Sinay: Nun and Entrepreneur," in *Struggle and Survival in Colonial America,* ed. David G. Sweet and Gary B. Nash (Berkeley: University of California Press, 1981), 258; Agustín de la Madre de Dios, *Tesoro escondido en el Monte Carmelo Mexicano: Mina rica de exemplos y virtudes en la historia de los Carmelitas Descalzos de la Provincia de la Nueva España,* ed. Eduardo Báez Macías (Mexico City: UNAM, 1986), 245–46; John Frederick Schwaller, *The Church and Clergy in Sixteenth-Century Mexico* (Albuquerque: University of New Mexico Press, 1987), 106.

2. The monarchies generally limited their use of this privilege to appoint people to high-level offices, such as bishops and archbishops.

3. Francisco Morales, *Social and Ethnic Background of the Franciscan Friars in the Seventeenth Century* (Washington D.C.: Academy of American Franciscan History, 1973).

4. Sabine Hyland, *The Jesuit and the Incas: The Extraordinary Life of Padre Blas Valera, S.J.* (Ann Arbor: University of Michigan Press, 2003), 34–36.

5. William B. Taylor, *Magistrates of the Sacred: Priests and Parishioners in Eighteenth-Century Mexico* (Stanford, Calif.: Stanford University Press, 1996), 87.

6. D. A. Brading, *Church and State in Bourbon Mexico: The Diocese of Michoacán, 1749–1810* (New York: Cambridge University Press, 1994), 118.

7. Taylor, *Magistrates of the Sacred,* 109.

8. Ibid., 95.

9. Margaret Chowning, *Rebellious Nuns: The Troubled History of a Mexican Convent, 1752–1863* (New York: Oxford University Press, 2006).

10. Susan A. Soeiro, "The Feminine Orders in Colonial Bahia, Brazil: Economic, Social, and Demographic Implications, 1677–1800," in *Latin American Women: Historical Perspectives,* ed. Asunción Lavrin (Westport, Conn.: Greenwood Press, 1978), 185.

11. Kathryn Burns, *Colonial Habits: Convents and the Spiritual Economy of Colonial Peru* (Durham, N.C.: Duke University Press, 1999); Ann Miriam Gallagher, R.S.M. "The Indian Nuns of Mexico City's *Monasterio* of Corpus Christi, 1724–1821," in Lavrin, *Latin American Women* (Westport, Conn.: Greenwood Press, 1978).

12. Karen Melvin, "Urban Religions: Mendicant Orders in New Spain's Cities, 1570–1800," Ph.D. dissertation, University of California, Berkeley, 2005, 163; Asunción Lavrin, "Female Religious," in

Cities and Society in Colonial Latin America, ed. Louisa Schell Hoberman and Susan Migden Socolow (Albuquerque: University of New Mexico Press, 1986), 175.

13. Dauril Alden, *The Making of an Enterprise: The Society of Jesus in Portugal, Its Empire and Beyond, 1540–1750* (Stanford, Calif.: Stanford University Press, 1996), 219–20.

14. Several orders were required to practice the *alternativa,* whereby important positions alternated between people of the two "nationalities." European leadership established the *alternativa* to keep the numerically superior creoles from shutting out the *peninsulares* from offices, which some Europeans feared would lead to the loss of discipline and good practices.

15. Melvin, "Urban Religions," 193.

16. Taylor, *Magistrates of the Sacred,* 79.

17. Chowning, *Rebellious Nuns,* 187.

18. Susan Migden Socolow, *The Women of Colonial Latin America* (Cambridge: Cambridge University Press, 2000) and Taylor, *Magistrates of the Sacred,* 78.

19. Angelico Chávez, ed., *The Oroz Codex* (Washington D.C.: Academy of American Franciscan History, 1972), 115.

20. Alsono Franco, *Segunda parte de la historia de la Provincia de Santiago de México: Orden de Predicadores en la Nueva España* (Mexico City: Museo Nacional, 1900), 205.

21. Daniel T. Reff, "Critical Introduction," in Andrés Pérez de Ribas, *History of the Triumphs of Our Holy Faith amongst the Most Barbarous and Fierce Peoples of the New World,* trans. Daniel T. Reff, Maureen Ahern, and Richard K. Danforth (Tucson: University of Arizona Press, 1999), 33.

22. Madre de Dios, *Tesoro escondido,* 56.

23. Pérez de Ribas, *History of the Triumphs,* 306.

24. Ibid., 33.

25. Taylor, *Magistrates of the Sacred,* 183, 192.

26. Brading, *Church and State in Bourbon Mexico,* 115.

27. Asunción Lavrin, "Espiritualidad en el claustro novohispano del siglo XVII," *Colonial Latin American Review* 4, no. 2 (1995): 155–79. Quoted in Chowning, *Rebellious Nuns,* 63.

28. Burns, *Colonial Habits,* especially chapters 2 and 5.

29. "Sor Juana Inés de la Cruz's Letter to Sor Filotea (1691)," in *Colonial Latin America: A Documentary History,* ed. Kenneth Mills, William B. Taylor, and Sandra Lauderdale Graham (Wilmington, Del.: SR Books/Scholarly Resources, 2002), 208.

6

The Holy Office of the Inquisition
and Women

Jacqueline Holler

The Holy Office of the Inquisition, one of the best-known arms of the Catholic Church, played a significant role in the development of colonial societies in Latin America. The Inquisition also had a considerable effect on colonial women, who despite their general status as legal minors were responsible for their conduct as Christians and fully subject to inquisitorial authority. The history of the Inquisition's relationship with women is therefore of great interest to scholars, and exceptionally detailed inquisitorial records have proven a great boon to those interested in women's history.

The American tribunals came into existence as an outgrowth of the Iberian (Spanish and Portuguese) Inquisitions. The Spanish Inquisition was founded first. Spain's Holy Office was distinct in its aims and procedures from the Inquisitions established in other parts of Catholic Europe. Though the kingdom of Aragon had a tribunal dating to the thirteenth century, the institution known as the Spanish Inquisition was a later development. Founded in 1478 "to examine the disposition of genuine religious observance," the Inquisition was created largely to police the religious lives of New Christians (or *conversos*).[1] *Conversos,* or *marranos,* were individuals of Jewish ancestry whose familial conversions to Christianity generally dated to the violent pogroms of the late fourteenth and early fifteenth centuries. The *conversos* were the only group specifically named in the founding decree issued by King Ferdinand and Queen Isabella, who were ceded jurisdiction over the Aragonese and Castilian Inquisitions by Pope Sixtus IV.

Two elements of the Spanish Inquisition's foundation are particularly noteworthy. First, the Holy Office was an instrument of the state as much as of the church, under monarchic rather than papal jurisdiction. Indeed, many scholars have pointed to the institution's role as an instrument of nationalism and state power. Second, the specific mention of *conversos* is significant. The targeting of this long-Christianized group and the virulence of its persecution have led one scholar to portray the Spanish Inquisition as an institution founded on race-based anti-Semitism rather than a desire for religious purity.[2] Certainly, the racism evident in

115

contemporary accounts of "stinking Jews" lends credence to this claim.[3] Whatever the motivation behind the Inquisition's creation, it devastated the *conversos* of Spain between 1480 and 1520. This was by far the most violent and deadly period in the Spanish tribunals' more than three centuries of existence, and a period in which the Inquisition focused nearly exclusively on the persecution of *conversos*.[4] During this initial phase, women were a significant focus of inquisitorial activity, accounting for roughly half of prosecuted *conversos*, in part because of women's role in maintaining Jewish cultural and religious practices.[5]

Though "crypto-Jews" would continue to be sporadically persecuted both in Spain and in Spanish America, the Inquisition expanded its activities to encompass many other aspects of religious purity, beginning in the 1520s with attacks on Christian heresies such as illuminism,[6] or *alumbradismo*. The religious atmosphere of the decade was highly experimental and reformist, and the influence of women among the experimenters made them doubly suspect. Holy women, such as the Third Order Franciscan Isabel de la Cruz, found themselves arrested, condemned, and penanced (though never executed) for propositions and practices considered heretical.[7] Despite illuminism's notoriety in the sixteenth century, it was not statistically significant, accounting for fewer than 1 percent of all trials between 1540 and 1700.[8] From the 1520s until the middle of the following decade, the Inquisition cast its net ever more broadly for vaguely defined heterodoxy.

This amplification of mandate continued from 1547 to 1566, when inquisitor general Fernando de Valdés pursued cells of suspected Protestants. Lutheranism was overwhelmingly associated with men, and particularly with soldiers and foreigners. Protestant women, however, were subject to full punishment: in 1559, María de Borboques was burned in Seville as a Lutheran heretic.[9] Still, women were a small minority among those disciplined for this reason. While ferreting out Protestants, the Inquisition also began to pursue those guilty of offenses against Christian morality. Indeed, after the Council of Trent (1545–63), the Spanish Inquisition focused more on policing the behavior and morality of Christians than on persecuting so-called crypto-Jews or heretics. Thus while the vast majority of cases tried before 1540 involved major heresy, after 1540 a substantial majority of cases concerned moral infractions of less serious tenor.[10]

By the beginning of the seventeenth century, Spanish tribunals were well versed in all kinds of prosecutions, hearing cases of sodomy, fornication, witchcraft, blasphemy, and other sins familiar to Old and New Christians alike. This instituted what has been called a "culture of control" in early modern Spain[11] and gave the Holy Office broad jurisdiction over surprisingly varied aspects of social and cultural life. For example, in 1605, when the hermaphrodite Eleno/a de Céspedes of Ciempozuelos (in central Spain) was accused of bigamy, sodomy, and impersonating a man, the Holy Office was the body that heard the allegations and eventually convicted the prisoner.[12] The institution founded to extirpate the so-called "Mosaic heresy" had become, by the end of its first century, an institution with great influence and an ample mandate to monitor the boundaries of Christian society and culture.

During the forty years in which the Spanish Inquisition so zealously persecuted the *conversos* of Spain, no Inquisition was constituted in Portugal. As a result, many New Christians fled Spain for Portugal, as did Jews after Spain's expulsion order of 1492. But Portugal issued its own expulsion decree in 1496, thereby stimulating both a new wave of conversions and emigration to Portuguese Asia and particularly to the Low Countries. In 1531, the Inquisition was extended to Portugal by papal assent, though controversy over implementation and papal disapproval of the harsh measures to be taken against *conversos* delayed full establishment until 1536. Nonetheless, in 1541 the first Portuguese *auto da fé* took place, inaugurating a period of *converso* persecution that was as virulent as anything seen in Spain and that stimulated emigration both to Brazil and, perhaps ironically, to Spain. The popular perception that the Portuguese Inquisition was gentler or less dogged in its pursuit of suspected Judaizers than the Spanish is therefore without solid foundation. Indeed, throughout its history the Portuguese Inquisition remained focused on the New Christian population, with the vast majority of trials involving converted Jews and their descendants subject to often "ferocious" persecution.[13] Women were prominent among the accused. In some jurisdictions, such as that covered by the Evora tribunal, there were more women than men among convicted *conversos*.[14]

Distinctions emerged, however, in the American Inquisitions' creations and structures. The Spanish Inquisition had been founded with authority over all the kingdoms that Spain comprised. With the establishment of Spanish hegemony in the Americas, inquisitorial authority fell to friars, who received papal assent to exercise this power in 1521 and 1522, and later to bishops as they were appointed in various areas. Finally, in 1570–71, Philip II ordered the constitution of two tribunals of the Holy Office, one in Mexico City and one in Lima. The latter was given jurisdiction coextensive with the viceroyalty of Peru, thus encompassing much of South America, while the former exercised authority over what is now Mexico, Central America, the American Southwest, and the Philippines. In 1610, a further tribunal was added, at Cartagena, to police the Caribbean and the northern coast of South America.

The creation of formal tribunals in Spanish America thus followed colonial population and institutional growth in a fairly orderly fashion. Nonetheless, these tribunals, called upon to exercise jurisdiction over impossibly vast territories with minimal resources, had a difficult task. The Mexican Inquisition, for example, held sway over a region larger than that policed by all of the tribunals in the Iberian peninsula.[15] Moreover, the population of America was more diverse than Spain's, and included many individuals exempt from the institution's authority, as we shall see below. Finally, scholars have argued that the Spanish American tribunals were less regular in practice and possibly more prone to corruption and foot-dragging than their Spanish antecedents.[16] Thus the apparently orderly and systematic establishment of tribunals in Spanish America did not necessarily produce institutional vigor.

The Portuguese Inquisition, like the Spanish, was extended across the Atlantic with the incorporation of Brazil into the Portuguese domain. The process, however, was both slower and less fully developed. In 1551, the Lisbon tribunal (one of three tribunals in Portugal) received authority over cases arising in Brazil, Africa, and Portugal's Atlantic islands. No nonpeninsular tribunal was established in Portuguese lands except in Goa (1560). Thus throughout the colonial period, Brazil was policed not by a resident tribunal but by sporadic visiting tribunals relying upon the assistance of local secular and religious authorities.[17] The first of these inquisitorial visits occurred in 1591, some forty years after Lisbon attained jurisdiction over Brazil.[18] The absence of a permanent Brazilian tribunal undoubtedly led to a perception of the colony as a refuge for *conversos* and Jews;[19] nonetheless, Brazilians were not exempted from the Holy Office's supervision despite the institution's relatively tenuous position in the colony. Close to eleven hundred prisoners were sent from Brazil to Lisbon for trial, and recent estimates suggest that over eighteen hundred people were accused of secret Jewish practices in the eighteenth century alone.[20] Thus the significant differences between Brazilian and Spanish American Inquisitions are not indicators of their relative rigor or efficiency. In both Portuguese and Spanish colonies, however, inquisitorial surveillance and control were less effective than the Holy Office might have hoped, and the institution generally failed to instill orthodoxy and compliance with church edicts.[21]

Like the Spanish tribunals, the Inquisitions of Latin America focused originally on major religious crimes. This was particularly true of the monastic and episcopal Inquisitions of the sixteenth century. Nonetheless, in the early years, inquisitors were broadly empowered to deal with all kinds of offenses against the faith, and with the entire population regardless of ethnicity or conversion status. In New Spain, for example, the early monastic inquisitors tried indigenous people (almost all of them men) for misdeeds ranging from improper burial to idolatry, though the number of Indians tried was small relative to the total number of trials conducted. Many high-profile cases, particularly those of former priests in indigenous religions, did involve indigenous people. In fact, the first inquisitorial proceedings in New Spain (1522) involved an indigenous man accused of bigamy. A far more significant case, however, was the trial of Don Carlos Ometochtzin, the leader of Texcoco, who was garroted and burned in 1539 for his active opposition to Christianity. The case resulted in the 1540 censuring of Archbishop Fray Juan de Zumárraga for the harshness of Don Carlos's punishment. In addition, the Don Carlos affair, and the brutal Mani Inquisition carried out by the Franciscans in Yucatán,[22] played an important role in Philip II's decision to formally exempt indigenous people from the jurisdiction of the Holy Office in 1571.[23] This exemption notably failed to prevent inquisitorial proceedings against indigenous people, which continued to be carried out under the authority of bishops and even Audiencia judges throughout the colonial period.[24] Indigenous people still appear in Inquisition cases as denouncers and witnesses; nonetheless, in overwhelmingly indigenous areas such as Central Mexico more than three-quarters of the population was technically exempt from prosecution by the Holy Office.[25]

Indeed, despite the infamy of their interactions with indigenous people, even the early Inquisitions spent most of their energy policing the nonindigenous inhabitants of the colonies. Certainly, the concerns of the Spanish Inquisition were replicated in the American context; therefore, Judaizing and heresy figure prominently in the early period as they did in Spain. Other concerns, however, were at least as important. In New Spain, for example, trials for blasphemy outnumbered those for any other cause, and were often used as a political tool.[26] Similarly political in its aims, the first Brazilian inquisitorial visit paid particular attention to the powerful *mamelucos* (persons of mixed European and indigenous descent), both because of their suspect Christianity and, probably, because the Jesuits wanted to challenge the *mamelucos'* power and role in the trade in captured indigenous slaves.[27]

The tribunals of Lima and Mexico, which began their work in 1571, were instituted precisely at the moment when the recommendations of the Council of Trent (1545–63) were being implemented. The American tribunals thus possessed an unmistakably Tridentine character. This dictated, foremost, a focus on the banning of "dangerous" books and the eradication of heresy, particularly "Lutheranism" in any form. The latter concern was evident on February 28, 1574, when the Holy Office staged its first American *auto de fe* in Mexico City. Huge crowds gathered to watch the disciplining of a number of penitents, most notably French and English pirates captured during the previous eight years and found guilty of Protestantism. Two of the corsairs were executed.[28] This exemplary punishment was a powerful object lesson on the dangers of heterodoxy.

To further ensure that Latin Americans were not contaminated by unorthodox thought, the Holy Office used its power to censor and condemn books. Despite inquisitors' efforts, however, books circulated in a lively fashion, to the extent that books cited by the Index of Forbidden Books were to be found in Latin American libraries. The Holy Office reserved most of its censure for Protestant and, in the seventeenth century, astrological treatises.[29] While efforts to censor books might have profound effects on the lives of individual booksellers and collectors, there is little evidence that the Inquisition succeeded in controlling the flow of ideas from Europe to America, either in the early colonial period or later when tribunals attempted to stem the tide of reformist sentiment in the aftermath of the French Revolution. Finally, inquisitors remained alert to any expression of thought that smacked of heretical tendencies. Trials for "propositions" generally ended in light penances if no intransigent commitment to heresy was uncovered; such cases were exceedingly common, accounting for some ninety-three cases in the first year of the Mexican tribunal's functioning.[30]

Less common, and immeasurably more serious, were cases of major heresy (including Judaizing), which tended to occur in sporadic outbursts; for example, in Mexico Judaizing prosecutions peaked in the 1590s when the Carvajal family came under scrutiny. Nine family members were eventually executed in the *auto de fe* of 1596. From 1639 to 1650, another massive offensive was launched against the *converso* community of New Spain. In 1649, eight prominent citizens of Mexico City, many of them Portuguese merchants, were executed at the "costly and grandiose" *auto de fe* that marked the apex of the Mexican tribunal's zeal.[31] At the same time, eleven convicted Judaizers were executed in Lima.[32] Roughly contemporary with this wave of persecutions, the Holy Office also moved against the New Christians of Cartagena.[33] These convulsions were, however, rare in America relative to the levels attained in the Iberian peninsula, though Brazil's consistent persecution of New Christians may be an exception to this generalization. The comparison is clearer when Spanish American tribunals are compared to their Spanish counterparts. In Spain, for example, cases of heresy (including Judaizing) accounted for 42 percent of all cases pursued by the tribunals, while approximately 8 percent concerned sexual crimes (including solicitation). In Mexico, on the other hand, heresy cases formed no more than 27 percent of the total, while sexual crimes accounted for at least 20 percent.[34] The overall character of the American tribunals, then, emphasized Tridentine morality to a greater degree than was characteristic of Spain. Through a combination of repressing inflammatory printed materials, correcting unorthodox propositions while disciplining their promoters, and resorting to deadly violence against a minority of obdurate heretics, the Holy Office hoped to mold a population of faithful Tridentine Catholics immune to the temptations of Protestantism and purged of any "Mosaic" tendencies.

The reform of the Catholic population's morality and behavior was therefore a central plank of the Holy Office's work, in America as in Iberia. Indeed, this reformative activity may be said to have formed the bulk of the Inquisition's work. One key area of reform, as evidenced by the statistics cited above, involved sexual morality. For example, the Holy Office conducted investigations into concubinage and fornication, sometimes subjecting unmarried sexual partners to discipline, financial penalty, and separation. Indeed, five fornicators appeared in Mexico's first *auto de fe* in 1574.[35] Yet despite the frequency of illicit unions in Latin America, cases involving fornication and concubinage form a tiny proportion of the total number pursued by inquisitors between 1522 and 1700.[36] These cases were, however, also prosecuted by diocesan officials, and inquisitors may have therefore felt it appropriate to leave minor offenses to be dealt with in that arena. Though fornication and concubinage were of little interest to the Holy Office, it did pursue some people who denied the sinfulness of such activities. For example, European beliefs were sometimes newly elaborated in the context of colonial domination; thus in America the Inquisition found itself dealing with men who claimed that fornicating with an indigenous or African woman was not a sin, prompting a flurry of prosecutions at the end of the sixteenth century both in Spanish America and in Brazil. Though this particular claim was associated almost exclusively with men, women were denounced for denying the sinfulness of fornication more generally. The Holy Office appears to have expressed relatively little interest in such assertions.

The Inquisition reserved its serious interest in sexual morality for those offenses with clear religious impact. Solicitation in the confessional (priests' sexual advances toward parishioners) was one of these. Though obviously involving only men as suspects, solicitation is of interest here only as it involved women as witnesses and complainants.[37] The decrees of the Council of Trent increased the number of obligatory confessions; at the same time, frequent communion became a popular religious practice, particularly among women. Counter-Reformation piety also dictated a fuller self-examination and thus produced greater intimacy in the confessor-confessant relationship. Perhaps this led to an increase in priests' sexual approaches within the confessional. Whatever the case, the Tridentine church was concerned about the sanctity of the sacraments, and anything that contaminated their administration was dangerous to the faith. Thus, precisely as the American Inquisitions were beginning to work, solicitation *intra confessionem* became a matter of concern for the church.

Priests often used intimidation and trickery when soliciting sex from female penitents. For example, an eighteenth-century Mexican nun denounced her confessor for telling her that sexual acts with him were not sinful, as he had the power to relieve her of any sin she incurred. In other cases, priests refused to absolve women if they refused to grant sexual favors, or changed the venue of confession from the church to the priest's dwelling in order to gain sexual access to their spiritual daughters.[38] In 1590, a chaplain of Mexico City's Regina Coeli convent attempted to seduce an eighteen-year-old nun by reproducing a sonnet from a printed text, telling her he had written it in her honor.[39] While the church had long turned a blind eye to sexual misconduct by priests, particularly fornication and concubinage, the Counter-Reformation church would not tolerate solicitation. The abuse of a sacrament, rather than sexual coercion of women, motivated inquisitors' pursuit of priests who used the confessional as a sexual opportunity. Because the sacramental relationship was imperiled by priests' sexual predation,

121

the Holy Office heard cases against not only those who had made advances during confession, but any priests who engaged in sexual relationships with their parishioners. These *solicitantes* were pursued regularly and vigorously on both sides of the Atlantic.[40] For women, then, the Inquisition was not only a prosecuting institution — indeed, cases of solicitation show that women looked to the Holy Office for protection and even revenge.

Concern over the sanctity of a sacrament, in this case marriage, also fueled the prosecution of bigamy, which was pursued vigorously and generally punished harshly, whether committed by a man or a woman. However, bigamy was a crime overwhelmingly associated with men because of men's greater geographic mobility and women's greater financial dependence and vulnerability to retributive violence.[41] Clearly, however, many women were affected by bigamy cases, either as abandoned spouses or as new spouses who faced the invalidation of marriages and the loss of any claim to support. Sodomy was another serious crime policed by the Inquisition, as was bestiality; again, these crimes were almost entirely associated with men.[42] The policing of sexual morality was undoubtedly a central component of the Holy Office's effort to reform the diverse and unruly population of the New World and instill appropriate Catholic piety and comportment. These efforts, however, emphasized the most serious crimes against Catholic morality, most of which were associated with men, and left much behavior at most sporadically policed.

Policing diverse and innumerable crimes in such a vast terrain taxed the policies, practices, and personnel of the Holy Office. First, the Inquisition's regular staff was meager. According to the policies codified in Iberia before the implantation of the American tribunals, each tribunal was required to have two inquisitors; by the end of the sixteenth century tribunals commonly employed three. Aside from the inquisitors, the personnel included a prosecutor, a treasurer, a constable or bailiff, a warden, a prison quartermaster or dispenser, a notary who transcribed testimony, a notary who recorded sequestered goods, a general secretary, and scribes.[43] In addition, though not formally employed by the Holy Office, theologians were called to act as assessors and consultants. These personnel were truly the office staff of the Inquisition.

In order to police their territories adequately, inquisitors also relied on a network of allies known as *comisarios* (commissioners) and *familiares* (lay officers). *Comisarios* were the highest Inquisition officials in their regions and reported directly to the inquisitors. Generally drawn from the ranks of secular and regular clergy, commissioners were empowered to read edicts of faith, to undertake regional visits, to receive denunciations, to take testimony, and to refer cases to the tribunals. They also ordered the arrest, transport, and sequestration of goods belonging to suspects. Arrest and transport was conducted by the *familiares*. The latter were a much larger group than the *comisarios* and had a looser affiliation with the Holy Office. Appointment as a *familiar* followed an individual's application and was available only to those who could prove their purity of blood (*limpieza de sangre*) and the absence from their family line of individuals disciplined by the Inquisition. Applicants were regularly turned down, but the prestige associated with the appointment ensured a steady flow of applicants and, eventually, a large network of *familiares* in most Latin American regions. Between 1571 and 1646, for example, the Mexican tribunal could rely upon a total of 314 *familiares,* including 24 in the Philippines.[44] One hardly need mention that both *familiar* and *comisario* appointments were available only to men.

Familiares and *comisarios* played an important role in the process by which individuals came to the attention of the Holy Office, particularly in areas without resident tribunals, that is, outside the cities of Lima, Mexico City, and Cartagena, and throughout Brazil. Partly a "spy network" as has occasionally been suggested, *familiares* and *comisarios* more generally processed denunciations received in response to church edicts. Indeed, edicts and denunciations were the principal instruments by which the Inquisition instituted its culture of control. Printed edicts were sent out by the tribunals (Lisbon in the case of Brazil) and were read in all local churches and convents, more frequently during Lent. Edicts generally identified unlawful practices and beliefs and charged all Christians with reporting suspicions or knowledge of unorthodox activity. Most denunciations were of others, often for causes that seem trivial to modern observers, but sometimes individuals came forward to denounce themselves. Occasionally the denunciation was made to a clergyman, who then brought the case forward to a *comisario* or to the tribunal itself.

Once a denunciation was made, inquisitors interviewed suspects and decided whether to pursue the case. Thousands of cases never proceeded past this point; indeed, one of the apparent distinctions between American and Iberian tribunals is the large proportion of abandoned prosecutions in Latin America. When a formal case was made, however, suspects were generally imprisoned and their goods sequestered. They were not told of the charges against them, but were interviewed and exhorted to search their consciences for any and all sins against their faith. The interrogation aimed not at gaining answers to a set group of questions, but at producing a full and authentic confession and an understanding of the context in which sins had occurred. The interrogation was therefore wholly unlike those conducted in modern courtrooms, and the confessions obtained were also *sui generis.* Not surprisingly, given this procedure, much new information often emerged during the interrogation of a suspect, as did new denunciations, particularly in cases of sodomy and heresy. When suspects were not forthcoming, or when the charges were serious, torture might be employed. It was seldom used, however, because inquisitors recognized its distorting effects on testimony, and the fact that suspects who confessed under torture often refused to ratify their testimony later, thus invalidating their confessions.

Once interrogation had elicited the fullest possible confession, suspects were presented with summaries of accusations and testimony against them, and at this point they were given legal counsel and permitted to prepare a defense. The defense having been heard, a definitive sentence was pronounced and enforced. Despite being less arbitrary and violent than the popular stereotype, any inquisitorial proceeding was nonetheless a terrifying ordeal for the suspect. And formal disciplining by the Holy Office became a "criminal record" that left a permanent stain on one's life and lineage. Moreover, while the Inquisition deployed the death sentence only rarely, the humiliation of appearing in an *auto de fe* could accurately be described as social death, particularly for those of high status. In honor-obsessed colonial Latin America, public humiliation was sometimes more feared than torture.[45] Beyond sentence of death and participation in an *auto de fe,* the Holy Office could also pronounce sentences ranging from two hundred lashes to banishment and loss of property.

Despite following the general colonial practice of excluding women from positions of responsibility, the Holy Office held women fully responsible for their conduct as Christians. One should note, however, that women generally formed an absolute minority of suspects; for the Mexican tribunal, Solange Alberro has found that women did not exceed 30 percent of suspects in any year between 1571 and 1700;[46] women were defendants in only 16 percent of the cases that went to trial.[47] Though the condition of the Peruvian records does not permit such detailed statistical analysis, women were also a small minority among those tried by the Lima tribunal.[48] This might lead one to conclude that the Inquisition was in some ways less interested in women than in men, or that women were granted protective treatment, or even that women were seen as minors and were therefore not taken seriously as deviants. But women appeared much more often before the Inquisition's courts than, say, before contemporary civil courts. Their relative "underrepresentation," therefore, should not be taken as evidence of any lack of interest on the part of inquisitors. Indeed, the Holy Office was concerned with women both as suspects in the most serious crimes and as Christians liable to less serious deviations from orthodox norms. Despite offering leniency in many of the latter cases, the Holy Office moved with utter rigor against women accused of the crimes it considered dangerous.

As has already been noted, the most serious crimes policed by the Inquisition in Latin America were those involving major heresy or Judaizing. As in Iberia, women were heavily represented among convicted Judaizers. The presence of Doña María de Carvajal and her four daughters among the nine Carvajal family members burned in 1596 in Mexico City is evidence of women's continued "equality" in this one realm of Inquisition activity.

Women were also active members of the few heretical groups uncovered in colonial Latin America. Illuminist groups, for example, tended to coalesce around prophetic holy women. In Mexico in 1598, the Holy Office uncovered an illuminist cell stretching from Puebla to Mexico City, in which the *beata* Marina de San Miguel was prominent.[49] The punishment of this group was severe, and the Holy Office continued its occasional prosecutions of *alumbrados* well into the seventeenth century. *Beatas,* or semi-religious laywomen, were particularly suspect, since their religious path tended to be "individualistic." In general, Latin American *beatas* took no vows, or only simple ones, and lived alone, without the formal supervision of a male confessor or a properly constituted religious community. Far from being a rarity, holy women were a fixture of the colonial religious scene. *Beatas* were important members of colonial neighborhoods and were relied upon for counsel on matters both sacred and secular. Moreover, not only the ignorant poor but the wealthy, and even priests and friars, were in the thrall of these women, who seemed to enjoy frequent favors from God. The *beata's* lifestyle was thus undeniably attractive to women and was one of the few options that allowed single women to survive respectably.

While trials of holy women were relatively rare among Inquisition proceedings, such trials were important in the control of popular religious expression. In 1575 the Spanish Holy Office had warned of the many dangers posed by *beatas.* The phenomenon, according to the warning, was an invention of the *alumbrados,* who used it to free daughters from obeying their parents and wives from obeying their husbands. The inquisitors cautioned, "Because this is a new way of life, not encountered previously in the Church, one must suspect that it is an invention of the Devil and of vain men who, under cover of holiness and religion, want to be served and obeyed by simple-minded women."[50] The mention of "vain men who want to be served" is no accident. Inquisitors suspected, and confirmed in many trials, that the relationships between holy women and the many men who surrounded them were sometimes sexual in nature. In the case of the *alumbrados* disciplined in Mexico in 1598, Marina de San Miguel was found to have engaged in a variety of sexual activities, including "indecent touchings," with her "spiritual brother" Juan Núñez. Moreover, Juan Plata, a churchman also central to the group, had solicited the sexual favors of the nuns in his pastoral care.[51] Even outside the ranks of confirmed heretics like the *alumbrados, beatas* were suspect because of the very nature of their mystical religiosity. *Beatas* frequently went into trances, received bodily visitations, and suffered either their own or God's mortification of the flesh.[52] Visitors, particularly men, viewed all of this with rapt attention. The religious fervor of the *beata* and the intense relationship between her and male supporters could, and occasionally did, blur into erotic passion. Contemptuous of what they saw as the religiosity of the ignorant and suspicious of the potential for sexual sin, inquisitors viewed *beatas* distrustfully.

From 1575 until the end of the Holy Office's tenure, inquisitors regularly examined and tried holy women for a variety of infractions. In the second half of the seventeenth century the Mexican tribunal moved against several *beatas* with illuminist tendencies, punishing them relatively severely.[53] In Lima, St. Rose herself was subjected to rigorous examination before being exonerated of any heretical tendencies; ironically, her hagiographers would someday present her as an enemy of heresy and idolatry.[54] Other holy women in St. Rose's circle were not so fortunate; six were disciplined in the Lima *auto de fe* of 1625.[55] In the late seventeenth century, the Lima tribunal also disciplined the remarkable Angela de Carranza, whose spiritual diary amounted to thousands of folio pages, many devoted to the theme of the Immaculate Conception. Her heretical errors were considered so dangerous that she was subjected to a lengthy trial and interrogated under torture.[56]

After 1650, holy women not suspected of true heresy were sometimes pursued as charlatans or *ilusas* who staged fraudulent shows of religious devotion and divine favor in pursuit of wealth and fame.[57] More than seventy such individuals, both men and women, were denounced to the Mexican Holy Office.[58] One of the most famous *ilusa* trials is that of Teresa de Jesús, or Teresa Romero Zapata, a young woman from a poor Cholulan family whose spiritual gifts were promoted by her father. Her ten-year trial ended in her condemnation, in 1659, for numerous crimes including fakery and sexual license.[59] Despite her ultimate punishment, Romero's success in attaining financial rewards and fame for her holiness demonstrates the credulity of the public, which seems to have had an almost insatiable hunger for holy women and men. Indeed, by the eighteenth century, the *beata's* career had become a well-trodden path, with holy women relying upon male "managers" to assist them in staging their "bodily theater."[60] Not surprisingly, *beatas* were a majority among convicted *ilusas*.[61] The Inquisition continued to prosecute these women throughout the eighteenth century, though increasingly it viewed them as suffering from medical problems such as hysteria and depression linked to feminine bodily weakness, rather than as heretics or cunning hucksters.[62] Major heretics and *ilusas* were a more important target for inquisitors than the number of documented trials would suggest and have been an important focus of Inquisition scholarship.

Women also figure as suspects in other kinds of trials, accounting, for example, for approximately 20 percent of all blasphemy cases brought before the Mexican tribunal.[63] Though women of varying status were accused of this offense, slave women (and men) were particularly vulnerable to charges of renouncing God, usually during the course of horrific abuse and punishment, and sometimes in a deliberate bid to escape tyrannical owners.[64] Blasphemy was by far the most frequent cause for which slaves were prosecuted by the Mexican tribunal. Among slaves, moreover, blasphemy was not the gendered crime that the more general statistics would suggest; male and female slaves were roughly equal among accused blasphemers. This emphasizes the importance of recognizing the complexity of the category "women" in colonial Latin America. Blasphemy trials also caution against any simplistic understanding of female solidarity. In 1606, for example, the slave Esperanza described being cruelly whipped, leading to her desperate renunciation of God and trial for blasphemy; the owner who scourged her so pitilessly was a woman.[65]

A relatively unusual form of feminine blasphemy involved invoking the sacred to ensnare or satisfy lovers; this blasphemy thus blurred with the love magic associated with women in colonial Latin America, which is discussed below. In Brazil, some women confessed to using the words of the Catholic Mass to bind lovers to them; for example, during the first inquisitorial visit to Bahia in the late sixteenth century, Guiomar de Oliveira confessed to speaking the words *hoc est enim corpus meum* (this is my body) into her lover's mouth during intercourse to "make him mad with love and desire."[66] In Mexico in 1604, the Spanish captain Garci Pérez de Salas became alarmed when his lover Catalina de Chávez spoke similarly sacred words during intercourse with him. According to the captain, Catalina on several occasions expressed her sexual delight with the words, "I'm doing this not with you but with God, and you are my eternal God, and I renounce God." When Pérez's admonitions failed to reform Catalina's erotic outbursts, he denounced her to the Holy Office, suggesting that either the devil had inspired her or she was trying to make him love her. Despite involving what might seem relatively serious blasphemy, including the renunciation of God, Catalina's case was not pursued.[67]

In most areas of the Inquisition's jurisdiction, then, women appeared as suspects and were held fully accountable for their behavior as baptized Christians. Women also appeared as accusers, most significantly in cases of solicitation but also in cases involving other crimes. The Holy Office was therefore neither obsessed with nor dismissive of the crimes of women. Indeed, as discussed above, it paid attention to crimes associated with women, such as the charlatanism of the *ilusas,* whenever it considered those crimes disruptive of social and religious order.

There is controversy over the significance of the largest group of trials of women, that is, those for witchcraft and superstition. Certainly this is the area in which women were dominant, and witchcraft trials were also of great interest to inquisitors, judging from their numbers. In contrast to trials for major heresy, trials for witchcraft were conducted on a regular basis throughout the Inquisition's tenure in Latin America. Still, it must be emphasized that only 7 to 14 percent of trials in Mexico involved witchcraft and magical practices,[68] far less than those for either heresy or sexual crimes. In Brazil, the proportion seems similar, if Pernambuco is taken as typical; in any case, only 5 of the 556 Brazilian individuals punished in Portuguese *autos da fé* were disciplined for witchcraft and/or demonic pact.[69] In Lima, the situation may be slightly different. There, 60 of the 184 trials between 1650 and 1700 were for witchcraft, a substantial proportion compared with other American tribunals or those in Iberia. The Cartagena tribunal was also relatively active, with 55 cases between 1610 and 1660, as discussed below. Regardless of these variations, however, any discussion of witchcraft brought before the tribunals of the Holy Office must begin with an acknowledgment that the Inquisition was not particularly obsessed with or credulous about the existence of diabolic witchcraft, at least not as compared with the various secular and clerical courts that were condemning thousands of women to death for witchcraft in non-Iberian Europe at the same time. This acknowledgment, however, should not obscure the American tribunals' interest in suppressing witchcraft and their general acceptance of the demonological models provided by European witch hunts.

Iberian precedent acknowledged the criminality of witchcraft. In Castile, sorcery had been declared a crime involving heresy in 1370 and 1387. Laypeople were to be tried for this crime by secular courts, clergy by church courts. The Catholic Church, however, adamantly maintained the position that witchcraft was a delusion rather than a practice until the publication of the *Malleus Maleficarum* (*The Witches' Hammer*) in the late fifteenth century, which yielded several well-known effects. It not only promoted the veracity of witches' claims of malefice and Satanic Sabbaths, but also popularized among the learned the association of women with witchcraft and the particularly sexual nature of women's relationships with the devil. While many inquisitors remained skeptical, after 1520 edicts of faith began to append magic and sorcery to the list of heretical beliefs and activities proscribed by the church. Nonetheless, throughout the sixteenth century the Spanish Holy Office remained relatively hostile to persecution of witches, which tended to occur in sporadic outbursts directed by civil authorities.[70] Indeed, the established church viewed witchcraft not in terms of malefice, but as a matter of idolatry.[71]

The Latin American Inquisitions thus inherited the church's skepticism about the wilder claims of witch hunters. Still, accusations of witchcraft and sorcery presented before the Holy Office had currency and importance in the American territories, particularly because of their purportedly corrupt nature. As is well known, diabolism was imputed to precontact religions, particularly in Mesoamerica. America was regarded by many as a land peculiarly corrupted by centuries of demonic influence.[72] At the same time, the Holy Office had limited scope to act against this influence. As has already been noted, after early Inquisitions' attacks on indigenous shamans, indigenous people were exempted from the jurisdiction of the Holy Office. Episcopal and secular Inquisitions attempted to suppress indigenous magico-religious practices, as when a seventeenth-century Guatemalan parish priest staged an informal *auto de fe* to punish accused indigenous sorceresses. Borrowing the dramatic methods of the Inquisition, the priest ordered his indigenous bailiffs to bring the women into the church wearing penitential dress; they were then stripped to the waist and whipped in front of the congregation.[73] The Holy Office, however, was powerless to do more than attempt to prevent the spread of indigenous practices to the nonindigenous population, for example, by prohibiting the use of peyote and other hallucinogens.

The presence of a large indigenous population with a substantial herbology and a relatively intact magical tradition gave colonial Latin American witchcraft a different character from its Iberian counterpart. Moreover, the relatively large-scale importation of African slaves after the late sixteenth century introduced another set of magical and curative practices. Like indigenous people, Africans (whether slave or free) were presumed more susceptible to demonic influence.[74] By the first third of the seventeenth century, a complex multiethnic world of magical practice had coalesced. The peak of witchcraft persecutions in various locations thus coincided with other concerns about caste, race mixture (*mestizaje*), and the disintegration of social order. This may explain why in Mexico, for example, denunciations for witchcraft grew steadily after 1650. The significance of witchcraft and magic in a multiethnic colonial society, coupled with concern over American demonism, may also help explain the Holy Office's consistent interest in the prosecution of witches. Rather than claiming that the American Inquisitions were consistently skeptical about witchcraft, therefore, one might more accurately describe a dual inquisitorial impulse. On one hand, the American Inquisitions acknowledged the influence of the devil and moved to punish demonically inspired witchcraft wherever they found it. On the other, the Holy Office in America, regardless of location, faced a vast complex of multiethnic magical practices that it viewed as characteristic of superstition and worthy of minor discipline.

The world of Latin American witchcraft is thus more complex than its European counterpart. The witch/woman association in Latin America was also less automatic than in Europe.[75] Many men, particularly those of *mestizo*, indigenous, or African descent, were charged with offenses that would be considered witchcraft in Europe. However, they were more likely to be charged with making a pact with the devil than with witchcraft per se. The multiethnic and bigendered character of Latin American witchcraft has led one scholar to describe the magical world of colonial Mexico as an "unsanctioned realm" of power in which normal caste and gender hierarchies were inverted.[76] Notably, many accused witches were African; indeed, for almost the first half of the seventeenth century, slaves in Cartagena were more likely to be accused of witchcraft than of any other crime. Of the fifty-five witchcraft cases tried by the Cartagena tribunal in its first half-century of activity, fully fifty-one involved individuals of African descent.[77] But if Latin American witchcraft was a terrain complicated by ethnicity and class, one must note that a substantial majority of witchcraft trials involved women as suspects. For example, of the sixty accused witches tried by the Lima tribunal between 1650 and 1700, forty-nine (or 82 percent) were women.[78] Of the fifty-five Cartagenan cases discussed above, forty-seven involved women. Thus while recognizing that caste played an important role in witchcraft practice and persecution, one must acknowledge the central role of gender in both arenas.

Women who appeared before the Holy Office accused of illicit magical practices were described as being superstitious (*supersticiosas*), or as healers (*curanderas*) or witches (*hechiceras*). These groups, of course, were not mutually exclusive. There is disagreement about the class status of accused witches; in seventeenth-century Peru, they seem to have been marginal characters, mostly without occupation and with limited kin networks.[79] In sixteenth- and seventeenth-century Veracruz (New Spain), however, accused witches seem to have been a relatively well-off group, though, notably, most were single.[80] Certainly, the one group exempt from such accusations was the elite, though elite women and men do appear in cases as witnesses to and consumers of witchcraft.

In colonial Latin America, the most common form of witchcraft appears as a crime committed against men, generally with the aim of subduing them and, in effect, reversing the gendered social order.[81] This further differentiates colonial Latin American witchcraft from the forms characteristic of the European witch panics. Nevertheless, the dominance of what is often called "love magic" in colonial Latin American witchcraft does not mean that witchcraft was seen as trivial by the people who were ensorcelled. Men who denounced the women they believed to have bewitched them were definitely convinced that witches caused harm. Even comparatively learned men could be convinced of the potency of women's magic. In 1733, for example, the friar Diego Núñez accused his *mulata* slave of bewitching him, causing him to expel from his body human and animal hair, stones, wool, and a paintbrush.[82]

Furthermore, colonial Latin Americans believed in, and denounced others for, malefice taken directly from the classic demonological treatises. To appreciate the population's credulity regarding the efficacy of malefic practices, one need only remember that the church itself upheld a variety of magical beliefs, for example the utility of saintly relics against sickness. There was no clear divide, then, between magic and medicine, magic and religion, or magic and science.[83] The boundaries of the licit, moreover, changed relatively rapidly. In the sixteenth century, astrology was taught alongside mathematics at Mexico City's university, but by the seventeenth century, the discipline was viewed as dangerous, and astrological works were censored and forbidden. In such a context, most people believed in the power of magical practice to influence events. They attempted to deploy magic themselves, often consulting practitioners, and they feared the similar efforts of acknowledged or unrecognized enemies. They particularly feared the witchcraft of social inferiors and, ironically, of those they called upon to help them manipulate magical forces. Witches were often denounced by their own clients.

These circumstances made women healers, in particular, vulnerable to charges of witchcraft. Most of the colonial population, regardless of ethnic status, relied on male barbers and folk healers of both genders rather than on the rare, trained, male physicians. Like other nonprofessional healers, *curanderas* were vulnerable to charges of witchcraft when cures went wrong or relationships broke down. Among healing women, midwives were probably most at risk. Their practices customarily involved magical and quasi-magical practices, and in their capacity as facilitators of the mysterious process of birth, they mediated between worlds.[84] When pregnancies ended in an infant's death, deformity, or illness, midwives were often the first to be blamed, either by the mother or by her husband. What might often have been simple incompetence or bad luck was sometimes construed as malefice. The particular vulnerability of infants produced anxieties about the "evil eye," which midwives and healers might promise to combat, but which they might also be accused of using themselves. A child who exhibited nursing problems or failed to thrive was often diagnosed as *ojeada,* or cursed with the evil eye. While midwives were not the only ones suspected of culpability in these cases, they were especially at risk.

Thus both in cases of "love magic" and in cases of classic malefice, colonial Latin Americans believed in the efficacy of witchcraft and denounced it to the Holy Office. The response of the American Inquisitions varied. With regard to the regularly deployed spells to attract and maintain love or to tame violent husbands, the Holy Office seems to have done little, often failing to follow up on denunciations. In the cases that were pursued, discipline was light. In the more serious cases of alleged malefice, the Holy Office generally took action. As noted above, however, the Holy Office was not particularly credulous about claims of malefice. The principal concern of inquisitors was religious; witchcraft might spill over into idolatry, even without an explicit demonic pact; and such idolatry was a constant threat to orthodoxy, particularly among ethnic groups viewed as susceptible. In such cases, the Inquisition tended to impose harsh punishments, particularly on slaves; for example, three of the four Cartagenan witches convicted in 1620 were sentenced to perpetual imprisonment in the dungeons of the Inquisition (though they were later transferred to a convent).[85] So the American Inquisitions were not by any means dismissive of witchcraft. Moreover, inquisitors accepted many of the tenets of the *Malleus Malificarum,* including the ubiquity of sexual contact between witches and the devil.[86] There were, moreover, cases that conform closely to the stereotypes associated with European witch panics, and in those cases inquisitors often persecuted witches. Any claim that the Holy Office completely disregarded witchcraft, or viewed it simply as the superstition of the ignorant, is therefore flawed. Nonetheless, the absence of European-style witch panics in colonial Latin America is testament to the Inquisition's focus on religion, rather than malefice, as the central issue in the discovery and disciplining of witches.

The Holy Office's skepticism about cases of demonic witchcraft increased over time. By 1691, when the famous case of the demoniacs of Querétaro (New Spain) came to light, the Mexican tribunal seemed to have lost patience with popular conceptions of diabolism. In the course of a Franciscan religious revival in the city, a group of women were "possessed" by the devil. Among the many demons who occupied the women's bodies were several quick-witted enough to tell the Franciscan friars that they had been placed there by a group of witches, including a woman called the "Mice-Sucker" (*La Chuparratones*). While many of the Franciscans viewed these events as proof that their mission was bearing fruit, since the devil had become so angry, others were more skeptical. When a young possessed maiden gave birth, the inquisitors had all the proof they needed that events in Querétaro had human rather than demonic causes. Rather than examining the possessed women, the inquisitors forbade any discussion of exorcism or possession and formally charged the "demoniac" women with fraud and blasphemy. In the following years, allegations of demonic pact were likely to be regarded as mental imbalance rather than evidence of the devil's work, and the Mexican tribunal ceased serious investigation of diabolism.[87] In 1739, when Felipa de Alcaraz of Oaxaca denounced herself for blasphemy, sodomy, and Satanism, the Holy Office declined even to investigate, ordering instead that the Oaxacan commissary find her a "learned and prudent" confessor.[88]

This attitude is evidence of the changes in the Inquisition's goals and rationale over time. The peak activity of the Holy Office in America lasted from 1571 to 1649, a small number of years relative to the institution's long life. The year 1649, with its dramatic and deadly autos de fe, marks the peak of the Holy Office's power and vigor, after which the American Inquisitions may be said to have entered a phase of relative decline. Cases were increasingly left hanging, or were treated as less significant than they might have been in the period of peak activity. By the eighteenth century, the Holy Office itself seems to have exhibited a decline in credulity. Increased reticence in diabolism cases also evidenced itself in other areas. As noted above, *beatas* who in the seventeenth century were punished as dangerous charlatans capable of infecting the population with heterodoxy were increasingly perceived as mentally ill or simply deluded. Even cases of sodomy seem, in New Spain at least, to have been infrequently pursued.[89] Moreover, the Holy Office's jurisdiction seems to have contracted in favor of secular authorities; by 1803, when a Guatemalan hermaphrodite was tried for "double concubinage" with men and women, s/he was tried neither by the Holy Office nor by diocesan court, but by the criminal court of the Audiencia of Guatemala.[90]

The ultimate suppression of the Holy Office came after a long period of decline. Like the initial establishment of the American tribunals, suppression came from the metropolis. The Portuguese Holy Office, established second, was suppressed first. The Marquis de Pombal, the eighteenth-century radical reformer, eliminated rules regarding purity of blood in 1768. In 1771, the Portuguese Inquisition's powers were further limited. In Spain, the institution lasted longer, though by the late eighteenth century it was greatly diminished in power and activity, concentrating more on censorship than on active prosecutions. The last person put to death by the Holy Office, ironically a convicted witch, was executed in 1781.[91] The Inquisition was suppressed in 1812 by the liberal Cadiz constitution, restored by Ferdinand VII, and then suppressed again in 1820. The final abolition came at the hands of the regent María Cristina in 1834. Still, purity of blood legislation remained intact in Spain until 1865.[92] In America, the tribunals largely followed the fortunes of their peninsular counterparts. In Peru, the Holy Office was abolished in 1813. Some evidence of the "esteem" in which the Inquisition was held at that time appears in the accounts of those who entered the official buildings to destroy instruments of torture and to finally uncover the secrets that the Inquisition had guarded so effectively. According to William Bennett Stevenson, who accompanied a group into the Inquisition palace, "the rack and the pillory were soon demolished, for such was the fury of more than a hundred persons who had gained admittance, that had they been constructed of iron they could not have resisted the violence and determination of their assailants."[93] Despite popular sentiment, the Lima tribunal was reestablished in 1814, only to be finally suppressed in 1820. Events in Mexico followed a similar course, though not before the Holy Office had disciplined the Independence leader and priest Miguel Hidalgo, who was defrocked in 1811 and turned over to secular authorities to be executed by decapitation.

The Inquisition exercised enormous power over colonial Latin American society between its establishment in the sixteenth century and its elimination in the early nineteenth. Despite its failure to impose conformity to orthodox Catholic belief and behavior, the Inquisition participated significantly in the shaping of colonial society both in Spanish America and in Portuguese Brazil. Though women were a minority among those formally charged by the Holy Office in every American jurisdiction, their interactions with the Inquisition also shaped expectations for and beliefs about women's behavior and role. To some degree, the importance of the Inquisition's interactions with women is borne out by the reams of documentation concerning colonial Latin American women's lives and thoughts. That these documents now serve as one of the foremost sources for the history of women in colonial Latin America is a pleasant irony.

Notes

1. This translation of the original Latin mandate "Exigit sincerae devotionis affectus" can be found in Georgina Dopico Black, *Perfect Wives, Other Women: Adultery and Inquisition in Early Modern Spain* (Durham, N.C.: Duke University Press, 2001), 10.

2. See Benzion Netanyahu, *The Origins of the Inquisition in Fifteenth Century Spain* (New York: Random House, 1995).

3. See Document 1 in Lu Ann Homza, ed. and trans., *The Spanish Inquisition 1478–1614: An Anthology of Sources* (Indianapolis: Hackett Publishing Company, 2006), 4.

4. R. Po-chia Hsia, *The World of Catholic Renewal, 1540–1770* (Cambridge: Cambridge University Press, 2005), 50.

5. Stephen Haliczer, *Inquisition and Society in the Kingdom of Valencia, 1478–1834* (Berkeley: University of California Press, 1990), 213, *http://ark.cdlib.org/ark:/13030/ft958009jk/*.

6. Illuminism (*iluminismo* or *alumbradismo*) was a tendency that emerged from the general late medieval religious revival and that emphasized internal prayer, the uselessness of good works, and the importance of unmediated contact with God among many other propositions that church authorities viewed as perilously close to Lutheranism.

7. Mary Giles enumerates these propositions in *Book of Prayers of Sor María de Santo Domingo* (Albany: State University Press of New York, 1990), 69.

8. William Monter, "*Women in the Inquisition: Spain and the New World*" (review), *Church History* 68, no. 4 (1999): 1015–17.

9. Mary Elizabeth Perry, "Beatas and the Inquisition in Early Modern Seville," in *Inquisition and Society in Early Modern Europe*, ed. Stephen Haliczer (London: Croom Helm, 1987), 147–69.

10. Hsia, *The World of Catholic Renewal*, 50.

11. See the essays in Anne J. Cruz and Mary Elizabeth Perry, eds., *Culture and Control in Counter-Reformation Spain* (Minneapolis: University of Minnesota Press, 1992).

12. Lisa Vollendorf, *The Lives of Women: A New History of Inquisitional Spain* (Nashville: Vanderbilt University Press, 2005), 13.

13. Stephen Haliczer, "The First Holocaust: The Inquisition and the Converted Jews of Spain and Portugal," in Haliczer, ed., *Inquisition and Society in Early Modern Europe*, 12–15.

14. Hsia, *The World of Catholic Renewal*, 46.

15. Solange Alberro, *La actividad del Santo Oficio de la Inquisición en Nueva España, 1571–1700* (Mexico City: Instituto Nacional de Antropología, 1981), 257.

16. Ibid., 259–62; Irene Silverblatt, "Colonial Conspiracies," *Ethnohistory* 53, no. 2 (2006): 259–280.

17. See James E. Wadsworth, "In the Name of the Inquisition: The Portuguese Inquisition and Delegated Authority in Colonial Pernambuco, Brazil," *The Americas* 61, no. 1 (2004): 19–54.

18. Alida Metcalf offers a sustained discussion of the visit in chapter 8 of her *Go-Betweens and the Colonization of Brazil 1500–1600* (Austin: University of Texas Press, 2005).

19. Laura de Mello e Souza, *The Devil and the Land of the Holy Cross: Witchcraft, Slavery, and Popular Religion in Colonial Brazil*, trans. Diane Grosklaus Whitty (Austin: University of Texas Press, 2003).

20. Wadsworth, "In the Name of the Inquisition," 40.

21. For example, see Kathleen Higgins, "*Licentious Liberty*" in a Brazilian Gold-Mining Town: Slavery, Gender, and Social Control in Eighteenth-Century Sabará, Minas Gerais* (University Park: Pennsylvania State University Press, 1999), especially chapter 3.

22. The classic account is Inga Clendinnen's *Ambivalent Conquests: Maya and Spaniard in Yucatán, 1517–1570* (Cambridge: Cambridge University Press, 1987).

23. For an analysis of pre-1571 Central Mexican inquisitorial trials of indigenous people, see J. Jorge Klor de Alva, "Colonizing Souls: The Failure of the Indian Inquisition and the Rise of Penitential Discipline," in *Cultural Encounters: The Impact of the Inquisition in Spain and the New World*, ed. Mary Elizabeth Perry and Anne J. Cruz (Berkeley: University of California Press, 1991),

3–22. See also Richard Greenleaf, "The Inquisition and the Indians of New Spain: A Study in Jurisdictional Confusion," *The Americas* 22, no. 2 (1965): 138–66.

24. For example, see the trials of indigenous shamans and prophets uncovered by Serge Gruzinski in his *Man-Gods in the Mexican Highlands: Indian Power and Colonial Society, 1520–1800,* trans. Eileen Corrigan (Stanford, Calif.: Stanford University Press, 1989). Michael Francis details a 1595 Audiencia inquisition in New Granada in "'the Service of God I Order These Temples of Idolatrous Worship Razed to the Ground': Extirpation of Idolatry and the Search for the *Santuario Grande* of Iguaque," in *Colonial Lives: Documents on Latin American History, 1550–1850,* ed. Richard Boyer and Geoffrey Spurling (Oxford: Oxford University Press, 2000), 39–53.

25. Solange Alberro, *Inquisición y sociedad en México 1571–1700* (Mexico City: Fonda de Cultura Económica, 1988), 26.

26. Klor de Alva provides a useful breakdown of trials by cause; for discussion of the political motivations behind many monastic and episcopal Inquisition trials, see Richard Greenleaf, *The Mexican Inquisition of the Sixteenth Century* (Albuquerque: University of New Mexico Press, 1969).

27. See Metcalf, *Go-Betweens and the Colonization of Brazil,* 237–41.

28. For a description of the 1574 *auto de fe* and the Tridentine character of the tribunal, see Stafford Poole, C.M., *Pedro Moya de Contreras: Catholic Reform and Royal Power in New Spain, 1571–1591* (Berkeley: University of California Press, 1987), 28–37.

29. See Irving Leonard, *Baroque Times in Old Mexico: Seventeenth-Century Persons, Places, and Practices* (Ann Arbor: University of Michigan Press, 1959), 98. Documents relating to censorship in the sixteenth century are collected by Francisco Fernández del Castillo in *Libros y libreros en el siglo XVI* (Mexico City: Fondo de Cultura Económica, 1982).

30. Richard Boyer, *Lives of the Bigamists: Marriage, Family, and Community in Colonial Mexico* (Albuquerque: University of New Mexico Press, 1995), 18.

31. Jonathan I. Israel, *Race, Class, and Politics in Colonial Mexico, 1610–1670* (Oxford: Oxford University Press, 1975), 124.

32. Irene Silverblatt, "New Christians and New World Fears in Seventeenth-Century Peru," *Comparative Studies in Society and History* 42, no. 1 (2000): 524–46.

33. Stephen Haliczer, "The First Holocaust," 14.

34. Alberro, *Inquisición y sociedad en México,* 207.

35. Boyer, *Lives of the Bigamists,* 257 n. 21.

36. Ibid., 31.

37. However, for cases that involved a number of male complainants, see John F. Chuchiak IV, "The Sins of the Fathers: Franciscan Friars, Parish Priests, and the Sexual Conquest of the Yucatec Maya, 1545–1808," *Ethnohistory* 54, no. 1 (2007): 69–127.

38. Jorge René González Marmolejo, "Confesores y mujeres en el Obispado de Puebla, siglo XVIII," in Seminario de Historia de las Mentalidades, *El placer de pecar y el afán de normar* (Mexico City: Instituto Nacional de Antropología e Historia, 1987), 147–66.

39. The case is described in Jacqueline Holler, *Escogidas Plantas: Nuns and Beatas in Mexico City, 1531–1601* (New York: Columbia University Press, 2005), 331–32.

40. Adelina Sarrión Mora, *Sexualidad y confesión: La solicitación ante el Tribunal del Santo Oficio (siglos XVI–XIX)* (Madrid: Alianza Editorial, 1994). See also González Marmolejo, "Confesores y mujeres."

41. Boyer's *Lives of the Bigamists* remains the definitive study of the Mexican bigamy cases; for Lima, see the microhistorical study by David Noble Cook, *Good Faith and Truthful Ignorance: A Case of Transatlantic Bigamy* (Durham, N.C.: Duke University Press, 1991).

42. However, the Holy Office remained concerned with sodomy whether it occurred within a same-sex or opposite-sex relationship. For discussion of Mexican cases in which women were

forced or coerced to participate in anal sex with their husbands, see Zeb Tortorici, "'Heran Todos Putos': Sodomitical Subcultures and Disordered Desire in Early Colonial Mexico," *Ethnohistory* 54, no. 1 (2007): 35–67. However, Bishop Zumárraga considered homosexual anal sex more sinful than heterosexual; see Martin Nesvig, "The Complicated Terrain of Latin American Homosexuality," *Hispanic American Historical Review* 81, no. 3–4 (2001): 694.

43. Homza, *The Spanish Inquisition,* xxii.

44. Alberro, *Inquisición y sociedad en México,* 53.

45. Ibid., 269.

46. Alberro, *La actividad del Santo Oficio,* 130.

47. Stacey Schlau, *Spanish American Women's Use of the Word: Colonial through Contemporary Narratives* (Tucson: University of Arizona Press, 2001), 30.

48. María Emma Mannarelli, *Hechiceras, beatas y expósitas: Mujeres y poder inquisitorial en Lima* (Lima: Ediciones del Congreso del Perú, 1999), 14.

49. Jacqueline Holler, "More Sins Than the Queen of England: Marina de San Miguel before the Mexican Inquisition," in *Women in the Inquisition: Spain and the New World,* ed. Mary Giles (Baltimore: Johns Hopkins University Press, 1999), 209–28.

50. Quoted in Fernando Iwasaki Cauti, "Mujeres al borde de la perfección: Rosa de Santa María y las alumbradas de Lima," *Hispanic American Historical Review* 73, no. 4 (1993): 583. Translation by author.

51. Holler, "More Sins Than the Queen of England," 220, 224.

52. Nora Jaffary cautions against an exclusive focus on *beatas'* embodied religion, however, emphasizing that many holy women who appeared before the Inquisition produced reams of text. See *False Mystics: Deviant Orthodoxy in Colonial Mexico* (Lincoln: University of Nebraska Press, 2004), 13.

53. Solange Alberro studies three cases in detail in her *Inquisición y sociedad en México,* 491–530.

54. See Ronald Morgan, *Spanish American Saints and the Rhetoric of Identity, 1600–1810* (Tucson: University of Arizona Press, 2002), 94–96.

55. Hsia, *The World of Catholic Renewal,* 153–54.

56. Mannarelli, *Hechiceras, beatas, y expósitos,* 54–74.

57. This phenomenon is studied in Jaffary, *False Mystics.*

58. Ibid., 4.

59. See Alberro, *Inquisición y sociedad en México,* 491–99; see also Schlau, *Spanish American Women's Uses of the Word,* 32–44.

60. Alejandra Araya Espinoza, "De espirituales a histéricas: Las beatas del siglo XVIII en la Nueva España," *Historia* 37, no. 1 (2004): 5–32. See also Jaffary, *False Mystics,* 141–44.

61. Jaffary, *False Mystics,* 90.

62. Araya Espinoza, "De espirituales a histéricas," 30–31. See also Mannarelli, *Hechiceras, beatas, y expósitas,* 46.

63. Kathryn McKnight, "Blasphemy as Resistance: An African Slave Woman before the Mexican Inquisition," in Giles, *Women in the Inquisition,* 229–53; 230.

64. Generally, however, the Holy Office punished the slaves themselves. See Javier Villa-Flores, "'To Lose One's Soul': Blasphemy and Slavery in New Spain, 1596–1669," *Hispanic American Historical Review* 82, no. 3 (2002): 435–68.

65. Archivo General de la Nación (hereafter AGN), Mexico. Inquisición 471, especially 52ff., 171–72.

66. de Mello y Souza, *The Devil and the Land of the Holy Cross,* 74–75.

67. AGN, Mexico. Inquisición 368, especially 129ff., 490–91.

68. Based on three databases, Alberro gives figures of 7, 8, and 14 percent, the former two more plausible. See Alberro, *Inquisición y sociedad en México,* 207.

69. Wadsworth, "In the Name of the Inquisition," 40–43.

70. Henry Kamen, *The Spanish Inquisition: A Historical Revision* (New Haven: Yale University Press, 1999), 270–71.

71. See Fernando Cervantes, *The Devil in the New World: The Impact of Diabolism in New Spain* (New Haven: Yale University Press, 1994), 20–21.

72. See Jorge Cañizares-Esguerra, *Puritan Conquistadors: Iberianizing the Atlantic, 1550–1700* (Stanford, Calif.: Stanford University Press, 2006), 96–97 passim; and Cervantes, *The Devil in the New World,* 5–39.

73. Greenleaf, "The Inquisition and the Indians of New Spain," 148.

74. See Heather Rachelle White, "Between the Devil and the Inquisition: African Slaves and the Witchcraft Trials in Cartagena de Indias," *North Star: A Journal of African-American Religious History* 8, no. 2 (2005), 1–15.

75. One should note, however, that recent European scholarship challenges the automatic association of witchcraft with femininity, particularly in the British context; see E. J. Kent, "Masculinity and Male Witches in Old and New England, 1593–1680," *History Workshop* 60 (2005): 69–92.

76. Laura Lewis, *Hall of Mirrors: Power, Witchcraft, and Caste in Colonial Mexico* (Durham, N.C.: Duke University Press, 2002), 6 passim.

77. White, "Between the Devil and the Inquisition," 12.

78. Mannarelli, *Hechiceras, beatas y expósitas,* 24.

79. Ibid., 30–31.

80. Solange Alberro, "Templando destemplanzas: Hechiceras veracruzanas ante el Santo Oficio de la Inquisición, siglos XVI–XVII," in Seminario de Historia de las Mentalidades, *Del dicho al hecho: Transgresiones y pautas culturales en la Nueva España* (Mexico City: Instituto Nacional de Antropología e Historia, 1989), 77–89.

81. See Mannarelli, *Hechiceras, beatas y expósitas,* 33; Alberro, "Templando destemplanzas," 81.

82. Ruth Behar, "Sexual Witchcraft, Colonialism, and Women's Powers: Views from the Mexican Inquisition," in *Sexuality and Marriage in Colonial Latin America,* ed. Asunción Lavrin (Lincoln: University of Nebraska Press, 1989), 178–206; 195.

83. See Cervantes, *The Devil in the New World,* 58–59.

84. Martha Few, *Women Who Live Evil Lives: Gender, Religion, and the Politics of Power in Colonial Guatemala* (Austin: University of Texas Press, 2002), 94.

85. White, "Between the Devil and the Inquisition," 11.

86. Mannarelli, *Hechiceras, beatas, y expósitas,* 17.

87. Cervantes, *The Devil in the New World,* 113–27.

88. Ibid., 138.

89. Martin Nesvig, "The Complicated Terrain of Latin American Homosexuality," 710 n. 89.

90. Martha Few, "'That Monster of Nature': Gender, Sexuality, and the Medicalization of a 'Hermaphrodite' in Late Colonial Guatemala," *Ethnohistory* 54, no. 1 (2007): 129–57.

91. Joseph Pérez, *The Spanish Inquisition: A History* (New Haven: Yale University Press, 2005), 85.

92. Haliczer, "The First Holocaust," 15–16.

93. Stevenson's description is reproduced in Lee M. Penyak and Walter J. Petry, eds., *Religion in Latin America: A Documentary History* (Maryknoll, N.Y.: Orbis Books, 2006), 142–44.

7

Church-Sponsored Education
in Latin America, c. 1800–c. 1930

Grover Antonio Espinoza

In 1881 Isaac Christiancy, U.S. minister to Peru, wrote U.S. Secretary of State James Blaine: "If there is anything for which you and I and the great mass of the American people ought to be more thankful than any other, it is that we were not born and raised under the dominion of the Catholic Church, which, wherever it prevails, makes all permanent or settled popular government impossible."[1] Christiancy's opinion was common among foreign visitors to Latin America during the nineteenth century and leads us to ask two important questions: What was the nature of the relationship between Latin American states and the Catholic Church after independence from Spain and Portugal? And, more specifically, what were the resulting advantages and disadvantages of the church's prominent role in education for those Latin American states?[2] This chapter provides preliminary answers to these questions by analyzing the interaction between the political government and the church in the educational realm from the late colonial period through the first decades of the twentieth century. During this long century Latin American societies were creating the independent nation-state while the church was attempting to maintain and, where necessary, reassert its role in society.

When the Iberian monarchies undertook the conquest of the Americas they entrusted a number of responsibilities to the Catholic Church, including the education of the various social classes. Later, after independence from Spain and Portugal, the new political elites expected the educational institutions run by the church to continue to support the local political, social, and cultural objectives of the state. But that was not the expectation or intent of the church in all instances. Thus, by the mid-nineteenth century the appropriate role of the Catholic Church in society became a matter of debate between the liberal and conservative parties that represented the interests of the elites. In some instances government officials tried to loosen the grip of the Catholic clergy on the schools and universities. Hostility to this control was motivated by liberal ideology and resentment of the economic power and cultural influence of the church. In the late nineteenth century new ideologies, strongly anticlerical in orientation, such as positivism, spread among intellectual and liberal elites. Nevertheless, the social and economic changes that Latin American nations experienced in the early decades of the twentieth century forced the state to reach an accommodation with the church that became evident by the 1930s.

The Colonial Background

During the colonial period the Catholic Church served to legitimate the political power exercised by the Spanish and Portuguese monarchies over their New World colonies. The papacy approved the conquest of the New World because it represented an opportunity to incorporate its territory and peoples into Christendom. After the conquest the church upheld and inculcated the principle that the Iberian monarchs ruled over their colonial subjects by divine right. In reciprocity political authorities supported the activities of the clergy, patronized their missionary activities, and promoted their near monopoly of primary, secondary, and higher education.[3]

According to some historians, the colonial regimes intentionally limited access to education to the Spanish and creole (upper class of European descent) minorities because learning by the masses was considered dangerous to the maintenance of the social order.[4] The colonial elites believed that there was an appropriate level of education for each of the many racial groups. Nevertheless, it is difficult to sustain the argument that crown and church deliberately established a policy to prevent parts of the populace from becoming educated. Neither institution had sufficient economic and human resources to instruct all of the population effectively (nor would such a project be conceivable anywhere until the twentieth century). In addition, some Spanish and creole landowners and entrepreneurs actually hampered the educational and religious efforts of the clergy in furtherance of their own economic and political interests.[5]

From the Spanish monarchy the church had accepted the responsibilities of teaching the Spanish language to the indigenous, converting them to Catholicism, and indoctrinating them in its principles.[6] However, though political authorities periodically passed laws ordering the establishment of elementary schools in indigenous towns, implementation of the regulations was limited. In the early colonial period there was such a shortage of clergy that churches and monasteries in Mexico would group hundreds of native children on their porches and patios and attempt to teach them the Christian catechism as well as reading and writing. And there were some successes. The clergy were even able to establish a few short-lived schools for girls in Mexico, teaching them Catholic doctrine and domestic skills.[7] In Peru the Society of Jesus sought to educate the indigenous population through their missions. In Juli (close to Lake Titicaca) the Jesuits learned the native language of the Indians in order to indoctrinate them and teach them reading, writing, arithmetic, and music.[8]

The clergy also opened boarding schools to prepare the indigenous elite for positions as native officials, teachers, and ecclesiastics. In Mexico members of the Order of St. Francis founded the Colegio of Santa Cruz of Tlatelolco in 1536, which taught Spanish, Latin, and Greek to male children of the Aztec nobility. Santa Cruz was active until the mid-seventeenth century, when it was closed because of administrative problems, rivalries among religious orders, and growing hostility toward educating the Indians.[9] In Peru the Society of Jesus had founded the Colegio Real del Príncipe in Lima (1619) and the Colegio of San Francisco de Borja in Cuzco (1621). Both taught Christian doctrine, reading, writing, arithmetic, music, and Latin to the children of indigenous *caciques* (chieftains).[10]

The Society of Jesus was the religious order that was most involved at all educational levels. In addition to its efforts to educate the indigenous population, the Jesuits ran primary schools, *colegios,* or boarding schools, that provided secondary and higher education, and "minor" universities for Spaniards, creoles, and *mestizos* (males of mixed ancestry). Two years after their arrival in Mexico in 1572 they founded the Colegio of San Pedro and San Pablo in the capital city; and by the end of the century they had established five more *colegios* in other Mexican cities. The first Jesuit priests arrived in Peru in 1568 and founded the Colegio of San Pablo and San Pedro in the city of Lima. By 1613 the Jesuits had a total of eight *colegios* in the viceroyalty of Peru. From 1599 on the authorities of the Society of Jesus ordered all their *colegios* throughout the world to follow the *ratio studiorum,* a pedagogical system that focused on moral and intellectual training, and that emphasized discipline and loyalty. The minor Jesuit *colegios* taught Spanish grammar and the basics of Latin; intermediate boarding schools added humanities (Latin grammar, literature, and rhetoric) and arts (logic, physics, and mathematics); the higher-level *colegios* taught all of these subjects plus philosophy. Higher education included professors' lectures, student recitations, and debates about controversial points.[11]

Colonial universities, like their medieval predecessors and contemporaries in Spain (and elsewhere in Europe), were conceived of as professional schools to train students to become public officials, priests, lawyers, and, to a much lesser extent, physicians.[12] Religious orders such as the Jesuits and Dominicans generally administered universities of minor rank, focusing on the teaching of the liberal arts as a preparation for further professional studies. Major universities, usually sponsored by the crown, had faculties of theology, civil and canon law, and medicine. The first colonial universities were those of Mexico City and Lima, which were chartered by the crown in 1551 and opened classes two years later. According to C. H. Haring, by the end of the colonial period there were a total of eight major and twenty to twenty-five minor universities.[13] Education was intended for the white elites, though some boys from the original indigenous ruling class received this opportunity as well. According to Mark A. Burkholder and Lyman L. Johnson, class and race considerations helped some and stymied others: "The racially mixed children of wealthy or well-connected Spaniards had little trouble overcoming the racial proscriptions designed to exclude all persons with 'tainted blood.' Blacks and mulattoes had the greatest difficulty entering universities. They repeatedly met prejudice and protest and found it difficult to receive degrees even after completing the required coursework and examinations."[14] Although university regulations generally required purity of blood and legitimacy for men to matriculate and receive degrees, these measures were not thoroughly enforced during the sixteenth and seventeenth centuries. By the late eighteenth century, however, as the number of students of mixed ancestry increased, colonial authorities had become especially vigilant regarding the requirements for blood purity and legitimacy.[15]

The teaching methods and curricula of Spanish-American universities were modeled on those of the University of Salamanca in Spain. Like the other great medieval European universities, it was a center of Catholic orthodoxy. To give a minor example, professors had to swear to defend the doctrine of the Immaculate Conception. They were also required to maintain modest personal conduct. Memorization and deduction rather than experimentation and induction were the accepted methods of learning since the curriculum followed medieval tradition. Students had to take a course of arts or general studies before entering a specific school — theology, law, medicine less often — that they had chosen.[16] Courses included Latin grammar and rhetoric, and scholastic philosophy, physics, and mathematics, all based on Aristotle and his medieval commentators. Theology students studied the "sentences" of Peter Lombard (c. 1100–1160), writings of St. Thomas Aquinas (c. 1225–74), John Duns Scotus (c. 1266–1308), and Francisco Suárez, S.J. (1548–1617). Scholars destined for the law studied Roman law including *Digesta* and *Institutiones,* two parts of the collection of jurisprudence issued by Byzantine Emperor Justinian I from 529 to 534. Students of ecclesiastical law had to examine the *Decretales,* or juridical decisions of the popes. Schools of medicine taught the theories of the ancient Greek physician Galen (c. 200–c. 130 BC).[17] From the seventeenth century onward academic scholasticism flowered into a baroque intellectual style, characterized by its intricacy and formality. Colonial scholars and writers became fond of literary devices such as allegory, illusion, conceit, and a "distant" stance.[18]

The Catholic Church had played an even greater role in education in colonial Brazil than in Spanish America. The Portuguese crown was initially uncertain about the profitability of its South American colony and it was slow to develop a bureaucratic apparatus. As a consequence, the religious orders of the Jesuits, Benedictines, Franciscans, Carmelites, and Mercedarians dominated the cultural and educational activities there. The Society of Jesus, which first arrived in Bahia in 1549, played a prominent role in providing education to the indigenous population while endeavoring to protect it from enslaving expeditions, or *bandeiras*. The Jesuits established *aldeias de indios* (new villages for Indians) and taught reading, writing, catechism, and vocational training to the natives.[19] They also provided primary and secondary education to the elites of Portuguese descent. Shortly after arriving in Bahia and commencing basic education, the Jesuits offered classes in grammar, literature, and mathematics. In 1553 they introduced a three-year course in the liberal arts (logic, physics, ethics, mathematics, and philosophy), and a four-year course in theology. One year later they opened the Colegio of São Paulo of Piratininga which laid the foundations of the city of São Paulo. In 1564 the Portuguese crown assigned 10 percent of all taxes collected in Brazil to the support of the schools of the Society of Jesus. By the mid-eighteenth century the Jesuits had thirty-six missions, nine *colegios*, and five seminaries. The crown never supported the creation of a university in Brazil and those with the means and the desire had to attend the University of Coimbra in Portugal.[20]

Colonial education experienced both ideological and institutional changes during the late seventeenth and eighteenth centuries. In the late 1600s the ideas of the Polish astronomer Nicolaus Copernicus (1473–1543) and the French scientists and philosophers Pierre Gassendi (1592–1655) and René Descartes (1596–1650) were introduced into Latin American *colegios* and universities. Cartesianism was compatible with scholasticism because, although it encouraged the methodical questioning of previously accepted truths, God remained the vital element in its rationale. It became acceptable for colonial scholars to criticize Aristotelian writings but not those of St. Thomas Aquinas. Already in the first half of the eighteenth century the works of the progressive Spanish Benedictine Benito Jerónimo Feijóo (1675–1764) began to popularize philosophical and scientific ideas of the European Enlightenment. These included post-Cartesian natural philosophy, as well as criticism of historical sources as developed by members of the Benedictine order, and the physics of Isaac Newton (1642–1727).[21]

The spreading of new ideas paralleled the growing interest of the Spanish and Portuguese monarchies in strengthening their political power and increasing colonial revenues. Both crowns concluded that in order to accomplish these goals they needed to exercise greater control over the Catholic Church and reform educational institutions by promoting the new sciences that characterized the intellectual revolution that was taking place in Europe. Some groups within the church itself, influenced by regalist and Gallican theories, supported the monarchy's growing absolutism.[22] Other ecclesiastical sectors including the Society of Jesus opposed these initiatives. In response, the Portuguese monarchy, led by the Marquis of Pombal, expelled the Jesuits from Brazil in 1759, and eight years later Charles III forced the Society of Jesus to leave his Spanish dominions.

The expulsion of the Jesuits and the effects that this event had on education remain a controversial subject in Latin American history. The most evident consequence was the increased control it gave Spanish and Portuguese civil authorities over a large number of educational institutions. Some historians consider the expulsion positive because it freed education from Jesuit scholasticism and opened it to enlightened methodology.[23] The expulsion, indeed, gave the Iberian monarchies the opportunity to promote their official version of the Enlightenment through a revised educational curriculum. Other historians point out that enlightened ideas were already found in colonial educational institutions before the expulsion. Still other scholars claim that the expulsion of the Jesuits led to a decrease in the quality of education because some of their former schools declined and a few closed prior to Independence. Although some schools formerly owned by the Society of Jesus were mismanaged by colonial authorities, other new institutions flourished under the administration of lay officials, secular priests, and other religious orders.

After the expulsion of the Jesuits the Spanish and Portuguese crowns propagated an official reform program characterized by its eclecticism, regalism, and utilitarianism. In Brazil emphasis on Greek and Latin decreased in favor of the study of Portuguese. Authorities opened *aulas régias* (royal classrooms) to teach mathematics and natural sciences. The Seminario of Olinda (founded in 1800) emphasized analysis rather than memorization; history and geography were added, as were arguments about international commerce, all within the rhetoric requirement.[24] In Spanish America former Jesuit *Colegios* became the main vehicles of curricular reform. In philosophy the emphasis on Aristotle's writings was replaced by interest in the history of philosophical schools of thought and the study of encyclopedias of philosophical ideas. Practical sciences such as physics, chemistry, mineralogy, botany, natural history, and medicine were now included in the curriculum. Academics defended the use of Spanish over Latin as the scholarly language. Law schools became more interested in natural law and Spanish jurisprudence, especially the laws introduced by Visigothic kings and the Catholic monarchs. Professors of ecclesiastical law adopted Gallican and regalist doctrines. In general, baroque formalism was repudiated and a new preference shown for a more restrained classicism.[25] An increased desire for professionalism became the goal of the university by the end of the colonial era.

The church in colonial Spanish America did not have only one position regarding the expulsion of the Jesuits. A certain rivalry had existed between the Society of Jesus and other religious orders over financial resources, political influence, and public prestige, so not all members of the clergy disagreed with the expulsion. In the educational realm, it became clear that those priests who supported the institutional and curricular reforms would have better professional opportunities than those who opposed them. Outstanding clergy such as José Celestino Mutis

(Bogotá), Juan Díaz de Gamarra (Mexico), José Antonio Caballero (Havana), Toribio Rodríguez de Mendoza (Lima), and Dean Gregorio Funes (Córdoba) were among the main defenders of the changes. In terms of educational content, even faculties of theology criticized accepted Catholic historical interpretations without questioning traditional Catholicism. The writings of the Jesuit Francisco Suárez were eliminated from the curriculum and emphasis on Scripture became more prominent than the study of scholastic textbooks. In moral theology, authorities tried to replace Jesuit casuistry with a more rigorous approach.[26]

According to historian Mario Góngora, the Bourbon reforms, including the educational ones, actually weakened the hold that the Spanish monarchy had over its colonies. The reforms reduced the personal charisma of the monarch by emphasizing his role as representative of state power and sovereignty. The kind of political analysis that grew out of the Enlightenment eroded the basis of royal authority and diminished the intellectual prestige of Spain by focusing on the achievements of other European countries. The acceptance of the Enlightenment by the educated creole elite paradoxically caused a deeper cultural division between them and the popular sectors of mixed and Indian ancestry.[27]

From Independence to the Mid-Nineteenth Century

Once the former colonies became independent nations the new governments continued to rely on the educational institutions of the church for several reasons. First, the possibility of priests spreading monarchical ideas was unlikely, since the majority of those who supported the crown had left for exile in Europe. Second, many of the clerics who remained in Latin America accepted the subordination of church to state because of their regalist and Gallican ideas. Third, the creole elites who controlled the new nations considered church-sponsored education a means of social control that could prevent major economic and social changes and allow them to continue to maintain the privileges they enjoyed before independence.[28] Finally, although the majority of the new independent governments declared primary education mandatory, they did not have sufficient financial resources or political will to create and sustain an extended network of public schools.[29] Therefore, they, with some trepidation, allowed the Catholic Church to retain its traditional educational responsibilities.

As students of the new republics have argued, the early independent governments followed an ambivalent policy toward the Catholic clergy. On the one hand, during the first half of the nineteenth century, political authorities in Mexico, Guatemala, Colombia, Peru, and Bolivia closed the houses of religious orders deemed useless because they had too few priests or nuns. On the other hand, the same authorities ordered convents and parishes to establish free elementary schools and appointed priests to teaching positions.[30] However, religious houses and parishes were not always responsive to these demands because they lacked the resources. At the same time financial difficulties and political instability hampered the ability of national governments to expand their own institutions. Thus those governments frequently resorted to appointing priests to staff both their schools and school administrations. Among the clerics who held such posts in the early postindependence decades were Saturnino Segurola in Buenos Aires, José Antonio Jiménez in Puebla, and José Francisco Navarrete in Lima. Navarrete was an excellent example: he occupied several positions in school administration in Lima from 1822 to 1850. During his long tenure he was vice-principal of the training school for teachers, later its principal, and finally director of primary instruction for the whole capital city.[31]

The Catholic Church not only had direct management of a large number of primary schools throughout Latin America, but also determined the content for dame schools, private schools run by lay entrepreneurs, and municipal and provincial schools. Children in dame schools memorized the Catholic catechism, and the curriculum of other private and public primary schools also included Catholic doctrine, with subjects such as the life of Jesus and the history of the church.[32] Since the colonial period, elementary school teachers taught students to read by using books with religious content. Children thus learned to read while imbibing religious doctrine.[33] In the decades after independence, political and educational authorities continued to promote such practices. Schools continued to use traditional catechisms such as *Doctrina Cristiana y documentos de crianza* (1576) by Jesuit priest Gaspar Astete and *Doctrina Cristiana con una exposición breve* (1586) by fellow Jesuit Jerónimo Ripalda. Other catechisms written by Latin Americans were published, e.g., *Catecismo histórico-dogmático* by the aforementioned José Francisco Navarrete, which first appeared in 1845 and was still in use in the 1870s.

The catechism, emphasizing uncritical obedience and respect for rank, had to be memorized.[34] Such traditional values would presumably help creole elites maintain their political dominance and preserve social and economic hierarchies. In 1865 Paraguayan dictator Francisco Solano López reprinted a political catechism written by the bishop of Córdoba (Argentina), José Antonio de San Alberto, and originally published in 1784. Solano López's regime adapted San Alberto's catechism, which preached absolute obedience to the king, to the new political framework, and continued the demand for total obedience to authority.[35] Catechisms took pains to encourage students to obey the fourth commandment: "Thou shalt honor thy father and thy mother," and thus obey, help, and revere their parents as well as all government officials, judges, priests, and teachers.[36] Questioning the contents of any of these catechisms, especially where religious doctrine was concerned, was not permitted.[37] Navarrete, for instance, went so far as to say that no individual could interpret the Bible without the approval of the church, because the church was the sole legitimate proprietor and interpreter of the Gospels.[38]

Liberal Reforms (c. 1850–c. 1880)

In the mid-nineteenth century Latin America experienced a number of economic, political, and ideological changes that had major impact on relations between church and state. The gradual recovery of the Latin American economies after the destruction caused by the Wars of Independence and the increasing demand for raw materials in Europe and the United States provided the governments with growing fiscal resources. In order to take advantage of these economic changes and to insure their own continued dominance, the governing elites sought to modernize and strengthen the apparatus of government. There were disagreements, however, over issues such as the nature of political sovereignty, access to labor and land, the relationship between central and local government, and the rights of the Catholic Church. National elites fell into two political tendencies, liberal and conservative. Liberals upheld popular sovereignty (understood to include the newer elites but not "lower" social strata), free labor and land markets, greater autonomy for local government, and limitations on the judicial privileges of the Catholic Church. Liberals resented the enormous wealth of the church. Conservatives supported political participation based on wealth and education, corporative ownership of land, an executive stronger than the legislature, and preservation of the traditional prerogatives of the church.[39]

The effects of the rivalry between liberals and conservatives on the educational role assigned to the Catholic Church varied according to the wealth and strength of the national clergies.[40] In Mexico and Colombia, for example, where the Catholic Church possessed a good measure of both, the disagreements over the prerogatives of the clergy led to serious armed conflicts. Mexican liberals took power in 1855 and initiated an uncompromisingly radical reform program (*La Reforma*) including abolition of ecclesiastical courts. In reaction to this and other measures, conservatives rebelled militarily, and this action ended only with the unsuccessful French intervention (1862–67). The liberals, still in control, then incorporated all the restrictions of La Reforma against the Catholic Church into the Mexican constitution in 1873, and in 1880 they eliminated religious instruction from the public curriculum.[41] In Colombia, liberals, who dominated national politics from 1861 to 1885, passed an education law in 1870 mandating freedom of conscience and religion in schools. According to this law, instructors were not obligated to teach religion, and parents who wanted their children to learn the catechism had to hire a priest.[42] The initial reaction of the Colombian clergy to this law was to promote absenteeism, but once this failed, they and the Conservative party rebelled in the so-called "War of the Schools" in 1876. The liberals won this armed confrontation at great human and material cost, but by 1880 the new liberal leadership had come to an agreement with the conservatives and abandoned its education reforms.[43] In effect, the government acknowledged the difficulty of providing a sufficient number of teachers and other resources for their expanding educational systems, including church-run schools and other institutions.[44] In other Latin American nations conflicts between the Catholic Church and the state were not as serious or violent as in Mexico and Colombia, in part because the church was not as powerful and was willing to compromise with the political authorities.

The increasing educational needs of Latin America coincided with a missionary revival in France. Renewed religious zeal, lack of opportunities in the public sector, and pride in the civilizing mission of Europeans produced a new wave of missionaries who were gladly accepted by many Latin American governments. Local ecclesiastical authorities, of course, welcomed these fresh human and financial resources, which enabled them to counter liberal secularism, evangelize the indigenous populations in remote areas, and expand their network of schools.[45] Argentina received French and Irish nuns; in 1854 the Chilean government granted the Order of the Sacred Heart of Jesus the management of a new school for women teachers; and Paraguay received French priests and sisters in the 1870s.[46]

While the governments of these Latin American countries were open to these newcomers from European religious orders willing to operate primary and secondary schools, many local lay educators criticized this development. The lay owners of and teachers in private schools resented the competition posed by European missionaries who reduced the number of potential fee-paying students.[47] In Peru, private-school owner Teresa González de Fanning complained that some Peruvian-born lay teachers who had obtained their teaching licenses were unable to gain public school appointments.[48]

Most foreign missionaries focused on the education of the elites, believing that by indoctrinating them Catholic virtues would filter down to the masses. Others catered to the educational needs of the urban and rural poor. The Christian Brothers, for example, noted for their commitment to educating boys from poor families, arrived in Ecuador in 1863 and were paid a fee by the government for each child they instructed.[49] Franciscan and Dominican missionaries resumed the evangelization of the indigenous population in the rural areas of Bolivia, Peru, Chile, Argentina, and Mexico in the latter part of the nineteenth century.[50]

New Ideologies and Their Impact (c. 1880–c. 1930)

In the last decades of the nineteenth century, Latin American nations underwent a new series of economic, political, and social transformations. Among them were the consolidation of the export-oriented economy, the emergence of new elites associated with foreign capital, the growth of the middle class, and the appearance of industry and an incipient working class. In order to cope with these transformations, the different social classes adopted new and varied ideologies such as positivism, socialism, and anarchism, all of which would affect the relationship between church and state in the educational sphere.

According to the supporters of positivism in Latin America, earlier liberalism had focused on written constitutions and abstract ideals such as freedom and democracy, but had been unable to either bring about stability or make significant progress. Positivists promoted the establishment of strong and pragmatic governments that could address specific problems. They believed it important to bring a new generation of leaders up to date in the natural and social sciences. These leaders would be prepared to guide their nations to the level of cultural and material well-being already achieved by Western Europe and the United States. Some European positivists thought that the racial makeup of Latin America doomed the region to backwardness and instability and Latin America itself had its share of such thinkers as well. Some, however, believed that education could improve prospects for their countries, fostering racial harmony and national feeling and, as a consequence, promote material progress. French philosopher Auguste Comte, the founder of positivism, had argued in favor of a new Religion of Humanity and a Universal Church that would replace Catholicism. Although many Latin American positivists were critical of the Catholic Church, few of them supported Comte's religious theses because they recognized that the church for better or worse was an important element of national culture and cohesion.[51]

The majority of Latin American governments tried to implement their positivist agenda without replacing the role played by the church in education. They wanted to create greater allegiance to the state and to the traditional values imparted by the church, such as respect for authority and obedience to superiors.[52] The civil authorities opened more primary public schools and sought greater supervisory control over private ones, including church schools, which represented a growing percentage of private schools.[53] At the levels of secondary and higher education, governments founded a number of new institutions to teach science to elite youth: the National Preparatory School in Mexico (1867), the Normal School of Paraná in Argentina (1870), the Military School in Brazil (1874), and the Pedagogical Institute at the University of Chile (1889).[54]

Anarchism was another ideology that gained a following in Latin America during the late nineteenth century. It was a radical doctrine that advocated revolution against the state, capitalism, and the social hierarchies, with the purpose of establishing an egalitarian society run by the workers. Anarchism was brought to Latin America by native intellectuals who had traveled in Europe, as well as by Italian, Spanish, and Eastern European immigrants. Anarcho-syndicalism viewed trade unions as the main vehicle for bringing about revolutionary change and as the major basis for postrevolutionary society. Both anarchism and anarcho-syndicalism held the Catholic Church to be an ally of the capitalist state and an enemy of the working class.

148

One of the harshest anarchist critics of the Catholic Church was the Peruvian writer Manuel González Prada, who particularly opposed the large ecclesiastical presence in education. In 1892 he argued:

The state and the Church maintain a continuing secular and apparently irreconcilable conflict; but in the war against individual human rights, Church and state become allies, tacitly defend each other, proving that all tyranny is based on fanaticism, just as fanaticism is supported by tyranny. In the history of nations, every new outbreak of despotism coincides with an exaltation of superstition. Religion serves as a powerful instrument for servitude: with resignation, it chains the spirit of rebellion; with hope of a posthumous reward, it lulls the immediate pain of the disinherited.[55]

In response to such radical criticism the Catholic clergy advanced new arguments for the continued place of religion in private and public education.[56] In Peru, Franciscan priest Bernardino González answered González Prada's attack, arguing that the religious orders had extensive experience in teaching, respected the official curriculum, and taught the subjects prescribed by authorities. González stated that learning Catholic dogma contributed to the moral and intellectual development of children. He also claimed that the introduction of a purely secular instruction in France had led to a rise in criminality.[57]

A few years earlier the Colegio of Belén in Lima, administered by the nuns of the Sacred Heart, commissioned the writing of a play comprising a dialogue among Science, Faith, and Virtue. While Science presented itself as the primary authority in the world because it unlocked the secrets of nature, Faith criticized it as arrogant and evil, and as having caused Eve to commit "original sin." While Science might control perishable matter, Faith claimed control over the immortal soul. Faith also inspired willingness to defend the native country. At the end of the play, Virtue appeared and encouraged Science and Faith to support each other since both were creatures of God.[58] This drama commissioned by the Sacred Heart nuns, as well as Fray Bernardino González's response to González Prada, provide good examples of the church's campaign against positivist and anarchist attacks.

State and church developed a mutually beneficial relationship in Mexico, Colombia, and Peru during the transition from the nineteenth to the twentieth centuries. Dictator Porfirio Díaz, who ruled Mexico from 1876 to 1911, gained political support from the Catholic hierarchy and in exchange allowed the church to recover some of the freedoms it had enjoyed before the mid-nineteenth-century *Reforma*. He accepted an increase in new priests and left Catholic schools undisturbed as he did the anticlerical legislation that remained on the books. In Colombia the church supported the conservative regimes that held power from 1886 to 1930. With official government support, the clergy provided most of the education available to the lower, middle, and upper classes.[59] In Peru the number of Catholic schools increased significantly in the late nineteenth and early twentieth centuries. According to historian Jeffrey Klaiber, the factors that contributed to this phenomenon were the interest of elite families in providing a "good Catholic" education for their children, the church's combating the advance of anticlerical ideas, and the missionary zeal of religious orders. Although liberal anticlericalism did not collapse, the national government continued its tradition of welcoming the educational activity of the Catholic clergy while at the same time showing increasing tolerance for Protestant missions.[60]

In other Latin American countries such as Brazil, Argentina, and Chile, the state imposed some restrictions on church-sponsored education. In Brazil the establishment of the Republic in 1889 made official the separation of state and church. The liberals in power introduced secular education and ended subsidies for religious instruction. The Argentine constitution recognized the Catholic Church as the official church while also guaranteeing freedom of worship. In 1884 political authorities removed religious instruction from public schools, a measure that was implemented in spite of the opposition by the hierarchy. In Chile, since 1865, the state subsidized church education but also guaranteed freedom of worship. Protestants took advantage of religious tolerance and opened schools for the Chilean elites in the late nineteenth-century. In 1888 the archbishop of Santiago founded a Catholic university in order to provide higher education for the elites. The government finally separated state and church in 1925, canceling official subsidies, but it also took steps to soften the effects of the change.[61]

Any "relationship" between the Catholic Church and the state in Mexico ended with the Mexican Revolution (1910–20). Revolutionary leaders condemned the church for its tacit alliance with dictator Porfirio Díaz. They also resented the support that Catholic conservatives provided Victoriano Huerta, who overthrew and ordered the assassination of elected president Francisco Madero in 1913.[62] General Venustiano Carranza and his allies attacked priests and churches during their victorious war against Huerta and later implemented the fierce anticlerical measures in the constitution of 1917. Article 3 of the constitution specifically prohibited the teaching of religion in both private and public schools and forbade religious orders from founding or operating schools in the following terms:

> Instruction is free; that given in public institutions of learning shall be secular. Primary instruction, whether higher or lower, given in private institutions shall likewise be secular. No religious corporation nor minister of any religious creed shall establish or direct schools of primary instruction.[63]

Other constitutional articles declared that religious establishments were the property of the state; restricted public worship to inside the churches; and forbade foreign clergy to reside in Mexico, thereby affecting those priests who were dedicated to teaching.[64] A recent study has shown that from 1917 to 1926 the enforcement of these regulations was left to the discretion of regional and local leaders, some of whose policies were draconian.[65] Nevertheless, the restoration of peace and order and the expansion of the educational system were high priorities for the postrevolutionary leaders. In fact, the government and the church held similar educational goals: fostering nationalism; providing each class with instruction suited to its political and social roles; preparing the population for economic modernization; and improving the morals and character of the lower class. Under Secretary of Public Education José Vasconcelos (1920–24) the revolutionary government even provided subsidies to schools sponsored by the church.[66]

Still in 1925 the Mexican government led by President Plutarco Elías Calles (1924–28) adopted a strongly confrontational stance toward the church. The anticlericalism of political leaders was encouraged by radical members of the labor movement. In February 1926 a newspaper published an interview in which Archbishop José Mora y del Río of Mexico City criticized the anticlerical constitutional provisions and their recent application in some states. The government reacted by closing religious houses, deporting foreign priests, and announcing the imminent inspection of all primary schools to guarantee compliance with the ban on religious affiliation. In June the president decreed the "Calles Law," which demanded the enforcement of the constitutional regulations on religious education and gave government the right to ban religious orders, appoint and dismiss clergy, determine the number of priests, punish priests for their political activities, and finally, the right to confiscate all ecclesiastical property in the capital city.[67]

In response the Catholic bishops suspended church services, a prohibition that remained in effect for three years. In January 1927 zealous Catholics in Colima, Guanajuato, Jalisco, Michoacán, and Nayarit openly rebelled against the government. They placed their movement under the protection of Christ the King and called their action the Cristero rebellion. Catholic guerrillas burned government schools and killed their teachers; government forces reacted by killing one priest for every assassinated teacher. In spite of the determined and violent response of the Mexican army, the Cristeros grew from about twenty thousand in 1927 to some fifty thousand by mid-1929. Political and ecclesiastical authorities held peace negotiations under the sponsorship of U.S. diplomatic officials. In late June 1929 the government and the church reached a compromise with ecclesiastical leaders, agreeing that priests would register with the government and that schools would not offer religious instruction. In turn the government declared that it was not seeking to destroy the integrity of the church and that religious instruction would be allowed within church edifices.[68] Although tensions between state and church reappeared in the following years they never again led to serious episodes of violence.

Conclusions

During the colonial period the Spanish and Portuguese monarchies entrusted the Catholic Church with legitimating their political dominance, evangelizing the indigenous peoples, ministering to the spiritual needs of other racial groups, and providing education to all social classes. The regular and secular clergy fulfilled these responsibilities within the limits of their human and financial resources, the varying degrees of support granted by political authorities, and the interests and demands of Peninsular and creole elites. In both Spanish America and Brazil the Society of Jesus was the religious order most involved in educational endeavors. During the sixteenth and seventeenth centuries colleges and universities espoused traditional scholasticism and a baroque intellectual style that was highly rhetorical, clever, and flamboyant. In the late seventeenth and early eighteenth centuries colonial educational institutions, including those managed by the Jesuits, welcomed Cartesian and Newtonian theories, which competed with traditional scholasticism. In the second half of the eighteenth century both the Portuguese and Spanish monarchs expelled the Society of Jesus from their colonial dominions as part of an effort to increase their political authority and gain more direct control over education. After taking over the educational institutions formerly run by the Jesuits, colonial authorities promoted ideals of the European and specifically Spanish Enlightenment, which was characterized by regalism, eclecticism, and utilitarianism. The results of the educational reforms were mixed, especially in Spanish America: some institutions thrived while others decayed; many priests welcomed and others opposed the new curricula. In the long run, the new intellectual currents weakened the authority of the Spanish monarchy.

After independence from Spain and Portugal, Latin American nations maintained collaboration with the Catholic Church for institutional, financial, and political purposes. In institutional terms, the Catholic clergy had seconded the initiatives of administrative authorities since the colonial period. The continuing dominance of the church in education provided the postindependence states with the human and material resources that they initially lacked, the main disadvantage of this situation for the state being its minimal control over the curricula. Since creole elites were not interested in introducing social or economic reforms and church-sponsored education seemed to guarantee respect for existing privileges and hierarchies, this collaboration was deemed an acceptable instrument for social control.

By the mid-nineteenth century Latin American liberals were fostering an agenda that restricted the economic and political influence of the church in society. In countries such as Mexico and Colombia, where the church was powerful, liberal measures led to civil wars initiated by the conservative elite. In the majority of the other Latin American countries the church made efforts to accommodate itself to the new needs and demands of the state. Increasing demand for education and the state's continued need to rely on church schools coincided with vigorous efforts by European Catholic religious orders to establish schools in the New World and to educate and evangelize the poor and indigenous. These schools were a source of income for the clergy as well as a defense against the liberal agenda and a means of preserving the church's traditional presence in society.

In late nineteenth-century Latin America many politicians and intellectuals embraced positivism, while anarchism acquired some popularity among urban workers. Positivists favored increased control of, and in some cases restrictions upon, the educational activities of the church. The clergy opposed these policies, but ultimately had to accept their implementation. The threat represented by such a radical ideology as anarchism encouraged the church to accommodate itself to the new conditions imposed by the breaking up of the preindustrial social order.

In the early decades of the twentieth century Latin American nations experienced increased political and social instability. Although this affected the Catholic Church it did not put an end to its prominent educational role. Even in Mexico, where mid-nineteenth-century liberals had been able to restrict the economic and political privileges of the church after a prolonged and violent civil war, early twentieth century revolutionary leaders could not really abolish the church's educational activity because of the popular support it enjoyed.

Notes

1. Christiancy to Blaine, May 4, 1881, Dispatches from Peru, National Archives T52/R36, quoted in Lars Schoultz, *Beneath the United States: A History of U.S. Policy toward Latin America* (Cambridge, Mass.: Harvard University Press, 1998), 95.

2. Among the various travelers who criticized the influence of the Catholic Church on Latin American politics and society we can mention Americans William Ruschenberger (1807–95) and William Carpenter, and French-born writer Flora Tristán (1803–44). William Ruschenberger, *Three Years in the Pacific: Containing Notices of Brazil, Chile, Bolivia, Peru, ... By an Officer in the United States Navy* (London: Richard Bentley, 1835), 2: 202–35; William W. Carpenter, *Travels and Adventures in Mexico: In the Course of Journeys of Upward of 2500 Miles, Performed on Foot: Giving an Account of the Manners...* (New York: Harper and Brothers, 1851), 236–39; Flora Tristán, *Peregrinaciones de una paria,* 1838 (Lima: Fondo Editorial de la Universidad Nacional Mayor de San Marcos, 2003), 252–53.

3. Mario Góngora, *Studies in the Colonial History of Spanish America* (Cambridge: Cambridge University Press, 1975), chapter 2; John Charles Chasteen, *Born in Blood and Fire: A Concise History of Latin America* (New York: W. W. Norton, 2001), 69–71.

4. Bailey W. Diffie, *Latin American Civilization: Colonial Period* (Harrisburg, Pa.: Stackpole Sons, 1945), 494.

5. Thomas J. La Belle and Peter S. White, "Educational and Colonial Language Policies in Latin America and the Caribbean," *International Review of Education* 24, no. 3 (1978): 246–47.

6. Ibid., 252–54.

7. Diffie, *Latin American Civilization,* 495; C. H. Haring, *The Spanish Empire in America* (New York: Oxford University Press, 1947), 209, 211.

8. Roberto MacLean y Estenos, "Sociología educacional peruana: Universidades, colegios, seminarios y escuelas en el Virreinato del Perú," *Revista Mexicana de Sociología* 5, no. 2 (1943): 246–47.

9. Haring, *The Spanish Empire in America,* 210.

10. MacLean y Estenos, "Sociología educacional peruana," 245–46. For an in-depth study on the education of indigenous elites in colonial Peru, see Monique Alaperrine-Bouyer, *La educación de las élites indígenas en el Perú colonial* (Lima: Instituto Francés de Estudios Andinos–Instituto Riva-Agüero, 2007).

11. Haring, *The Spanish Empire in America,* 212; MacLean y Estenos, "Sociología educacional peruana," 232–33. Pilar Gonzalbo Aizpuru presents a detailed analysis of the principles of Jesuit education and the values that it spread in colonial Mexico in *La educación popular de los jesuitas* (Mexico City: Universidad Iberoamericana, Departamento de Historia, 1989).

12. Diffie, *Latin American Civilization,* 498; James Lockhart and Stuart B. Schwartz, *Early Latin America: A History of Colonial Spanish America and Brazil* (Cambridge and New York: Cambridge University Press, 1983), 159–60.

13. Haring, *The Spanish Empire in America,* 213–15. John Lanning presents a different total number of colonial universities than Haring and also dates the actual opening of the University of Lima much later. John Tate Lanning, *Academic Culture in the Spanish Colonies* (London: Oxford University Press, 1940), 14, 33.

14. Mark A. Burkholder and Lyman L. Johnson, *Colonial Latin America,* 6th ed. (New York: Oxford University Press, 2008), 285.

15. Diffie, *Latin American Civilization,* 499; Lanning, *Academic Culture in the Spanish Colonies,* 38–40.

16. On the medieval origins of the Spanish and Spanish American universities see Lanning, *Academic Culture in the Spanish Colonies,* 6–9.

17. Haring, *The Spanish Empire in America,* 215–16; Góngora, *Studies in the Colonial History of Spanish America,* 178, 188–89.

18. Lockhart and Schwartz, *Early Latin America,* 124, 161–64.

19. Diffie, *Latin American Civilization,* 704–6.

20. Heloisa Suzana Santos Tomelin, "Access to Higher Education in Brazil," M.A. thesis, Ohio University, 2002, 11–17; Diffie, *Latin American Civilization,* 707.

21. Diffie, *Latin American Civilization,* 547–49; Lanning, *Academic Culture in the Spanish Colonies,* 64–68; Góngora, *Studies in the Colonial History of Spanish America,* 178.

22. Regalism defended the preeminence of the political government over the church, while Gallicanism upheld the supremacy of the king over the pope in temporal matters.

23. Diffie, *Latin American Civilization,* 552.

24. Santos Tomelin, "Access to Higher Education in Brazil," 21–22.

25. Góngora, *Studies in the Colonial History of Spanish America,* 179–91; Diffie, *Latin American Civilization,* 550.

26. Góngora, *Studies in the Colonial History of Spanish America,* 191.

27. Ibid., 185–86.

28. Pilar García Jordán, *Iglesia y poder en el Perú contemporáneo 1821–1919* (Cuzco: Centro de Estudios Regionales Andinos Bartolomé de Las Casas, 1991), 14–15, 25–26.

29. John Lynch, "The Catholic Church in Latin America, 1830–1930," in *The Cambridge History of Latin America,* vol. 4, ed. Leslie Bethell (Cambridge: Cambridge University Press 1986), 529.

30. Carlos Newland, "La educación elemental en Hispanoamérica: Desde la independencia hasta la centralización de los sistemas educativos nacionales," *Hispanic American Historical Review* 71, no. 2 (1991): 348–49.

31. Grover Antonio Espinoza, "Education and State-Building in Peru: The Primary Schools of the Departamento of Lima, 1850–c. 1920," Ph.D. dissertation, Columbia University, 2007, chapter 3.

32. Angela Thompson, "Children and Schooling in Guanajuato, Mexico, 1790–1840," in *Molding the Hearts and Minds: Education, Communications, and Social Change in Latin America,* ed. John A. Britton (Wilmington, Del.: Scholarly Resources, 1994), 22, 26.

33. For a brief examination of elementary school books in eighteenth-century Spain see Paulette Demerson, "Tres instrumentos pedagógicos del siglo XVIII: La cartilla, el arte de escribir y el Catón," in *L'enseignment primaire en Espagne et en Amérique Latine du XVIIIe siècle à nos tours: Politiques éducatives et réalités scolaires,* ed. Jean-René Aymes (Tours: Université de Tours, 1986), 31–40.

34. Thompson, "Children and Schooling in Guanajuato, Mexico, 1790–1840," 31.

35. Newland, "La educación elemental en Hispanoamérica," 341.

36. Luis Resines, ed., *Catecismos de Ripalda y Astete* (Madrid: Biblioteca de Autores Cristianos, 1987), 134–35, 304–6; Joaquín Lorenzo de Villanueva, *Catecismo de moral* (Lima: Imprenta Republicana, 1825), 46–47; José de Urcullu, *Lecciones de moral, virtud, y urbanidad* (Paris: Lecointe y Laserre, 1838), 30; Lucas Huerta Mercado, *Lecciones de religión y moral extractadas de autores clásicos* (Arequipa: Imprenta del Gobierno, 1840), 12; José Francisco Navarrete, *Catecismo histórico dogmático para el uso de la juventud peruana* (Lima: Lib. Hispano-Francesa, n.d.).

37. Resines, *Catecismos de Ripalda y Astete,* 65; Eugenia Roldán Vera, "Reading in Questions and Answers: The Catechism as an Educational Genre in Early Independent Spanish America," *Book History* 4 (2001): 24, 27, 41.

38. Navarrete, *Catecismo histórico dogmático,* 165.

39. Chasteen, *Born in Blood and Fire,* 152; Charles Hale, "Political and Social Ideas in Latin America, 1870–1930," in *The Cambridge History of Latin America,* ed. Leslie Bethell (Cambridge: Cambridge University Press, 1986), 378.

40. Lynch, "The Catholic Church in Latin America, 1830–1930," 562–63.

41. Mexican liberals began *La Reforma* in 1855. Carlos Newland, "The Estado Docente and Its Expansion: Spanish American Elementary Education, 1900–1950," *Journal of Latin American Studies* 26 (1994): 461.

42. Jairo Ramírez Bahamón, "Vicisitudes de la utopía escolar del radicalismo en el Tolima (1863–1886)," *Bulletin de l'Institut Français d'Etudes Andines* 28, no. 3 (1999): 333.

43. Ibid., 336.

44. Newland, "La educación elemental en Hispanoamérica," 346–47.

45. Lynch, "The Catholic Church in Latin America, 1830–1930," 544–45; Claude Pomerleau, "French Missionaries and Latin American Catholicism in the Nineteenth Century," *The Americas* 37, no. 3 (1981): 351–55, 358.

46. Newland, "La educación elemental en Hispanoamérica," 349.

47. Pomerleau, "French Missionaries and Latin American Catholicism in the Nineteenth Century," 355; Newland, "La educación elemental en Hispanoamérica," 351.

48. Teresa González de Fanning, *Educación femenina: Colección de artículos pedagógicos, morales y sociológicos* (Lima: Torres Aguirre, 1898), 14–16.

49. Eduardo Kingman Garcés, "Del hogar cristiano a la escuela moderna: La educación como modeladora de habitus," *Bulletin de l'Institut Français d'Etudes Andines* 28, no. 3 (1999): 350.

50. Lynch, "The Catholic Church in Latin America, 1830–1930," 547–49.

51. Hale, "Political and Social Ideas in Latin America, 1870–1930," 385–86.

52. Mary Kay Vaughan, *The State, Education, and Social Class in Mexico, 1880–1920* (DeKalb: Northern Illinois University Press, 1982), 28.

53. On the increasing number of church schools in Mexico see ibid., 55.

54. Hale, "Political and Social Ideas in Latin America, 1870–1930," 384–85.

55. Manuel González Prada, *Free Pages and Hard Times: Anarchist Musings* (New York: Oxford University Press, 2003), 91.

56. Lynch, "The Catholic Church in Latin America, 1830–1930," 560–61.

57. F. B. González, *Páginas razonables en oposición a las páginas libres* (Lima: Centro de Propaganda Católica, 1895), 2:5, 10, 21–22.

58. Lastenia Larriva de Llona, *La ciencia y la fe* (Guayaquil: Imprenta de La Nación, 1889).

59. Lynch, "The Catholic Church in Latin America, 1830–1930," 576, 582–83.

60. Jeffrey Klaiber, S.J., *The Catholic Church in Peru, 1821–1985: A Social History* (Lima: Catholic University of America Press, 1992), 93–95, 136–39.

61. Lynch, "The Catholic Church in Latin America, 1830–1930," 564–67, 569–71.

62. Jan Bazant, *A Concise History of Mexico from Hidalgo to Cárdenas 1805–1940* (Cambridge: Cambridge University Press, 1977), 167.

63. *The Mexican Constitution of 1917 Compared with the Constitution of 1857...* (Philadelphia: American Academy of Political and Social Science, 1917), 2.

64. Ibid., 15, 19, 104–7.

65. Patience A. Schell, *Church and State in Revolutionary Mexico City* (Tucson: University of Arizona Press, 2003), 12–14.

66. Ibid., 21–33, 94, 109.

67. Michael C. Meyer et al., *The Course of Mexican History*, 6th ed. (New York: Oxford University Press, 1999), 567; Schell, *Church and State in Revolutionary Mexico City*, 176–80.

68. Jean Meyer, "Revolution and Reconstruction in the 1920s," in *Mexico since Independence*, ed. Leslie Bethell (Cambridge: Cambridge University Press), 213–15; Meyer et al., *The Course of Mexican History*, 570–71.

8

Anticlericalism in the Nineteenth and Early Twentieth Centuries

Jeffrey Klaiber, S.J.

Anticlericalism was a widespread and deeply felt sentiment in Latin America throughout the nineteenth century and well into the twentieth. The anticlericals, most of whom were intellectuals or politicians, looked upon the Catholic Church as a major obstacle to progress and democracy. Although anticlericalism is usually associated with liberalism, in fact it had antecedents in the kings of Spain and Portugal who aimed to curb church influence, limit its capacity to acquire property, and reduce the number of regular clergy and women religious. Some strong-arm caudillos, military or hacienda owners who seized power in the early republics, like Juan Manuel Rosas in Argentina or Dr. Francia in Paraguay, were as overbearing as any Bourbon or Braganza king in their strict control of the church. From the point of view of both caudillos and liberals the church was a powerful institution that wielded too much influence over all social classes, and hence had the power to promote or retard change. In this context, the liberal-conservative contention in the nineteenth century may be understood as a struggle over legitimacy, each side supported by its own tradition: the newer liberal one, born during the Enlightenment and inspired by the American and French revolutions, and the longer Hispanic authoritarian and centralist tradition fashioned over the entire colonial period. In this battle over legitimacy, religion was a key factor. The liberals represented a progressive minority, but, especially in countries with large Indian or black populations, the clergy were closer to the religious feelings and attitudes of the majority.[1] Indeed, for Indians, *mestizos,* blacks, and the lower classes in general, cold rational liberalism constituted an assault on their cultural identity.

Anticlericalism may also be understood in the context of the struggle to modernize Latin American societies. Liberals looked to revolutionary France or to Protestant England and the United States as models for their constitutions and laws, but their laws frequently clashed with older customs and traditions and were largely irrelevant to the social reality and were ignored. The church was the only institution that reached almost every corner of the nation, whereas the new republican states were weak and had no presence in distant Indian communities or in the remote areas of the Amazon basin. The church was present at every important moment in life. It recorded all baptisms, marriages, and funerals, and owned most of the cemeteries. For the liberals, control of the church, or at least eliminating its spheres of influence and control, was an absolute prerequisite for establishing a modern state that could exercise real authority throughout the republic.

This struggle often took the form of tension between progressive centers and conservative hinterlands. Capital and port cities were centers for new ideas from Europe and the United States and were the strongholds of the liberals. But in rural areas life continued unchanged with religion maintaining a vital presence. For example, in Argentina, Buenos Aires was the center of liberal influence, whereas the interior provinces produced the caudillos. In Mexico, in contrast to the capital, a liberal bastion, Guadalajara was the haven for Catholic sentiment during the nineteenth century, and this circumstance continued into the twentieth. In Ecuador Gabriel García Moreno, the conservative president and former seminarian, was closely aligned to upper-class Quito, whereas General Eloy Alfaro, the liberal president, represented the commercial interests of Guayaquil. In 1856 Manuel Ignacio Vivanco, with the full support of Bishop José Sebastián de Goyeneche of Arequipa in southern Peru, the "Rome" of America, led an insurrection against the liberal constitutional assembly in Lima, which had passed several anticlerical measures.

Liberalism also divided families: men who were liberals considered themselves rational thinkers free from superstition and myth, as opposed to women, whom they classed as sentimental and prone to fanaticism. As a result, many middle-class men ceased to practice Catholicism, while their wives and women in general became the mainstays of the church.

Jesuits and Masons

Liberals looked somewhat benevolently on new congregations like the Daughters of Charity and the Sisters of the Good Shepherd that provided social services. And the Franciscans, especially the non-Spanish Franciscans, were not perceived as threatening. But the Society of Jesus was the bête noir of the liberals, and was universally viewed as dangerous to the development of a modern sovereign nation. Although the Jesuits were known in colonial times for their progressive ideas, and the Peruvian Jesuit Juan Pablo Viscardo y Guzmán openly summoned fellow creoles to embrace independence, nineteenth-century Jesuits had become allies of the conservatives and were perceived as harbingers of papal interference in the new states. To understand this change in the Jesuits it must be remembered that they had all been expelled from Brazil in 1759 and from Spanish America in 1767. The Portuguese and Spanish monarchs and their advisers deemed that the Jesuits wielded too much influence in society and acted far too independently. Their economic success in ranching and influence over the Indians in the missions created envy and suspicion among the colonial elite. In 1773 they were suppressed as a religious order by Pope Clement XIV. The Jesuit order was resurrected in 1814, but in very different circumstances. Catholic monarchs, beginning with Ferdinand VII of Spain (1813–33), saw the Jesuits as intellectual allies in their efforts to restore absolutism and combat liberalism, and the Jesuits undertook this role.

When the Jesuits trickled back to Latin America, they faced unrelenting hostility from the liberals and were repeatedly expelled: Argentina, 1843; Paraguay; 1844; Colombia, 1850 and again in 1861; Mexico, 1856; Uruguay, 1859; Ecuador, 1852; Guatemala, 1871; Peru, 1886. When he expelled the Jesuits from Colombia in 1850 President Hilario López commented: "Our young civilization and industry, and our nascent institutions, do not have sufficient strength to fight advantageously for our social regeneration against the lethal and corrupting influence of Jesuitism."[2]

Among the liberals the Masons were the most passionate and vehement. Politically, they shared the same agenda as most liberals, but their animosity against institutional religion, and especially the Jesuits, was more intense, no doubt in part because Masonry was shaped by the Enlightenment's deism, which rejected institutionalized and dogmatic religion. Like most liberals they had fought hand in glove with liberal clergy during the wars for independence and worked together with them to write the new constitutions. Prominent Masons included Simón Bolívar, José de San Martín, and Bernardo O'Higgins, but none of these champions of independence was anticlerical or antireligious. However, as we shall see, during the nineteenth century the church grew increasingly conservative and the Masons, in turn, grew more critical of the church. In 1869 Francisco Javier Mariátegui, one of the founders of Freemasonry in Peru, exclaimed: "What I wouldn't give for the clergy of today to be like that of 1820 in patriotism and virtue."[3] Masonic invective was especially directed toward the Jesuits. In 1879 a Mason in Uruguay summoned all Masons to form a bulwark of resistance against the Jesuits:

> Today, as the cursed sons of Loyola are invading our land, we trust that Uruguayan Masonry will be up to the task of building a dike to stem this sinister invasion. The principles on which Masonry is founded are the antithesis of the all-absorbing spirit of the selfish and tyrannical order of Jesus. For these reasons, Masonry is called upon to be in the front lines to block this black invasion.[4]

First Generation Liberals

Anticlericalism emerged in stages: postindependence liberalism, mid-century anticlericalism, and, in the latter part of the century, radical anticlericalism. As we mentioned above, the early liberals after independence were not generally anticlerical. Although the pope and most bishops condemned the various independence movements, liberal priests everywhere supported them. Many of these priests, such as Francisco Javier de Luna Pizarro in Peru, Gregorio Funes in Argentina, and Servando Teresa de Mier in Mexico, were elected to the constitutional assemblies of their respective republics. The new governments claimed the right to exercise national patronage, as a continuation of the *patronato real* (by which the crown had the right to name all bishops) of the colonial era. But Pope Leo XII (1823–29) and initially Gregory XVI (1831–46), deeply suspicious of liberal movements, especially after the papacy's experience with the French revolution, refused to recognize that right. Finally, both sides agreed to compromise: the new governments would present a list of episcopal candidates, and Rome would make the final choice. Increasingly, Catholics, who once depended upon the commitment of the kings of Spain and Portugal to promote the interests of the church, now looked to the papacy for inspiration, strength, and support. Pope Pius IX (1846–78) became a rallying point for a Catholicism in Europe and Latin America embattled against liberalism, Masonry, positivism, socialism, and other modern forces. Papal infallibility, declared a dogma at the First Vatican Council (1870), served as a final bulwark of defense against these foes. But the efforts of the papacy to take charge of the church in Latin America, known as "Romanization," had another important consequence. The new bishops, although they were no longer Spanish, were almost all conservatives, and they in turn formed a new and more conservative clergy in their seminaries.[5]

The first generation of liberals was often termed "ideological" because it was more interested in defining the legal framework for the new republics than in promoting social change. The majority of liberals were lawyers and priests, who passionately believed in the power of constitutions and constitutional law to modernize society. They were fatally unaware that without social change the new republics were destined to come under the sway of economic elites. In many cases the republics of Latin America were born as divided societies: small white minorities versus the vast majority of Indians, blacks, and peoples of mixed racial ancestry who were virtually excluded from all aspects of the new system. Liberals were not revolutionaries: they believed that change would come about through the law, education, and good moral example. For this reason most believed that religion was a stabilizing force, which would cement social cohesion. Manuel Lorenzo de Vidaurre, the first president of the Supreme Court of Peru (1825), even proposed expelling atheists, justifying this draconian measure by stating: "A person who denies the power of a Higher Being is capable of any crime."[6] In the same vein liberals also feared social revolution. In Peru in 1780 Túpac Amaru had led a well-planned revolution during which he abolished slavery and other social abuses. The specter of an Indian-led revolution persuaded many leaders of independence movements to exclude and marginalize the Indian. It is somewhat telling that most of the soldiers who fought for the king in Peru were Indians, though, of course, many were undoubtedly drafted against their will. Miguel Hidalgo's insurrection in Mexico in 1810–11, during which thousands of Indians invaded haciendas, justified suspicion of the Indian in the eyes of the governing elites.

The anticlericalism of these early liberals may be demonstrated by their hostility toward the religious orders (Dominicans, Franciscans, Augustinians, etc.), which included priests, brothers, and nuns. The liberals believed there were too many religious and that the religious way of life was unproductive and useless for the life of the new nations. In 1826, both Peru and Bolivia enacted the Reform of Regulars decree by which convents and monasteries were confiscated and converted into military fortresses or schools. The reform also declared that no one under twenty five could join a religious order. That many male religious were Spanish justified suspicion of their loyalty to the new republics. In 1824 Bolívar expropriated the Franciscan monastery of Santa Rosa de Ocopa near Huancayo in the highlands. The nineteenth-century Peruvian historian Mariano Paz Soldán explained that Ocopa was "a purely Spanish establishment."[7] As a result of such measures, convents and monasteries were expropriated, and by mid-century those that remained were half-empty. By way of contrast, liberals viewed many secular clergy as model patriots since they had fought for independence, championed the cause of democracy, and preached civic virtue in the pulpit.

Mid-Century Anticlericalism

By mid-century liberals had become full-fledged anticlericals. Latin American societies were experiencing important social and economic changes. Each country had discovered a product, which enabled it to enter the world market: Peru, guano; Brazil, coffee; and the Central American republics, coffee and, later, bananas. Still later nitrates and copper would give rise to important industries in Chile. In Peru, Brazil, and Colombia a landed oligarchy exported sugar and coffee and wielded great power in their respective congresses. In this context liberals, with the support of many businessmen, merchants, and modern landowners, saw the church, with its extensive properties and colonial mentality, as an obstacle to the changes needed for a modern open society. Liberals sought to restrict the church's influence by separating church and state and by passing other laws that eliminated state support for the church, abolished mortmain (by which the church could not sell its own properties), secularized cemeteries, laicized education, made civil marriage mandatory, and allowed for divorce. In addition, liberal governments in many countries confiscated the wealth of the confraternities and other lay associations and turned it over to the new state-supported beneficent societies. The church resisted every one of these measures and church-state or conservative-liberal confrontations became typical in the political landscape of Latin America. Separation

161

of church and state usually occurred as the result of these confrontations as were the cases of Colombia in 1853, Mexico in 1857, and Ecuador in 1906.

Religious toleration was nonexistent in most countries and the church resisted any encroachment by Protestants on Latin American soil. But the liberals, who looked with envy at the progress of Protestant England and North America, saw toleration as a way of attracting non-Catholic European immigrants from advanced industrial nations. Liberals like Benito Juárez in Mexico and Eloy Alfaro in Ecuador favored Protestant missionary activity. But in other cases the newcomers were met with hostility and rejection. In 1890 Francisco Penzotti, a Uruguayan born in Italy and a representative of the Bible Society, was imprisoned in Callao (Lima) for public preaching. His imprisonment provoked a cry of indignation from both the liberals and the government of the United States. Penzotti was released and Peru's nontoleration laws were never again enforced. Finally, after many battles and heated debates, toleration was achieved in country after country: Argentina, 1853; Mexico, 1859; Chile, 1865; Brazil, 1890; Ecuador, 1904; Bolivia, 1905; Peru, 1915.[8] In the latter part of the nineteenth century Protestant missionaries, principally Methodists and Baptists, began arriving in large numbers. In Brazil, Argentina, Uruguay, and Chile, European Protestants, especially German Lutherans, established "transplanted" churches, that is, colonies of immigrants who simply relocated to parts of South America similar to their homelands, but who had no intention of proselytizing.

Antireligious Anticlericalism

During the second half of the nineteenth century, anticlericalism entered a new and more radical phase under the spell of positivism which, as expounded by Auguste Comte, represented the culminating phase in human evolution. During the first phase, humanity was held sway by religion and superstition. In the second phase, beginning with the Greek philosophers and reaching a high point in the Enlightenment, reason replaced superstition. Then, in the nineteenth century, science became the third and highest level of evolution. Reason, guided by the scientific method, had produced machines and inventions that were finally securing humankind's control over nature. In Comte's view, religion had no place in this world. To be sure, Comte actually spoke of a new religion of humanity, though it was more of a slogan or a moral imperative than something formal. Curiously, in Brazil, small groups of followers gathered together in the countryside to ritually celebrate the wonders of nature and the overall harmony of the universe, but Comte's "religion" had no appeal for the vast majority of Latin Americans.[9] Many intellectuals in Europe and Latin America embraced positivism as an obvious and logical step for achieving rapid progress. Most believed that, at least for free and rational men, religion was a private affair. The public practice of religion was merely a social necessity providing a moral framework for lesser educated members of society: Indians, blacks, peasants, workers, and children; and it satisfied the sentimental longings of women. Many positivists were also influenced by new racial theories emanating from Europe, especially those of Arthur Gobineau and Gustave Le Bon who classified all races according to their degree of evolution: white Europeans at the top, Latins lower, and black Africans at the bottom. For the positivists, religion and race were two obstacles in the way of progress.

In Latin America such ideas were received with uncritical certitude. In his 1894 lecture inaugurating the academic year at San Marcos University in Lima, Javier Prado y Ugarteche dwelt upon these themes. He pointed out that for three hundred years Spain had fostered a "religion of fanaticism" which stifled intellectual progress and moral development.[10] It had, he said, replaced Indian superstitions with a new set of superstitions, and the arid dogmas of scholasticism produced a new breed of intolerant clerics who fought to restrain the advance of science. Finally, Prado y Ugarteche called for the immigration of the "superior races" of Europe to Peru.[11]

But the Peruvian who most openly excoriated religion, and by doing so became that country's most famous anticlerical, was Manuel González Prada (1844–1918). After Peru's bitter defeat by Chile in the War of the Pacific (1879–84) he raised his voice in protest against all the social groups and forces that he held responsible for the defeat: the oligarchy, inept politicians, the military, and the church. He traveled to France and immersed himself in radical literature, especially the literature of positivism and anarchism. When he returned to Peru in 1898 he was one of the first voices in favor of social revolution.[12] For González Prada, Catholicism, especially Spanish Catholicism, bred fanaticism and intolerance. He took Peruvian liberals to task for not confronting the question of religion and for their continued support of church state union, and for sending their children to religious schools. He accused them of failing to understand that "every political question comes down to a moral one, and all moral questions come down to religion."[13] By criticizing only some practices of the church, but not religion itself, liberals, he said, legitimized the status quo. In particular, he emphasized, the church mentally subjugated three groups of "slaves" to religious dogmatism: women, children, and Indians. He especially singled out the unholy "trinity" of the Andes: the town mayor, the judge, and the priest, who conspired together to exploit the Indians. Although he praised the Adventists in the southern highlands for their schools and clinics and believed that Protestantism was a moral step up from Catholicism, he nevertheless concluded that, "as far as religions go, they are like diseases: none is good."[14] Furthermore, although he rejected formal religion, he considered atheism a sort of religion in the service of social justice. As such, he believed that atheists who fought for justice could also be models of "abnegation and virtue."[15]

An overview of anticlericalism in five countries will demonstrate similarities and differences in church-state relations in the nineteenth and early twentieth centuries. For this survey we will look at Mexico, which represented a very aggressive anticlericalism; Uruguay, historically the most secular country in Latin America; Chile, where church and state separated harmoniously; Ecuador, an Andean country characterized by a deep polarization between liberals and conservatives; and Brazil, whose unique development after independence from Portugal in 1822 allowed it to avoid most of the liberal-conservative clashes typical of Spanish America.

Mexico

In 1821, according to historian Jan Bazant, the church owned between one-fifth and one-fourth of all landed wealth in Mexico.[16] It also exercised considerable influence over all social classes, especially the Indians. These two characteristics enraged Masons, who were stronger in Mexico than in most other Latin American countries. Valentín Gómez Farías, a leading Mason, attempted to reform the church when he served as Mexico's de facto president, 1833–34. One of Latin America's first true anticlericals, he suppressed religious orders, secularized (turned over to the secular clergy) the missions in California, excluded the clergy from public education, and eliminated tithes. All of this came to naught, however, when Antonio López de Santa Anna regained control of the government in 1834. Nevertheless, the liberals continued to grow in strength and in 1855 they seized power, ushering in the period known as La Reforma. Among their first actions they passed two relatively mild laws: the Ley Juárez (1855), which abolished church *fueros* (church tribunals for clerics), and the Ley Lerdo (1856), which put an end to mortmain (by which the church could not sell or give away its own properties). However, they also convoked a constitutional assembly (1856–57) which proposed far more radical measures, such as the elimination of religious orders and the establishment of religious toleration. The depth of feeling and the mentality of the liberals can be sensed in the acrimonious exchanges in the assembly between liberals and conservatives. One major issue centered on the distinction between the private practice of religion and its public expression. Liberals claimed that the state had the obligation and right to regulate what they called "external" or public manifestations of religion, while conservatives, who spoke for the church, objected that the liberals wanted to impinge on their basic right to practice religion.

Two other important issues concerned marriage and religious vows. In the case of the former, the liberals argued that the state had the right to impose obligatory civil marriage and norms to protect the young. In the latter case, liberals insisted that no one had the "right" to abdicate his or her liberty, even under the guise of religious vows, and especially in the case of young women who were sent to convents by their families. The liberals also argued that no one should be forced to live in a state of "eternal desperation," which would be the case if these women decided to leave their religious order, since the church did not allow such a change. One liberal, José Antonio Gamboa, claimed that as a medical doctor he had visited several convents where he had seen nuns between the ages of twelve and fourteen. He favored the passage of a law that would allow only mature women to take religious vows.[17] For their part, the conservatives argued that religious vows were a covenant between God and the individual and that the state had no right to interfere. But liberals won the day. Article 12 of the 1857 constitution contained much of the liberal program regarding religion:

> No one may be forced to render personal service without just compensation and without their full consent. No contract or promise can have as its object the loss or the irrevocable sacrifice of one's liberty, whether it be for reason of work...or a religious vow. No one may sign away their life and liberty nor those of their children or students.[18]

The issue of religious toleration itself revealed deep differences among liberals. Many favored religious toleration for purposes of fostering immigration. Others supported toleration to create competition and incentives for a lazy and corrupt clergy. José Antonio Gamboa, a liberal deputy from Oaxaca, suggested that the government should bring in the clergy of "another religion" to shake the Catholic clergy out of their complacence. Francisco Zarco, the editor of a liberal newspaper, argued that the church did not need any special protection, although, he pointed out sarcastically, the clergy needed to be protected from their own corrupt ways.[19] In the end, the constitutional assembly of 1855–56 voted against religious toleration for the moment in the belief that it would be too unsettling for the general population.

When the constitution of 1857 was officially promulgated, the bishops exhorted the faithful to reject it. The bitterness between liberal and conservative parties soon erupted in a civil war, initiated by conservatives, that emboldened the liberals to take radical measures. In 1859 the minister of the treasury, Miguel Lerdo de Tejada, decreed the expropriation of all church properties and the suppression of all monasteries. When the liberals finally triumphed in 1860 under Benito Juárez, they promptly issued new laws: all cemeteries were secularized, the state assumed control of the civil register (by which all births, marriages, and deaths would be recorded in government offices), and, finally, religious toleration was granted.

The liberal triumph was interrupted by the French invasion in 1862, which was strongly supported by the conservatives. Maximilian, the Austrian prince who ruled from 1864 to 1867, thanks to French support, initially courted the church, which looked to him as a savior. But the church and the conservatives were soon disillusioned when it became clear that the new emperor entertained liberal ideas and had no plans to restore the church's privileges and wealth. When the liberals returned to power in 1867, Juárez expelled several bishops, including the archbishop of Mexico City, who had supported Maximilian. Juárez's successor, Sebastián Lerdo de Tejada (1872–76), eliminated religion in public schools in 1874 and expelled the Daughters of Charity in 1875, even though these women were nurses who tended the sick. Of the 410 women expelled, 315 were Mexicans.[20]

In 1876 General Porfirio Díaz overthrew Lerdo de Tejada and had himself elected president. During the Porfiriato (1876–1911) Mexico enjoyed stability, economic growth, and the development of a prosperous upper class. Díaz, a pragmatist and ex-seminarian, allowed the church to function without enacting changes to the reform laws. The church prospered: new religious congregations arrived, native vocations flourished, and processions and other displays of popular devotions were well attended. On the eve of the 1910 revolution official statistics declared that 99.6 percent of Mexicans were Catholics.[21]

But the pent-up hostility of peasants, urban workers, and middle-class professionals against the authoritarian regime was finally released. Revolutionaries viewed the church as an accomplice of Díaz, and ignored a Catholic reformist movement that also called for social change. The northern revolutionaries under Venustiano Carranza and Alvaro Obregón prevailed, and their radical ideology was embodied in the 1917 constitution, which became the most anticlerical constitution in the history of the Western hemisphere. At the onset of the constitutional convention, anticlerical orators branded priests as "eternal exploiters of household secrets," "filthy bats," and "insatiable vultures."[22] Given this highly charged atmosphere, the church could expect no quarter.

The anticlerical clauses of the constitution were sweeping and profound. Article 3 excluded the church or any religious group from participating in primary or secondary education. Article 5 forbade the existence of religious orders, and Article 24 prohibited the public exercise of religion. Article 27 declared that "those associations called churches" could not own or acquire property.[23] Article 130 stripped churches of juridical personality and decreed that all clergy must be Mexican born. Furthermore, this article deprived the clergy of the right to vote and to express criticism of the constitution or civil authorities. Finally, it declared that no party could henceforth associate itself with any religious group, thereby disbanding el Partido Católico, the Catholic political party. In short, the constitution totally marginalized the church from public life and reduced it to Sunday worship and dispensing the sacraments.

President Plutarco Elías Calles (1924–28) fully implemented these draconian laws, precipitating a major uprising in the countryside. In 1927, in response to the new articles and multiple acts of anticlerical violence (which included an attempt to bomb the image of Our Lady of Guadalupe in the basilica of the same name), several thousand peasants rose up in arms against the government with the cry

"Viva Cristo Rey!" The Cristero rebellion lasted until 1929, cost the lives of some fifty thousand Cristeros and federal soldiers, and the execution of many priests, including Jesuit Miguel Pro, who was falsely implicated in a plot to assassinate ex-president Obregón.[24] Obregón was subsequently assassinated by Catholic activist José León Toral. Violence on this scale persuaded the church and the state to agree to a peace pact in 1929. The church promised to stay out of politics and the state to cease overt persecution of the church. Finally and much later, in 1992, after many meetings with church leaders and two papal visits, the government removed most of the anticlerical articles from the constitution and signed a new agreement with the Catholic Church and other denominations.[25]

What is striking in the case of Mexico is that this country, steeped in popular religiosity and known for its religious fervor, experienced the most intense anticlericalism at a time when it was on the wane elsewhere in the hemisphere.

Uruguay

The contrast between Mexico and Uruguay could hardly be greater. Uruguay became a completely secular state without any resistance from the populace and without an iota of violence. A small, isolated colony, founded relatively late (Montevideo in 1726), the *Banda Oriental* (the "Eastern Bank," of the Rio de la Plata, its colonial name) emerged in the nineteenth and twentieth centuries as one of the most European of all the Latin American republics. Its small Indian population declined sharply upon contact with Iberian colonizers. During the nineteenth century the country attracted an enormous diversity of European and Near Eastern immigrants who worked on farms and haciendas.[26]

Uruguay had no bishop until 1859, and in 1887 there were only 161 priests for this country of approximately 250,000. A century later, in the 1965 census, only 52 percent of men and 66 percent of women claimed Catholic affiliation.[27] Within this context, a large immigrant European population and no Indians, liberalism advanced very rapidly with little opposition. The national university, founded in 1838, had become completely positivist by 1900. The Jesuits had been expelled in 1859, obligatory civil marriage was decreed in 1885, and European religious orders were prohibited from entering the country in 1901. Under José Batlle y Ordóñez, president from 1903 to 1907 and from 1911 to 1915, liberalism reigned triumphant. In 1907 the constitution was amended to remove mention of God, and incoming members of parliament were no longer obliged to swear on the Bible. In 1909 the teaching of religion was eliminated in public schools, and in 1917 a new constitution separated church and state and secularized all religious holidays. Christmas became "Family Day" and Holy Week became "Tourism Week." Under Batlle a social welfare state was instituted, which completely marginalized the church from public life.

167

Through all this hostility the church struggled to defend itself by organizing Catholic congresses and organizations like the Civic Union (1912), a small political party. After Vatican II (1962–65) the Uruguayan church made an important contribution to the human rights movement during and after the civilian-military dictatorship (1973–85).[28]

In Uruguay, unlike Mexico, there had been no resistance from a silent Catholic majority, much less a popular uprising in the countryside. By the same token, although liberals excluded the church as much as possible from public affairs, there had been no need for violent persecution.

Chile

Unlike its status in Uruguay, Catholicism had made a deep impact on Chileans of all social classes during the colonial era and continued to wield considerable influence during most of the nineteenth century. Chile is thus an example of a confessional state with close ties to its church that was able to achieve secular status with minimum disruption and vituperation. Conservatives dominated the political scene from 1800 to 1920 with a brief liberal incursion during the presidency of Domingo Santa María (1881–86), who successfully moved forward the secularizing of the state. The state, however, continued to support the church. Although the institutional church was weak in the countryside, popular devotions flourished there. The church was much stronger in the cities among the middle and upper classes. Chile experienced the same tensions between the church and the liberals as did the rest of Latin America, but quite unlike Mexico those tensions were resolved through reasonable dialogue.

Exploitation of the nitrate fields and copper mines in the north gave rise to a workers' movement, which became a force by the early twentieth century. Social tensions deepened: between 1911 and 1920 there were three hundred violent clashes between workers and the police.[29] The workers also directed their protests against the church, which was allied closely to the conservatives, whose fortunes were based on land, mines, and commerce.[30] Liberal-church tensions came to a climax in 1925 when President Arturo Alessandri, supported by both the lower and middle classes, proposed separation of church and state. After a brief period of political chaos and Alessandri's self-exile in Europe, he returned with a proposal for separation of church and state that was, atypically, approved by the Vatican, which feared a repetition of the Mexican debacle. The archbishop of Santiago at the time, Crescente Errázuriz, was a man of moderate views who had long been opposed to priests as political candidates and who favored social reform. Although he did not favor separation of church and state, he did not oppose the new constitution, which included that separation.[31] After the constitution became the law of the land, the bishops issued a remarkably generous statement:

In Chile the state has separated itself from the church, but the church will not separate itself from the state and it will always be there to serve it promptly; it will attend to the good of the people, seek social peace, and come to the aid of all, whether they be adversaries or not, in times of stress.[32]

Chile was not the first case of church-state separation in Latin America, but it serves as an example of a friendly separation agreed upon by both parties. Subsequent history has proved the wisdom of that course. The church removed itself from state interference and the overbearing influence of the Conservative Party, which no longer felt the need to protect the church. This new freedom allowed the Chilean church to become one of the most socially progressive in Latin America after Vatican II.

Ecuador

Ecuador experienced an intense polarization between liberals and conservatives throughout the latter half of the nineteenth and the beginning of the twentieth centuries, which culminated in irrational violence. Two men personified this extremism: Gabriel García Moreno (president, 1861–65, 1869–75) and Eloy Alfaro (president, 1896–1901, 1906–11). They also personified the rivalry between coastal Guayaquil, the bastion of the anticlerical liberals, and mountainous Quito, stronghold of pro-clerical conservatives.

The first constitution of Ecuador (1830), a tiny nation with an Indian majority, established Catholicism as the official religion to the exclusion of any other. Between 1830 and 1860, liberals and conservatives reversed each other's religious policies whenever they resumed power. After a series of weak presidents, Gabriel García Moreno seized power in 1860 and remained the dominant force in the country until 1875. He believed that only religion, and specifically Catholicism, could unite Ecuadorians — whites, *mestizos,* Indians, and blacks — and forge a new national identity. He signed a concordat with the Vatican that enormously strengthened the church's authority. He brought in French religious to found schools for both the upper and lower classes. He also allowed the Jesuits to return (they had been exiled in 1852) to found schools and work among the Indians in the eastern Amazonian region. He was ultimately assassinated by liberals in 1875, who viewed him as the incarnation of fanaticism and intolerance. Though he was authoritarian and Catholic, he was a "modernizer," providing education for women and Indians, reforming the clergy, and building hospitals and roads.[33]

During the twenty years following García Moreno the liberal-conservative seesaw resumed. The period between 1895 and 1912 was dominated by General Eloy Alfaro, who was supported by Guayaquil interests. He imposed a liberal regime that totally dismantled García Moreno's Catholic authoritarian state. Once in power, some liberals resorted to violence. In 1897, for example, a mob in Riobamba, incited by anticlerical military, stormed the Jesuit school and killed one of the priests. Eloy Alfaro expelled bishops who criticized him, exiled the Jesuits and French religious, secularized the cemeteries, and took charge of the civil registry. A new liberal constitution established religious toleration and a penal code forbade the clergy to criticize that constitution and other laws. Alfaro's successor permitted divorce, mandated civil marriage, and expropriated lands belonging to religious orders. Alfaro returned to power in 1906 and formally separated church and state. He was forced out of office in 1911 and killed by a mob of conservatives in 1912, which brought full circle the killing of the Jesuit priest in 1897 by a mob of liberals.

Ecuador's political history, then, was characterized by extremism on one side provoked by extremism on the other. Peace was finally achieved in 1937 when the state and the Vatican signed a *modus vivendi*.

Brazil

Brazil is a special case in Latin America: after achieving independence (in 1822), it did not become a republic, but remained a monarchy under the control of the Braganza family. When Napoleon invaded Portugal in 1807 the royal family fled to Brazil. When the king returned to the mother country in 1821, he left his son, Pedro, behind. In 1822 Pedro declared the independence of Brazil and had himself recognized as emperor, albeit within the framework of a constitutional monarchy. He fell out of favor with contending political forces and abdicated in 1831. His son, Pedro II, who came of age in 1840, managed to unite most Brazilians into a single cohesive body. As a native of Brazil with liberal tendencies he pleased the liberals; as a monarch with royal blood he pleased the conservatives.

By and large the clergy, which supported independence and accepted the monarchy, was not affected by the process of Romanization that marginalized liberal clergymen in all Spanish America. The emperor assumed the role of protector of church interests and resisted any efforts by Rome to control the church. As a result of this unique set of circumstances, as well as the prevailing atmosphere of tolerance in Brazilian society, the acrimonious clashes between liberals and conservatives, so typical of the rest of Latin America, did not take place in nineteenth-century Brazil. The imperial constitution of 1824 established Catholicism as the official religion, but granted religious toleration. In fact, the evidence suggests that clergymen in Brazil, unlike those in Spanish America, even enjoyed amicable relations with their usual "foes": Protestants and Masons. In 1845 a Protestant missionary, Rev. James C. Fletcher, made this rather startling statement in a letter: " ... there is not a Roman Catholic country on the globe where there prevails a greater degree of toleration or a greater liberality of feeling toward Protestants."[34]

Fletcher developed strong friendships with many Catholic clergy. At the same time he noted "the shameful immorality" and "practices...so corrupt as those of the priesthood."[35]

Equally surprising was that the same amicable feeling existed between Catholics and Masons until Pope Pius IX precipitated a crisis by denouncing Freemasonry and other "evils" in his encyclical *Quanta Cura* (1864). Until then, priests in Brazil regularly celebrated Masses in Masonic lodges, and Masons joined Catholic confraternities. It was precisely this New World accommodation, so different from the bitter clashes between Masonry and Catholicism in Europe and the rest of Latin America, that alarmed Rome. The emperor refused to allow the publication of *Quanta Cura*. Certain zealous bishops, however, notably Vital Maria Gonçalves de Oliveira of Olinda (near Recife), carried out the papal instructions and ordered Catholics to end all relations with Masons. This in turn provoked the emperor's ire because the bishops were openly defying the constitution, which held that no papal document had validity if it had not been previously approved by the emperor. In 1873 Pedro ordered the arrest and imprisonment of the ultramontane (extreme papalist) bishops of Olinda and Pará. His heavy-handed treatment of the two bishops caused resentment among the clergy. Although they were released in 1875, this incident, known as the "religious question," served to discredit the monarchy, and contributed, among other factors, to its collapse in 1889.

The army, supported by conservative landowners who would not forgive the emperor for abolishing slavery in 1888, overthrew the monarchy and established a republic. The 1891 constitution, written by liberals and positivists, separated the church from the state and removed the church from public education. Yet unlike Mexico or Ecuador, the new republican state did not expropriate church properties and allowed the church to operate its own schools. Church leaders, although they criticized the state, imbued as it was with positivist ideas, were relieved to be freed from the tutalege of the monarchy, which in the end proved to be as overbearing as the Braganzas in the age of absolutism.

A Final Comment

In 1928 José Carlos Mariátegui, the Peruvian Marxist, wrote: "We have definitively left behind the days of anticlerical prejudice, when the 'free-thinking' critic happily discarded all dogmas and churches in favor of the dogma and church of the atheist's free-thinking orthodoxy."[36] By this Mariátegui meant that liberal anticlericalism had run its course, that it was no longer meaningful to a new generation of social reformers. But his criticism was much more acute and severe: he implied that liberal anticlericalism, obsessed with controlling the church, had actually missed the whole point, which was to change society. Mariátegui's criticism may have been too harsh. The liberals did aim to redeem the Indians from backwardness, and they proposed education as a key instrument. On the other hand, they did not propose land reforms to extricate the Indians from the control of oppressive landowners. In fact, whenever they expropriated church lands, they usually divided them up among themselves and other landowners.[37] Nevertheless, by granting religious toleration, secularizing cemeteries, and allowing for civil marriages, they opened the door to non-Catholic immigration. And by separating the church from the state they paved the way for a more open, pluralistic society. Once the liberals had accomplished these goals, they had little more to do. To touch religion itself would have been a mistake. For Indians, blacks, lower-class peasants, and some workers, religion, whether it be orthodox or syncretic Catholicism, was an integral part of their cultural identity. Furthermore, religious belief and practice did not impede the popular classes from rising up against abuses and exploitation.[38] This was a lesson that the Mexican liberals never learned.

Anticlericalism faded when the church itself began to change, slowly after World War II and rapidly after Vatican II (1962–65). By then the new Latin American church openly called for religious liberty, social justice, and respect for human rights. Perhaps in the long run independence from the state and anticlericalism played a positive role by forcing the church to shift its focus from defense of its own narrow interests to these other priorities.

Notes

1. On the role of the rural clergy in nineteenth-century Peru, see Jeffrey Klaiber, *The Catholic Church in Peru, 1821–1985: A Social History* (Washington, D.C.: Catholic University of America Press, 1992), 172–206.

2. Daniel Restrepo, S.J., *La Compañía de Jesús en Colombia, 1539–1940* (Bogotá: Imprenta del Corazón de Jesús, 1940), 197.

3. Francisco Javier Mariátegui, *Anotaciones a la historia independiente de Don Mariano Felipe Paz Soldán* (Lima: Imprenta de El Nacional, 1925), 16.

4. *La Razón* (Montevideo), September 3, 1879, quoted in Charles E. O'Neil, S.J., and Joaquín María Domínguez, S.J., directors, *Diccionario histórico de la Compañía de Jesús* (Rome: Institutum Historicum S.I.; Madrid: Universidad Pontificia de Comillas, 2001), 4:3865.

5. For more on Romanization, see Antonine Tibesar, "The Peruvian Church at the Time of Independence in the Light of Vatican II," *The Americas* 26 (April 1970): 349–75.

6. Manuel Lorenzo de Vidaurre, *Proyecto de un código penal* (Boston: Hiram Tupper, 1828), 147.

7. Mariano Paz Soldán, *Historia del Perú independiente* (Lima: Alfonso Lamale, 1874), 2:106.

8. The best overall study of the history of religious toleration in Latin America is J. Lloyd Mecham, *Church and State in Latin America*, 2nd ed. (Chapel Hill: University of North Carolina Press, 1966).

9. On positivism in Brazil, see Claudio Véliz, *The Centralist Tradition in Latin America* (Princeton, N.J.: Princeton University Press, 1980), 196–99.

10. Javier Prado y Ugarteche, *Estado social del Perú durante la dominación española* (Lima: Librería Imprenta Gil, 1942), 108.

11. Ibid., 205.

12. He himself proposed no program for change. He assumed the role of an "apostate," a term Peru's national historian Jorge Basadre applied to him, because he believed his mission consisted in preparing the way for a new future by denouncing and exposing the evils in society. Jorge Basadre, *Perú: Problema y posibilidad,* 5th ed. (Lima: Fundación M. J. Bustamante de la Fuente, 2000), 163.

13. Manuel González Prada, *Horas de lucha* (Lima: Fondo de Cultura Popular, 1964), 107.

14. Manuel González Prada, *Prosa menuda* (Buenos Aires: Ediciones Imán, 1941), 51.

15. Manuel González Prada, *Nuevas páginas libres* (Santiago: Editorial Ercilla, 1937), 58.

16. Jan Bazant, *Los bienes de la Iglesia en México, 1856–1875: Aspectos económicos y sociales de la revolución liberal,* 2nd ed. (Mexico City: El Colegio de México, 1977), 293.

17. Francisco Zarco, *Historia del Congreso Constituyente, 1856–1857* (Mexico City: El Colegio de México, 1956), 517.

18. Ibid., 331.

19. Ibid., 572.

20. Alfonso Alcalá Alvarado, "El triunfo del liberalismo, 1860–1873," in *Historia general de la Iglesia en América Latina,* 5:262.

21. Carlos Alvear Acevedo, "La Iglesia en México en el período 1900–1962," in *Historia general de la Iglesia en América Latina,* 5:314.

22. Ibid., 324.

23. *Constitución política de los Estados Unidos Mexicanos* (Mexico City: Secretaría de la Presidencia, 1971), 43.

24. Romero de Solís, *El aguijón del espíritu,* 311. For an in-depth study of the Cristeros, see David Bailey, *¡Viva Cristo Rey! The Cristero Rebellion and the Church-State Conflict in Mexico* (Austin: University of Texas Press, 1974).

25. On the 1992 rapprochement between the state and the church and the new law on religion, see Jeffrey Klaiber, S.J., *The Church, Dictatorships, and Democracy in Latin America* (Maryknoll, N.Y.: Orbis Books, 1998), 249–50.

26. Jan M. G. Kleinpenning, *Peopling the Land: A Historical Geography of Rural Uruguay, 1500–1915* (Amsterdam: CEDELA, Centre for Latin American Research and Documentation, 1995), 228.

27. Enrique Sobrado, *La Iglesia uruguaya: Entre pueblo y oligarquía* (Montevideo: Editorial Alfa, 1969), 63. A more contemporary estimate puts the number of Catholics at 47 percent. Néstor Da Costa, "El Catolicismo en una sociedad secularizada: El caso uruguayo," *Religión e Società* 57 (January–April 2007), 31.

28. For example, the Jesuit Luis Pérez Aguirre founded the Peace and Justice Service, which defended people detained by the military. He later organized a movement to vote against amnesty for the military. See Klaiber, *The Church, Dictatorships, and Democracy in Latin America,* 116–20.

29. Hernán Godoy, *Estructura social en Chile* (Santiago de Chile: Editorial Universitaria, 1971), 243.

30. A few clergy called for a more radical response on the part of the church. Rafael Edwards Salas, a secular priest named a bishop in 1935, was an early champion of the church's social message. Fernando Vives Solar, a Jesuit, taught that message in the Jesuit school in Santiago and founded Christian unions for chauffeurs, milkmen, and seamstresses. Father Alberto Hurtado, one of the shining lights for social justice in Catholic circles in the thirties and forties (and canonized by Benedict XVI in 2006), attributed his vocation as a Jesuit to Vives.

31. Fidel Araneda Bravo, *Historia de la Iglesia en Chile* (Santiago de Chile: Ediciones Paulinas, 1986), 711.

32. Ibid., 712.

33. Derek Williams, "The Making of Ecuador's Pueblo Católico," in *Political Cultures in the Andes, 1750–1950,* ed. Nils Jacobsen and Cristóbal Aljovín de Losada (Durham: Duke University Press, 2005), 207–29.

34. Mecham, *Church and State in Latin America,* 269.

35. James Fletcher and D. P. Kidder quoted in Lee M. Penyak and Walter J. Petry, eds. *Religion in Latin America: A Documentary History* (Maryknoll, N.Y.: Orbis Books, 2006), 189.

36. José Carlos Mariátegui, *Seven Interpretive Essays on Peruvian Reality,* trans. Marjory Urquidi (Austin: University of Texas Press, 1971), 124.

37. This was certainly the case in Ecuador. See José Tamayo Herrera, *Liberalismo, indigenismo y violencia en los países andinos, 1850–1995* (Lima: Universidad de Lima, 1998), 66–67.

38. For a study of the religious factor during Indian rebellions, see Jeffrey Klaiber, *Religion and Revolution in Peru, 1824–1976* (Notre Dame, Ind.: University of Notre Dame Press, 1977), 45–70. For an overall assessment of Latin American liberalism, see David Bushnell, "Assessing the Legacy of Liberalism," in *Liberals, Politics, and Power: State Formation in Nineteenth-Century Latin America,* ed. Vincent C. Peloso and Barbara A. Tenenbaum (Athens: University of Georgia Press, 1996), 278–300.

9

"Not to Be Called Christian"

*Protestant Perceptions of Catholicism
in Nineteenth-Century Latin America*

Monica I. Orozco

*A land with one-third of its people purely aboriginal and one-half its people on
the plane of the Eurasians of India, and three-quarters unable to read a line of
Scripture, is not to be called Christian on account of the presence of a degraded
Romanism.* — The Church at Home and Abroad (1887)[1]

*I consider missionary work in Mexico, as in all papal countries, more difficult
than it is in pagan lands. The Gospel has not to encounter and overcome a base
system of heathenism, but a shameful counterfeit of itself, a public sentiment
bitterly prejudiced against it by a system worse than heathenism that it has
palmed itself upon a people as Christianity.* — Rev. Milton Greene (1893)[2]

Many Protestants in North America in the nineteenth century viewed Latin American Catholicism as politically and spiritually moribund, a faith encumbered with a medieval past, steeped in superstition and idolatry, only nominally Christian in character, and tainted with indigenous and African influences. Some intellectual and political elite in Latin America shared these sentiments. They associated Catholicism and its clergy with values that ran counter to the republican ideals of the newly independent states and to "modernization." They could not fathom how such a distorted version of Christianity could command the devotion of a majority of the population nor how so misguided a clergy could continue to play so integral a role in daily life. The following accounts by North American missionaries in central Mexico illustrate Protestant perceptions of Catholicism in Latin America, the changing intellectual and political climate in both Latin America and the United States, and the aggressive evangelization pursued by mainline Protestants in the late nineteenth century.

The Western Mexican Mission of the Congregationalists under the American Board of Commissions of Foreign Missions (ABCFM) was established in Guadala-

175

jara, Jalisco, in 1872. Two missionaries, John Stephens and David Watkins, both graduates of the Pacific Theological Seminary in Oakland, California, volunteered for the assignment there and wrote optimistically about their new posts. Their 1873 report reflected the enthusiasm and naiveté of many U.S. Protestant missionaries who believed they could evangelize all of Latin America into a proper, that is, non-Catholic, Christianity. They described the support they received from people in "influential circles," such as the governor, the superintendent of public instruction, and the growing number of converts to Protestantism from members of the professional classes. But this same report suggested serious obstructions in the way of long-term success.

> Of course the priests and the fanatics are bitter against us; and a few evenings ago a letter was thrown into our window, stating that the Mexicans did not want Protestant rascals here to deceive and cheat them, and warning us to take care, for we would be punished and killed. Mr. Stephens is living in the same house as the commander-in-chief of the Mexican army, and he mentioned the fact to him, as he is a Liberal. The commander desired to see the letter. He intends publishing it in the poor English in which it is written, also a translation of it into Spanish, and his orders underneath, that if any dare to touch us he will bring his whole army, if necessary, to bear upon them. It is said there are six men paid by the priests to kill us, but the "Lord is on our side, what can man do unto us?"[3]

Other sections of the report refer to hostile reactions from members of the local Catholic clergy and menacing Catholics who resented Protestant incursions into this Catholic stronghold.

> The Catholics are now printing eight different papers weekly, whose great object is to attack us. From the pulpit, also, people are warned from visiting or speaking with us; but the very violent language used in mentioning Protestants has been (with but little exception) more in our favor than against us. Only once have we been pelted in the street. One afternoon, as Mr. and Mrs. Watkins and I were returning from a visit, we were attacked by a party of men and boys, who commenced throwing stones, two of which struck Mr. Watkins, confining him to his bed three days. The entire city was indignant at the outrage, and some of the papers said plainly, "The rascals did it to please their confessors." It was a bad blow for Catholicism, even if it did hit Mr. Watkins. We know there will be hard fighting for some time, but it must melt away before the Spirit of God. We are happy in having the governor and the State officers on our side, they aiding us in every possible way.[4]

Despite the serious harm experienced by the missionaries, they put complete trust in the providential and spiritual nature of their mission and in their influential political contacts in high places.

In November, Stephens visited the town of Ahualulco, Jalisco, population five thousand, including two thousand indigenous. He encountered extreme hostility from the local population under the direction of a Catholic priest. "The first few days we met some opposition," he wrote. "The doors were defaced, stones were thrown at the windows, and there was shouting during the speaking. But all this has entirely ceased; I sleep as safely as in California."[5] Unfortunately, Stephens's sense of security misled him: he was murdered shortly after that report. His attackers, allegedly shouting, "Long live the curate, death to the Protestants," killed Stephens, severed his head, and mutilated his body.[6]

Despite Stephens's murder and other recurring physical and economic threats to their well-being, the Protestants were resolved to continue their process of evangelization. New generations of Protestants confronted verbal and physical attacks, which they blamed on the pernicious influence of priests. The missionary journal *The Church at Home and Abroad* noted in 1895 that some local Catholic officials assessed excessive taxes in order to deter Protestants from owning property or operating businesses. A Presbyterian missionary in Mexico City, for example, reported that he was taxed fifty cents per month for preaching to fellow United States citizens. Missionaries also accused priests in Saltillo of cajoling local authorities to impose a tax of five dollars on anyone who testified to his or her religious conversion at a Baptist meeting. According to *The Church at Home and Abroad,* this tax "amounted to a prohibition of the meetings."[7] Presbyterian minister Anthony Graybill detailed the difficulty he and his family experienced when they attempted to rent a house in Monterrey in 1888.

> The owner, a polite old lady of one of the first families, showed me a very suitable house for fifteen dollars per month. I agreed to the price. She handed me the key, and told me to return at 3 p.m. for the written contract. I did so, but she shook her head, and said she had learned we were Protestants, and she could not rent her house to us.[8]

Graybill's unpleasant experience was repeated several times. The local priest had exerted pressure on his parishioners not to rent to Protestants.

Militant Protestant evangelism derived from two biblical commands: the first to spread the gospel and the second to live a life similar to Christ's, that is, to love others as Christ loved them. It was therefore incumbent upon Christians to commit themselves to the spiritual and physical welfare of others, especially those spiritually malnourished, and to provide the "men and means" for proselytization. Historic factors also contributed to the Protestant fervor to spread the gospel in the Americas. The eighteenth-century religious revival, the "Great Awakening"

(1726–56), compelled many mainline Protestants, including Congregationalists, Presbyterians, and Methodist Episcopalians to engage in missionary work in the United States, especially among enslaved blacks and Native Americans.[9] By the early nineteenth century, U.S. Protestant missionaries took the next logical step and looked outside their own country.[10]

In light of the ongoing worldwide missionary effort, some Protestant churchmen debated the wisdom of spending precious resources in Latin America, which had already been Christianized, albeit by misguided Catholic churchmen. Those dedicated to evangelizing Latin America, while acknowledging the urgent need for Protestant missionaries in "unharvested fields" in Asia and Africa, claimed that evangelization was demanded in Latin America because of the "appalling need of Roman Catholic lands" and their "virtual heathenism."[11] They believed that Spanish Catholicism had both helped and hindered the spread of Christianity. Latin Americans, they argued, had only rudimentary knowledge of basic Christian tenets and had received improper religious instruction from poorly trained and morally lax Catholic clergy. Presbyterian missionary Melinda Rankin visited Mexico in the mid-nineteenth century and lamented, "Indeed a pure Christianity had never penetrated these dark regions, as all the previous history of Mexico clearly proved."[12] Isaac F. Holton, a Presbyterian minister who visited New Granada (present-day Colombia) from 1852 to 1854 had little regard for Catholic practices. Claiming to provide a "candid statement of facts" he wrote, "If the reader charge me with irreverence, my plea is that I find not reverence among the faithful here, and the less can therefore be expected in me."[13] He derided the rituals attached to the sacraments of the Catholic faith and claimed that the church fostered "mere ceremonies irrespective of any exercises of the heart." He ridiculed the sacrament of infant baptism since newborns do not enter the faith willingly, and he denigrated the role of priests, some of whom he described as "drunk or stupid" during the ceremony at which they were officiating.[14]

Reverend Robert Walsh, a chaplain attached to the British Embassy in Brazil in 1828–29, noted the shortage of suitable candidates and inadequate training for those who did aspire to the priesthood. Walsh attributed these shortcomings to the lack of educational support in Catholic seminaries and to insufficient "inducements" for young men from wealthy families to join the priesthood. Regarding the latter point, Walsh believed that the stipends usually afforded priests, though small, made it more likely for males from poorer families to become candidates for the priesthood. Much to his chagrin, moreover, this appeal of the priesthood to members of the lower classes in Brazil meant that men of African descent had been permitted to join the clergy. In his estimation, "the admission of the poor despised race, to the highest functions that a human being can perform" was evidence of the sad state of the Catholic clergy in Brazil.[15] Despite Walsh's negative view, he noted the mitigating influence of outsiders and acknowledged the presence of a few exceptional members of the Catholic hierarchy, such as the Portuguese bishop of Rio, José Caëtano da Silva-Cutinho, described by Walsh as favorably inclined to improve the moral and spiritual status of his fellow clergy and as unusually tolerant of English Protestant clergy there.[16]

Protestant observers of Catholicism in Latin America relished the opportunity to criticize processions, religious festivals, and other ceremonies that they believed hindered spirituality. The frequency of elaborate religious processions confirmed the problematic nature of Catholicism to John Clark Brigham, who toured South America in 1824–25. "It is indeed a mystery," he stated "how the simple religion of Christ, the most simple of all systems, was ever transformed into such an unmeaning show."[17] John Lloyd Stephens, a well-educated and well-traveled resident of New York City who once served as ambassador to the United Provinces of Central America, also witnessed the important role that processions and religious festivals played in Latin America. The following account describes the eight-day festival of Santiago in Jalacho, Yucatán, which he attended in 1840. Stephens noted the easy commingling of the Holy Spirit and the "spirit of commerce" in these elaborate ceremonies and criticized those priests who profited from the latter.

> The doors of the church were constantly open; the interior was thronged with Indians, and a crowd continually pressing to the altar. In the doorway was a large table covered with candles and small figures of arms and legs in wax, which the Indians purchased as they entered at a *medio* a piece, for offerings to the saint. Near the altar, on the left, sat an unshaved *ministro*, with a table before him, on which was a silver waiter, covered with *medios, reales,* and two-shilling pieces showing to the backward what others had done and inviting them to do the same. The candles purchased at the door had been duly blessed, and as the Indians went up with them, a strapping Negro, with linen particularly dirty, received and lighted them at one burning on the altar, whence with his black hands he passed them to a rusty [*sic*] white assistant, who arranged them upon a table, and, even before the backs of the offerers were turned, puffed out the light, and took the candles to be smoothed over and resold at the door for another *medio* each.[18]

Prior to Mass, Stephens noted, parishioners lit candles and made significant monetary contributions. Upon the ringing of bells, he continued, the faithful left the church to witness the procession of a statue of Santiago through the town, clothed with great splendor and accompanied by "Indians with lighted candles; then the *ministro* with the large silver salver and money upon it, presenting it on either side to receive additional offerings."[19] Stephens depicted the congregation's priest as the embodiment of excess and materialism, especially when compared to its indigenous members who made great sacrifices to sustain the church and its clergy. Stephens remarked,

Throughout the state, this class of inhabitants pays annually a tax of twelve *reales* per head for the support of the *cura;* and it was said on the ground that the Indians at this fiesta had paid eight hundred dollars for *salves,* five hundred for *aves,* and six hundred for masses, which if true, was an enormous sum out of their small earnings.[20]

James Fletcher and D. P. Kidder made similar observations during their extensive stay in Brazil in the mid-nineteenth century. They noted the plethora of religious festivities and the methods used to extract funds to pay for processions, fireworks, and orchestras. In preparation for the ceremonies, they stated, "begging-processions go through the streets, a long while in advance, in order to secure funds" and "some *festa* is always in anticipation."[21] In both Spanish America and Brazil, therefore, Protestants expressed awe and chagrin at the emphasis placed upon ceremony and ritual in the Catholic faith, and their cost.

Some Protestant observers, Stephens, for example, were favorably impressed by some Catholic clergy and praised those priests whom they believed labored earnestly amid their parishioners' grinding poverty. Stephens's picture of excess and materialism in the religious ceremonies in Jalacho, Yucatán, for example, was juxtaposed against the material impoverishment but spiritual wealth he witnessed at a church in Ticul, Yucatán. There the once grand facilities had fallen into disrepair, but in contrast to the corpulent and unkempt priest Stephens encountered in Jalacho, the priest in Ticul had an "open, animated, and intelligent countenance, [and was] manly, and at the same time mild."[22] Stephens's admiration for this poor friar was obvious as he noted that "Cura Carillo," in keeping with the Franciscan vow of poverty, turned over the income of his parish to the order, deducting only a small amount for his subsistence. The good priest

> never expected to be rich and did not wish to be; he had enough for his wants and did not desire more. He was content with his village and with the people; he was the friend to everybody, and everybody was his friend; in short, for a man not indolent, but, on the contrary, unusually active in both mind and body, he was, without affectation or parade, and entirely more contented with his lot than any man I ever knew.[23]

The dynamic political, cultural, and economic development in countries where Protestantism was dominant resonated with nineteenth-century Latin American liberals, who deplored the overwhelmingly tranquilizing influence of the Catholic Church in Latin America. They linked the church to the colonial legacy of monarchy, authority, and privileged corporate entities in contradiction to their own ideals of republicanism, private property, and individualism. Though most Latin American liberals remained at least nominally Catholic, they viewed Protestantism as an important addition that would open up the social fabric of society. Protestantism would introduce modern ideas into indigenous communities, which they perceived as backward, as barriers to development and progress. Mexico's president Benito Juárez, himself a Zapotec Indian from Oaxaca, even stated, "I would like to see the Indians converted to Protestantism; they need a religion that will teach them to read and not to waste their pennies on candles for the saints."[24] These liberals faced strong opposition from conservative elements in society — the church hierarchy, religious orders, landowners, and most military. Conservatives sought to maintain social, political, and religious stratification in order to preserve traditional values and to solidify their own privileged social positions. They opposed instituting republican forms of government, which they believed would inevitably lead to upheaval.

The ideological divisions between liberals and conservatives produced protracted civil conflict and instability throughout most of Spanish America especially in the first generation after independence.[25] But once liberal governments proved stable during the second half of the nineteenth century, they usually stripped the church of its economic wealth, secularized education, created civil institutions, and endeavored to restrict the role of the church to purely spiritual concerns. In some countries these reforms allowed for separation and divorce, the creation of civil registries, religious toleration, and freedom of the press.[26] Mid-nineteenth-century Mexican liberals, for example, sponsored La Reforma, which secularized and sold church properties. This movement benefited foreign missionaries such as the Methodist Episcopal Church, which was able to acquire the former monastery of San Francisco in Mexico City as its mission headquarters.[27] Ironically, however, because of the lack of funds and teachers for state schools, liberals were forced to accept the continued existence of Catholic schools.

Despite the welcoming atmosphere provided by liberal governments, some intellectuals questioned the role Protestant missionaries should play in society. Mexican liberal and presidential advisor Justo Sierra, for example, expressed appreciation in 1883 for Protestantism's promotion of a strong work ethic, but feared that the missionaries' cultural links to the United States promoted "Americanism," which would lead to further political and economic domination by the United States.[28] This apprehension had been aroused by the pronouncement of the Monroe Doctrine (1823) and exacerbated by the celebration of "Manifest Destiny" as a guiding principle of U.S. expansionism; the war waged by the United States against Mexico (1846–48); the Gadsden Purchase (1853); attempts by the United States to purchase Cuba; American filibusterers in Central America; and later by the so-called Spanish-American War (1898).[29]

Reports written by American Protestant missionaries in Mexico suggest that they did in fact combine secular cultural, political, and economic programs with their religious ideals. They argued that Mexicans needed a strong dose of "American Protestantism" and that close religious ties would benefit both countries economically, as suggested in the 1890 "Monthly Concert of Missions": "Great railroad lines have already crossed the border at different points, and the two countries are bound by a thousand commercial bonds."[30] While U.S. missionaries recognized the suspicion that such ideas aroused, they were nevertheless convinced of the providential nature of their mission. They believed that the advance of Protestantism was part of a long-term shift in the global balance of power from Catholic states to Protestant ones. As the editor of the journal *Missionary Review of the World* observed in 1890, the most powerful countries were no longer Austria, France, and Spain, but rather England, Germany, and the United States.[31] Some missionaries argued that the Monroe Doctrine lent itself to Protestant evangelization in Latin America:

> We have charged ourselves publicly with the obligation of giving to these neighbors the only secret of stability and strength for a free nation. This at least the Christian man dare not refrain from reading into the Monroe doctrine, as in its highest sense, a missionary declaration. By the traditions of the past and the necessities of the present we are more closely bound to Mexico than to any other American nation, and we owe to her on many counts a pure faith and a Bible for all.[32]

The initial goal of these missionaries was to convert the elites, and they assumed that once the elites were converted, the lower orders would follow. But the traditional, thoroughly conservative elites were not drawn to Protestantism and would not have contemplated such a conversion. Even liberals, though they resented the power of the institutional church and shared Protestant values of education, individualism, and republicanism, still retained a nominal allegiance to Catholicism. Though anticlerical and resentful of the prominent role that the church played in society, they were not hostile to Catholicism as such.

Nineteenth-century Latin American liberals were actually most enthusiastic about the ideas of a contemporary European utopian thinker, the French philosopher and sociologist Auguste Comte (1798–1857). Comte's doctrine of positivism taught that only a scientific approach could solve the problems of society, once order was established there. In Latin America, as elsewhere, these ideas fused with the social Darwinism articulated by Herbert Spencer (1820–1903) and resulted in the formulation of racial doctrines that devalued indigenous peoples and cultures and often resulted in their political and social repression.[33]

U.S. Protestant missionaries and Latin American liberal governing elites shared these views about human and societal development. While they believed that indigenous populations could theoretically benefit from acculturation into the more "modern" values of Protestantism, most mission societies did not aim to work among that population. Missionaries perceived those exhibiting fewer European traits as more difficult to reach, and the more "Indian" a person, the more rooted in Catholic practices and beholden to Catholic clergy. The following statement by missionary Melinda Rankin illustrates the positivist, "scientific" approach to social analysis:

> Aside from the demoralizing influence of Romanism, the Mexicans are simple, inoffensive people. Being a mixture of races, we find characteristics which scarcely exist in any other nation of people. Probably the Indian element predominated, as their habits correspond more with that race; yet there are exhibited many distinctive traits of Spanish character. Sometimes a very favorable combination is observed, where the cold blood of the Indian is happily blended with the hot blood of the Spaniard. Mexicans are found [to be] of calculating mind with quick and ingenious penetration, whom, if born and reared under other circumstances, might have become lights unto the world.... Unlike the North American Indians, they are easily made subjects of others.[34]

In order to establish a coherent procedure for achieving the goals of evangelization, missionaries first identified three groups of people: (1) those dissatisfied with their economic and social condition and open to a new faith; (2) a larger group of practicing Catholics who actively supported the church and its activities; and (3) the vast majority of the population who seldom attended church but were unwilling to question their allegiance to their ancestral faith.[35] Missionaries focused their attention on members of the first group, found especially in areas of economic and social transition, who generally believed that their political participation was stymied by traditional elites. This group comprised what missionaries termed the "nascent middle class" and scholars called "the amorphous middle strata."[36] In other words, potential converts included small-scale merchants, advanced students, teachers, doctors, bureaucrats, lawyers, and other urban professionals.[37] These groups would value Protestantism's message of the importance of the individual and education and could be confident about their future role in society. An 1890 report from *Missionary Review of the World* suggests this:

> The old bonds are yielding and breaking away. The abolition of slavery, the surrender of class privileges, the spread of republican ideas, closer contact with Protestant civilization, and the necessities of material improvement and development of natural resources, are influences working together to bring forward the despised laboring man to a new position of importance and power. Here, then, is our second strategic point, *Get hold of the middle class,* for it is destined to play an important, if not a leading part in the future history of Spanish America.[38]

For Protestant missionaries, establishing a successful mission mandated the erection of church buildings, the founding of schools and hospitals, the distribution of Bibles, the training of native-born ministers, and the publication of Spanish-language newsletters that included sections on morals and ethics. Missionaries viewed the strengthening of Christian character as an integral part of general education. Converts were to be educated to become better Christians and witnesses for Christ, to qualify for well-paid jobs in business and the professions, and to serve as role models for further recruitment, as stated in the following 1891 statement from *The Encyclopedia of Missions:*

> But long experience…proves that Christian education is not only a valuable adjunct or complement to evangelistic effort — it is itself a means of evangelism. *First,* it prepares the way for the Gospel by undermining the old systems.…*Second,* Christian education is indispensable to the highest type of Christianity. Men have had saving faith in Christ while in a state of utter illiteracy and ignorance; but their influence as Christians will be narrow and their usefulness restricted. They must have training in the various branches of learning to fit them to be exponents and propagators of Christianity in the various spheres of life.…*Third,* Christian education is necessary to fit men for business and professional positions in their own country.[39]

Schools and hospitals were especially useful for attracting a wide sector of the population, since these missionary-sponsored institutions were often the only accessible options. Many denominations established presses for publishing newspapers as well as instructional material, as the following report from a Congregational missionary in Mexico in 1884 noted: "Since February, a small weekly paper has been published with an exposition of the Sabbath-school lesson, and a few simple stories of a moral and religious character."[40] Protestant youth clubs and organizations also played an important role in cities undergoing urbanization and economic development.[41]

Missionaries established schools at the kindergarten, elementary, preparatory, and collegiate levels. Classes at the kindergarten and elementary levels were usually day schools while boys and girls sometimes boarded at preparatory schools. Men in theological seminaries took coursework in Bible studies, theology, medicine, and industrial arts, and usually undertook practical field training. Women more typically went to normal or teacher-training schools (and men were allowed to attend these schools in some countries). By 1891 missionaries in Mexico had established 123 elementary schools, 24 "higher or special educational institutions," 5 hospitals and dispensaries, and 7 publishing houses or printing establishments.[42]

While preaching and leadership positions in missions were restricted to men, women played important roles in evangelization and education in nineteenth-century Protestant missionary movements. Stereotypes of women in the United

States and in Latin America as nurturers and caretakers helped them to establish a foothold in the teaching profession, as well as becoming "bible women."[43] Missionaries also viewed female converts to Protestantism as especially important since child rearing, they assumed, would aid in the transfer of religious culture to the next generation.[44] Ambitious female missionaries recognized that teaching provided one of the few and satisfying career options for women. "As teaching is really the only avenue open to the women by which they can earn enough to be above want," noted the writer of one missionary report, "we saw that our opportunity had come to prove to the people that we were ready, as far as possible, to meet this deeply felt need."[45] Anglo and Latin American bible women could also enter homes and interact with women, a sphere in which male ministers were frequently restricted or prohibited. Methodist Bishop R. K. Hargrove discussed the role of female missionaries in *The Methodist Review* (1896). While he prefaced his remarks with "There is nowhere in the Old Testament nor in the New an indication that God intended woman for priestly or ministerial functions," he also contended that

> it is foreign to the spirit and intent of [Scriptures and our church] to depreciate or discount womanhood and its important relation to the Church of God and the salvation of the world. Woman's relation to the Church is in perfect analogy and agreement with her relation to man.... Woman has been conspicuous in her devotion to Christ and his Church. Full two-thirds of his followers on earth today are of that sex... and that too without recognition as an office-bearer in the organized body.[46]

Women's missionary boards in the United States played an important role in funding and staffing mission schools and charitable organizations in Latin America. They trained and provided salaries to young Anglo women interested in evangelizing in Latin America and held fundraisers to establish schools for girls in the region. The Women's Board of the Episcopal Church South, for example, funded various educational opportunities for students in Mexico, such as those in Saltillo (1888), Durango (1889), San Luis Potosí (1890), Chihuahua (1892), Guadalajara (1893), and Mexico City (1897).[47] Carrie Carnahan, in her report to the Women's Board of Missions of the Methodist Episcopal Church in 1913, noted that additional schools had been established throughout Mexico and other Latin American countries such as Uruguay, Argentina, and Peru, some becoming financially self-sufficient.[48]

As suggested by some of the cities listed above, the spread of Protestant missions close to the Mexican–U.S. border proved especially successful. The American Baptist Missionary Society (1870), Cumberland Presbyterian Board (1872), Associate Reformed Presbyterian Church of the South (1880), Southern Baptist Convention

(1880), Christian Missions (1890), Seventh-Day Adventists (including the International Medical and Benevolent Association, 1894), and the Christian Woman's Board of Missions (1897) established themselves in northern Mexico during the final decades of the nineteenth century.[49] By 1900 fifteen different U.S. Protestant denominations had missions within Mexico alone, though the number of Protestant converts represented less than 1 percent of the total population. An 1891 report in *The Encyclopedia of Missions* stated that there were 22,010 "Professing Christians" in Mexico and 66,069 in Central and South America. This same source claimed 424 "Places of Regular Worship" in Mexico and another 480 in Central and South America.[50] Most converts in Mexico became members of the Presbyterian Church North and South, the Methodist Episcopal Church and ME Church South, the Congregationalists (ABCFM), or the Southern Baptist Convention. Those converts in Central and South America joined the Moravian Missions, the ME Church, the Presbyterian Church North and South, or the African Methodist Episcopal Church.

A final consideration of one of the major concerns and successes of liberal governments as the nineteenth century drew to a close will end this brief survey on a note of irony. Protestant missionaries became increasingly aware of the general trend toward educational reform in Latin America, recognizing the greater number of schools available to the public, more government funding, and more teaching supplies. But in spite of positive comments in Protestant journals regarding these efforts by various liberal governments, some missionaries became concerned with the total absence of religious instruction in the new secular curriculum. One 1892 report noted the benefits of secularized education in Mexico, but also commented on its shortcoming: "The system of public education recently adopted and made obligatory throughout the Republic is admirable, except that it is purely rationalistic."[51] Ironically, therefore, while the separation of church and state had paved the way for the entrance of Protestantism into most Latin American countries, Protestant missionaries shared the same frustrations as Catholics at the lack of emphasis in the curriculum on ethics and morals, as traditionally understood by Christians.

Despite these misgivings, however, nineteenth-century Protestant missionaries believed that the spiritual and political influence of Catholicism was waning, and that Catholicism itself was becoming obsolete in a modern world. These perceptions resonated with the liberal elites in Latin America as they endeavored to distance their nations from their colonial pasts and to integrate their economies into the world market. These elites viewed Protestantism, with its emphasis on education and individualism and its historic fostering of the entrepreneurial spirit that so animated Protestant nations, as a valuable ally in their move toward modernization. For the popular sectors, however, loyalty to the Catholic Church remained strong while advance of mainline Protestant churches continued weak.

Liberal elites and Protestant missionaries would not see their visions fulfilled until the dramatic surge of evangelical Protestantism in the late twentieth century.

Notes

1. "Opportunity and Acceptance," *The Church at Home and Abroad* [*CHA*] (March 1887): 265.

2. J. Milton Green, "Mexico's Twofold Curse," *Missionary Review of the World* [*MRW*] (March 1893): 204.

3. "Annual Report," American Board of Commissions of Foreign Missions [ABCFM] (1873): 110.

4. ABCFM (1873): 111.

5. ABCFM (1874): 93.

6. ABCFM (1874): 94; The Mexican government's response was immediate and resulted in the conviction and punishment of the participants, including the execution of some of its leaders. See the *American Journal of International Law, volume I, part I* (New York: Baker, Voorhis and Company, 1907): 5–6. This source erroneously cites Watkins as the victim of the attack.

7. *CHA* (May 1895): 439. Apparently, Protestants were not above using the same tactics. For example, in 1898 a Presbyterian missionary in Guerrero, Mexico, reported a "unique method" of ensuring conversion to Protestantism: a local landowner with extensive holdings would tell prospective tenants that they could rent land from him on the condition that they would convert to Protestantism within a year. If they failed to do so, they would be evicted. See *CHA* (October 1898): 312. President Porfirio Díaz ordered the governor of Coahuila to rescind the law requiring that Protestant converts pay five dollars for professing their religious affiliation.

8. "No Protestants in My Parishioners' Homes," quoted in *Religion in Latin America: A Documentary History,* ed. Lee M. Penyak and Walter J. Petry (Maryknoll, N.Y.: Orbis Books, 2006), 192 (insert).

9. For additional information on the Great Awakening, its impact on a variety of Protestant denominations, and the emphasis on missions to North American Indians and blacks, see J. William T. Youngs, *The Congregationalists* (New York: Greenwood Press, 1990); William W. Sweet, *Revivalism in America: Its Origin, Growth and Decline* (New York: Scribner's Sons, 1944); and John F. Thornbury, *God Sent Revival: The Story of Asahel Nettleton and the Second Great Awakening* (Grand Rapids: Evangelical Press, 1977). For an outline of the eighteenth-century missionary effort and its influence on the leaders of the nineteenth-century missionary movement, as well as work among North American indigenous peoples, see "Moravian Mission," *Methodist Quarterly Review* [*MQR*] 15, no. 2 (July 1893): 243–56.

10. Other missionaries argued that increased Mexican emigration to the United States demanded that Protestants re-Christianize Latin America, lest the ills of Mexican Catholicism contaminate U.S. society. See "Monthly Concert of Missions," *MRW* (March 1889): 224–25.

11. "Christian Missions and the Highest Use of Wealth," *MRW* (January 1892): 11–23; "Mexico as a Mission Field," *MRW* (March 1895): 198–202; "Missions in Papal Europe," *MRW* (August 1890): 625.

12. Melinda Rankin, *Twenty Years among the Mexicans* (Cincinnati: Chase & Hall, 1875), 22.

13. Isaac F. Holton, *New Granada: Twenty Months in the Andes* (New York: Harper & Brothers Publishers, 1857), 180.

14. Ibid., 181.

15. Robert Walsh, *Notices of Brazil in 1828 and 1829,* vol. 1 (Boston: Richardson, Lord, & Holbrook et al., 1831): 203–4.

16. Ibid., 367–69.

17. "Mission: Reconnaissance," quoted in Penyak and Petry, *Religion in Latin America,* 184.

18. John Lloyd Stephens, *Incidents of Travel in Yucatán* (Norman: University of Oklahoma Press, 1962), 1:126.

19. Ibid., 1:137.

20. Ibid., 1:137–38.

21. James Fletcher and D. P. Kidder, *Brazil and Brazilians* (New York: AMS Press, 1867), 155.

22. Stephens, *Incidents of Travel in Yucatán,* 1:173.

23. Ibid., 1:174.

24. Benito Juárez quoted in Justo Sierra, *The Political Evolution of the Mexican People* (Austin: University of Texas Press, 1969), 348.

25. The case of Brazil was much different from its Spanish American counterparts. Its relatively easy transition from colony to independent empire was coupled with an extraordinary degree of political, economic, and social continuity. As such, Brazil generally escaped the civil conflicts of its neighbors. This absence of ideological disputes also contributed to the more receptive atmosphere for Protestants coming into that country. See Leslie Bethell, "Independence of Brazil," in *Brazil: Empire and Republic, 1822–1930,* ed. Leslie Bethell (Cambridge: Cambridge University Press, 1989), 42.

26. Conservative factions remained in control throughout much of the nineteenth century in Guatemala, Nicaragua, El Salvador, Ecuador, and Paraguay. David Bushnell and Neill Macaulay, *The Emergence of Latin America in the Nineteenth Century* (New York: Oxford University Press, 1994); Richard N. Sinkin, *The Mexican Reform, 1855–1876: A Study in Liberal Nation-Building* (Austin: University of Texas Press, 1979).

27. William Butler, *Mexico Coming into the Light: Mexico in Transition from the Power of Political Romanism to Civil and Religious Liberty* (New York: Eaton and Mains, 1907): 287–90. This property was sold to Methodist missionaries after Mexican politicians first sold the building to a theater company.

28. Sierra, "Polémica sobre la instrucción obligatoria," *La Libertad* (Mexico City) (March 6, 1883), and "Americanismos," *La Libertad* (Mexico City) (December 22 and 27, 1883) reprinted in *Obras Completas,* vol. 8 (Mexico City: Universidad Nacional Autónoma de Mexico, 1948), 114, 133–39.

29. Ronald Takaki, *Iron Cages, Race and Culture in 19th-Century America* (New York: Oxford University Press, 1979); Joseph Smith, *The United States and Latin America: A History of American Diplomacy, 1776–2000* (New York; Routledge, 2005), 28–32.

30. "Monthly Concert of Missions," *MRW* (March 1890): 228.

31. "Foreign Missions in the Seventeenth and Eighteenth Centuries," *MRW* (February 1890): 260.

32. "Mexico, Her Need and Our Duty," *MRW* (March 1896): 177.

33. Leopoldo Zea, *The Latin American Mind* (Tulsa: University of Oklahoma Press, 1963); Leopoldo Zea, *Positivism in Mexico* (Austin: University of Texas Press, 1974); Charles Hale, *The Transformation of Liberalism in Late Nineteenth-Century Mexico* (Princeton, N.J.: Princeton University Press, 1990); Robert H. Jackson, *The Liberals, the Church, and Indian Peasants: Corporate Lands and the Challenge of Reform in Nineteenth-Century Spanish America* (Albuquerque: University of New Mexico Press, 1997).

34. Rankin began distributing Bibles in 1863 along the U.S.-Mexican border before any concerted missionary efforts began. She later extended her work further into northern Mexico. Rankin, *Twenty Years among the Mexicans,* 206.

35. Edwin Bliss, *A Concise History of Missions* (New York: Fleming H. Revell, 1897), 265–66.

36. Deborah Baldwin, *Protestants and the Mexican Revolution: Missionaries, Ministers, and Social Change* (Urbana and Chicago: University of Illinois Press, 1990), 53–54.

37. Baldwin, *Protestants and the Mexican Revolution,* especially 52–60; Jean-Pierre Bastian, *Breve historia del Protestantismo en América Latina* (Mexico City: Casa Unida de Publicaciones, 1986).

38. "General Missionary Intelligence: South America — Strategic Points," *MRW* (August 1890): 608.

39. Rev. Edwin Bliss, ed., *The Encyclopedia of Missions* (New York: Funk & Wagnalls, 1891), 220 (emphasis in original).

40. *ABCFM* (1884): 75–76.

41. Baldwin, *Protestants and the Mexican Revolution,* especially 34–52; Jean Meyer, *Historia de los cristianos en América Latina, Siglos XIX y XX,* trans. Tomás Segovia (Mexico City: Editorial Vuelta, 1989).

42. Comparable statistics for Central and South America include: 175 elementary schools, 27 higher or special educational institutions, 4 hospitals, and 9 publishing houses. See Bliss, *The Encyclopedia of Missions,* 840.

43. Dana L. Robert, *American Women in Mission: A Social History of Their Thought and Practice* (Macon, Ga.: Mercer University Press, 1996) for a thorough discussion of women's missionary theory and practice especially in Asia and Africa.

44. "The Spiritual Movements of the Century — Woman's Work at Home and Abroad," *MRW* (September 1897): 646.

45. See this missionary report sent to the Woman's Board of the Methodist Episcopal Church South, in 1893 and found in Sara Estelle Haskins, *Women and Missions* (Nashville: ME Church South, 1920), 141.

46. *MR* (March–April 1896): 5–7.

47. Haskins, *Women and Missions,* 134–60.

48. Carrie Carnahan, "Women's Work in Latin Lands," *Conference on Missions in Latin America* (New York: Foreign Missions Conference of North America, 1913): 123–29.

49. While some British missionaries operated in Latin America, most did so under U.S. mission boards. For a list of denominations operating in Latin America at the end of the nineteenth century, see Bliss, *The Encyclopedia of Missions.*

50. Bliss, *The Encyclopedia of Missions,* 840.

51. *CHA* (March 1892): 234.

10

"Like a Mighty Rushing Wind"

The Growth of Protestantism
in Contemporary Latin America

VIRGINIA GARRARD-BURNETT

The conventional wisdom holds that Latin America has always been inextricably "Catholic" in religion, culture, and worldview, and to some extent, this is still true. Latin America today remains overwhelmingly Catholic. In 2006 there were an estimated 490 million Roman Catholics in Latin America, making the region home to more Catholics than any other part of the world. Yet Protestantism, specifically Pentecostalism, has been making significant gains in Latin America during the last forty years, becoming what is arguably the single most important social movement to sweep though the region in the late twentieth and early twenty-first centuries. Such a claim may appear extreme, but consider the following: there are more than twenty times as many members in one large metropolitan Pentecostal church in Guatemala City (15,000) than there are Catholic priests (644) in the entire country.[1] In El Salvador, ten times more people converted to Protestant churches during the 1980s than were killed during that nation's civil war (1980–92). There were more Protestants in Nicaragua during the Sandinista decade than there were members of Catholic Christian base communities (CEBs). Or ponder this: one study found that in the mid-1990s, some ten thousand Brazilian Catholics abandoned the Catholic Church *per day*, mostly to become Protestants, known in Brazil and elsewhere as *evangélicos* or, simply, *crentes* (believers).[2]

A little more than a century ago, there were some fifty thousand Protestants in all Latin America, a figure made up exclusively of foreigners — English Anglicans, German Lutherans, and the occasional wandering Mennonites — who happened to live and worship in that part of the world. By 1995, in contrast, a reliable study estimated that 40 million Protestants were spread across Latin America, the vast majority of whom belonged to independent Pentecostal denominations.[3] Brazil, in particular, offers a striking case of religious transformation. In 1950, its population surpassed that of Italy, making Brazil the largest Catholic country in the world. During the next three decades, however, evangelical religion began its expansion, so that the 1980 census reflected, for the first time in the history of the Brazilian census, that less than 90 percent of the population claimed to be Catholic. By the time of Pope Benedict XIV's May 2007 visit, Brazil's Catholic population had reached an all-time low of 74 percent.[4] By contrast, between 1970 and 2007, Protestantism increased from 5.2 percent to 16.2 percent, a numerical increase of more than 22 million people.[5] While Brazil today is the largest Catholic country in the world, it is also, numerically speaking, one of the largest Protestant nations as well.

Other Latin Americans nations besides Brazil claim sizeable Protestant populations. Guatemala, for example, one of the first countries in Latin America to experience what political scientist Roland Ebel has called a "Protestant awakening," is just over one-third Protestant, while Chile and El Salvador are both about one-quarter Protestant. Other countries, however, can be considered staunchly Catholic. This is especially true of Mexico, a nation where, despite a long tradition of anticlerical legislation and anti-Catholic government policies, the population has maintained a fervent devotion to a popular Catholicism. According to the 1990 census, Protestants represented less than 10 percent of the population, while 88 percent identified themselves as Catholic in 2000.[6] But even in the case of a highly "Catholic" country like Mexico, deep pockets of Protestantism can be found in critical areas; Chiapas, for example, is heavily Protestant, with some indigenous *municipios* claiming nearly total Protestant homogeneity.[7] According to Mexico's Instituto Nacional Indigenista, only 54 percent of the indigenous population of Chiapas is Catholic; the other 46 percent is primarily *evangélico*.[8] A similar pattern is evident for a Catholic citadel like Ecuador, where, though the national total is only 3 percent Protestant, nearly the entire populations of several northern Andean villages have reportedly converted to the Church of Jesus Christ of Latter-day Saints (Mormons).[9]

What is perhaps most remarkable about this movement — and it does seem valid to refer to Protestant conversion as a social as well as a religious movement — is its existence as a phenomenon only since 1960, a period when many social scientists were distracted by other types of social and political currents — Marxism, authoritarianism, dependency theory, praetorianism, developmentalism, even radical Catholicism — that seemed to many academics to be more intellectually engaging, and perhaps, even more "authentic" to the Latin American experience than Protestantism. Yet hidden in plain sight, Protestantism has engaged "ordinary" Latin Americans more than any of these other "isms." Failure to consider the movement perhaps stems less from its apparent small impact than its aesthetic: as David Stoll, whose 1990 *Is Latin America Turning Protestant?* was a pioneering work on this subject, once remarked, "No one who loves Latin America goes there to see nondescript little concrete churches with loudspeakers blasting out 'Onward Christian Soldiers.'"

Protestantism traditionally does have a strong North Atlantic and North American cachet. As we will discuss, the implications of conversion are indeed great in societies where a Catholic worldview has long prevailed. Moreover, Protestantism was introduced into Latin America by forces that have been traditionally hostile to the Hispanic experience. It is not insignificant that British pirates taken before the Spanish colonial Inquisition two centuries ago were tried as heretics rather than as thieves, rapists, and murderers.[10] But the Protestant presence in Latin America — the "invasion of the sects" as it is still sometimes referred to by hostile observers, including the late Pope John Paul II — really began in the second half of the nineteenth century, during an era of enormous expansion of U.S. political and economic influence in Latin America and the Caribbean. During this period, North American and, to a lesser extent, British missionaries of the historical denominations of the Reformation, often called "mainline denominations," such as the Methodists and Presbyterians, came to the region bearing a message of salvation that was deeply imbedded in the cultural norms and behaviors of Victorian society and wrapped in the flag of political imperialism. Foreign Bible societies and Protestant missionaries, most originating in Great Britain and later the United States, worked in Latin America from the nineteenth century onward but generally failed in their efforts to convert a significant number of Latin American Catholics to Protestantism.

Presbyterian, Methodist, Quaker, and Baptist missionaries, many of whom equated the Protestant religion with social and economic development, produced an extensive network of mission-run schools, clinics, hospitals, and literacy programs throughout the region.[11] In some countries, for example Mexico, Guatemala, and Peru, the liberal governments of the late nineteenth century actively encouraged Protestant educational initiatives to replace Catholic parochial education.[12] The Anglican and Lutheran churches also expanded in Latin America in the late nineteenth century, ministering primarily to expatriate populations. This was particularly true after the 1910 World Missionary Conference held in Edinburgh discouraged Anglicans from proselytizing in Roman Catholic countries but also led to the eventual formation of the foremost international ecumenical Protestant organization, the World Council of Churches. While liberal and positivist leaders in the last decades of the nineteenth century often welcomed Protestant missionaries as harbingers of modernity and counterweights to Catholic political power — as evidenced by Benito Juárez's earlier *sub rosa* remark that North American missionaries might "teach Indians to read rather than light candles" — it is little wonder that the population at large tended vigorously to reject both the foreigners and their alien (and for them, alienating) message.

Thus, despite the long and diligent efforts of missionaries, Protestantism did not take root in any significant way among the local populations in Latin America until the second half of the twentieth century. This is not to say that missionary work went unnoticed during the earlier period. To the contrary, mission-run hospitals and clinics were among the first to bring then modern medicine to much of Latin America, and mission schools educated a generation of future statesmen and leaders, including, but by no means limited to, the radical Peruvian political theorist Raúl Haya de la Torre, Mexican statesman Moisés Sáenz, and Guatemala's progressive president Jacobo Arbenz. Yet despite the missions' influence in establishing schools, clinics, etc., they largely failed in their primary goal, which was to evangelize and convert the people of Latin America. Although missionaries consoled themselves by turning to the parable of the sower of seeds that would someday be "ripe for the harvest," by the late 1950s, not a single Latin American nation had a Protestant minority larger than 5 percent of the native population, and in many places it was less than 2 percent.

The limited successes in conversion notwithstanding, the historic Protestant missions were a permanent fixture in Latin American society by the mid-twentieth century, their institutional presence, evinced in hospitals and schools, evident in every major city in the region. However, the fate of mission work in Latin America for the mainline denominations by mid-century seemed in some ways to be tenuous. By the late 1940s and 1950s, the pioneering missionaries, whose zeal and confidence had begun to decline, were replaced by a new generation of workers who had begun to seriously question the methodologies and motives of their predecessors, especially their unchallenged equation of Protestant mission work and "modernity." Younger missionaries found the paternalistic language and Victorian worldview of old school mission work to be no longer relevant enough to withstand a series of contemporary challenges.[13] These included rising nationalism, increased political activism (especially from the Left), and emerging anti-imperialism within the host countries. The wholesale expulsion of Christian missionaries from China in the wake of the Maoist revolution in the late 1940s served as a wake-up call for foreign missionaries working in all parts of the world. While the Latin American mission field temporarily benefited from the Chinese expulsions (as funds and personnel originally destined for Asia were diverted instead to the region), Mao's ability to shut down virtually overnight what had once been the largest mission field in the world offered clear warning that the missions needed to devise new methods and strategies to cope with the rising tide of Marxist and nationalistic revolutions.

The mainline denominations found one solution in the nationalization of their work: new administrative structures established in-country so that churches could be accountable to a local *iglesia nacional* instead of to a U.S.-based Board of Foreign Missions. This meant that each in-country denomination would become technically autonomous from its parent denomination in the United States, with leadership of the "national church" given to local administrators and pastors. In reality, the "national churches" tended to maintain close ties to the parent denomination, and many — even in the early twenty-first century — still depend on the U.S. denomination for at least some of their funding, training, and personnel.[14]

Because it often took place somewhat prematurely or under duress, in many cases the nationalization of missions proved to be a mixed success. Cuba, after the triumph of Fidel Castro's revolution in 1959, provides a good example. Cuba had been widely evangelized after the 1898 Spanish-American War; indeed, between 1898 and 1900, more than two dozen denominations sent missionaries to the island. Virtually all the denominations (with one exception, the Quakers), were from mainline Protestant groups — Methodists, Presbyterians, Baptists, and Episcopalians. The Cuban missions were unusually well supported, since many American policy makers and ordinary citizens considered missionaries to be a "third force" of U.S. interests in Cuba (along with the military and business), a vanguard poised to provide Cubans with the religious and cultural components of a general "civilizing mission."

By the mid 1930s, pressed by economic concerns, by the new mandates of the Good Neighbor Policy, and especially by emerging Cuban nationalism, the missions began to adopt a program of "indigenization" (early, for such an initiative), in which they gradually turned the running of the schools over to educated Cuban leaders. As part of indigenization, the home mission boards continued to closely monitor, support, and to some extent, control the Cuban Protestant institutions, but the churches nonetheless began to develop a local identity and leadership. By the late 1940s, Protestant work — including actual church attendance — had grown dramatically, especially in the eastern part of the country. By the early 1950s, Cuba had one of the largest Protestant populations and the most indigenized Protestant church establishment of any country in Latin America.[15]

Because they were already innovators and outside the conventional venues of power, Cuban Protestants were among some of the early supporters of the Revolution. Even today the government-sanctioned Cuban Council of Churches, a Protestant body, continues to endorse the regime. Yet what could potentially have been a symbiotic relationship between Protestant churches and the new communist government quickly soured, to the lasting detriment of the missionary denominations. The revolutionary government's early ideological opposition to religion resulted in the arrest and detention of active Christians (including Catholics) in reeducation camps in the early 1960s. The repression of religion, combined with the Cuban churches' isolation from their home denominations, has meant that even in Cuba, a former "success story," the mainline denominations have not fared well. In the early twenty-first century, Christianity is on the rise again in Cuba, but primarily among Pentecostals and Catholics, and only to a lesser extent within the historic Protestant churches.[16]

In a few other countries, however, the national churches took root and have become fully vibrant and independent entities, with only slender ecclesial ties to the original missionary denomination. In 1997, for example, the Anglican (Episcopal) Church of Central America severed its subordinate status as a missionary province of the American Episcopal Church to form the autonomous Iglesia Anglicana de la Región de Centro América, a title that indicates the church's full and independent status within the worldwide Anglican communion.[17] To some extent, the full separation of the Central American Anglican church from its missionary mother church reflects a fissure that is common today between the heritage churches of Latin America and their U.S. missionary counterparts. Such divisions, sometimes formal and sometimes not, occur because, as elsewhere in the developing world, Latin American churches, even of the historic denominations, tend to be significantly more theologically and socially conservative than their North American counterparts.[18]

As Philip Jenkins has shown in his recent work, Christians in the "global South" (Latin America included) tend to read the Bible literally and use it as a central guide for informing their behavior, moral outlook, and lifestyle.[19] Without doubt, one the great legacies of missionary work is Bible translation, enabling believers to read and interpret the Bible in their own language (not only Spanish and Portuguese, but also indigenous languages). Latin American Protestants believe this grants them full privileges as Christians. One scholar notes that people who have a Bible in their own language "have as much claim to it as does the nation that first brought it to them."[20] As the Episcopal case shows, this sense of hermeneutical authenticity can and sometimes does cause the historic mainline Protestant churches of Latin America to differentiate themselves from their sister churches in the global North, where Christians are more likely to contextualize their behavior and reading of the Bible in light of modern theology and scholarship, and position it within contemporary society.[21]

But the real growth of Protestantism within Latin America in recent decades has not taken place in the historic mainline denominations, and the 1960s are a pivotal aspect of the Protestant story in Latin America. In the wake of the success of the Cuban Revolution in 1959, a new type of missionary from North America began to operate in Latin America, promoting Protestantism as a "spiritual alternative to communism." In the early 1960s, a variety of new nondenominational Protestant agencies, usually based in Latin America but often financed from the United States, began elaborate "salvation campaigns" across the two continents. Among the largest of these proselytizing groups, Latin American Mission (LAM), along with its imitators, utilized for the first time the latest advertising and telecommunications techniques, including stadium-size revivals, door-to-door evangelism based on market research, the extensive use of radio and, to a lesser extent, television to spread their message. It is worth noting that this saturation marketing came at a time when the Catholic Church was suffering from a severe shortage of clergy. Thus, due to a favorable convergence of sociological, political, and even spiritual factors, the efforts of such interdenominational agencies quickly bore fruit and, by the middle of the decade, and for the first time, locally run Protestant churches began to sprout in the urban slums and rural villages of Latin America.

This effort coincided with the massive social and political dislocations that affected so many countries in the region during the same period: population explosions and "demographic inversions" occurred in which the rural populations began their large-scale exodus to Latin America's burgeoning cities; antigovernment insurrections and counterinsurgencies were initiated; and economic developmental programs transformed peasants into low-paid workers or the unemployed. So powerful and transformative were these changes that one anthropologist has referred to them as "a bombardment of twentieth century forces."[22] Added to this were profound sea changes within the Mother Church: the Second Vatican Council and emergence of liberation theology — which within Latin America transformed ordinary Catholics from fatalists to activists and shifted the focus of the church from the hereafter to the here and now. One additional aspect of Vatican II, little noticed in Latin American scholarly circles at the time, was a new spirit of ecumenism, for, in Vatican II, the Roman Catholic Church first recognized Protestants as "separated brethren" rather than heretics. For future converts, the distinction was critical, for it inadvertently provided a means by which Catholics could expose themselves to other faiths without fear of losing their place in the kingdom of heaven.[23]

The "radicalization" of the Catholic Church in the 1970s and 1980s has led many to the not incorrect assumption that the growth of Protestantism is tied inextricably to politics. At the most facile level, this model pits Catholic progressives against conservative *evangélicos*, who receive money and support from the Christian Right in the United States. There is ample evidence of this sort of collusion, a notorious example taking place in Guatemala in the early 1980s. There, born-again general Efraín Ríos Montt, claiming he ruled by the will of God and with substantial financial support from U.S. televangelist Pat Robertson, presided over an eighteen-month scorched-earth sweep of the highlands to rout those whom he called "the Anti-Christ, the communists." Ríos Montt's crusade left tens of thousands dead, most of them indigenous and Catholic activists.[24] In a case such as this, Guatemalans could hardly be blamed for assuming that there was at least a modicum of safety in Protestant churches, which as a rule tended to subscribe to the biblical injunction to "submit to the authorities in power" (Rom. 13:1) and to shun political action of any kind.[25]

Although Guatemala represents only one specific case, there is a substantial body of literature that draws direct parallels between political behavior and religious affiliation. These suggest that Protestant churches in the post 1960s period grew in part because of Cold War era political interests, and that Protestant missions and churches promoted the interests of U.S. foreign policy.[26] This explanation, however reductionist, raises some important issues. First is the question of agency: in this interpretation, Latin Americans are either passive agents in their own religious destiny, or "empty vessels" into which foreign religious and political notions can easily be poured — an idea not at all borne out by the much chronicled resiliency of popular religion throughout Latin America's history from the colonial period onward. Second is the issue of contextual relativity: there is an implicit notion that Protestant religion, when transferred to the Latin American context, retains the same focus, style, and associations that it has in North America or northern Europe. By this definition, a member of the Assembly of God in Atlanta thinks, believes, and acts similarly to a member in highland Guatemala, or the Amazon, or Buenos Aires, or Seoul, Korea, *ad infinitum*. Even taking into account the increasing homogeneity of global culture, a literal transference is not possible, given the subdermal level at which religious beliefs operate. Even Catholicism, whose clergy has gone to great pains throughout its long history to maintain orthodoxy, has nonetheless witnessed fundamental changes in alternative cultural milieus.

Contrary to the notion that Latin American Protestant churches operated under the strict paternalistic control of North American missions, by the late 1960s, they were established, pastored, and attended exclusively by local converts. These indigenous churches quickly took root, and as they branched out, Protestantism began to assume a more Latin face. This is not to say that Protestantism in Latin America today is completely independent of North American evangelicalism; to the contrary, many Latin American churches — especially those that draw their congregations from the urban middle and upper classes — are cheek by jowl with the beliefs and worldviews of North American Christians, especially those of politically conservative evangelical fundamentalists. At the same time, many other Latin American *congregaciones evangélicas*, perhaps even the majority, do not claim missionary origins, and indeed, some of the largest and most influential Protestant denominations in Latin American today, such as Brazil's mega-church, the Igreja Universal do Reino de Deus (which currently has a presence in at least twenty-seven foreign countries, including the United States and Europe), point proudly to their autochthonous origins.[27] Most church growth in Latin America since the 1960s has occurred not in established, historic denominations, but in small splinter churches that have only minimal or no ties at all to traditional Protestant denominations. They are, by design, local in pastorate, custom, and belief, since the pastor usually obtains his insights from his own experience and revelation rather than from formal theological training in some far-off seminary.

The establishment of a new church or denomination requires three essential elements: a leader with a revelation; a congregation of at least one who believes in his revelation; and a place in which to meet.[28] Local churches tend to be theologically idiosyncratic, sometimes to a degree that startles outsiders, who often mistake the austerity of the worship spaces — whether in small houses or in stadium-size sanctuaries — for orthodoxy. Yet given the latitude and heterodoxy of the beliefs that are called "Protestantism" in Latin America, especially in indigenous areas, it should not come as a surprise when Mayan Presbyterians believe that Jesus is raingiver and vanquisher of the evil eye, or that Quichua Pentecostals perform an *acción de gracia* to the life-force, Pachamama, when piercing the earth to plant their corn.[29] This is not to declare that Protestantism is undergoing syncretism — at least not yet — but it does support the simple proposition that Latin American Protestantism is informed by the local views of the ineffable, not by the Ur-images and archetypes of ancient Europe and the Middle East.[30]

Protestant churches almost everywhere in Latin America differ from their North American counterparts on another central point: they are overwhelmingly Pentecostal. According to the 2006 World Christian Database, 73 percent of Latin American Protestants are Pentecostal.[31] To be a Pentecostal is not to belong to a particular denomination, but to subscribe to a particular body of belief that places great emphasis on the power of the Third Entity of the Trinity, the Holy Spirit, who is the major presence in the Book of Acts. Pentecostals believe they must receive "baptism in the Holy Spirit," which is typically manifested by such "signs and wonders" as "speaking in tongues" (glossolalia), miraculous healing, and spirit possession exhibited through dance, shouting, song, or more exotic forms of ecstatic behavior.

Pentecostalism is by no means unique to Latin America; it has its roots in the bitter debates that fractured Western Christianity at the end of the nineteenth century, as modernists and fundamentalists wrestled with the issues of the "higher criticism" of biblical texts and the conflict between faith and science brought to the fore by Darwin's *On the Origin of Species by Means of Natural Selection* (1859) and *Descent of Man* (1871). As a highly emotional practice and a transcendental system of belief, Pentecostalism provided a tonic to those who shunned the modernists' efforts to quantify faith through science.[32] Although Pentecostalism in the United States has historically been popular among subaltern groups such as poor whites, rural Southerners, and African-Americans, it is one of the fastest-growing varieties of Christianity in the United States today, where it draws increasingly from the affluent middle class.[33] Even so, the growth of Pentecostalism in the United States cannot compare with that in Latin America, where upward of three-quarters of all Protestants are Pentecostal.[34] The longstanding tension, dating back to the days of the missionaries, between Pentecostals and mainline Protestants stems as much from competition as from genuine theological differences. As Pentecostalism has become the norm in Latin America, however, many of the traditional denominations have "Pentecostalized" their worship and liturgy to some extent in order to compete effectively in the religious marketplace. This is also true in the Catholic Church, where charismatic worship has far outpaced liberation theology as the dominant movement within that church.

The specific appeal of Pentecostalism raises the larger issue of the cause of Protestant growth in Latin America at this particular time in history. Some of the earliest scholarly analysis of this phenomenon in Latin America is based, not surprisingly, on the work of early sociologists of religion, such as Emile Durkheim and Max Weber. Scholars continue to rely on Durkheim's understanding of Protestantism as a bridge toward secularism as societies become more complex, and especially on Weber's explication of the "elective affinity" between the rise of Protestantism and the development of capitalism.[35] One such classic study is Christian Lalive d'Epinay's *Haven of the Masses*, which examines Protestantism among immigrants in urban Chile in the late 1960s. He suggests that small *evangélico* congregations, with their personalistic and often dictatorial pastors, served the function of "replicating the authoritarianism of the old hacienda system."[36] Another pioneering study by Emilio Willems, *Followers of the New Faith*, analyzes Protestants in both urban and rural Chile and Brazil. He posits that Latin American converts are most likely to be found among people on the cusp of economic transition, such as those who migrate from agrarian to urban areas, usually because of dire economic circumstances.[37]

Bryan R. Roberts (1968), drawing on the determinist views of Lalive and Willems, describes how new immigrants from the countryside utilize Protestant churches as voluntary organizations that enable them to save money and insulate themselves from social ills such as alcoholism and abuse. Sheldon Annis (1989) demonstrates how Indian converts free themselves from "milpa technology," which permits them to save and enter more fully into the capitalist economy, and so allowing them to raise themselves *del suelo a cielo*.[38] An interesting variation on the idea of economic efficacy is Cecília Mariz's study (1994) in which she argues that among Brazilian *favela* dwellers, Protestant (and specifically Pentecostal) religion does not offer any particular material advantage, but does provide believers with certain new psychological strategies and attitudes that help them cope with the reality of their poverty.[39]

Two newer works appeared in 1990 that directly challenge this rather strict economic determinist paradigm: David Stoll's *Is Latin America Turning Protestant? The Politics of Evangelical Growth* and David Martin's *Tongues of Fire: The Explosion of Protestantism in Latin America*. Though different in many ways, each seeks to examine Protestant growth in Latin America from the inside out.[40] They both attempt to understand the kinds of comparative advantage that conversion offers believers from a cultural point of view. Martin is especially concerned with analyzing the kinds of changes — both positive and negative — that occur when the fabric of a society is rewoven and overshot with religious pluralism. These two books spawned a series of monographs that focus on specific aspects of conversion and its cultural impacts: Elizabeth Brusco's wittily entitled *The Reformation of Machismo*, for example, examines how family relations in Colombia are reformed when one member (usually the wife) converts, and family resources generally improve when the husband, because of his promise upon conversion, no longer spends his salary on alcohol or visits violence upon the family.[41] R. Andrew Chesnut, in his study of the Assembly of God in Amazonia, *Born Again in Brazil: The Pentecostal Boom and the Pathogens of Poverty*, takes the gender argument even further, suggesting that in the highly sensualized context of contemporary Brazil, Pentecostal worship assumes an intimate and even erotic quality — this based on the comments of local informants who describe their relationship with God in terms normally associated more with *Eros* than *Agape*.[42]

Other studies examine how Protestantism affects community relations. Historically, the effect of conversion on community and family life has tended to be divisive. While Eric Wolf's half-century old trope of the "close corporate community" may be passé, there is little dispute that the "traditional community" as an integrated social system did once define the countryside of much of Latin America, even if it has now largely ceased to exist in most areas. For some, Protestantism is one of the key culprits in this decline; that is, when people leave the system of *costumbre* that tends to be constructed around Catholic rituals and beliefs, they also abandon the historical patterns of living in community.[43] This abandonment may manifest itself in material ways: Annis's book, for example, suggests that Maya women who are Protestant are not as likely to wear the elaborately woven *huipiles* that have long been the index of Maya identity. In the case of Chiapas, moreover, the perception among traditionalists is that Protestants represent such a negative and divisive threat to the traditional "way of being" that they are systematically and violently forced to flee to the nearby city of San Cristóbal de las Casas. Others suggest that these displaced people have become more likely to join revolutionary groups such as the Zapatistas.[44]

For rural Pentecostals, the abandonment of traditional "ways of being" may well manifest themselves in a manner that indicates fundamental shifts in worldview. According to Annis, Protestant women did not completely stop wearing huipiles, but they were much more likely to wear ones embellished with simple cotton embroidered flowers, not the much more labor-intensive huipiles with ancient motifs woven directly into the cloth. The reason? The thousand-year-old woven designs no longer carried any religious value for Protestant women. And in general, Protestants do not typically participate in the rituals that have historically defined community identity. They do not attend fiestas; they do not drink; they do not belong to religious brotherhoods. They may be systematically excluded from community life, but even more importantly, they exclude themselves. As David Martin notes, for Protestants and Pentecostals in particular, "[their congregation] is its very own fiesta."[45]

I have elsewhere suggested that some Latin Americans choose Protestantism because the old identities that once designated one's place in life fell away over the course of the twentieth century.[46] In Guatemala, ancient verities, though not always appealing, at least placed one solidly and inextricably within a static context. But that context no longer seems genuine: the *patrón* is gone, the *cofradía* is powerless, the young are abroad, and snow peas are planted in the milpa. Even the Catholic Church, the locus of eternal truth, buffeted in some regions by violence against the faithful and challenged by liturgical and theological renovations in others, has changed. In such a context, Protestant churches can provide a new locus of meaning and identity: the new community is one of *hermanos* and *hermanas* and is both geographically smaller and metaphysically larger than the community of old.[47]

While the descriptions of the attractions of Protestantism, and of Pentecostalism in particular, may explain its advance among the rural poor, these descriptions do not account for the expansive gains made by Protestants in Latin America's cities. For this we turn to historian R. Andrew Chesnut's recent work *Competitive Spirits: Latin America's New Religious Economy,* where he offers an understanding of religious conversion in Latin America based on what some have called the "religious supermarket" theory.[48] Building on this rational choice theory first devised by Rodney Stark and Roger Finke, Chesnut devises an economic model for clarifying religious choice in simple terms: consumers of religious goods select from competing "producers."[49] This has resulted in Pentecostalism, with its emphasis on immediacy, experience, and healing, becoming Latin America's most competitive religious product. It provides, as one member of a Brazilian Pentecostal church described it, "a God you can use."[50] The model also helps explain why charismatic Catholicism, which some have called "Catholic Pentecostalism," is also one of the most rapidly expanding faiths in the region in the early twenty-first century.[51]

The most literal example of the market model is the form of Pentecostalism that has grown quickly since the turn of this century in Latin America among the urban middle and upper classes, or at least among the larger sector of people who aspire to those classes. These are the neo-Pentecostals who espouse what is known as "prosperity theology," a belief that God rewards his faithful through good health and material well-being. Although prosperity theology has its origins (and a following) in the United States, some of the theology's most avid proponents are in Latin America.[52] Included among these is the Brazilian Igreja Universal do Reino de Deus (IURD), which has become a significant and controversial force within contemporary Brazilian culture, especially in the media.[53] Unlike the first generation of Pentecostal churches in Latin America, the health-and-wealth churches cater to a prosperous and influential constituency and have brought Pentecostalism out of the shadows of rural poverty. This new generation of aptly named "mega-churches" (the sanctuary of Guatemala City's Fraternidad Cristiana, dedicated in May 2007, for example, has seating for over twelve thousand, making it one the largest Protestant worship spaces in the world)[54] and their influence among Latin Americans with access to money and power strongly suggests that Pentecostalism is becoming a significant social, cultural, economic, and perhaps even political driving force within Latin America.[55]

Although using the religious supermarket approach to explain the expansion of Pentecostalism has its detractors — some of whom believe that its clinical diagnoses and anti-numenist views of religious motivations are demeaning — the model usefully includes a truism of contemporary Latin American religious behavior: once people begin to convert, their religious identities are no longer fixed. In contrast to trends in North America, where church members who leave the religion of their birth are likely to convert only once or twice in their lifetime, Latin Americans who leave the Catholic Church are likely to change their religious affiliation many times, to fit their changing circumstances and perceptions of need.[56] This migration, which Dutch scholar Henri Gooren calls a "conversion career," might actually take a convert from Catholicism through three or four Pentecostal denominations, then to Mormonism or Adventism, and back again to Catholicism.[57] While conversion careers may suggest that Latin American converts are not committed to their latest religion or are spiritually opportunistic, the converts themselves see this movement in a different light. While their self-identification as Christians may not change, Latin American converts are less likely to see a particular church or set of beliefs as a final destination than as a way station where they may linger for a while, before continuing along on their spiritual journey.

The rapid expansion of Protestantism in Latin America in recent decades, then, flatly contradicts the secularization theory, whose pioneers in the discipline of the sociology of religion, from Emile Durkheim to Max Weber to David Martin, and whose secular theorists, including Karl Marx and Antonio Gramsci, all predicted religion's demise in the face of modernity. Instead, Christianity has actually flourished in modern Latin America. This is explained in the relatively recent work of social scientist Philip Jenkins, who argues in *The Next Christendom: The Coming of Global Christianity* that in the twenty-first century, Christianity will be a forceful spiritual, social, and political movement with its locus in the global South (Latin America, Africa, Asia) instead of the global North, where, he believes, historical Christianity, especially in Western Europe, is largely moribund.[58] It is in the global South that Latin America's "new" Christianity — Pentecostal Protestantism — continues to advance rapidly even in an environment of hyper-modernization and globalization by providing order and meaning to lives that might otherwise be overwhelmed by change.

Notes

1. For the Catholic figure, see *www.adherents.com*; the Fraternidad christiana in Mixco (Guatemala City) claims fifteen thousand members. See also *www.frater.org*.

2. Eugene L. Stockwell, "Open and Closed, Protestantism in Latin America," *Christian Century* 112, no. 10 (March 22, 1995): 317. The estimates of Protestant membership come from Patrick. J. Johnstone, *Operation World*, 4th ed. (Bromley, Kent: STL Books and WEC International, 1986), 62, and David Stoll, *Is Latin America Turning Protestant?* (Berkeley: University of California Press, 1990), 335–36.

3. Stockwell, "Open and Closed, Protestantism in Latin America."

4. *www.fgv.br/cps/religioes*.

5. Marcelo Neri, "A ética pentecostal e o declínio católico" (May 2007), *www.fgv.br/cps/religioes*.

6. Instituto Nacional de Estadística, Geografía e Informática: *La diversidad en México XII, Censo General de Población y Vivienda 2000* (Aguascalientes, Mexico: Instituto Nacional de Estadística, Geografía e Informática, 2005).

7. Estados Unidos Mexicanos, *Resumen general tabulados complementarios, XI censos general de la poblacíon y vivienda, 1990* (Mexico City: Instituto Nacional de Estadística, Geografía e Informática, 1993). The regional estimate comes from the Rev. Raúl Ruiz, the Methodist bishop of Chiapas, who estimates that some 980,000 Indians in Chiapas have converted or been born into Protestantism over the past twenty years. See David Luhnow, "Protestant Indians' Lands Taken: The Other War Waging in Chiapas," *San Francisco Chronicle*, January 21, 1994.

8. Enrique Serrano et al., *Indicadores socioeconómicos de los pueblos indígenas de México, 2002* (Mexico City: Instituto Indigenista, 2002).

9. For the purposes of this study, certain groups that claim many adherents in Latin America such as the Church of Jesus Christ of Latter-day Saints (Mormons), the Seventh-Day Adventists, and the Jehovah's Witnesses will be classified as non-Catholic Christian groups, but not as Protestant, and as such they are largely outside the scope of this particular work. Webster's defines "sect" as "a dissenting or schismatic religious body," a definition that, given the autonomy, high level of organizational structure, and well-established theology of all three of these groups, suggests to this writer that they do not merit this designation. Sources on Ecuador include David Stoll, "Estimates of Protestant Representation in Latin America and the Caribbean," in *Is Latin America Turning Protestant?* 333; and Gregory Knapp, unpublished religious mapping project on Ecuador.

10. Gonzalo Báez-Camargo, *Protestantes enjudiciados por la Inquisición en Iberoamérica* (Mexico City: Casa Unida de Publicaciones, 1960).

11. There are several good country-specific studies on this topic. See, for example, Luis Martínez-Fernández, *Protestantism and Political Conflict in the Nineteenth-Century Hispanic Caribbean* (New Brunswick, N.J.: Rutgers University Press, 2002), as well as some of the other works sited in this article.

12. See, for example, Juan Fonseca Arize's excellent account of the influence on Protestant institutions, especially mission schools in Peru. Juan Fonseca Arize, *Protestantismo y modernización en el Perú, 1915–1931* (Lima: Pontificia Universidad Católica del Perú, 2002). There are surprisingly few dispassionate accounts of institution-building by Protestant missionaries in Latin America, but a good recent work is Todd Hatch, *Missionaries of the State: The Summer Institute of Linguistics, State Formation, and Indigenous Mexico, 1935–1985* (Tuscaloosa: University of Alabama Press, 2006).

13. For more on this perspective, see Mark A. Noll, "Evangelical Identity, Power and Culture in the 'Great' Nineteenth Century," in *Christianity Reborn: The Global Expansion of Evangelicalism in the Twentieth Century,* ed. Donald M. Lewis (Grand Rapids: William B. Eerdmans Publishing, 2004), 31–51.

14. The Iglesia Evangélica Presbiteriana de Guatemala provides a good example of some of the challenges and successes that can come with the nationalization of a missionary denomination. See Heinrich Schäfer, *Entre dos fuegos: Una historia socio-política de la Iglesia Presbiteriana de Guatemala* (Guatemala City: CEDEPCA, 2002).

15. Jason M. Yaremko, *U.S. Protestant Missions in Cuba: From Independence to Castro* (Gainesville: University of Florida Press, 2000).

16. Ira Rifkin, "Cuba's Other Christians: Island's Protestant Population Is Climbing," *www.wfn.org/ 1998/01/msg00139.html,* January 30, 1998.

17. With the exception of Costa Rica and Belize, all of Central America was, prior to 1997, part of Province Seven of the American Episcopal Church. The church was introduced into Costa Rica, Belize, and the Miskitu (Atlantic coast) region of Nicaragua not by the American Episcopal Church, but by the British Society for the Propagation of the Gospel, and peoples in these areas were therefore missionized by the British branch of the Anglican communion, the Church of England. The current Anglican Church of Central America is comprised of the dioceses of Guatemala, El Salvador, Nicaragua, Costa Rica, and Panama. See *www.anglicancommunion.org/tour/province.*

18. That said, the Anglican Church of Central America is less conservative than its African counterparts. The Anglican Church of Nigeria under the leadership of Archbishop Peter Akinola demanded that the American Episcopal Church be forced to withdraw from the Anglican Communion because of the Episcopal Church's willingness to consecrate an openly gay bishop in 2003. Although the Central American Church agreed with the Africans that this action was not in keeping with biblical teaching, the bishops took a more moderate position. In May 2007, the Central American bishops met in Panama from whence they issued a letter called the "global center," calling for reconciliation and for the American Episcopal Church's continued membership within the worldwide communion. See *www.alcnoticias.org/artículo.*

19. Philip Jenkins, *The Next Christendom: The Rise of Global Christianity* (New York: Oxford University Press, 2002).

20. See Lamin O. Sanneh, *Translating the Message* (Maryknoll, N.Y.: Orbis Books, 1989); Lamin O. Sanneh, *Encountering the West* (Maryknoll, N.Y.: Orbis Books, 1993), cited in Jenkins, *The New Christendom,* 24.

21. See Philip Jenkins, *The New Faces of Christianity: Believing the Bible in the Global South* (New York: Oxford University Press, 2006), and Jenkins, *The New Christendom.*

22. Sheldon Annis, *God and Production in a Guatemalan Town* (Austin: University of Texas Press, 1987).

23. See Phillip Berryman, *The Religious Roots of Rebellion: Christians in Central America's Revolutions* (Maryknoll, N.Y.: Orbis Books, 1984).

24. See Ricardo Falla, *Massacres in the Jungle: Ixcán, Guatemala, 1975–1982* (Boulder, Colo.: Westview, 1994).

25. See Enrique Domínguez and Deborah Huntington, "The Salvation Brokers: Conservative Evangelicals in Central America," *NACLA* 17, no. 1 (1984): 2–36.

26. See, for example, Søren Hvalkof and Peter Åby, *Is God an American? An Anthropological Perspective on the Missionary Work of the Summer Institute of Linguistics* (Copenhagen: International Work Group for Indigenous Affairs, 1981); Juan Miguel Ganuza, *Las sectas nos invaden* (Santiago: Ediciones Paulinas, 1983).

27. See Ari Pedro Oro, André Corten, Jean-Pierre Dozon, eds. *Igreja Universal do Reino de Deus: Os novos conquistadores da fé* (São Paulo: Paulinas, 2003).

28. The use of the male pronoun is intentional. While women often take active roles in Protestant worship in Latin America, they rarely serve as pastors.

29. David Scotchmer, "Symbols of Salvation: A Local Mayan Protestant Theology," *Missiology* 17, no. 3 (1989): 293–310.

30. See Gary H. Gossen, *Symbol and Meaning beyond the Closed Community: Essays in Meso-american Ideas,* Institute for Mesoamerican Studies, Studies on Culture and Society 1 (Albany: State University of New York, 1986).

31. World Christian Database, cited in "Spirit and Power: A Global Survey of Pentecostal and Charismatic Christians," Pew Forum on Religion and the Public Life, October 2006, *http://pewforum .org/surveys/pentecostal/latinamerica/.*

32. See Donald Dayton, *Theological Roots of Pentecostalism* (New York: Oxford University Press, 1987).

33. See Harvey Cox, *Fire from Heaven: The Rise of Pentecostal Spirituality and the Reshaping of Religion in the Twenty-First Century* (Reading, Mass.: Addison-Wesley, 1995).

34. See Edward L. Cleary and Hannah Stewart-Gambino, *Power, Politics, and Pentecostalism in Latin America* (Boulder, Colo.: Westview Press, 1997).

35. Emile Durkheim, *The Elementary Forms of the Religious Life* (New York: Free Press, 1915); Max Weber, *Protestantism and the Spirit of Capitalism* (London: Allen and Unwin, 1930).

36. Christian Lalive d'Epinay, *Haven of the Masses: A Study of the Pentecostal Movement in Chile* (London: Lutterworth Press, 1969).

37. Emilio Willems, *Followers of the New Faith: Culture, Change, and the Rise of Protestantism in Brazil and Chile* (Nashville: Vanderbilt University Press, 1967).

38. Bryan R. Roberts, "Protestant Groups and Coping with Urban Life in Guatemala," *American Journal of Sociology* 73 (1968): 753–67; Annis, *God and Production in a Guatemalan Town.*

39. Cecília Loreto Mariz, *Coping with Poverty: Pentecostals and Christian Base Communities in Brazil* (Philadelphia: Temple University Press, 1994).

40. Stoll, *Is Latin America Turning Protestant?;* Martin, *Tongues of Fire.*

41. Elizabeth Brusco, *The Reformation of Machismo: Evangelical Conversion and Gender in Colombia* (Austin: University of Texas, 1995).

42. R. Andrew Chesnut, *Born Again in Brazil: The Pentecostal Boom and the Pathogens of Poverty* (New Brunswick, N.J.: Rutgers University Press, 1997).

43. See Duncan Earle, "Authority, Social Conflict, and the Rise of Protestant Religious Conversion in a Mayan Village," *Social Compass* 39, no. 3 (1992): 379–89.

44. Diego Ribaldeneira, "In Mexico's South, a Religious Divide: Non-Catholics, Seen as a Threat to the Social Order, Are Expelled from Majority Maya Towns," *Boston Globe,* February 2, 1994.

45. Martin in Virginia Garrard-Burnett and David Stoll, eds., *Rethinking Protestantism in Latin America* (Philadelphia: Temple University Press, 1993), 285.

46. Virginia Garrard-Burnett and Carlos Garma Navarro, "Protestantism(s) and Mayan World-views in Chiapas and Guatemala in the Context of Civil Violence, *Social Science and Missions/Sciences sociales et missions* 20 (2007): 99–116.

47. Virginia Garrard-Burnett, *Living in the New Jerusalem: A History of Protestants in Guatemala* (Austin: University of Texas Press, 1998).

48. R. Andrew Chesnut, *Competitive Spirits: Latin America's New Religious Economy* (New York: Oxford University Press, 2003), 3–4.

49. Anthony Gill, "The Institutional Limits to Catholic Progressivism: An Economic Approach," *International Journal of Social Economics* 22 (1995): 135–48; and Laurence Iannaccone, "Voodoo

Economics? Reviewing the Rational Approach to Religion," *Rationality and Society* 34, no. 1 (1995): 76–88; Laurence Iannaccone, "The Consequences of Religious Market Structure: Adam Smith and the Economics of Religion," *Rationality and Society* 3, no. 2 (1991): 156–77; Laurence Iannaccone, "Religious Participation: A Human Capital Approach," *Journal for the Scientific Study of Religion* 29, no. 3 (1990): 297–314.

50. Jenkins, *The Next Christendom*, 77.

51. Barbara Boudewijnse, "The Development of the Charismatic Movement within the Catholic Church of Curaçao," in *Popular Power in Latin American Religions,* ed. Andre F. Droogers et al. (Saarbrucken, Germany: Breitenbach, 1991).

52. Neo-Pentecostalism, as its name implies, is a variety of Pentecostalism, which is itself a form of Christianity that emphasizes the Third Person of the Trinity, the Holy Spirit, as displayed in miraculous manifestations such as "baptism in the Spirit," physical healing, and ecstatic behavior such as speaking in tongues. Modern Pentecostalism is predominantly a Protestant phenomenon, having its origins in the holiness movement of the late nineteenth century and in the Azusa Street Revival of 1906. By contrast, neo-Pentecostalism has its origins in the charismatic movement, which started in the Catholic Church during the 1960s. Although many of their beliefs and practices are similar, Spirit-filled Catholics are generally known as "charismatic," while Protestants are Pentecostals or neo-Pentecostals. Neo-Pentecostalism differs from "traditional" Pentecostalism primarily in its emphasis on the temporal world as opposed to the traditional Pentecostal preoccupation with Christ's return and on the afterlife.

53. See Leonildo Silveira Campos, *Teatro, templo e mercado: Organizaçao e marketing de um empreendimento neopentecostal* (Petrópolis: Voces e São Paulo, Umesp e Simpósio, 1997); Daniel Míguez, "Pentecostalism and Modernization in a Latin American Key: Rethinking the Cultural Effects of Structural Change in Argentina," paper presented to the Latin American Studies Association, Washington, D.C., 2001, 4.

54. Fraternidad Cristiana claims that its new Mixco church has the largest sanctuary in the world, but Joel Osteen's Lakewood Community Church in Houston, Texas, meets in a converted sports stadium that seats sixteen thousand. See *www.frater.org.*

55. See Paul Freston, *Evangelicals and Politics in Asia, Africa and Latin America* (New York: Cambridge University Press, 2001).

56. Roger Fink and Rodney Stark, *The Churching of America, 1776–1990* (New Brunswick, N.J.: Rutgers University Press, 1992). Chesnut discusses this theme in *Competitive Spirits,* but see also Peter S. Cahn, *All Religions Are Good in Tzintzuntzan: Evangelicals in Catholic Mexico* (Austin: University of Texas, 2003).

57. Henri Gooren, "Conversion Careers in Latin America: Entering and Leaving Church among Pentecostals," in *Conversion of a Continent: Contemporary Religious Change in Latin America,* ed. Timothy Steigenga and Edward Cleary (New Brunswick, N.J.: Rutgers University Press, 2007), 52–71.

58. Jenkins, *The Next Christendom*.

11

Charismatic Competitors

Protestant Pentecostals and Catholic Charismatics
in Latin America's New Religious Marketplace

R. Andrew Chesnut

After a half-century of explosive growth, charismatic Christianity has attained hegemonic status in Latin America's religious economy. The great majority of church-attending Christians in the region worship at services in which the Holy Spirit occupies an eminent place. Among Protestants, Pentecostalism has enjoyed such success that at least 75 percent of all *evangélicos* (the preferred term for Protestants in Latin America) belong to Pentecostal denominations such as the Assemblies of God or Pentecostal-style charismatic mainline churches. Across the Christian divide, the Catholic Charismatic Renewal (CCR) has mushroomed to the point that in just three decades since its arrival in Brazil, the largest Catholic nation on earth, it can claim at least half of all practicing Catholics among its ranks.[1] Such is the hegemony of charismatic Christianity that those Catholic and Protestant groups that do not offer some form of pneumacentric (spirit-filled) worship face stagnation and even decline.

The main objective of this chapter is to explore the reasons for charismatic Christianity's unparalleled success in the region's free-market economy of faith. The roughly 75 million Latin American Pentecostals represent the same number of adherents as their chief competitors, the Catholic charismatics.[2] Through examination of the elements that determine the success or failure of any religious organization competing in an unregulated religious economy, Pentecostalism's and the CCR's recipes for success will become clear. Analyses of products, marketing, and consumers will illuminate the determining factors in ecstatic Christianity's commanding position in the free religious market.[3] A few introductory remarks on Pentecostalism and a brief profile of the CCR, which has received far less academic attention, will allow for a better understanding of the two groups that dominate the Christian marketplace of Latin America.

As the premier non-Catholic religion of Latin America, Pentecostalism has been the primary religious architect and developer of the region's new free market of faith. If the region's popular consumers are now free to choose to consume the religious goods that best satisfy their spiritual and material needs, it is largely due to the unparalleled growth of Pentecostal churches since the 1950s. This charismatic branch of Protestantism single-handedly created religious and social space where Latin Americans from the popular classes are free not to be Catholic. Given Catholicism's historic role as one of the constituent elements of Latin American national identities, Pentecostalism's construction of an alternative religious identity for those unhappy with their inherited faith is no minor achievement. For more than four centuries to be Brazilian or Mexican, for example, was to be Catholic. The tiny minorities who converted to historic Protestant denominations, such as Methodism and Presbyterianism, in the latter half of the nineteenth century, and then to the faith missions around the turn of the century, risked social ostracism and sometimes even violence at the hands of Catholics who viewed Protestant converts as traitors to the One True Faith, if not to the nation itself.[4] Not surprisingly, Protestant converts during this period tended to be those Latin American men and women who had the least religious, social, political, and financial capital to lose in abandoning their native church. Very rarely did members of the privileged classes shed their Catholic identity.

That not more than 1 percent of Latin Americans identified themselves as Protestant as late as 1940 is evidence of the failure of historic Protestantism and the numerous faith missions to attract a critical mass of converts. Since Pentecostal churches currently account for approximately 75 percent of all Latin American Protestants after almost a century of evangelization, the obvious conclusion is that Pentecostalism's predecessors did not offer attractive religious goods and services to popular religious consumers.[5] If the stigma attached to shedding one's Catholic identity had been the only factor impeding conversion to Protestantism, the historic churches and faith missions would be thriving at present. However, the only historic Protestant churches able to effectively compete with the Pentecostals are those that have Pentecostalized and embraced spirit-filled worship. In Brazil these schismatic churches generally maintain their denominational title but distinguish themselves from their noncharismatic brethren by adding the term "renewed" (*renovada*) to their name.

Pentecostal Catholics

While mainline Protestants, such as Methodists and Presbyterians, and Catholic base Christian communities (CEBs) struggle to maintain a presence throughout Latin America, another Catholic movement easily fills soccer stadiums in the major cities of the region with tens of thousands of fervent believers. At the beginning of the twenty-first century, the CCR stands as the largest and most dynamic movement in the Latin American Catholic Church. Even leaders of the liberation wing of the Catholic Church, who often view charismatics as alienated middle-class reactionaries, admit that no other ecclesial movement has the CCR's power to congregate and mobilize the faithful.

The region's most vibrant Catholic lay movement nevertheless has received very little academic attention. If the CCR's popular appeal has yet to register among students of Latin American religion, it is because liberation theology and CEBs have captured the hearts and minds of many North American and Latin American social scientists during the past quarter century. The notion of a "preferential option for the poor" and the attempts to initiate the kingdom of heaven on Latin American soil through political and social transformation proved far more appealing to many scholars than a socially disengaged movement dedicated to transforming individual lives through conversion. Academic sympathies aside, however, the charismatic Renewal demands scholarly attention because of its extraordinary appeal among Catholic laity and its unanimous approval by national episcopacies. If the perennial shortage of priests has eased somewhat in the last two decades and if the Catholic Church is finally employing mass media, especially television, as a tool for evangelization, it is because of the charismatics, whose missionary zeal rivals that of their chief competitors in the religious marketplace, the Pentecostals.

Although the CCR manifests diverse local and national characteristics, it is generally a Catholic lay movement that seeks to revitalize the church through the power of the third person of the Trinity, the Holy Spirit. That both U.S. and Latin American charismatics initially called themselves Pentecostal Catholics is revealing: Catholic charismatics share the same ecstatic spirituality as Protestant Pentecostals and, like Pentecostals, Catholic charismatics are pneumacentrists, that is, the Holy Spirit occupies center stage in believers' religious praxis.

Through baptism in the Holy Spirit, individual charismatics believe that they are endowed with gifts of the Spirit, such as glossolalia (speaking in tongues) and faith healing.[6] For charismatics and Pentecostals alike, these charismata are powerful and palpable proof of the presence of the Spirit in their lives. In addition to pneumacentrism, charismatics tend to share, though to a lesser degree, the biblical fundamentalism and asceticism of their Pentecostal progenitors. Of course, what most distinguishes charismatics from other Catholics is their special emphasis on the transformative power of the Holy Spirit.

The most recent figures from the International Catholic Charismatic Renewal Services (ICCRS), the CCR's international headquarters at the Vatican, indicate that some 120 million Catholics belong to the movement in over two hundred countries. Latin American charismatics, according to the ICCRS, number around 74 million, accounting for almost two-thirds of the global total.[7] A recent survey discovered that at least half of all Brazilian and Guatemalan Catholics are charismatic.[8] Data for other Latin American countries are lacking, but the CCR is the largest and most active Catholic lay movement in most nations and in all likelihood can claim at least a third of the region's practicing Catholics.

Like Pentecostalism, its Protestant forbear, the Catholic Charismatic Renewal is a religious product imported from the United States. In the late 1960s, the same charismatic spirituality that had given birth to Pentecostalism in the first decade of the twentieth century and had led to the formation of charismatic communities among mainline Protestants, such as Episcopalians and Presbyterians, in the 1950s and 1960s finally penetrated the U.S. Catholic Church. The CCR specifically traces this genesis to the "Duquesne Weekend" in February 1967, when some twenty-five students at Duquesne University in Pittsburgh (a Catholic institution that, appropriately, was founded by members of the Congregation of the Holy Ghost) gathered for a spiritual retreat with two professors who had already been baptized under the direction of Presbyterian charismatics. Many of the students were baptized in the Holy Spirit and received charismata, marking the first event in which a group of Catholics experienced Pentecostal spirituality.

From Duquesne the nascent movement spread to other college campuses, foremost of which were Notre Dame and Michigan State Universities. During the next decade, the Renewal grew rapidly, spawning charismatic prayer groups and "covenant communities," in which members sought to develop their spiritual lives in a communal setting. By the mid-1970s, the CCR had expanded to the point that it could pack stadiums. In 1974 approximately twenty-five thousand believers attended a CCR international conference at Notre Dame. Three years later in Kansas City, some fifty thousand Protestant and Catholic charismatics participated in an ecumenical assembly, which drew extensive press coverage.[9]

These two events are significant not only for their size but also for two major themes that they underscored. At the Notre Dame convention, a mass healing ritual, led by Dominican priest Francis MacNutt, propelled the spiritual gift of faith healing to the center of charismatic religious praxis. Father MacNutt, who already was a pioneer in exporting the CCR to Iberoamerica, consolidated his position as a leading proponent of faith healing in the movement with the publication that year of his book *Healing*.[10] At the Kansas City gathering it was the ecumenism of the assembly that took the most prominent position. From its inception, the CCR in the United States had been strongly ecumenical, particularly with mainline Protestant charismatics (known as neo-Pentecostals in the United States). Many CCR prayer groups included Protestants, and even some covenant communities counted "separated brethren" among their ranks.[11] Although many, if not most, of the original CCR groups in Latin America were founded by ecumenical pastoral teams, faith healing has proven to be a much more attractive feature than ecumenism south of the Rio Grande.

Mirroring the pattern of Pentecostal expansion to Latin America more than a half-century earlier, the CCR was brought to the region by evangelists only a few years after its birth in the U.S. city of steel. In this case, Catholic priests, mainly Dominican and Jesuit, exported the CCR to major cities throughout Latin America in the early 1970s. Francis MacNutt played a pivotal role in establishing the CCR in several Latin American nations, including Mexico, Colombia, Peru, and Chile. True to the movement's ecumenism in the United States, MacNutt's pastoral teams often included North American Protestant ministers.[12]

Dolores Campos, an Archetypical Pentecostal Consumer

Since the tastes and preferences of religious consumers largely determine the fate of any given religious enterprise in a competitive economy, consideration of the large class of popular religious consumers who have purchased the Pentecostal product is imperative. In other words, who are these millions of Brazilians, Paraguayans, Peruvians, and Guatemalans, among others, who have converted to Pentecostalism since it first sunk roots in Latin American soil in the initial decades of the twentieth century? Sufficient research on Ibero-American Pentecostalism has been conducted over the past decade to allow for a fairly accurate socioeconomic profile of believers.

The archetypical Latin American Pentecostal is Dolores Campos, a poor, married woman of color in her thirties or forties living on the urban periphery. She works as a domestic servant in the home of a privileged compatriot and was a nominal Catholic before converting to the Assembly of God during a time of personal crisis related to her poverty. Of course charismatic Protestantism is so widespread and differentiated now that there are hundreds of thousands of believers who possess none of these constituent elements of the Pentecostal archetype. For example, many of the members of the neo-Pentecostal denominations in Guatemala, such as Shaddai and El Verbo, are upper-middle-class professional men.[13] Nonetheless, Dolores Campos personifies the most common socioeconomic traits found among the vast population of believers.

Most salient among the socioeconomic characteristics of Latin American *crentes* (or believers, as they are often called in Brazil) are poverty, a nominal Catholic background, and female gender. Historically, the great majority of Pentecostal converts have been poor, nonpracticing Catholics. Numerous studies, including my own in Brazil, have shown that not only are Latin American Pentecostals poor, but that they tend to have lower incomes and less education than the general population.[14] The largest study ever conducted of Latin American Protestantism, the 1996 ISER (Instituto Superior da Religião) survey of the Protestant population of Rio de Janeiro found *crentes* to be considerably more likely to live in poverty and have less schooling than the *carioca* population at large.[15] Although Pentecostalism has ascended the region's socioeconomic pyramid, particularly since the 1980s, it continues to be predominantly a religion of the popular classes.

In addition to social class, most Latin American Pentecostals share a common former religious identity. The majority of *creyentes* (the Spanish for "believers") had been nominal or cultural Catholics before converting.[16] Most would have been baptized in the Catholic Church and perhaps had even taken First Communion, but their contact with the institutional church was minimal. However, their weak or nonexistent ties to the church in no way meant that their worldview had become secularized or disenchanted. In times of both need and celebration, nominal Catholics, like their practicing coreligionists, would send prayers of supplication or thanksgiving to the Virgin Mary or one of the many saints. Due to their estrangement from the church and the perennial shortage of clergy, no priest or pastoral agent would likely be present at the time of their poverty-related crisis, which so often leads afflicted individuals to the doors of a Pentecostal temple. It is among this vast field of nominal Catholics, who compose the majority of the Ibero-American population, that Pentecostal evangelists have reaped such bountiful harvests of converts.

While the third conspicuous characteristic of the Pentecostal consumer market, the great female majority among believers, is not peculiar to the faith, it merits discussion because of the religion's status as the most widely practiced faith among women of the popular classes. Hence, product development and marketing strategies naturally must take into account the fact that women believers outnumber men by a ratio of two to one. In one of Brazil's largest and fastest growing Pentecostal denominations, the Universal Church of the Kingdom of God (IURD), the ratio climbs to four to one.[17] Male believers, of course, continue to monopolize the pastorate and high-ranking church offices, but Pentecostalism is largely sustained and spread by sisters in the faith.

Ivonne Ferrer, an Archetypical CCR Consumer

In contrast to the Pentecostals, the first adherents to the CCR were disproportionately middle-class, practicing Catholic women, and those who joined during the 1970s and well into the 1980s tended to share the characteristics of class, gender, and active religious practice. Although the CCR is now expanding among the first of these, the Latin American popular classes, the movement during most of its short history has been solidly middle-class. Thus the Catholic charismatic counterpart to Dolores Campo would be Ivonne Ferrer, a forty-something stay-at-home mom who was already a devout Catholic before joining a CCR prayer group during a marital crisis. In one of the first studies conducted on the CCR in Latin America, researcher Pedro Oliveira in the early 1970s found the majority of Brazilian Catholic charismatics to be middle- and upper-middle-class, like Ivonne Ferrer. More than half the charismatics surveyed had at least a secondary education, and only 1 percent were illiterate.[18] Even twenty years later, Brazilians averaged only five years of primary school education. In Mexico, the Holy Ghost Missionaries, who introduced the CCR in Mexico City, had historically directed their pastoral activities toward the middle and upper classes. Indeed, Santa Cruz, their principal parish, is located in the Pedregal, one of the city's most exclusive residential districts.[19]

After social class, gender also has been one of the marked demographic characteristics of the charismatic community in Latin America. Precise figures do not exist, but since the CCR's arrival in the region, women have comprised approximately two-thirds of the movement in Iberoamerica. Oliveira's study reported women as 71 percent of Brazilian CCR membership.[20] A 1994 Brazilian survey found the gender ratio had remained constant at 70 percent female. The same poll found that women also predominated in Brazil's base Christian communities, but at the significantly lower rate of 57 percent.[21] In Mexico, the archdiocesan coordinator of the Renewal in Latin America's largest city, Miguel Ramírez, estimated that the country's female charismatics outnumber their male brothers in faith by two to one.[22]

The third major characteristic that CCR members have in common is their prior status as active Catholics. Oliveira's study confirms that the great majority of Brazilian charismatics had been active Catholics before joining; furthermore, 80 percent had participated in other church lay groups, particularly *cursillo*.[23] Barbara Boudewijnse discovered the same pattern of CCR expansion in Curaçao (Dutch Caribbean) while CCR lay leaders in Guatemala and Mexico reported the same recruitment strategy of focusing on active Catholics in those two countries.[24] Thus, in its initial phase the CCR rarely attracted nominal Catholics, much less Pentecostal converts.

Practical Products

The above profile of Pentecostal and CCR consumers contributes to a better understanding of the religious products that pneumacentric Christians purchase and consume in churches and in their daily lives. Defining religious products as the doctrine and worship services of faith-based organizations, this section of the chapter considers the spiritual goods and services that have resulted in charismatic Christianity's unmatched success in the free market of faith. The task at hand, then, is not to identify every religious product but to scrutinize those whose popularity among consumers has led to pneumacentric Christianity's dramatic expansion in Latin America since the 1950s.

The utilitarian nature of Pentecostalism and popular religion in general means that the spiritual products offered to consumers of the divine must prove useful in their daily lives. Products that do not relate to believers' quotidian existence will find few purchasers in the popular religious marketplace. This does not mean that consumers of the popular classes are only religious instrumentalists who evaluate spiritual products solely on the basis of their capacity to provide relief from the afflictions of everyday poverty. Spiritual products that hold little relevance to the social reality of impoverished believers will collect dust on the lower shelves of the market. Since most Latin American religious consumers are much better acquainted with Catholic products, rival spiritual firms, in order to compete, must offer goods that are simultaneously familiar and novel. That is, the non-Catholic product must distinguish itself from the Catholic doctrine or worship to maintain the potential consumer's comfort level. At the same time, the product must distinguish itself from the Catholic product. Pentecostalism possesses exactly this type of product in its doctrine and practice of faith healing. More than any other of its products, it is the Pentecostal belief that Jesus and the Holy Spirit have the power to cure believers of their spiritual, somatic, and psychological ills that impels more Latin Americans to affiliate with *crente* churches. All Catholics, whether practicing or nominal, are familiar, if not experienced, with the healing powers of the saints and the Virgin Mary. In fact, it is their status as powerful agents of divine healing that has won such world renown for Virgins such as Guadalupe, Lourdes, and Aparecida.

Pentecostal faith healing thus is really not a new product per se but a greatly improved one. With the great exception of the Catholic Charismatic Renewal, divine healing had continued to exist on the fringes of the twentieth-century Ibero-American Catholic Church. The curing of all types of ailments through promises and petitions to the Virgin and saints has customarily taken place beyond the pale of the institutional church, and if any human mediators were involved at all, they were more likely to be *curanderas* (folk healers) than priests. In striking contrast, Pentecostal preachers from the earliest days made *cura divina* a centerpiece of both doctrine and practice. Indeed, it was an act of faith healing in 1911 that led to the birth of the Western Hemisphere's largest Pentecostal denomination, the Brazilian Assembly of God.[25] Whereas Catholic Masses offered little liturgical space for the healing of believers' everyday afflictions, Pentecostal worship services and revivals in which Jesus or the Holy Spirit failed to operate through the congregation to cure worshipers of their illnesses are almost unimaginable. Of such importance is faith healing to the mission of the Brazilian Universal Church of the Kingdom of God that two days of its weekly schedule of services are devoted to it. Hence, Latin American Pentecostalism took what had been a marginal product in institutional Catholicism and turned it into the sine qua non of its own religious production.

While faith healing, more than any other product, induces religious consumers to join the Pentecostal enterprise, it is still another benefit that facilitates the recovery and maintenance of believers' health over the long term, namely, conversion, in which joining a Pentecostal church is conceptualized as part of a process of spiritual rebirth, allowing the believer to be born again into a healthy new environment where the demons of poverty can be neutralized. Conceived as a "positive transformation of the nature and value of a person," religious conversion appeals most to those individuals and groups who have been stigmatized or negatively evaluated by society.[26] A conversionist religion, then, which offers the possibility of a new life far removed from the afflictions of the old, would be understandably popular among those millions of Latin Americans, especially women, seeking to turn away from family conflict, alcoholism, and illness.

This element of the conversion process is of such importance that two-thirds of my male informants in Brazil mentioned the repudiation of "vice" as the most important change in their life since conversion. And, not surprisingly, they cited worldly temptations as their second greatest problem after financial hardship.[27] Since the streets of Latin America, especially on the urban margins, are still largely a male domain, it follows that the rupture caused by conversion to Pentecostalism is greater for men. As practicing Pentecostals men must leave the temptations of the street behind and focus on their home and family life. In short, this product of conversion allows believers to reclaim and maintain their health through their rebirth into a salutary new environment, largely devoid of the demons of the street.

If believers find themselves assailed by such demons, their religion offers them a specific brand of faith healing to exorcise them. Exorcism, usually referred to as liberation, *libertação* in Portuguese, has been practiced by Pentecostal preachers since its early days, but over the past two decades, neo-Pentecostal churches have brought it from the fringes of religious practice to its present prominence. Indeed in its weekly calendar of worship, the Universal Church devotes Fridays to *cultos de libertação* (exorcism services).

Pentecostalism shares its final salient product, ecstatic power, with its main religious rivals, African diasporan faiths and charismatic Catholicism, but emphasizes it in greater measure. Just as the dialectic between illness and faith healing attracts millions of converts, so too does that between socioeconomic impotence and spiritual power. With direct access to the Holy Spirit through baptism in the Spirit and charismata, such as glossolalia and prophecy, impoverished Latin American Pentecostals experience intense spiritual power. Filled with the might of the Holy Spirit, impoverished believers are fortified to do battle with the demons of deprivation, which can make life for those on the urban and rural margins a living hell.

The CCR and Pentecostalism have multiplied exponentially for similar reasons. A slight modification to the Pentecostal dialectic makes plain the mass appeal of the Catholic Charismatic Renewal. While the thesis of affliction or illness is the same for both the Renewal and Pentecostalism, the higher social class position of CCR adherents translates into a less direct relationship between misfortune and poverty. The afflictions that compel middle-class Latin Americans to join the CCR may stem less directly from material deprivation and more often from psychological problems, such as those that may stem from early childhood trauma. It follows, then, that the distinct origins of the Pentecostal and CCR dialectical theses lead to different manifestations of the same antithesis of faith healing. Whereas the *cura divina* practiced in Pentecostal churches has tended to focus on healing the physical illnesses that plague the Latin American poor, the *sanación* offered at charismatic Masses and assemblies in the 1980s more often involved the "inner healing" (*sanación interior*) of painful memories and past psychological stresses.

Inner healing has been the predominant form practiced in the CCR, but two other types complement the charismatic typology of illness and healing. According to charismatic etiology, illness is of three types: emotional, physical, and spiritual. Physical illness arises from disease and accidents, while spiritual malaise results most often from personal sin and less frequently from demonic oppression. The corresponding methods of healing are straightforward for emotional and physical illnesses. Prayers for inner healing are directed toward the former, while petitions for a physical cure are made for the latter. Because spiritual afflictions have two distinct origins, personal sin and satanic oppression, there are two different methods of treatment. Spiritual problems diagnosed as originating in personal sin require prayers of repentance, while afflictions caused by the devil or his minions demand a much stronger medicine: exorcism.

Since the late 1980s, competition with Pentecostalism has led to the formation of a cadre of priests who specialize in "liberation" or exorcism ministries. So strong is current consumer demand for release from demonic possession that some priests, such as the Brazilian charismatic superstar Marcelo Rossi, even celebrate weekly "liberation Masses" (*missas de libertação*).[28] Acknowledging his pastoral debt to Pentecostal leader Bishop Edir Macedo, whose Universal Church of the Kingdom of God (IURD) brought exorcism to the fore of pneumacentric Christianity in Latin America, Padre Marcelo observed, "It was Bishop Edir Macedo who woke us up."[29] As the CCR proceeds down the Latin American class scale, both exorcism and physical healing will continue their advance from the margins of charismatic practice to the center.

The Virgin in the Vanguard

To ensure the Catholic identity of the CCR, the bishops have emphasized the role of the Virgin as defender of the faith and guardian of orthodoxy. The Virgin, particularly Guadalupe (the "Queen of Mexico"), is the most potent and visible symbol of Catholic identity in Latin America. For a movement rooted in Pentecostal spirituality, which has historically been radically anti-Catholic in Latin America, what better way to preserve the Catholic identity of the Renewal than through emphasis on the element that most distinguishes the church from its

Protestant competitors? Thus the Virgin, in her myriad national and local incarnations, has, over the past decade and a half, come to constitute the dividing line that separates Catholic charismatics from Pentecostals.

Episcopal emphasis on the importance of the Virgin, represented by the Virgin of Guadalupe and Our Lady of the Immaculate Conception, among other images, is a clear example of the marginal differentiation of an otherwise standardized religious product. In the figure of the Virgin, the church's chief religious producers offer an appealing variant to the pneumacentric spirituality shared by both Catholic charismatics and Pentecostals. Without the Mother of God to differentiate them, only the Roman pontiff is left to guard the bridge leading to Pentecostalism.

Faith in Marketing

As any business student knows, it is not sufficient for a firm to simply possess an appealing product. In modern consumer societies where prospective customers are presented with a dizzying array of goods and services, businesses must aggressively market their product to get their message to consumers. So important is marketing, particularly in affluent consumer societies such as the United States, that a product's packaging and advertising often have greater bearing on sales than the quality of the product itself.

Admittedly, the science of marketing is not as developed in religious economies as commercial ones. But without a successful strategy of evangelization that offers doctrine and worship directly to prospective believers, spiritual firms operating in a free market of faith will find it hard to compete with these rivals who actively and creatively evangelize. And in the religious economies of present-day Ibero-America no religion has evangelized as successfully as charismatic Christianity. If in less than a century spirit-centered Christianity has become hegemonic in the region, it is in no small measure due to the skillful marketing of the faith. This section, then, considers the ways in which Pentecostal denominations and the CCR have successfully advertised and packaged their religious products to spiritual consumers. Using evangelical idiom, the next section of this chapter examines the methods of evangelization that have won so many "souls for Jesus."

Like their Pentecostal brethren in the United States, Latin American *crentes* are the most skilled marketers in the region's new religious economy. They have utilized diverse media to deliver the simple but potent message to prospective converts that affiliation with Pentecostalism will imbue them with sufficient supernatural strength to vanquish the demons of poverty. It is the dynamic and controversial Universal Church of the Kingdom of God that has captured the essence of Pentecostal advertising in its evangelistic slogan, "stop suffering." The pithy phrase *pare de sofrer*, typically printed in bright red letters, calls out to the afflicted poor of Brazil from the church walls, pamphlets, and newspapers of this innovative denomination. A combination of low- and high-tech media invite religious consumers, mainly nominal Catholics, to relieve their suffering by embracing Jesus and the Holy Spirit within the walls of the church that advertises its product.

One of the most effective means of marketing the Pentecostal product is the oldest method of *creyente* evangelization in Latin America, home visits. The founders of the Assembly of God in Brazil, the Swedish-American immigrants Gunnar Vingren and Daniel Berg, proselytized in early twentieth-century Belém through visits to victims of a yellow fever epidemic and other maladies.[30] Since then, hundreds of thousands of Pentecostal pastors and lay persons have knocked on flimsy doors throughout Latin America's urban periphery and countryside to spread the good news of healing to those suffering from poverty-related afflictions. In the Assemblies of God, lay women evangelists, called *visitadoras* (visitors) proselytize not only door to door but also in hospitals filled with those who are especially predisposed to accept a prescription for divine healing. Until the charismatic renewal developed its own home visit campaign in the 1980s to target nominal Catholics, Pentecostals and neo-Christians, such as the Mormons and the Jehovah's Witnesses, were the only groups who brought their products directly to the homes of Latin American spiritual consumers.

For those Ibero-Americans who do not come into contact with Pentecostalism through low-tech marketing, evangelists have made it difficult to avoid exposure to their product through its advertisements in the mass media and the Internet. Despite the rapid growth of Pentecostal televangelism in the region since the early 1980s, it is the oldest form of electronic media, radio, that continues to account for the bulk of *crente* broadcasting. While Pentecostal-owned television stations, such as the IURD's Rede Record, transmit mostly commercial programs, many radio stations broadcast nothing but Pentecostal preaching, music, and conversion testimonials, twenty-four hours a day.

Radio has a twofold advantage over television as a marketing tool for the Pentecostal product. It is significantly cheaper than television. Only the largest denominations, such as the Assemblies of God, IURD, and Foursquare Gospel Church can afford the high costs associated with proprietorship of a station or production of programs. In contrast, some smaller churches that could never dream of appearing on television possess the funds to purchase small amounts of air time, particularly on the AM band of some one thousand radio stations in Latin America that carry Protestant programming.[31] In addition, while TV antennae have become a growing fixture on the skyline of the urban periphery, radio is ubiquitous among the Latin American popular classes.

Following in the footsteps of their North American brethren who dominate religious broadcasting in the United States, a few large Pentecostal denominations enjoy a commanding position in the transmission of spiritual programs.

With the exception of the pioneering but short-lived programs of the Brazil for Christ denomination in the 1960s and the IURD in the early 1980s, Latin American owned and produced Pentecostal television did not take root until the late 1980s. Since the early part of that decade, U.S. televangelists, such as Assembly of God members Jimmy Swaggart and Jim Bakker, had dominated Protestant broadcasting in Latin America. Given the superior resources of the North American televangelists, it was only natural that they served as the trailblazers in Latin American Pentecostal television.

By the end of the decade, however, a few major *crente* churches, particularly in Brazil, such as the Assemblies of God, Foursquare Gospel, IURD, and International Church of the Grace of God (Igreja Internacional da Graça de Deus) were producing their own programs and, in the case of the IURD, purchasing its own station. In November 1989, the IURD made Latin American history when it bought the Rede Record television and radio stations for US$45 million. With Record now owned by the IURD and Globo, Latin America's largest broadcasting corporation, owned by the staunch Catholic impresario Roberto Marinho, the battle for Christian market share has played out on the small screens of Brazil. Both networks have aired *novelas* (evening soap operas) satirizing and even demonizing each other. And Padre Marcelo, the dashing young star of the Catholic charismatic renewal, appeared frequently in the late 1990s on Rede Globo's variety and talk shows.

Ever seeking novel ways to market their products, large Latin American Pentecostal churches have joined the revolution in information technology and have developed Internet websites.[32] The IURD website even has its own chatroom in which members and the curious can discuss matters of faith in "real time." The small but increasing minority of Latin American believers who have Internet access can take pride in the fact that their denominations have embraced the latest mass medium as a novel way to market their religious product to those in need of healing. The plethora of Internet cafes throughout the region has made it even easier for believers, especially technologically savvy youth, to go online even if they do not own a computer.

The Pentecostal product sold in the mass media is particularly appealing when packaged in the form of testimonials, music, and exorcism. Whether on television, on the radio, or at rallies in soccer stadiums, the conversion narrative of a Pentecostal convert is often a powerfully emotive account of how Jesus or the Holy Spirit restored the believer's health or saved her from one of the demons of deprivation. Listeners and viewers experiencing their own crises hear or see someone from the same or similar social class dramatically turn his life around through acceptance of Jesus and affiliation with the church broadcasting the program. Such advertising, of course, is ubiquitous among commercial firms. Dramatic before and after photos, along with testimony of consumers who supposedly used a particular diet product, invite obese Latin and North Americans to remake themselves as slim and fit men and women.

Pentecostal sales representatives also package their product in the emotional form of music. In addition to worship services, romantic ballads, pop songs, and regional rhythms all set to evangelical lyrics blare from Pentecostal radio and television stations. The most musical of all the major branches of Christianity, Pentecostalism rouses its believers and attracts new converts through its melodic electric guitars, drums, tambourines, and synthesizers. Whether background mood music or moving hymns, melodic rhythms constitute such an integral part of *crente* worship services that in Brazil they are sung and played during at least two-thirds of the typically two-hour long service.

Although not of the same caliber and sophistication as Pentecostal marketing, CCR advertising puts the movement at the forefront of Catholic missionary activities. The CCR responded to the call made at the 1992 meeting of the Latin American Bishops' Conference (CELAM) in Santo Domingo for more vigorous evangelization efforts by intensifying its proselytizing activities. Of course, faith healing in its multiple forms is probably the most effective form of evangelization, but beyond attracting nominal Catholics back to the ecclesial fold through the promise of restored health, the Renewal has taken specific pastoral measures to win new adherents. At the grassroots level, charismatics copy the Pentecostal competition by evangelizing through home visits and mass rallies. The "visitation ministry," as it is called in Brazil, sends lay missionaries, who are mostly charismatics, to the homes of the "target population" of vulnerable nominal Catholics to invite them to attend a prayer group or some other church function.

By the mid-1980s, rallies, revivals, and healing marathons, in which thousands of believers gathered at soccer stadiums and gymnasiums to receive the power of the Holy Spirit, were no longer peculiar to Pentecostalism. Annual national CCR assemblies, known as cenacles (*cenáculos*), filled stadiums throughout the region. The Mexican CCR packed the Estadio Azteca with some 70,000 charismatics several times in the middle and late 1980s while the Brazilian Renewal attracted 150,000 on Pentecost Sunday 1987 and again in May 1991.[33] Renowned international CCR leaders, especially those who specialized in healing ministries, such as North American priest Robert DeGrandis and his Canadian colleague Emiliano Tardiff, attracted thousands of impoverished believers to rallies that were propelled by faith healing sessions and much upbeat popular music.

The CCR also emulates its Pentecostal rivals in embracing mass media, particularly television and radio. Such is the Renewal's dominance of Catholic radio and television in many Latin American countries that there would be very little church programming without it. In Brazil, most of the programming on the country's 181 Catholic radio stations is produced by CCR members.[34] In Guatemala, the Renewal almost single-handedly has answered a 1983 papal call to the episcopacy to take to the airwaves to "counteract the pernicious influence of the proselytizing activities of groups with little authentically religious content that create confusion among Catholics."[35] Six of the seven Catholic radio stations in Guatemala are run by the CCR.[36] The Brazilian Renewal has moved far beyond the simple broadcast of charismatic Masses to the production of religious dramas akin to Latin America's popular *telenovelas.*

It is no coincidence that charismatic television is strongest in the Latin American nation that has the greatest amount of Pentecostal programming. As previously mentioned, the Universal Church of the Kingdom of God runs its own station, Rede Record. More than any other factor, it was Pentecostalism's dominance of religious broadcasting that compelled the Brazilian CCR to embrace television as a powerful evangelical medium. Father Edward Dougherty has made CCR history not only by importing the movement to Brazil but also by his pioneering work in Catholic TV. In 1983 his charismatic association, Associação do Senhor Jesus (Association of Lord Jesus) aired the country's first CCR program, *Anunciamos Jesus* (We Announce Jesus), which is currently the longest-running weekly charismatic program.

Over the past decade, "Padre Eduardo" has expanded his operation to include control of a large television production facility, O Centro de Produção Século XXI (Century 21 Production Center). Century 21, located in the small city of Valinhos, São Paulo, comprises three large studios, which employ the latest technology in video production and a spacious auditorium for hosting studio audiences. Its programs are shown on national television covering 85 percent of Brazil's territory, and recently Century 21 has started to export its product to other Latin American nations, the United States, and Europe.[37]

Also a skilled fundraiser, Father Dougherty finances his enterprise through a combination of contributions from the seventy thousand members of his Association of Lord Jesus, sales of television programs and religious articles, and occasional donations from wealthy Brazilian, North American, and European charismatics. Conspicuous among the latter is the Breninkmeyer family, which owns C&A, the international chain of department stores with a strong presence in Brazil.[38] In contrast to his initial efforts, which were spurned by the Conference of Brazilian Bishops under the influence of progressive bishops, Dougherty has won widespread episcopal support over the past decade for his starring role in bringing the Brazilian church into the homes of millions of TV viewers. "The Catholic Church went for a long time without investing in communication," commented Dougherty's local bishop, Monsenor Geraldo Azevedo of Campinas. "That's why we need an offensive to counterbalance the presence of Pentecostal churches in the mass media."[39] Beyond the world of Catholic television, the CCR has greatly benefited from increasing exposure on secular TV, especially on Latin America's largest network, Rede Globo. Since 1998 Padre Marcelo Rossi has appeared regularly on the *Faustão* show, one of Globo's most popular programs; and Father Zeca, a young charismatic priest idolized by CCR youth in Rio de Janeiro, has also received widespread secular media coverage.

Free Market Salvation

If at the beginning of the twenty-first century, Latin American Christianity has Pentecostalized to the extent that the Catholic Church's most dynamic movement is its own version of Pentecostalism, it is because charismatic Christianity has developed superior religious products and marketed them more successfully than its competitors in the free market of faith. Over the past four decades popular religious consumers in Latin America have exhibited a strong preference for pneumacentric spirituality in both its Christian and non-Christian forms.[40] It is no coincidence that the most successful Christian denominations in the region are those that revolve around direct contact with or even possession by the Holy Spirit. Charismatic Catholicism and Pentecostalism share the common element of pneumacentrism; and one of the primary functions of the Spirit is to heal individual believers of their earthly afflictions. In his study of the CCR in Curaçao, Armando Lampe makes the crucial point that religions of possession are also ones of healing; the two moments are inextricably intertwined.[41] Thus charismatic Christianity has prospered in the unregulated market of faith because its religious specialists produce the standardized products, faith healing and pneumacentric spirituality, that popular consumers demand. In contrast, organizations such as the CEBs and mainline Protestantism, which offer neither supernatural healing nor direct contact with the Holy Spirit, have failed to thrive in the popular religious marketplace.

Notes

1. *http://pewforum.org/surveys/pentecostal/latinamerica*.

2. Ibid.

3. In their groundbreaking study of the historical winners and losers in the U.S. religious economy, *The Churching of America, 1776–1990* (New Brunswick, N.J.: Rutgers University Press, 1992), Roger Stark and Rodney Finke demonstrate that the fate of religious organizations in a free market economy depends on their products, marketing, sales representatives, and organizational structure. Translated into the ecclesiastical idiom, doctrine, evangelization techniques, clergy, and polity are the four factors that determine the success or failure of any given religious enterprise in a pluralistic environment. Broadening Stark and Finke's narrow pairing of the religious product with doctrine, I include liturgy or forms of worship in my definition of the religious product.

4. Faith missions were nondenominational evangelical Protestant organizations that sought to convert Latin American Catholics. They were often more theologically and culturally conservative than mainline Protestant churches.

5. *http://pewforum.org/surveys/pentecostal.*

6. Baptism in the Spirit is the central tenet and experience of Pentecostal religion. It is based on an event in the book of Acts in which the Holy Spirit descended on the apostles in tongues of fire, causing them to preach in languages previously unknown to them. Pentecostals claim that the Holy Spirit possesses them similarly during the spiritual baptism.

7. *www.iccrs.org/CCR%20worldwide.htm.*

8. *http://pewforum.org/world-affairs/countries.*

9. Abelardo Soneira, "La renovación carismática católica en la Argentina," *Revista del Centro de Investigación y Acción Social* 477 (1998): 473–86.

10. Richard Bord and Joseph Faulkner, *The Catholic Charismatics* (University Park: Pennsylvania State University Press, 1983).

11. Covenant communities are CCR groups that live communally and often take vows of poverty, chastity, and obedience.

12. Edward Cleary, "Protestants and Catholics: Rivals or Siblings?" in *Coming of Age: Protestantsim in Contemporary Latin America,* ed. Daniel Miller (Lanham, Md.: University Press of America, 1994), 205–27.

13. Neo-Pentecostal denominations are those founded from the 1970s to the present that emphasize prosperity theology and exorcism while relaxing the strict moral codes of older Pentecostal churches such as the Assemblies of God. The Brazilian Universal Church of the Kingdom of God (Igreja Universal do Reino de Deus) is one of the fastest growing neo-Pentecostal denominations.

14. R. Andrew Chesnut, *Born Again in Brazil: The Pentecostal Boom and the Pathogens of Poverty* (New Brunswick, N.J.: Rutgers University Press, 1997).

15. The ISER survey included mainline Protestants whose higher income and educational levels raised the mean. If only Pentecostals had been surveyed the gap between believers and the general population would have been substantially larger. Instituto Superior de Estudos da Religião, *Novo nascimento: Os evangélicos em casa, na igreja, e na política* (Rio de Janeiro: ISER, 1996).

16. Daniel Míguez, "Exploring the Argentinian Case: Religious Motives in the Growth of Latin American Pentecostalism," in *Latin American Religion in Motion,* ed. Christian Smith and Joshua Propoky (New York: Routledge, 1999), 221–34.

17. ISER, *Novo nascimento.*

18. Pedro Oliveira et al., *Renovação carismática católica: Uma analise sociológica, interpretaçes teológicas* (Petropolis, Brazil: Vozes, 1978).

19. María Cristina Díaz de la Serna Braojos, "El movimiento de la Renovación Carismática como un proceso de socialización adulta," licentiate thesis, Universidad Autónoma Metropolitana, Unidad Iztapalapa, Mexico City, 1981.

20. Oliveira et al., *Renovação carismática católica.*

21. Reginaldo Prandi, *Um sopro do espirito* (São Paulo: Edusp, 1997).

22. Miguel Ramírez, interview by the author, Mexico City, July 13, 1999.

23. Oliveira et al., *Renovação carismática católica.* The Cursillo (little course) movement was founded in 1949 in Spain by Monseñor Juan Hervas. In Latin America, it sought to organize and train middle-class laity with the overarching goal of Catholicizing the workplace and society in general.

24. Barbara Boudewijnse, "The Development of the Charismatic Movement within the Catholic Church of Curaçao" in *Popular Power in Latin American Religions,* ed. A. F. Droogers et al. (Saarbrucken, Germany: Breitenbach, 1991), 175–96. Miguel Ramírez. Sheny de Góngora, interview by the author, Guatemala City, August 5, 1999.

25. Chesnut, *Born Again in Brazil.*

26. Rodney Stark and William Bainbridge, *A Theory of Religion* (New York: Peter Lang, 1987).

27. Chesnut, *Born Again in Brazil*.

28. "Não sou artista, nem quero ser ídolo de ninguem: Meu sonho era jogar futebol," *CARAS*, December 4, 1998.

29. Samarone Lima and Thais Oyama, "Católicos em transe" *Veja* (online), *www2.uol.com.br/veja/080498/p_092.html*, 1998.

30. Ibid.

31. Pedro Moreno, "Evangelical Churches," in *Religious Freedom and Evangelization in Latin America*, ed. Paul Sigmund (Maryknoll, N.Y.: Orbis Books, 1999), 49–69.

32. A search in August 2007 found the following churches to be running their own websites: the IURD, the Assemblies of God in Brazil, Luz del Mundo–México (Light of the World), Deus é Amor–Brazil (God is Love), Iglesia del Evangelio Cuadrangular–Chile (Foursquare Gospel Church), El Shaddai–Guatemala, and Iglesia Cristiana Verbo–Guatemala (Church of the Word).

33. Monique Hebrard, *Les Charismatiques* (Paris: Cerf-Fides, 1991). Luiz Roberto Benedetti, "Templo, Praça, Coração: A articulação do campo religioso católico," Ph.D. dissertation, Universidade de São Paulo, 1988.

34. "Não sou milagreiro" *Isto É*, December 24, 1997.

35. Conferencia Episcopal de Guatemala, *Al Servicio de la vida, justicia y la paz: Documentos de CEG 1956–1997* (Guatemala City: Ediciones San Pablo, 1997).

36. Sheny de Góngora, interview with the author, Guatemala City, August 5, 1999, and Father Hugo Estrada, interview with author, Guatemala City, August 8, 1999.

37. Brenda Carranza Dávila, "Renovação carismática católica: Origens, mudanças e tendências," M.A. thesis, Universidade Estadual de Campinas, Brazil, 1998.

38. Ibid.

39. Ibid.

40. The religions of the African diaspora, such as Vodou and Candomblé, are the main non-Christian pneumacentrists.

41. Armando Lampe, "The Popular Use of the Charismatic Movement in Curação," *Social Compass* 45, no. 3 (1998): 429–36.

12

Umbanda

Lindsay Hale

Make a wish. That's how we would say it. Make a wish. Dona Luciana's[1] instructions were a little more detailed. *Faça seu pedido á nossa mãe Iemanja, e logo solte o barco* (Make your request of Our Mother Iemanjá, and then let the boat go). My "boat" was a wooden tray, like a cafeteria tray but a little bigger, with higher sides. A few minutes before, on the brown sugar sand beach of Copacabana, I had piled on my boat seven white roses, tied with a light blue ribbon; some seashells I had collected that morning; a piece of paper on which I had written the name of a relative about whom I was very worried; and a champagne glass. I had dug two holes in the sand, one for me and one for Dona Luciana, whose arthritic old hands were no longer up to the task. In each I lit a candle. One always lights a candle when making an offering; placing them in the holes shielded their flames from the breeze blowing off the ocean. I popped the cork on the champagne, filled the glass on my boat, and the one on Dona Luciana's, which I carried into the gentle surf, as Dona Luciana held onto my arm with both hands to steady herself. Now it was my turn, on this late afternoon of New Year's Eve. I lowered my boat into the knee-deep water, steadied it as it rose and fell on the little swells, made my wish, and let it go. We watched as the tide took the boat out a little ways, a sign that Iemanjá accepted my gift. It hadn't gone far, maybe fifteen feet, when some swirling eddy or ripping current — or as Dona Luciana said later, Iemanjá herself — sucked my boat under, as though a big fish had opened its mouth and flared its gills and sucked it in like a little sparkling minnow. Dona Luciana gasped, and her nails bit into my skin, *Meu Deus! Viu como ela engoliu a coisa! Ela lhe deu um sinal, meu filho....* (My God! Did you see how she swallowed the thing! She gave you a sign, my child....)

This is an essay about Umbanda, a religion that incorporates elements of the African religions brought to Brazil by the slaves, Catholicism, French Spiritism, and a potpourri of other influences, ranging from the archetypes of Jung to tales of Atlantis. Although it draws on traditions that go back, in some cases, thousands of years Umbanda itself is not at all old, dating only to the first decades of the twentieth century. And while its popularity has dwindled in recent years, hundreds of thousands of Brazilians (and even some people across the borders in Argentina and Uruguay) actively and regularly participate, and many more do so on an irregular basis. Umbanda is mainly found in big cities, especially Rio de Janeiro, where it began. Most *Umbandistas* are working class, or poor, but many, such as Dona Luciana, are from the middle and upper middle classes. And Umbanda is by no means restricted to any racial or ethnic group; Black and white and everything in between are amply represented in Umbanda.

I have conducted field research on Umbanda since 1986. My longest stretch in the field, well over a year, occurred during 1990–91, and that was supplemented by several three month stays, along with a short visit, just over a month, in 1994–95, when Dona Luciana and I made our last offering together in the warm surf just as the sun began to set behind us. This essay is informed by that research, but because my concern here is to paint the big picture of Umbanda's origins and development and place it within the larger contexts of African diaspora religion and Brazilian society instead of presenting a detailed ethnographic study, I will mainly use my own observations and experiences to illustrate these larger themes, to show how they play out "on the ground."

Beginnings

When and how did Umbanda begin? A straightforward question, but anthropologists almost never have a simple answer for a simple question. It is good that culture is not a crime, because the expert witnesses, anthropologists, tend to give several answers to any question, not always mutually consistent, and what's worse, the answers often come in the form of stories. Culture would walk, because the jury could never reach a verdict. So here are some stories. The first three are stories Umbandistas tell; these are very interesting, imaginative, and tell us about a lot more than just how and when Umbanda began. The final one is my attempt at an objective, historical answer. I am afraid you will find the Umbandistas tell better stories than I.

Story One: Not Welcome at the Table

For this one you need a little background on two terms used in the story. The first of these is "spiritist." Spiritists are practitioners of *Espiritismo*, also known as *Kardecismo*, after its founder, Allan Kardec. Kardec, a Frenchman whose real name was Hippolyte Léon Denizard Rivall, was a science teacher who became interested in the possibility of communicating with spirits. In the mid-nineteenth century, there were many people in France who claimed that spirits communicated with them through various channels — by rapping on a table in response to questions, by speaking through mediums in séances, and through "automatic writing," that is, the spirit guiding the hand of the writer, who is unaware of what is being written. Skeptical at first, Kardec became convinced that spirits really do communicate with the living. Kardec posed questions to spirits "working" through mediums and compiled the results, which he published in a series of books, the first of which came out in 1857. The books described the spiritual realm and laid out the doctrinal basis for Spiritism.

Despite the obvious contradictions between Spiritism and Catholicism, Spiritism quickly took root in Brazil. Journalist Paulo Barreto, who wrote under the penname "João do Rio" at the turn of the twentieth century, reported that a Spiritist acquaintance claimed that if there were a hundred thousand Spiritists in Paris, Rio de Janeiro counted nearly as many. An exaggeration, no doubt — after all, the population of Rio at the time was a little less than seven hundred thousand. But there is no doubt that thousands of *cariocas* (inhabitants of Rio de Janeiro) attended the *mesas,* where participants would sit around a table (a *mesa*) and receive visitors from the beyond, often from highly illustrious, forward-thinking, educated members of the elite such as Victor Hugo, Benjamin Franklin, and Jean Jacques Rousseau.

The second term is *caboclo.* The word has multiple referents; a caboclo can be a "civilized" person of indigenous ancestry, a peasant from the arid backlands of the Brazilian Northeast, usually of both African and indigenous ancestry, or a person of mixed European and indigenous ancestry. In Umbanda parlance, a caboclo is the spirit of a Brazilian Indian.

Here's the story:

On November 15, 1908, seventeen-year-old Zélio Fernandes de Morais attended a session of the Spiritist Federation of Niteroi (Niteroi is across the bay from Rio de Janeiro). The day before, young Zélio had recovered from a mysterious ailment. His doctors, who could not find the cause of his illness, could not cure him. But a spirit did. So a friend suggested that he attend the Spiritist meeting. Zélio was invited to take a seat at the *mesa.*

When it came time for the illustrious spirits to arrive, some uninvited guests — spirits of Brazilian Indians and old black slaves — appeared instead. The director ordered them to leave, but Zélio, overcome by a strange force, heard himself arguing, demanding to know why these spirits were not welcome. Was it their race? It soon became clear that this was not the young man speaking. It was a spirit, a spirit who proudly proclaimed himself to be the Caboclo Seven Crossroads, so named, he said, because "for me, all roads are open!" He went on to proclaim his mission: to found a new religion, one that would welcome the spirits of Indians and blacks, symbolizing the equality that must attain between all men, a religion that would minister to the spiritual needs of the masses. That religion would be known as Umbanda.

227

Story Two: The Root

Several Umbandistas told me variants of the following story:

> A few centuries back, in the interior of Angola, slave traders captured a powerful sorcerer. Somehow he managed to hide on his person the root of a plant that was a source of his power. Auctioned on the dock at Rio, the sorcerer ended up a slave on a nearby plantation. He suffered years of hard labor, beatings, hunger, and sickness. Finally he managed to escape, hiding out in the wooded mountains. His freedom did not last long. Slave hunters caught up with him. As they closed in, with his bare hands he scratched a hole in the earth and buried the root he had kept with him all those years. From that root sprouted the Umbanda practiced at the *terreiro,* or Afrobrazilian worship center,[2] erected on that very spot in the latter part of the twentieth century.

Story Three: The Extraterrestrials

The spirit of an old slave told me this one:

> Long ago on a faraway planet they called Cabal lived a race of beings as advanced in comparison to us as we are to monkeys. Long ago the highest wise men of the planet Cabal took up the charitable mission of spreading truth and enlightenment outward to all the other inhabited planets in the universe. They selected their brightest, most educated, and most spiritual young people and sent them forth in all directions on space ships capable of light speed travel, so that they could search indefinitely for peopled planets; as Einstein demonstrated, time and therefore aging stops when one reaches those velocities. One such ship happened upon Earth, a raw and savage place inhabited by brutes lacking all but the rudiments of culture and language. The Cabalan missionaries set to work, the fruits of which we see in the inventions of writing and mathematics, the Neolithic revolution, and the almost simultaneous development of civilization in Syria, Egypt, and China, and a little later in the New World. The center of it all, their home base, as it were, was Atlantis, from which all spiritual, technological, and intellectual progress radiated. Unfortunately, a foolish experiment with nuclear power by arrogant scientists ended catastrophically, destroying Atlantis and its Cabalic civilization. A few citizens managed to survive, clinging to flotsam and drifting to black Africa, the one corner of the world the Cabalic enlightenment had not touched. The survivors weren't the best minds of Atlantis, but they were far above the Africans. They introduced metallurgy,

counting, and law — albeit, in simplified form, in deference to the limited capabilities[3] of the African people. They also introduced their spiritist religion, which they called Umbanda after the fundamental vibration Om. Unfortunately, the Atlantans soon succumbed to disease, to native violence, to the sheer despair at being surrounded by such barbarism. As a result, the Africans did not make any substantial advances, and even worse, the sublime Umbanda became mixed with fetishism, superstition, and generally barbaric practices. And that was what the slaves brought to Brazil. There was much truth and enlightenment in their religion — the parts from Cabal, by way of Atlantis — but much error and primitivism, from Africa. Our mission is to purge Umbanda of those impurities. Umbanda, the real Umbanda, isn't an African religion; true Umbanda is Umbanda without Africa.

The "Real" Story

Here is where I planned to give an objective, historical, and analytical account of the origins and development of Umbanda. The account would take these three stories, along with other, more factual if less imaginative, information into account. But now I think: before I do that, before I "explain" Umbanda, let's spend some pages exploring and experiencing this thing that brings a not so young man and an old woman to wade in the surf on New Year's Eve and launch little boats filled with signs of hope and reverence to be swallowed up by the goddess of the sea.

Doctrines and Spirits

Umbanda displays a remarkable diversity of beliefs and practices, but we can briefly state some underlying doctrine.

Ethical and moral values are consistent with the Catholicism that most Umbandistas grew up with and continue to profess. Much emphasis is placed on doing good works for others; this is known as *caridade,* or charity, and it is both an obligation and a source of spiritual reward. These ethical values are imbedded in an overarching, Spiritist cosmology.

Spirits are at the center of Umbanda practice and belief. Following the doctrinal lead of Spiritism, Umbandistas maintain that every living human being is endowed with a material body, and a spirit that preexists the body's birth and survives its death. Following death — or, rather, disincarnation, because the spirit after all does not die, and the spirit is what truly lives — the spirit returns to the *astral,* the realm of pure spirit. Further, the spirit maintains its individuality: thus the *astral* can be seen as a society of souls. This society is remarkably well organized, like a military or corporate bureaucracy, into units and subunits, known, in rather martial language, as "lines" and "phalanxes" or "legions." Like totemic clans, these go by such names as "The Legion of the Mermaids," "The People of Mozambique," "The Legion of the Guaraní" (the latter referring to the Tupi-Guarní, a broad family of indigenous Brazilians: the Caboclo Seven Crossroads would belong to this one), and "The People of the Orient." But unlike the totemic clans of egalitarian societies, the spiritual society of Umbanda is strictly hierarchical. The legions make up the lines, which are under the command of a superior spiritual entity — for example, Iemanjá, the sea-goddess who swallowed up my offering that late afternoon in the waters off Copacabana. And not only are the legions and lines of spirits under the command of a superior officer, so to speak, but spirits are ranked in terms of their level of "elevation," or enlightenment and goodness.

Spirits do not normally remain permanently in the *astral*. After an indefinite period the spirit returns to inhabit a new material body, presumably at the moment of conception. Through reincarnation, the spirit is given the opportunity to evolve by doing good and attaining a higher grade of enlightenment. Both can be achieved through Umbanda. In her work as an Umbanda priestess, Dona Luciana, for example, has helped countless individuals, while steadily gaining greater wisdom. Presumably, she has accumulated considerable good karma (Umbandistas use that term) and can expect to occupy a high position among the People of The Orient (to whom her spirit belongs) during her next tenure in the *astral*.

While disincarnated spirits are believed to inhabit the invisible realm of the *astral*, Umbanda practice brings them into the here-and-now, transforming them from abstract entities into tangible presences ready to help people with the practical, painful problems of their earthly existence. This is done, as you might have guessed from the story about the Caboclo Seven Crossroads, through mediums. In Umbanda (as in Spiritism) some participants — mediums — receive spirits. Through hymns, and in many Umbanda *terreiros,* through drumming as well, the spirits are invited to "descend," to "incorporate," that is, to act and speak through the bodies and mouths of individuals who have developed the gift of mediumship. This occurs during what we would call an "altered state of consciousness," or a "trance," though Umbandistas do not use those terms. In their view, normal consciousness is suspended or submerged as the spirit takes over the medium's body and mind. Some mediums, among them Dona Luciana, are called "unconscious mediums" because they remember nothing of what happens during the trance. Others report having fragmented, vague, or confused memories; one medium told me that the experience of trance was somewhat like a half-remembered dream. In either case, the medium takes on the personality of a disincarnated spirit, and the spirit can then communicate through the medium with the living. This is what people come to Umbanda for, mainly. If you are having marital problems, if you have lost your job, haven't been feeling well, are suffering emotionally, whatever the problem — you can tell the spirit, the spirit can get to the root of it, give you advice, offer spiritual protection and support. The spirits are willing to help you, to perform *caridade,* "charity" which earns the spirits — and their mediums — karmic credit.

Let's meet a few of these spirits of Umbanda. We'll start with a kind of spirit that *doesn't* incorporate in Umbanda mediums, but is nonetheless of great importance to the religion.

Orixás

Iemanjá, to whom Dona Luciana and I made our offerings on that New Year's afternoon, is an *Orixá.* The Orixás are African deities, originally numbering in the hundreds, of which about a dozen survived in the hearts and souls of the slaves and their descendants. Especially in the Afrobrazilian religion known as Candomblé,[4] each Orixá is the subject of a rich mythology. As in the Greek or Norse or Roman mythologies, Orixás are associated with nature — in fact, they are often referred to as *forças da natureza,* forces of nature. Iemanjá, for example, is found in the dynamic forces of the sea, while culturally she embodies the ideal of the wise, strong, mother who gives without limit to her children. To offer just a few more examples, Ogum is the god of war, the patron of agriculture, and the indefatigable blacksmith whose forge gives humankind both swords and plowshares. His forces are found within human nature. Ogum is courage, drive, the forge-like heat of anger, the warrior's dual nature of sunny optimism and grim determination. His brother Oxossi is the hunter, and the forest. Xangô is the thunderbolt, the lord of justice and the master of stoneworking. Oxum is fresh running water, the cascade, fertility, and luxurious, domestic femininity. A rather different feminine ideal is expressed by Iansa, who lives in the whirling tempest, a warrior goddess, fierce and independent and beautiful, who, when she dances in the body of her medium, twirls like a tornado, a short, curved broadsword in one hand, a horsetail flywhisk in the other, a powderhorn slung over each shoulder.

The Orixás are at once very near and very distant in Umbanda. Very near, in that the Orixás are ever present in all aspects of our culture, and in the forces and features of our natural environment; Oxum in the clear running stream, Xangô and Iansa in the thundering, pelting storm, Omolu in the diseases that rack our bodies and the healing that, hopefully, soothes them. Very near, too, in the sense that each person is seen as being the spiritual offspring of Orixás. When Dona Luciana refers to Iemanjá as *mãe,* "mother," she is at one level using a conventional form of address — the female Orixás are often referred to as mother, the males as father — while at another she underscores her belief that Iemanjá is, indeed, her spiritual mother. (Her spiritual father is Ogum). Just as one's physical traits are in large part a mixture of the characteristics of one's biological parents, so the spirit, the soul, the character of the child bears the marks of its parents.

Very near — as close as the depths of one's being — but also very far. Umbanda, in contrast to Candomblé, does not invite the Orixás to manifest themselves through mediums. (The scene of Iansa dancing comes from my observations at an Umbanda center that occurred on a night devoted to the practice of Candomblé.) As Dona Luciana explained, the Orixás are so powerful, so beyond human strength and comprehension, that to bring them directly into our presence would be dangerous, like playing with lava. Not only that, the Orixás are too elevated and evolved to relate to the mundane concerns of primitive beings like ourselves. As she put it, they have an *astral* to run!

Caboclos

Before I go any further, let me explain how I write about mediums and spirits. When a medium like Dona Luciana is in a trance, receiving a spirit such as Jurema, I use the name of the spirit to describe her actions, words, dress, and so forth. Thus, I might say, "I told Jurema that I had been having some gastrointestinal troubles.... Jurema felt around my stomach and lower abdomen.... She then prescribed a tea made from *boldo,* a thoroughly nasty smelling herb I could obtain at the market...." I also use the spirit's name when I describe its personality, life history, etc; in short, I write as if the spirit is a person. That is in line with how Umbandistas talk about, believe about, and relate to spirits, and mediums receiving spirits. Whether you or I share those beliefs is beside the point; in anthropology, what matters is *their* cultural reality.

Seven Crossroads, the spirit that spoke through Zélio de Morais nearly a hundred years ago, establishing a religion that would welcome Brazilians and spirits of all colors and classes, was a caboclo. Caboclos are typically the spirits of Brazilian Indians. Generally, they are young, vigorous, brave, and they carry names that connect them to the realm of nature, the forest, and a romanticized past of "noble savages": Seven Arrows, Gilded Mountain, Tupinambá (a reference to the Tupi-Guaraní, the linguistic family to which many of the Brazilian tribes belong), and Coral Snake, to name a few. The songs that invite the caboclos to descend evoke such images as moonlit forests, waterfalls, anacondas and boa constrictors and other wildlife, and *aldeias,* villages nestled in the wilderness. Perhaps because they are so close to nature, and because they are conceived of as noble and strong, the caboclos represent or embody the Orixás in human form. A song that summons Dona Luciana's cabocla Jurema, for example, tells us that she comes from the sea, bringing with her the forces of Iemanjá.

The caboclos employ these forces to help people deal with their problems. Financial troubles, loss of a job, friction with a spouse or lover, fits of irrational anger or bouts of depression, drinking, a rebellious child or a string of bad luck: all these problems and more have a spiritual dimension, and the caboclos stand ready to help. The sufferer approaches the caboclo, who stands straight and tall, perhaps smoking a big cigar. Some caboclos will grasp the patient by the shoulders and forcefully embrace her, first to one side of the chest then the other, before proceeding with a *passé*, vigorously running the hands (or some leafy branches) over her body, from head to toe, an action that both cleanses and invigorates the spiritual body. The caboclo might blow smoke over the person as well, for the same purpose. The caboclo listens intently as the patient tells her troubles, interrupting the narrative to ask questions and urge the patient to get to the point. Caboclos, like mythical Indians, are spirits of few words. The caboclo gives his advice, often tough advice, and perhaps a prescription to make an offering. The caboclo might promise to look further into the matter, and usually requests that the person return on such and such a day, and that is it.

Dona Luciana receives a number of different caboclo spirits. One is called Rompe Mata (literally, "break [through the] forest"; Trail Blazer better captures the sense of the name). Dona Luciana's Rompe Mata[5] doesn't counsel people about their problems. His job, instead, is to bring the forces of the Orixá Ogum, god of war, to the ritual. Ogum's spirit protects and fortifies the ritual and those who participate. Another of Dona Luciana's caboclos, Jurema, does provide counsel. Her advice and spiritual intervention is, in fact, frequently sought after and highly acclaimed. But Jurema, who brings with her the powers of Iemanjá, Dona Luciana's spiritual mother, is much more than a wise counselor.

I met Jurema at the first Umbanda session I attended, in June of 1986. I knew from reading about Umbanda that caboclos were spirits of Brazilian Indians. So when I was introduced to Jurema, I thought that to make conversation (Jurema certainly seemed to be a woman of few words) I would ask her about her tribe. She fixed me a hard gaze, and, in no uncertain terms and in a rather indignant tone, informed me that she had no tribe, that, as anyone could tell, Jurema was not an Indian at all, but a white woman. Oops. *Desculpe, Eu não sou daqui* (Pardon me, I'm not from here, I said.) Jurema's expression softened. It turns out that this Jurema was born in Portugal, daughter of a court official, who brought her with him on a mission to the interior of Brazil during colonial times. Somewhere in the backlands, Jurema was bitten by a snake, and died.

I would come to know Jurema well over the years and learn that Jurema plays a very important role in Dona Luciana's life. She is, Dona Luciana says, her guardian angel, always looking over her, warning her of danger, through subtle signs and intuitions, pointing her in the right direction, and chastising her when she strays. Beyond their public, ritual role, caboclos often take on the very personal role of protector, advisor, and beloved spiritual companion. They can become, as we will see, a powerful symbol of the self.

The Old Slaves

I will refer to the *pretos velhos* (literally "old blacks") as the old slaves, because they are conceived of as the spirits of Afrobrazilian slaves, and it is the cultural fact of their slavery, and not the color of their skin, that stands out in their character. These old slaves are equally sought out as advisors. Perhaps more so, where the caboclos bring the forces of the Orixás and the qualities of boldness, courage, and strength, the old slaves stand out for their wisdom, patience, and compassion. If you are having problems with a relationship, or with your own emotions, the old slave will listen patiently, puffing away at an old pipe, maybe sipping some cheap red wine from a little black cup,[6] asking the occasional question, gradually getting to the bottom of the trouble. His or her comments and advice will be given with gentleness, sympathy, and humility. It is no wonder they are often called "the psychoanalysts of the poor."

I have also heard old slaves referred to as *sofredores,* sufferers. Their bodies are worn out. They walk hunched over, leaning on their canes; some shake with palsy. Their voices creak with age. Some tell stories of beatings, betrayals, exhaustion, hunger, longing for Africa, and for loved ones sold away or killed. Others won't talk about their "time in captivity," but their bodies tell the story. For example, an old slave that I came to know fairly well, Congo King, would break into a prolonged, violent stutter every several words (his medium is fluent), his eyes wide and terrified, before composing himself and going on. He wouldn't talk about the old times, but others speculated that beatings had damaged his brain, or his psyche, or both.

Exus

In West Africa, and in the traditional Afrobrazilian Candomblé, Exu is counted among the Orixás. A trickster, Exu amuses himself making fools of gods and human beings. For example, one day Exu spies two farmers bantering from opposite sides of the road separating their properties. Exu dons an exquisite leather cap, black on the left side, red on the right. He makes quite a spectacle as he dances up the road. Passing them, and just out of sight, he hides in the bushes, laughing himself silly as the two friends get into an argument about the strange fellow in the black — no red — no black — red, you fool! Fool is you, take that! Pow! And you take this! bam! — hat.

Despite his mischief and malice, Exu is essential. His tricks shake things up, push things forward. And, Exu, like Hermes or Mercury, is the messenger, mediating between human beings and Orixás. As they say in Afrobrazilian religion: *sem exu, não faz nada* (without Exu, nothing is done).

Exu is a little different in Umbanda. To begin with, there are exus, plural. Like the caboclos and the old slaves, these exus are conceived of as the spirits of once living human beings. And unlike the noble caboclos, or the humble and kindly old slaves, these exus are morally ambiguous — in fact, they are outright sinners. In life, it seems, they were colorful characters: bohemians, swindlers, prostitutes (in Umbanda, exu has a female counterpart, the *pomba gira*), low lifes of all kinds. Their colors are red and black, and sometimes they dress in black top hats and black and red capes, looking for all the world like Lucifers. But the exus who visit Umbanda are not really evil. They are ambiguous; like Exu's leather cap, they have two sides. A song, for instance, tells us that Exu has two heads — one is that of Satan from hell; the other, that of Jesus of Nazareth. By working for the good, by helping Umbandistas with their problems, the exus (like the caboclos, like the old slaves) improve their karma and better themselves spiritually. They are good advisors and powerful cunning allies. And they are lots of fun. Bawdy, exaggerated, earthy, raucous (though some are terribly grim), at once fools and tricksters, good and evil, formidable and flawed, the exus bring life and joy to Umbanda, and are much loved, no doubt because they are all too human.

Exus, old slaves, and caboclos — these are the spirits that people come to talk to when they have troubles. There are the Orixás, essential in terms of cosmology and the "folk psychology" of Umbanda. There are also child spirits, who are not advisors but rather emissaries of joy who typically appear to enliven and lighten the heavy atmosphere at the close of a long, difficult session.

We have seen how spirits come to "work" through mediums. How do mediums come to work with spirits in Umbanda?

"They Were Calling Me..."

Dona Luciana was in her forties and was in a world of pain. Her marriage was falling apart; the husband she had so loved since her youth, with whom she had three children, had become like a stranger, worse, a mean, tormenting stranger. They couldn't divorce; this was Brazil in the 1960s, and divorce was not a legal option. She was unspeakably sad, confused, hopeless, at the end of her rope. Dona Luciana, an educated and sophisticated woman of the upper middle class, sought the expert care of psychologists and medical doctors, but it did no good. A friend finally was able to get her to come with her to an Umbanda session, though Dona Luciana was highly resistant, believing it all to be superstition and ignorance.

From what Dona Luciana told me, and from the hundreds of Umbanda sessions I have attended over the years, I can vividly picture what must have transpired that night.[7] Arriving at the center, Dona Luciana and her friend briefly and quietly spoke with a woman, clothed in a white cotton dress, who gave them a number, wrote their names down on her clipboard, and directed them to be seated in one of the rows of benches facing the main ritual space. They took their seats, in the front row, alongside a number of other women, of various ages, classes, and colors. Men took seats on benches on the other side of the main aisle. Dona Luciana sat nervously, taking in the unfamiliar surroundings. In front of her, beyond a low railing, lay a freshly waxed floor. Elevated against the back wall, a large statue of Jesus, arms outstretched in the familiar pose of Christ the Redeemer who over-looks the city of Rio from his mountaintop. To his right, on an altar bedecked with images of St. Jerome, Santa Barbara, St. George, Our Lady of the Concep-tion, St. Ann, Saints Cosmo and Damien, and several statues of old black men, Indians, and even a bare-chested, leather-hatted Northeastern Brazil cowboy, sev-eral candles burned, while vases of roses and gladioluses freshened the view. A man dressed in white came out, approached the rail, blessed the audience, turned and prayed silently in front of the statue of Christ before taking a seat off to the side. From off to the right, twenty or so mediums, mostly women, all dressed in white, filed in, each in turn touching her forehead to the floor in front of the statue, then kneeling in front of the seated man, who touched her head, took her hands in his, and gave his word of blessing. The mediums assembled in a semi-circle, facing the man who, now standing and facing the audience, recited a brief Christian prayer, before leading the mediums in a series of songs, punctuated by handclapping, saluting the various Orixás, and then, finally, calling down the spir-its of the caboclos who would be performing their charitable mission of healing and guidance that night.

At some point during the singing and clapping, Dona Luciana went into a trance and became spontaneously possessed. I have seen this happen innumerable times; a member of the audience will, more or less suddenly, burst into a flailing, sometimes screaming fit. Quickly restrained, she will be brought into the ritual space, surrounded by mediums, who work to bring the trance under control. The possession is often quite violent, with weeping or cursing or moaning; this is because the possessing spirit is a bad spirit — indeed, often it is this entity that is causing the person's troubles. The mediums will admonish the spirit to leave, to stop tormenting this victim. The exorcism complete, the person returns to normal, drained but feeling much better. But with Dona Luciana, things went very differently. Far from a chaotic, uncontrolled, inarticulate attack, Dona Luciana was calmly possessed by a series of spirits, each articulately introducing herself or himself. Afterward, the leader told her that the Orixás were calling her to serve them, as a medium, as a vehicle by which caboclos and old slaves and exus and pomba giras and the spirits of little children could alleviate the suffering of people like herself. The unprecedented nature of her initial possession demonstrated that her calling was truly extraordinary. She could refuse the call, but surely her own suffering would increase until she gave in, or she could answer it. She did, and

Dona Luciana devoted the rest of her life to the charitable work of the spirits, both as a medium, and as the leader of her own Umbanda center.

Dona Luciana's story, in broad outline, is typical of dozens of detailed accounts I heard from mediums describing their entry into Umbanda. Almost always it begins with a person in crisis: it may be a physical ailment, alcoholism, or painful emotional illness. In most cases the person resists seeking the help of the spirits, but eventually relents. An old slave, or a caboclo, or it might be several spirits, give the diagnosis: the Orixás are calling. Or it might be put differently, that the person is unusually sensitive to the spiritual world, thus vulnerable to the attacks of bad spirits; the only cure is to learn how to use that sensitivity, to turn the curse into a gift of spiritual charity. In many of these stories, the person refuses the call and suffers a string of torments, before finally giving in. This begins a process of *desenvolvimento,* development, in which the person learns, through experience, the art of mediumship and the doctrines of Umbanda. The story has a happy ending; though life can never be without its troubles, the typical medium reports that she faces life with tranquility, knowing the spirits are there looking over her, that she is doing the good, charitable work that she was meant to do. Stepping away from this socio-spiritual explanation, an "objective," social-psychological explanation for the cure would be that learning to be a medium teaches the person about herself, and to accept herself; that it provides her outlets for self-expression; it surrounds her with a supportive community, while giving her a valued role within that community. Whether one accepts the spiritual explanation, the sociological-psychological explanation, or both, my observation is that mediums who have been at this for several years are, on the whole, well-adjusted, energetic, tranquil, and strong.

Umbanda in the Twentieth Century: Back to the Beginning

When anthropologists listen closely to myths they often hear hints and whispers of truths that go deeper than facts. Literal truth is not the issue. I do not believe in travelers from the planet Cabal, nor in Atlantis; and while I find it plausible enough that a sorcerer from Angola could escape from a plantation in Rio and then die at the hands of his captors, I don't believe that a religion sprouts from the cutting of a magical root. As for the caboclo Seven Crossroads...well, we know that Zélio de Morais existed, that he founded a Spiritist center where old slaves and caboclos were welcomed, and that he continued his work for several decades, but did the caboclo Seven Crossroads really make that dramatic declaration on the night of November 15, 1908? I don't know, and I don't believe it matters. What matters is that these three myths tell us a great deal about how Umbanda came to be what it is.

Let's start with the root. Enslaved peoples from West and Central Africa brought with them their religious traditions, which they kept hidden. For example, our sorcerer hid his root from the repressive gaze of white society. These traditions flourished, albeit oftentimes in secret, subjected to ridicule in the press, vehement attacks from the Catholic Church, and violent repression by the police — even during the twentieth century. You can read a fictional (but not for that a less true) account of such repression in Jorge Amado's wonderful novel *Tenda dos Milagres,* available in an English translation, *Tent of Miracles*, or you can just consider the fact that for years the Civil Police of Rio de Janeiro proudly displayed the religious artifacts they seized in raids on *terreiros.* In any event, in the early twentieth century, when Umbanda began, Afrobrazilian religion was a pervasive, though somewhat clandestine, presence in Rio de Janeiro.

The story of Zélio de Morais mythically (and with some factuality) dramatizes the key turn from the old Afrobrazilian traditions toward Umbanda. That was the incorporation of Spiritist doctrines and practices. Mediums, ideas about reincarnation, the concept of charity, the whole cosmological system of the *astral,* lines and legions — those are the fruits of the cross-fertilization of Spiritism and Afrobrazilian traditions. This is what makes Umbanda, Umbanda, however much it retains of its African roots. The traditional Afrobrazilian religions, such as Candomblé, are oriented mainly toward celebrating the Orixás; Umbanda aims mainly toward alleviating suffering through spiritual intervention and achieving individual spiritual growth and karmic improvement.

The Cabal story suggests two crucial facets of Umbanda's development. The first is its voracious appetite for compelling symbols and images and concepts from wherever it finds them. I am reminded of a seminal event in Brazilian cultural history, the Week of Modern Art, held in São Paulo in 1922. Writers and artists on the cutting edge of Brazilian high culture expounded a new project, what they called *antropofagia,* or "cannibalism." The idea was to devour whatever one could take from whatever sources and traditions one could find, and then digest them to produce a new, vital, and Brazilian art. Umbanda, which begins in the same epoch, shares this appetite. In my research I found not only African traditions, and Spiritism, and old slaves and Indians, but also Tarot cards, concepts such as archetypes from Jungian psychology, the powers of pyramids and crystals, spirits of Gypsies and Bedouins and even a Chinese scholar and a charming geisha from beyond the grave. Not to mention Cabalistic esoterica and tales of Atlantis.

The second facet is a darker one, and I am sure my reader was troubled by it as she read the story. Racism has certainly played an important role in the formation of Umbanda. The brilliant Brazilian sociologist Renato Ortiz some years ago wrote a book entitled *A morte branco do feiticeiro negro* (The white death of the black sorcerer). In it, he lays out the history of Umbanda as a process of "whitening" the stigmatized Afrobrazilian traditions. For decades, many Umbanda leaders sought to purge practices that carried the "taint" of Africa, associated as it was in the dominant (and racist) ideology with "superstition," "ignorance," and "barbarism." These leaders railed against such practices as animal sacrifice, "wild" dancing, and even drumming — all three of which are essential elements of Afrobrazilian religion. These leaders espoused a "Pure Umbanda" (as in, purified of the "contaminations" of Africa, as our Cabal story has it); it is telling that a different adjective, connoting purity, is often used instead, with unintended irony: "White Umbanda." I collected the Cabal story at just such a house of White Umbanda, one dating back, incidentally, to the 1940s. Far from all practitioners of White Umbanda are overtly racist; Dona Luciana, for example, is not. It is important also to point out that far from all Umbanda is White Umbanda; many, many Umbanda groups and Umbandistas valorize the African roots of Umbanda; practice the traditional drumming, dancing, and even blood sacrifice; are proud of their own Afrobrazilian ancestry, if they have that; and thoroughly oppose racism.

Umbanda experienced remarkable growth through much of the twentieth century. Anthropologist Diana Brown, who conducted field research on Umbanda in Rio de Janeiro in the 1960s, estimated that by the 1970s, it had "10 to 20 million adherents, that is, as much as 10 percent of the Brazilian population." Millions more no doubt participated on an occasional basis. Some reasons for this popularity are implicit in our discussion.

First, Umbanda offers help for the crises and chronic problems of everyday life. Life is hard, and it is very hard if you are poor, but even the well off are not immune from illness, depression, stress, broken hearts, troubled children, straying spouses, and all the rest. Whether or not old slaves and caboclos can intervene spiritually is not really the question; what matters is that they listen, they advise, they support, and the rituals they do on people's behalf give sufferers hope, and that all-important assurance that they are understood and that they are cared for. The great French social theorist Emile Durkheim told us that when old mores and values and ways of life are torn asunder by rapid social change, anomie — a profoundly alienated, disorienting normless-ness — can take hold. The twentieth century was certainly a time of rapid, and often chaotic and overwhelming, change in Brazilian society, especially for the urban masses. As an antidote to anomie, Umbanda offered a rich and dynamic structure of meaning.

Second, Umbanda's appeal is not restricted to any particular racial group or social class. Umbandistas I have worked with include residents of the favelas (slums) that dot Rio's mountainsides and its far flung, impoverished suburbs, working-class men and women with solid jobs, white collar professionals, and a few wealthy lawyers and businessmen. A medium that I came to know well was married to a general. Umbanda can make this broad appeal because it comes in different flavors. One of the groups I worked with was very strongly African in its orientation. They honored the major Orixás in annual all-night celebrations where they made blood sacrifices to them. Dona Luciana, while respecting those traditions, rejected them — not her style of Umbanda. And at least some members of the group from which I collected the Cabal story found such practices thoroughly repugnant, "backward," and ignorant. But they all call what they do Umbanda. Through much of its history, there have been attempts to standardize Umbanda; various strains have established "Federations" with codes and guidelines. None has really been able to establish hegemony, the result being that there are many rooms in Umbanda's house.

Third, Umbanda has been largely successful in avoiding repression. The "whitening" process that Ortiz describes played a part, but so has the willingness of Umbanda leaders to advocate for their religion in the press. Perhaps most importantly, Umbanda attracted powerful allies (and adherents), among the business class, politicians (who found that patronizing Umbanda leaders gave them entrée to voters in the congregation), and military officers, many of whom were strongly attracted to Umbanda's Spiritist doctrine, the cosmological vision of an *astral* ordered along military lines, as well as to Umbanda's nationalist flavor as a uniquely Brazilian religion.

Finally, Umbanda provides opportunities for self-expression, involvement with a community, self-realization, and a richly imaginative, engaging, spiritual life. Dona Luciana, for example, enacts a whole repertoire of spirits (of course, "enacts" is my term): a geisha, a *flamenca* dancer, a Spanish Crusader, an Indian princess, and a *pitoresco* slave by the name of Father Gerônimo. Over the years, I have come to see that these spirits may speak through her, but in important and rewarding ways, she speaks through them. When she was active as a medium and Umbanda leader, a whole community revolved around her, and she around it. And Umbanda gave her a set of practices and symbols and concepts with which to engage the spiritual, to reenchant her world, to make it a place where one wades from the brown sugar sand of Copacabana beach into the realm of Iemanjá.

Umbanda in the Twenty-First Century

As I write this, Umbanda seems to be shrinking in popularity. Diana Brown, who in the 1986 edition of her book talked about 10 to 20 million adherents, by 1993 noted that the enormous New Year's celebration of Iemanjá that she witnessed in 1970 had shrunk to about ten scattered groups performing rituals on the beach, amid great crowds of tourists there for the fireworks. After seeing Dona Luciana home that late afternoon in 1994, I returned to the beach and observed a much larger number of groups than that, some with as many as fifty people, making offerings and dancing. But their presence was underwhelming.

Where have so many Umbandistas gone? Those who have left seem to have gone in two major directions. Many have abandoned Umbanda in favor of the traditional Afrobrazilian Candomblé. In part this is because Candomblé has become a powerful symbol of Afrobrazilian identity — the "real thing," not "mixed" with the Spiritism and Catholicism of the oppressive white elites. Artists, especially musicians such as Gaetano Veloso, Gilberto Gil, Daniela Mercury, as well as writers and intellectuals celebrate the beauty, tradition, and wisdom of Candomblé. Large numbers of those who were, or would have become, Umbandistas, now find Candomblé more compelling, "deeper," more demanding, and more satisfying.

Equally important, Brazil (and Latin America in general) has seen an enormous growth in Pentecostal Protestantism over the last twenty years. As I write these lines, Pope Benedict is in the middle of a five-day visit to Brazil, and surely one of his major objectives is to try to stem the hemorrhage of Catholics into the storefront Pentecostal churches that proliferate in every poor neighborhood in the country. Only 72 percent of Brazilians now identify themselves as Catholics. Pentecostals have done at least as well, perhaps better, in drawing in Umbandistas. Millions of Brazilians over the years turned to Umbanda to make their lives better. For millions, like Dona Luciana, it has. But for further millions, especially those afflicted with poverty, the spirits may offer solace, but not solutions. Pentecostalism confidently claims to have the answer: a rigid moral code and deliverance from the demons of alcoholism, drugs, and the demons of Umbanda, for that is what they consider those caboclos and old slaves and exus to be. Pentecostalism promises salvation, community, and self-respect. And for many, many Brazilians, it has delivered.

I have worked in the field of religion in Brazil for the last twenty years. Perhaps I should make a wish to see what the next twenty years will bring — because I can't predict (without that help) what will happen.

Oh, about that other wish that I made that afternoon more than a decade ago. Dona Luciana told me to keep it in my heart and not tell anyone until it came to pass. It did, so I can tell it. At that time I had been feeling frustrated, sad, and somewhat unreal. I was done with graduate school, looking for work in a very difficult academic job market, listlessly rewriting my dissertation as yet another one of those academic books that practically no one would read, while my heart tried desperately to deny that a once great love was dying. Where I was I could not be. Or worse, I could be there for a long time, every day dying that much more. And yet I could find no way forward, it seemed. *O Iemanjá, fico bloqueado, abra meu caminho, quero chegar a ter uma vida da verdade....* Oh, Iemanjá, I'm stuck, open my road, I want to arrive at a true life...and gulp! The sea swallowed up my little boat.

My Umbanda friends would often say, when talking about dealing with the spirits and the Orixás, *isto aqui não é brincadeira, não....* This is no joke. Over the

241

next few years, Iemanjá would carry out my wish, though not as I had anticipated. She would swallow up and spit out a marriage; bounce me out of a high-paying but soul-killing job; kill some aspirations I once held dear but that were killing me; and shatter any number of illusions. Much that needed to die drowned in her waves, starting from that day. What was left was what I asked for that afternoon, a true life, and the open roads of Iemanjá's watery kingdom. Make a wish.

Notes

1. Names and certain details have been changed to protect the privacy of informants. "Dona" is a traditional term of respect used before the first name of a married or widowed woman. I have never heard anyone *not* use it in referring to Dona Luciana.

2. "Worship center" is an awkward construction, but the alternatives may be misleading. To call it a "church" risks bringing in a great deal of connotative baggage, while "sacred space" ignores the fact that in Umbanda, there are many kinds of sacred space, for example waterfalls and seashores and forests are all places for spiritual encounter.

3. This story was told me by an "old slave" spirit, by the name of Mané. His comment about "limited capacity" unfortunately reflects, I think, the medium's biases. Mané on other occasions gave a much different, simpler account of how the Cabalans came to inhabit Earth. It seems that the Cabalans were pure spirit, but spirit, apparently, follows a version of the laws of physics. Over thousands of years, they grew so numerous that the planet's gravitational field couldn't hold them all. Some were spun off into space, wandering through the cosmos until they happened on planet Earth.

4. "Candomblé" is a generic term referring to Afrobrazilian religions that more or less closely adhere to the African religions from which they derive. There are a number of different forms of Candomblé, corresponding to different regions in Africa. For example, the most famous Candomblés of Salvador, Bahia, follow the Nagô or Yoruba traditions, from what is now Nigeria. Others follow traditions derived from Angola, Congo, and various regions of West Africa.

5. I say "Dona Luciana's Rompe Mata" because that name, like many other spirit names, is used by any number of spirits at different Umbanda centers. Her Rompe Mata is not the same as, say, Dona Linda's Rompe Mata, who is in turn different from Seu Souza's Rompe Mata, both of whom do counsel visitors.

6. Some Umbanda centers strictly forbid drinking. At Dona Luciana's, for example, none of the spirits partake of spirits.

7. The description I offer, especially the visual details, is what I imagine: I wasn't there, I never saw the place where this occurred, and of course Dona Luciana did not provide a detailed, video-eye view of what transpired a quarter century earlier. The descriptive details are a composite of what I observed at a number of different Umbanda centers, but I must point out that there is considerable variation from place to place. For example, some places use drums to call down the spirits and dance the traditional dances of the Orixás; others do not. But it must have been something like this, or not much different.

13

The Catholic Church
and Social Revolutionaries

Jennifer S. Hughes

The 1970s and 1980s were a period of unprecedented upheaval in the Roman Catholic Church in Latin America, in particular with respect to the church's role in society and the political arena. These decades, troubled, turbulent, and full of hope, constitute the period during which the theology of liberation flourished and reached its maximum influence.[1] Shaped and inspired by this new and radical theology that emphasized political practice with justice as its aim for the poorest Latin Americans, what may be termed "Catholic social revolutionaries" appeared in varied and unexpected forms.

In 1968 a gray-haired group of men gathered in Medellín, Colombia, for the second meeting of CELAM, the Conference of Latin American Bishops. They came to pray for, discuss, and envision the future of Latin American Catholicism. The second Vatican Council, concluded in Rome just three years earlier, had explored the meaning of contemporary modernity for the Roman Catholic Church and charted a new, more open course, creating an opportunity for radical change within the church liturgically, theologically, and socially. At Medellín the bishops sought to translate the advances of Vatican II into the Latin American reality and to enlarge upon aspects of conciliar theology to better respond to demands from within their own cultural, social, and political context. Two concerns weighed heavily upon the bishops as the conference started: the grinding poverty of their flocks and the political instability of their countries, many of which were succumbing to military dictators or increasingly oppressive regimes.[2]

The official statements of the conference published under the title "The Church in the Present-day Transformation of Latin America in the Light of the Council,"[3] marked the beginning of a new era for the church. From its colonial origins, the Latin American church was an institution entrenched in systems of political and economic power, its bishops almost always identifying their interests with those of the economic and political elites. The Medellín documents represented a radical break with this history. They contain scathing criticisms of Latin America's ruling classes, of foreign capitalism, chronic poverty, and social injustice. Above all, the final statements articulate the church's primary commitment to the material and social liberation of the impoverished masses of Latin America. With these declarations, Medellín became the location of the first official, systematized articulation of the theology of liberation.

In the same decade, a thousand miles away, Ernesto Cardenal, Nicaraguan artist, poet, and ardent pastor, lived, worked, and prayed with the humble women and men of the rural fishing community of Solentiname, an archipelago in Lake Nicaragua. The priest met every Sunday with the local peasants to reflect upon and interpret the New Testament Gospels in light of the local experience of suffering and struggle. Together they formed a Christian base community, or CEB (as it is abbreviated in Spanish). At Medellín, these Christian communities, gaining in strength and popularity in Brazil and El Salvador, were posited as the fundamental expression of a newly conceived ecclesiology that emphasized the central role of lay believers to form the basis of a "popular church" and become agents of their own liberation, rather than mere objects of evangelization.[4] Father Cardenal could sometimes be found speaking animatedly and at other times listening intently to the group's reflections. Though the Solentiname peasants had no formal theological training and many were illiterate, Cardenal and other proponents of liberation theology considered these peasants and others like them privileged interpreters of the Scriptures because of their ability to grasp the message of the Gospels at a depth that eluded both formally trained theologians and middle-class and affluent Christians.

The god that emerged in the Solentiname dialogues desired not only their spiritual salvation but their earthly liberation: political, economic, and spiritual. Thus, the Solentiname community's specific reflections on the Bible in the 1970s quite logically emphasized the oppression of the Nicaraguan poor by the U.S.-backed Somoza dictatorship, which had ruled the country for decades. The community saw in Jesus their Nicaraguan brothers and sisters who had been arrested, tortured, and murdered by the military. They analyzed class structures and spoke of their desire for justice, love, and community, and ultimately they sympathized with the Sandinista rebels who were struggling to overthrow the Somoza regime. They contemplated the revolution and considered whether they as Christians should participate in that struggle. Their collective reflections (published in four volumes under the title *The Gospel in Solentiname*) eventually led many of them to take up arms — after the community was attacked by the Guardia Nacional — and join the Sandinistas in what became the successful defeat of Somoza in 1979.[5] For the peasants of Solentiname there was no contradiction between their Christian faith and the political agenda of the Sandinistas: indeed, some have observed that liberation theology provided the "overarching ideology" for the Sandinista revolution.[6]

Finally, in Brazil in the 1980s, the lay woman and Catholic social revolutionary Dona Margarida da Silva mobilized her local Christian base community in the small town of Bom Jardim in the impoverished and drought-ridden state of Pernambuco, Brazil. I met Margarida in the late 1980s, when I was an undergraduate student studying the popular church movement in Brazil. Strikingly tall and *india* (of indigenous descent), Margarida had no formal education or training other than what she received at occasional weekend workshops sponsored by ITER (the Theological Institute of Recife), a liberation theology seminary located in the state capital. Margarida, as I recall her, was a dynamo — full of faith, with no illusions about the plight of the poor, but indefatigably hopeful, and with an irreverent sense of humor — qualities that made her a famously successful *animadora* (or community organizer). "We've had enough of the church of *pregação e pecados*," she used to say, rejecting the church's traditional emphasis on individual sinfulness and salvation. "Now is the time of the new church, the church of hope and of the poor."[7]

Margarida often traveled to other communities in the region, strategizing with local women about how to overcome the many ills that plagued them: high infant mortality rates, chronic hunger, and terrifying "disappearances" wrought by government death squads. She spent several days in the rural community where I was living organizing the *lavadeiras* (the washer-women who worked for pennies a day laundering by hand the clothes of the wealthy) to unite and demand a living wage. Margarida always began her visits by leading small groups of women in prayer, Bible study, and song. I can still hear the hopeful urgency of those liberating hymns that echoed the Old Testament Psalms in their poetic and unrelenting condemnation of those who oppress the poor: "Open the door to Jesus, good people, for he arrives tired with the weight of the cross. There is no value in amassing wealth, stolen from the poor every blessed day. There is no value in pursuing power to rule over others, to make their cross heavier to bear. Open the door to Jesus, good people, open your hearts and share your life with your brother."[8]

These three examples, the revolutionary declarations of the bishops of CELAM, the Gospel as preached and practiced by Ernesto Cardenal and the peasants of Solentiname, and the ministry of Margarida the *animadora,* capture the depth and complexity of the faith-filled political radicalism that defined much of Latin American Catholicism during the latter third of the twentieth century. This liberating theology of grassroots and episcopal activism inspired and moved poor people, peasants, university students, priests, and bishops alike. It is best comprehended as a lived religion, that is, as a personal and collective practice of faith (both lay and clerical), worked out in the specifics of local cultural contexts, and in dynamic engagement with both the rich religious traditions and the ambiguous history of Christianity in Latin America.[9] The cultural-historical approach to the topic I offer here reveals that liberation theology is, in fact, highly local and varied in its expression, as frequently aesthetic in nature as it is political, and always, at every moment, authentically and uniquely Latin American.

In the next three sections of this chapter I will contextualize each of the examples in order to identify (1) the defining aspects of the liberation theology movement, (2) the meaning and significance liberation theology holds for individual believers and their communities, and (3) the movement's global and historical origins, impact, and relevance. My reading of the movement is sympathetic, although not uncritical, and it makes note of the heroism and even sanctity of its leaders.

The People's Bishops:
Saints and Martyrs for the Twentieth Century

A common interpretation posits liberation theology as, most importantly, an ecclesiastical event. Its origins, history, and fate are understood as the products of global, institutional, and intellectual forces birthed in meetings of cardinals and bishops in Europe and the largest Latin American urban centers, shepherded by priests, and brought to full maturity by highly trained theologians, with its fate determined by the policies and pronouncements of popes and presidents. In this interpretation local communities like Solentiname are sometimes regarded as theological laboratories: the social space where these policies and theologies are worked out and finally put into practice. This way of narrating the story of liberation theology is only partially accurate — it is limited by being disproportionately clerical, institutional, hierarchical, and Eurocentric.

And yet, it is not wrong to begin this discussion with the bishops gathered at Medellín. Many of them labored to create the infrastructure for liberation theology in their respective dioceses, and some were to become the saints, heroes, and martyrs of twentieth-century Latin American Roman Catholicism. These "people's bishops," called so because they won the trust and the affections of the poor, include most importantly Hélder Pessoa Câmara of Bahia, Samuel Ruiz García of Chiapas, Sergio Méndez Arceo of Cuernavaca, and Oscar Arnulfo Romero of San Salvador.

These and the other bishops who gathered at Medellín did much more than simply transform the Latin American church in accordance with the decrees of the Second Vatican Council.[10] In fact, several Latin American bishops, especially Hélder Câmara and Sergio Méndez, actually shaped the course of the discussion and the theology that emerged at Vatican II.

The diminutive, gentle but outspoken bishop from Brazil, Hélder Câmara, was a driving force at the council, though his greatest influence was outside the formal sessions, where he mobilized members to push an agenda especially meaningful to Latin America: the church's obligation to the poor. The so-called "church of the poor" was the subject of dozens of interventions (statements from the session floor) coming from a small, vocal, and persistent group of Latin American and European bishops who saw the council as an opportunity to call the church to account. They perceived that Catholic social teaching inherited from the 1891 *Rerum Novarum* was impotent to deal with the scale of poverty and suffering that plagued the twentieth century. Pope Leo XIII's anxious concern for defending private property against the perceived threat of socialism, Marxism, and class struggle diminished its otherwise powerful portrait of the plight of the industrial worker.

Dom Hélder Câmara and the "church of the poor" bishops at Vatican II worked to move the church toward a less defensive and more explicitly prophetic posture with respect to issues of social justice.[11] Dom Hélder spearheaded the Commission of the Poor, a group of multinational bishops and experts that met weekly outside formal council sessions to study the social and pastoral aspects of poverty.[12] Sowing the seeds, inside the sessions, for what would become the theology of liberation they advocated the development of a "theology of the poor" and pushed the church to recognize what they believed to be its obligation to improve economic conditions.[13] At the conclusion of the second session of Vatican II, the group delivered a petition to the pope requesting that these issues be taken up at the beginning of the third session. The influence of these bishops is clearly apparent in Vatican II's Pastoral Constitution on the Church in the Modern World, *Gaudium et spes* (1965). Câmara and others were planting seeds at the Second Vatican Council that would eventually mature into Puebla's "preferential option for the poor," arguably the fullest and most dynamic expression of Catholic social teaching.

Of all the Latin American bishops, perhaps Mexico's Don Sergio Méndez Arceo was the most consistent vocal presence at Vatican II. Though he would later become one of the most influential liberation-minded bishops in Latin America, his most pressing concerns during the council were liturgical. One of Méndez Arceo's greatest achievements was his ambitious renovation of the sixteenth-century Franciscan monastery that is today the cathedral of Cuerna-vaca. These renovations, which Méndez began in 1957, stripped away the baroque art and architecture of the building in an effort both to restore the church to its original Franciscan, monastic simplicity, and simultaneously to modernize the cathedral. For example, he replaced the more traditional image of the suffering Jesus with a crucifix depicting a resurrected, triumphant Christ. Don Sergio brought the lessons of his innovative and modernizing experiment to the Second Vatican Council, and his subsequent interventions in council sessions ultimately helped shape the council's vision for architectural and liturgical renewal within the church.[14]

The examples of Hélder Câmara and Sergio Méndez demonstrate that, far from being passive recipients of the Vatican II statements, Latin American bishops shaped the theology and influenced the outcomes of the council. These outcomes, the council's "constitutions," became a resource and authority for them as they continued to envision and implement a new and revitalized expression of Roman Catholicism in Latin America.

Building on their experience at Vatican II and the conclusions they had reached at Medellín, Latin American bishops put in place diocesan structures that provided the framework for the practice of liberation theology. Long before, in 1952, Dom Hélder Câmara began his episcopacy as the director of Brazilian Catholic Action.[15] The Catholic Action movement, which had emerged in Europe at the end of the nineteenth century but swept Latin America in the 1950s, is sometimes perceived, erroneously, as a precursor to liberation theology's base communities with which it shares a similar emphasis on lay activity in meetings with small groups. Catholic Action, however, labored under strong clerical supervision and was middle-class in its constituency. It is not surprising, therefore, that Câmara found it irrelevant to the needs of the increasingly large proletariat in the ever more urbanizing Brazil of the 1960s.[16]

Câmara's great contribution was as archbishop (1964–85) of the cities of Olinda and Recife in Brazil's impoverished Northeast. He founded the Theological Institute of Recife (the Instituto Teológico do Recife, or ITER), an urban seminary where priests and lay people were trained in the methods of liberation theology, and he restructured the existing Regional Seminary of the Northeast (SERENE II). Câmara required that all seminarians live not on campus, as was customary, but rather among peasants in rural areas or with the urban poor in one of the city's many shantytowns, or *favelas*. ITER emphasized the training of lay leaders, like the *animadora* Margarida, and broke tradition by hiring lay professors and religious sisters as instructors.[17] Of these, Ivone Gebara, feminist-liberationist theologian, became particularly well-known.[18]

At the same time, in Mexico, Don Sergio Méndez Arceo was creating similar institutional supports for the practice of liberation theology in his diocese. Most significantly, he transformed Cuernavaca's cathedral from a parish for the city's elite (a popular venue for high society weddings, for example) into the "people's cathedral." Members of the poorest parishes and Christian base communities gathered there for Mass each Sunday, and would offer their own reflections on the Christian Gospels in place of the priest's homily. Colorful banners with messages designed by the CEBs came to decorate its walls. But not only did the poorest members of the diocese flock to the cathedral Méndez had redesigned for them, he also traveled to the remote corners of the diocese to extend his ministry to the rural poor.[19]

Although Samuel Ruiz was also in attendance at Vatican II, he was more auditor than participant, perhaps because he was one of the youngest bishops in attendance.[20] Only in his late thirties when he returned from the council, he wasted no time implementing, with great imagination, the conclusions of his senior bishops. The crowning achievement of his forty-year tenure as bishop of Chiapas was the creation of a vibrant, highly successful, and extensive program of indigenous catechists and deacons.[21] Ruiz recognized that the ministry of the few Spanish-language priests of the diocese could hardly begin to reach the Maya-language majority of his diocese. He also realized that the centuries-old program of evangelization that pitted Roman Catholic faith against indigenous culture was not only doomed to failure but theologically incompatible with Vatican II and with his own understanding of the Christian gospels. His Indian catechists were not selected by priests, but rather chosen by members of their respective communities. Those who were eventually ordained deacons provided pastoral care in local languages and performed baptisms and marriages. By 2002, there were more deacons in Ruiz's diocese of San Cristóbal, Chiapas, than in any other Catholic diocese in the world, outnumbering priests by five to one.[22]

The Chiapas Indian deacon program was far from apolitical: Don Samuel and his deacons advocated indigenous rights and justice in the face of entrenched racism and exploitation. And in the 1980s, some of these catechists and deacons became supporters or members of the Zapatista rebels, who marched on the capital city of San Cristóbal on January 1, 1994, to protest the inauguration of the NAFTA agreement and to advance specific demands for achieving first-class citizenship of the indigenous. Ruiz, who had earned the trust of the Zapatistas, brokered a ceasefire between the rebels and the Mexican army. Following their initial armed uprising, the Zapatistas turned toward the media and the Internet to further their struggle for indigenous rights nationally and internationally. These efforts led to the signing of the San Andrés Accords in 1996, in which the Mexican government promised to recognize certain rights for indigenous Mexicans. Ruiz continued his efforts on behalf of these communities. In 1989, he had founded the Fray Bartolomé de Las Casas Human Rights Center to monitor ongoing human rights violations of the indigenous communities of Chiapas.[23]

Oscar Romero was neither present at the Second Vatican Council nor at Medellín, but he has come to be seen as the patron saint of liberation theology. Unlike Câmara, Ruiz, and Méndez, whose episcopacies spanned decades, Romero's ministry as archbishop of San Salvador was painfully brief: he was assassinated by a government-sanctioned death squad in 1980, barely three years after being named archbishop.[24] Rather than the creation of liberationist institutional structures then, Romero's legacy was his prophetic voice and witness. In his weekly radio addresses broadcast throughout El Salvador, he condemned the repressive violence of the Salvadoran military government and communicated hope to the poor and persecuted of his country. He also was a passionate advocate for peace in El Salvador, sending open letters demanding the cessation of U.S. aid to the Salvadoran military to then president Jimmy Carter. Perhaps most importantly, Romero was witness to the struggle and suffering of the Salvadoran people. Unlike many other religious and political leaders, he refused to turn a blind eye on the disappearances and tortures that devastated the impoverished nation. He insisted that this suffering be acknowledged and grieved publicly. Romero became the most famous and revered of the many martyrs El Salvador produced in the penultimate decade of the twentieth century. His tomb in the basement chapel of the cathedral of San Salvador became an immediate pilgrimage destination where the poor still flock to attend Mass rather than in the cathedral proper favored by the more politically conservative and economic elite of the population. The case for Romero's official canonization for Catholic sainthood was opened in 1997. Though the process has yet to be concluded, he is honored, beloved, and revered by millions of Latin Americans as San Oscar, St. Oscar Romero.

Over the course of almost two decades, often in the face of considerable resistance from political powers, Catholic elite, and Rome, Sergio Méndez Arceo, Hélder Câmara, Oscar Romero, and Samuel Ruiz García, created the infrastructure for liberation theology: its material, artistic, architectural, liturgical, educational, and institutional underpinnings. Though the grassroots origins of liberation theology have yet to be thoroughly understood, liberation theology could not have flourished without the commitment and protection of these four great ecclesiastics. Their labors also set in motion the closing of a centuries-long rift between the institutional hierarchs and the mass of poor believers.

The Prophets and Their People: Priests, Theologians, and the Christian Base Community Movement

The story of Ernesto Cardenal's relationship to the community of peasants in Solentiname provides an opportunity to explore the complex dynamics at work in the Christian base communities between lay believers and their priests. At grassroots meetings, highly trained and sometimes European-educated priests and theologians were transformed by immediate and unmediated encounters with the lives, struggles, suffering, and persistent faith of poor Latin Americans. In turn, these ordinary believers received and benefited from almost unprecedented access to the Christian scriptures (as well as support and aids for their interpretation), developed sophisticated analytical tools necessary for identifying the mechanisms of structural injustice, and explored and implemented strategies for dismantling these structures.

In theory, the CEBs were based on the methods of famed Brazilian educator Paulo Freire (1921–97), whose pedagogy subverted the traditional dichotomy between teacher and student.[25] As an administrator for the Federal University of Recife, Freire implemented his ideas through the creation of small learning groups, which he called "cultural circles" and which emphasized reciprocity in the learning process and a political awakening he dubbed *conscientização,* translated (somewhat awkwardly) as "conscientization" in English. Rather than Catholic Action groups, Freire's cultural circles were the true spiritual antecedents of the Christian base communities. Following the cultural circle model, the CEBs were the occasion for and the location of an intimate dialogue between priest and parishioner from which a new radicalized faith often emerged. This was a faith forged in common: CEB dialogue, as exemplified by Ernesto Cardenal's meetings with the peasants of Solentiname, was intended to stimulate a process of mutual conversion in which the line between clerical authority and lay adherence was subverted, and the faith of both was transformed and radicalized. Priest and community together studied the Scriptures in light of their specific historical context of oppression and struggle. The end result of conscientization was Christian praxis, intentional political engagement with the world in light of the Gospels.

This description of the CEBs is, of course, idealized and simplified. In fact, the dynamic between the priest and lay CEB member has always been complex and the nature, emphasis, and efficacy of individual CEBs has varied from community to community, country to country. In addition, many CEBs are almost entirely lay-driven, with only minimal clergy involvement. In practice, the CEBs sometimes do come close to (and even in some cases surpass) the ideal described above. But from their beginnings in the 1960s through the present, they have also had to grapple with challenges inherited from the colonial origins of Christianity in the New World, in particular the complicated history of strained lay-clergy relations.

The popular faith that priests encountered in the base communities sometimes created frustrations for the clergy as they pursued a more intimate relationship with the poor members of their parishes. In many regions, the perennial shortage of priests facilitated the development of semi-autonomous, local expressions of faith, and of structures of lay religious authority, which have sometimes been dismissively referred to as "folk Catholicism." In particular the civil-religious hierarchy of *mayordomías* and *cofradías,* or religious brotherhoods, that exists almost everywhere in Latin America, represented an alternative, and in some cases conflicting, model of lay authority and empowerment. These enduring structures of lay religio-political authority, with their origins in the colonial period, were perceived by liberationist priests as challenges to the founding of base communities and indeed as obstacles to the process of liberation. In this regard, the agenda of the church in the CEB movement proved similar to that of Catholic Action: in some regions (Guatemala in particular), the intended function of the groups was to undermine the "unorthodox religious beliefs and rituals of the Indian brotherhoods," replacing the *mayordomía* as the main institution of lay leadership in rural villages and towns.[26] Perhaps the most unfortunate area of friction between CEB members and liberation-minded priests was the pantheon of saints, official and popular, assembled by lay believers for their protection, healing, and general welfare. In the initial years of liberation theology especially, these traditional folk practices were frequently (dis)regarded by priests as oppressive and "anti-liberationist."

Therefore, liberation theology, in theory and practice, was not only a prophetic and revolutionary project but also a distinctly modern one in which the CEBs became a vehicle both for Christian evangelization and for the modernization of local faith. That is, some priests attempted to use liberation theology to guide and coax poor Christians away from the pitfalls of "superstition" and "idolatry," and to transform Latin American Christianity from a "folk religion," which, according to priests and theologians, mired believers in resignation and passivity, into an instrument for personal and social transformation. In many instances, local interpretations of liberation theology were pitted against traditional practices that were inherited from the colonial church: religious fiestas, devotion to saints, *mayordomías,* and the cargo system, in which adult males assumed financial responsibility for sponsoring elaborate and expensive community religious fiestas. Within a liberationist framework, the devotion of the poor to the Virgin Mary and to the suffering of Christ was even considered suspect. Some priests and theologians saw liberation theology as the fulfillment of Christian evangelization of the Americas begun in the sixteenth century, but which had been, up to that point, flawed and incomplete because of its original ties to the colonial project.

The modernizing aspect of liberation theology varied depending on region and context. In Brazil during the 1980s, for example, the CEBs were conceptualized as training grounds for electoral and participatory democracy: a place to practice and refine democratic skills that were underdeveloped due to a longstanding culture of patron-client relations and further weakened by more than twenty years of military dictatorship. In the CEBs, uneducated and illiterate peasants honed skills for participation in the political sphere: the free expression of political opinion and open debate without fear, social and political analysis, and even ballot-based voting.[27] In Chiapas, Mexico, the result was more ambiguous: while Bishop Samuel Ruiz's otherwise admirable indigenous deacons' program acknowledged the integrity and value of pre-Hispanic indigenous cultures and traditions, it directly challenged the authority of the *tradicionales,* those who practiced Christian–Indian syncretic religion (i.e., devotion to saints, participation in the cargo system, etc). Ruiz actively encouraged the indigenous to become candidates for catechist or deacon rather than pursue these local customary practices. Perhaps the most tragic outcome of the friction between liberation theology and "traditional" local practices of Catholicism occurred in highland Guatemala. There, the modernizing efforts of radical priests to "liberate" the faith of the people from "popular religion," which they labeled "the opiate of the masses," inspired peasant revolutionary guerrillas to publicly execute the head *mayordomo* of the Ixil region.[28]

In some locations, however, *mayordomías* functioned (alongside Freire's cultural circles) as a historical antecedent to the CEBs. In a small town in Morelos, Mexico, the site of my own research, the local *mayordomía* informally assumed the responsibility of running the CEBs. For the most part neither the *mayordomos* nor the liberationist clerics nor the community at large perceived any contradiction between or conflict in the overlap of the traditional mayordomal structure and the novel ecclesial communities, and the collaboration between the mayordomos and the liberationist priests ultimately contributed to the tremendous local success of the liberation theology movement.[29] Ruth Chojnacki's research on the Indian deacon program in modern-day Chiapas suggests that the work of the liberation theology-informed indigenous catechists was in part comprehended by the communities within the traditional cultural framework, as a sort of "cargo" with its own set of costs and sacrifices.[30]

Despite the apparent willingness of many indigenous and *mestizo* communities to accept the new evangelizing program of the CEBs, one of whose goals was to transcend the centuries-old friction between the Catholic hierarchy and the base of believers, in some cases the CEBs became an instrument for the reassertion of clerical authority at the local level. This was certainly true in Méndez Arceo's diocese of Cuernavaca wherein he saw liberation theology as an opportunity to reinvigorate the Mexican priesthood, which had grown weak and atrophied after decades of erosion by the anticlerical policies of the revolutionary nationalist state. Others, like Peruvian priest and theologian Gustavo Gutiérrez, imagined liberation theology priests as returning to the purity of purpose and passion for mission that motivated the first Christian friars who arrived to evangelize the New World.[31] One historian has even suggested that liberation theology achieved the "remasculinization of the Catholic priesthood in Latin America."[32] One might, then, identify two contradictory dynamics at work in liberation theology as it played out at the level of local parishes and communities. On the one hand it transferred religious authority to poor, lay believers as interpreters of the Bible and as agents of their own evangelization and liberation. At the same time, paradoxically, it reasserted the relevance, importance, and even authority of priests at the local level, although in their newly imagined capacity as defenders and liberators, witnesses, and revolutionaries.

In the CEBs, the agendas, desires, and vision of the priests and bishops met the reality of the people's own faith, practice, and understanding. Though some priests began with a modernizing agenda in the base communities, their eye-opening encounter with the suffering, oppression, and struggles of the poor often brought about a radical shift in perspective. In particular, priests were struck by the persistence of faith in the face of profound suffering. Their hearts were broken, as they sometimes described the process, when they witnessed the persecution of the poor, whom they began to understand collectively as the tortured and broken body of Christ. Religious leaders were both humbled and stirred by the sense of struggle, the *lucha,* with which poor people throughout Latin America faced the daily obstacles and devastations in their lives, as well as by the intimacy with the sacred that characterizes local faith. This was certainly the case with Catholic Maryknoll missioners from the United States who entered Central America in the 1960s and 1970s in the hopes of modernizing local Catholicism but, instead, found their own faith transformed into a faith defined by commitment to the poor.[33] Their growing awareness of the church's historical complacency coupled with the suffering of their parishioners radicalized many priests, even inspiring a few to collaborate with armed movements resisting oppressive military regimes, as was the case with the famed revolutionary priests Camilo Torres in Colombia and Gáspar García Laviana in Nicaragua.

Many highly educated parish priests engaged in the life of the CEBs had the intellectual tools to become the theorizers of the movement and thereby develop what has come to be called the "theology of liberation" as an academic and scholarly discourse. Latin American priests and lay scholars formalized and systematized this new approach within the Christian intellectual tradition.[34] They founded journals, met at scholarly conferences, and even launched new presses. Their labors sparked a true revolution within the academy, effectively shifting the center of production of theological knowledge from Europe to the third world, and to Latin America in particular.

Many of these thinkers had distinguished themselves in their studies as young seminarians and received further education and training at Europe's most respected institutions of higher learning. Gustavo Gutiérrez, Juan Luis Segundo, José Comblin, and Clodovis Boff all studied at the Louvain. Enrique Dussel and Pablo Richard studied at the Sorbonne, and José Míguez Bonino, Jon Sobrino, and Ernesto Cardenal at institutions in the United States. These theologians were mostly of European descent and middle-class. Therefore, when they returned to Latin America from their studies abroad their conversion to the poor necessarily meant that they had to transcend their class background and racial privilege in addition to shedding learned clericalism and recognizing the limitations of their European and North American education.

These theologians articulate the living and breathing faith of local communities when they truly engage in a "feet on the ground theology."[35] In this capacity they are less innovators than chroniclers documenting a grassroots movement. Toward this end, liberation theology's greatest resource is not in philosophy (which had been Christian theology's most important interlocutor for centuries), but rather in sociology and the social sciences. These theologians frequently used class analysis as a tool to understand and interpret the historical and social structures of oppression.[36] They also borrowed from Marx the concept that poor people are, in fact, agents of history.[37] But liberation theologians emphasize the Christian Gospels as the basis for imagining and envisioning an alternative social arrangement, that is, a vision for the world modeled after the kingdom of God.

Their collective efforts amounted to a reconsideration of the primary axes of Christian theology: Christology (theology of Jesus' relationship to human beings and God the Father), soteriology (theology of salvation), pneumatology (theology of the Holy Spirit), anthropology (theology of human beings and their relationship to God) and ecclesiology (theology of the church as an institution). In the area of theological anthropology, for example, liberation theologians shunned the two dominant ways of conceptualizing human beings. First, they did not primarily imagine humans as sinners in need of God's grace and salvation, but rather as sufferers in need of political and economic liberation. Second, they moved beyond the principal concern of twentieth-century theological thinking, which addressed human beings as "nonbelievers" (an approach that put the challenges of modern science and secularism at the center of theological concern). Instead, liberationist anthropology focused on the "nonpersons," those who had been regarded by society as if they were something less than human.[38]

These theologians and priests were the point of contact not only between poor communities and the institutional church but also between those same communities of the poor and the first world. Most theological works, as for example *The Gospel of Solentiname*, were written in large part for consumption by U.S. and European audiences. These texts functioned, very intentionally and with considerable success, to call to conversion affluent and privileged Christians in the first world. They inspired, for example, the Central American solidarity movements and the sanctuary movement of the 1980s, and they even affected U.S. foreign policy in Central America.

Margarida and the Faith of the People: Liberation Theology as Popular Practice and Belief

Many...people have imagined the theology of liberation as a "progressive" vision, when in fact it is a messianic one.
— Lancaster, *Thanks to God and the Revolution*, xxi

The ministry of the lay evangelist, Margarida da Silva, allows for a deeper exploration of the "popular" faith that priests encountered in Christian base communities. Her story is a reminder that the face of liberation theology was, and continues to be, not that of the bishops gathered at Medellín, nor the priests who shepherded their flocks through an ecclesial revolution, nor even the esteemed theologians who theorized the movement, but rather that of Margarida herself, poor, female, and of color. Lay participants in CEBs were most frequently women like her who had little or no formal education, worked as low-wage laborers, were peasants and farmers, or lived in shantytowns. Not only did poor women make up between 55 percent and 90 percent of CEBs; they were also the most active and engaged constituents.[39] These women and their male counterparts brought with them to the CEBs longstanding and vital religious beliefs, traditions, and practices, and their own theological interpretations of the world around them.

In spite of the anxious concern of some priests, theologians, and secular scholars that popular religion is fundamentally oppressive and anti-liberationist, liberation theology is best comprehended within the history of popular religious practice and belief in Latin America. Anthropologist Roger Nelson Lancaster argues that liberation theology is actually an "outgrowth or subset" of popular religion.[40] That is, the faith and Christian practice of the rank and file of the liberation theology movement were not originated in the twentieth century, but rather have deeper roots, predating the Second Vatican Council, the invention of the base communities, and the Medellín declarations. Indeed, this faith is colonial in origin, the result of a complex and ambiguous history and heritage defined above all by the conversion of indigenous people to Christianity and the concomitant process of their impoverishment and marginalization within colonial society. Furthermore, the CEB participants are the heirs of a rich and dynamic religious tradition influenced not only by the agenda of missionaries, but by the folk and Catholic practices of European colonials, the mores, worldviews, and sensibilities of indigenous cultures, and the experience of enslaved Africans brought to the New World. Thus, liberation theology is not without its spiritual and cultural antecedents, both resonating with and woven from strands inherited from these preexisting "folk" traditions.

It is risky to paint in broad brushstrokes the quality and character of religious belief across an entire continent, practiced over the course of centuries, and highly varied in its local expression. Latin American Christianity is famously plastic, characterized by an intense valuing of tradition and, simultaneously and paradoxically, by a tremendous capacity to absorb new ideas and practices. Although in theory Roman Catholicism is an exclusive religion, in practice it has proven to be surprisingly expansive, inclusive, and accommodating. Able to encompass and absorb not just religious practices external to the tradition, it has also been relatively pliant and available for religious innovation from within, of which liberation theology is just one example. This plasticity has frequently garnered a harsh and repressive response from the ecclesial hierarchy as it seeks to preserve uniformity of belief and practice.

Despite Latin American Catholicism's great diversity and dynamism, there are some identifiable common undercurrents present in popular religiosity with which the contemporary theology of liberation resonates. The first is a spirit of religious resistance, rebelliousness, and restlessness. The "messianism" to which Lancaster refers in the epigraph to this section alludes to the plethora of millennial movements, messianic prophets, and rebel folk saints that punctuate the religious history of Latin America. The breadth and depth of these diverse traditions is documented by Frank Graziano in his almost encyclopedic *The Millennial New World* (Oxford, 1999). Graziano's examples of utopian popular religious resistance are numerous, spanning centuries and the full geographic range of the continent. In the Andes, for example, during the last decades of the eighteenth century, the Indian noble José Gabriel Condorcanqui, taking the name Tupac Amaru II, led a movement of some fifty thousand against the entire colonial structure of forced tributes and taxes, all the while arguing that his Christianity was "superior to the ostentatious but morally vacant faith of the Spaniards."[41] In the Brazilian colonial period, communities of escaped slaves called *quilombos* were sometimes religious and utopian in nature. Under the charismatic leadership of the messianic prophet Antonio Conselheiro, rural Brazilians fleeing oppressive conditions in the drought-ridden Northeast established the utopian city of Canudos at the close of the nineteenth century.[42] An eighteenth-century adolescent mystic of Chiapas, Mexico, the young *india* María de la Candelaria, inspired by visions and speaking as the mouthpiece of a miraculous image of Mary called the Virgen del Rosario, galvanized an indigenous rebellion.[43] A talking cross advocated a rebellion by the Maya in the Yucatan in 1851 against the neocolonial exploiters leading these devout Mayan Catholics to attempt to drive out the European invaders once and for all from their land.[44] In many locales, this rich and diverse tradition of popular religious resistance complemented the radical political engagement encouraged by the liberation theology movement. Where present, local traditions of a millennial and utopian nature, expressing hope for real, dramatic, and unprecedented transformation of the social order, served as a spiritual resource for liberation theology's call for participation in transformative action to create a world more in keeping with God's own desires for humanity.

Liberation theology also spoke to a human tradition of daily struggle, of *lucha* (or *luta* in Portuguese), that in some ways has defined and shaped Latin American faith for centuries.[45] The perception that daily life is a struggle provides the interpretive framework for coping with the endemic poverty and suffering throughout Latin America. Faith is filtered and forged in the context of the survival of conditions of material misery. *Child of the Dark,* the diary of Carolina Maria de Jesus documenting the trials of life in a Brazilian shantytown, portrays something of this understanding as Carolina describes the ceaseless cycle of struggle, frequent defeat, and small but treasured triumphs that mark her existence. Thus the utopian hopefulness and otherworldly orientation of the Latin American millennial tradition is tempered by a quotidian experience of struggle and survival that yields a persistent and durable faith mystical in nature but also fundamentally immediate, concrete, and practical in its orientation toward the world. This matter-of-fact approach to the challenges of daily life, along with a corresponding faith-on-the-ground relationship to God, shaped the CEB's confrontation with the mundane problems that define the day-to-day struggle for survival.

Finally, a sense of intimacy with the sacred is another quality of Latin American popular faith, experienced and expressed in relation to the legions of local saints. This religious sensibility is also present in the immediacy of the Christian story within both popular tradition and liberation theology. The peasants of Solentiname offer pictorial representations of the passion of Christ as experienced in Nicaragua, representing Jesus as a Nicaraguan peasant who was arrested by military police.[46] As one older peasant explained to Lancaster:

> History is sameness. Christ is forever being killed by the Roman soldiers, here in the hills of Nicaragua, just as he was killed in the Bible five hundred years ago. And even now, at this moment, María is giving birth to Christ in the countryside, and his disciples are already walking the earth waiting for him. And the same Roman soldiers are already at the hill, waiting to kill him.[47]

This quote captures both the immediacy of the Christian story and the proximity of God in the daily lives and struggles of poor believers. The god of popular religion and the god of the theology of liberation are the same, defined above all by constant presence, and as a witness to human suffering.

Popular religious traditions and beliefs were not, in practice, exclusive to liberation theology. Quite often the two informed one another or lived side by side, the practice of local or "folk" traditions coexisting with the more explicitly "modern" and "progressive" vision. I was confronted with this simultaneous coexistence when, while in Pernambuco in the summer and fall of 1989, I participated in two very different "missions," both holy weeks of intense prayer, reflection, and community procession. This experience, discussed below, demonstrated how poor Catholics in Northeast Brazil absorbed two seemingly distinct versions of Christianity, which outside observers have seen as diametrically opposed, one ancient, penitential, and mystical, the other new, "this-worldly," and politically radical.

The first week of "mission" celebrated the twentieth-century religious mystic of the Brazilian *sertão*, Frei Damião. A crowd of several hundred of the community's poorest residents gathered at the entrance of the town to welcome the ninety-year-old popular saint and mystical figure, who arrived perched in the back of a brand new, cherry-red pickup truck. The monk, clad in his rough-hewn, brown Franciscan robes and worn leather sandals, was so short of stature and so gnarled and stooped with age that only his hunched back and a shock of gray hair were visible to the crowd. The welcome procession had an almost premodern, messianic quality that continued throughout the week. In his daily sermons preached from a makeshift stage erected in the town *praça*, Frei Damião called on the poor to renounce sin and the materialism of modern life. In the days that followed, so many thousands of people wanted to confess their sins at least half a dozen priests from neighboring towns were needed to assist. Some peasants waited hours so that Frei Damião himself could absolve them. Sometimes he would admonish a sinner with an angry roar. Nevertheless, trembling as they concluded their confessions, many of the faithful would reach out to touch the saint's gnarled foot for good luck. At the end of the week, Frei Damião left the same way he had come, riding high in his shiny truck and followed by a cheering crowd. For many, the monk possessed supernatural powers. Afterward rumors spread that some people had seen Frei Damião fly, and that a small girl who had doubted his saintliness had been struck dead.

During the final days of Frei Damião's visit, missionaries for the liberation theology "mission" began to arrive. While the previous week had emphasized repentance and spiritual redemption, the liberation theology week of mission was designed to reflect on and dramatize the poverty and violence of everyday life in the local *favelas*. Among the organizers was Margarida herself, by then a well-known activist. At one point, she joined Damião on stage to sing a favorite liberation theology hymn that called for a new church to replace the old. Some of Frei Damião's assistants were furious at what they correctly perceived to be a pointed criticism of their traditional conservative theology. But Damião himself, seemingly indifferent (or oblivious) to the political message of the lyrics, clapped his hands in utter, almost childlike, enjoyment to the rhythm of the music. Activists preparing for the liberation theology mission invited the elderly popular saint to bless a large wooden cross that they planned to use as a key symbol for their processions. His benediction lent the cross additional power and significance.

Padre Andres, leader of the liberation theology missions, was a priest and the editor of a liberationist journal published in Bahia. Like Damião, he led an ascetic existence, sleeping and eating very little. Yet his energy and enthusiasm seemed inexhaustible. Each morning for six days, Andres led a procession through the poorest neighborhoods. The large wooden cross that had been blessed by Damião was at the front of the procession, born aloft by teams of community residents that included the sick, children, manual laborers, and single mothers. The week culminated in an outdoor celebration of the Mass and a bonfire in the center of the community that included a collective confession. The emphasis was on social rather than individual sins: unemployment, poverty, poor health, issues that had been addressed and discussed all week. As each social sin was named, representatives from the community threw a symbol of each sin — of each oppression — onto the bonfire. A young man, an agricultural laborer, threw in a stalk of sugar cane. Dona Irene, whose two sons had been murdered by death squads, burned a sign that read "military violence."

People in this shantytown saw no contradiction between the penitential mission of Frei Damião and the liberationist mission of Padre Andres. To outside observers, the liberationist teachings of Padre Andres and the local popular devotion to Frei Damião may seem diametrically opposed, but both missions provided the townspeople with a week of contemplation, prayer, festivity, and celebration. To the people themselves, the two gods of the missionaries did not contradict one another. Instead, townspeople celebrated that the powerful God of Frei Damião, who could make men fly and who did not hesitate to exact punishment, was on their side, seeking the liberation of the poor, as Padre Andres assured them.[48]

The Undoing of Liberation Theology

In October 1989, on the eve of Brazil's first democratic elections in over twenty years, hundreds of peasants from the impoverished, drought-ridden state of Pernambuco protested the closing of a Catholic seminary, the Theological Institute of Recife (ITER). Outside the locked doors of the vacant seminary, some four hundred women and men, whose bodies were already half-broken by hunger and poverty, gathered to fast, sing, and pray for a reversal of the decision to close. As prayers were said, songs sung, and letters of support for the protesters read aloud, the whispered word "Ratzinger" passed from the lips of one person to the next. Cardinal Joseph Ratzinger (now Pope Benedict XVI) had ordered the closing, collaborating with the newly appointed conservative archbishop of Recife, José Cardoso, to shut down ITER and several other regional seminaries.[49] In his capacity as prefect of the Congregation for the Doctrine of the Faith (formerly the Holy Office of the Inquisition), the cardinal had deemed these seminaries theologically suspect and politically dangerous, radical training grounds for priests, sisters, and lay believers who took the "preferential option for the poor" too seriously. The closing of ITER was just one part of a larger institutional project of dismantling the infrastructure for liberation theology and the base communities.[50]

Starting in 1977 the Vatican attempted to create an agenda for the coming CELAM conference at Puebla that would temper the 1968 declarations of Medellín.[51] The pope himself traveled to Latin America to attend the CELAM gathering, at which he gave a speech criticizing both the "popular church" and the base communities. Some eighty priests and theologians, mostly liberationists, had been barred from attending the proceedings. Nevertheless, the bishops at Puebla (Mexico) reaffirmed the fundamental tenets of liberation theology and, for the first time, committed the Latin American church to a "preferential option for the poor." Undaunted, in 1984 Cardinal Ratzinger issued the famous "Instruction on Certain Aspects of the 'Theology of Liberation,'" a lengthy critique of what he perceived to be the errors and excesses of liberation theology. These Ratzinger identified as an emphasis on social sin above individual sin; the borrowing of some aspects of Marxist analysis; and liberation theology's commitment to build and strengthen the "church of the poor," a notion that Ratzinger took to be a direct criticism of the Magisterium.

Ratzinger also targeted specific theologians of the movement for censure. In 1995 the Vatican formally silenced Brazilian theologian Leonardo Boff, in particular for his criticism of the power structures of the institutional church.[52] Feminist Brazilian theologian, professor at ITER, and Sister of Notre Dame Ivone Gebara was also silenced for two years, beginning in 1995.[53] She initially attracted the Vatican's attention when she made public statements to the effect that abortion may not be a sin for desperately poor women. She was silenced when the Vatican further investigated her published writings and found problematic her interpretation of the image of God and her comments on the patriarchal nature of the church. The Vatican also urged, and in some cases even insisted upon, the retirement of many of the liberationist bishops, replacing them with conservative traditionalists and members of Opus Dei. This was the case for bishops Sergio Méndez of Mexico and Hélder Câmara of Brazil, who, upon retirement, were immediately succeeded by bishops who undid much of their predecessor's substantial and popular achievements. In February 2002 Rome moved to block Samuel Ruiz's successful program of the Indian diaconate, prohibiting the ordination of any further deacons for at least two years.[54] The Vatican reaffirmed this prohibition in October 2005 and then formally suspended the training program itself at the beginning of 2006.[55]

In addition to this process of institutional dismantling, liberationist communities and their leaders were subject to political violence wrought by the antidemocratic military regimes that they so often criticized and fought. Many clerics paid the ultimate price for their vigorous defense of the poor. For example, during Argentina's "Dirty War" (1974–85), two bishops and at least twelve priests were murdered, and five "disappeared," among other atrocities. I have already discussed the martyrdom of Salvadoran Archbishop Oscar Romero in March 1980. Later that same year, three American religious sisters and one lay missionary were raped, tortured, and murdered by Salvadoran death squads for their work among the poor and in the base communities. Several years later, in November of 1989, six Jesuit priests and their housekeeper and her daughter were murdered by the Salvadoran army at the Jesuit residence at the Universidad Centroamericana. Among them was liberation theologian Ignacio Ellacuría. The community of peasants of Solentiname was also attacked in 1977 and destroyed by Somoza's National Guard. Priests, nuns, and lay activists suffered similar abuses in Latin America during the military regimes of the 1970s and 1980s. This violent persecution, along with the church's process of critique and dismantling, has led to the weakening of the CEBs movement and to the decline of liberation theology's influence.

Conclusions

Much has been made, mostly by its critics, of the "failure" of liberation theology. Yet neither ode nor epitaph for the movement is called for. Indeed, on Ratzinger's first pastoral visit to Latin America as pope, he encountered in Brazil the reality that as many as eighty thousand base communities still exist as vital locations for the expression of a liberationist faith.[56] In El Salvador, as well, base communities remain an integral part of the religious landscape, especially in the rural areas. And in Chiapas, in spite of, and even indifferent to, Vatican censure, Ruiz's Indian deacons continue to serve as community leaders and advocates. In the last decade, a new generation of liberation theologians from Latin America and from U.S. Latino communities has begun to write, advocate, and publish, exploring the meaning of liberation theology for women, indigenous peoples, blacks, gays and lesbians, and U.S. Hispanics/Latinos.[57]

Nevertheless, in many local communities where liberation theology once flourished, today one notes a sense of loss and a longing as for a time past. But there is also a distinct sense of anticipation, of waiting at the margins, a persistent, even millennial, hope. This spirit is poignantly captured by one of the peasants of the Diocese of Cuernavaca, who remarked to me:

> The time of the CEBs passed with the change of the bishops. The ones that came after Don Sergio didn't want it....Now it is like we have lost our leaders, our spiritual guides. Some day, when there are again priests who involve themselves in the life of the poor, then the Base Communities will return. Let me tell you, even if I was in my grave, if the CEBs returned, I myself would rise from the dead to work with them.

In their many works, liberation theologians have offered interpretations of what this new movement of the Catholic poor, this "popular church," represented. For some thinkers, it was the culmination of Christian evangelization, for others, the fulfillment of the process of "inculturation" of Christianity into Latin America, a Christianity fully responsive to the Latin American reality — nothing less than the Latin Americanization of Roman Catholicism. For still others, liberation theology was Christianity itself come of age. Here I have argued that liberation theology is uniquely and authentically Latin American, drawing on some undercurrents perhaps common to the religious history of the continent, but always highly local in its manifestations, relevance, import, and experience. The local diversity of Christian practice and faith is always more complex, multifaceted, and dynamic than can be captured by a formal theological system, even one as encompassing and "close to the ground" as the formal scholarly field of liberation theology. Perhaps the hope and promise of liberation theology, along with the experience of persecution and defeat, will, in the long run, simply be folded back into and comprehended within the longstanding religio-cultural paradigm of millennial expectation and disappointment, encompassed and interpreted within the quotidian and cyclical experience of struggle, defeat, and survival that has marked Latin American faith for centuries. The struggle, *la lucha*, continues, as poor believers throughout Latin America often repeat. What may be unique about the liberation theology movement is that, for a moment in this cyclical history, the institutional church stood close to that struggle.

Notes

1. To date liberation theology's greatest impact has been in Brazil, Nicaragua, El Salvador, and Peru, but no Latin American country remained untouched or unaffected (Mexico, Guatemala, Haiti, Chile, and Ecuador are also noteworthy for their engagement). For a book-length historical background and overview of liberation theology see Pablo Richard, *Death of Christendoms, Birth of the Church: Historical Analysis and Theological Interpretation of the Church in Latin America* (Maryknoll, N.Y.: Orbis Books, 1987). See also David Tombs, *Latin American Liberation Theology,* Religion in the Americas series, vol. 1 (Boston: Brill Academic Publishers, 2002).

2. Statements about the physical misery suffered by most Latin Americans and the political instability of Latin American governments introduce and frame the published Medellín statements. For example, in Guatemala note the military overthrow of the democratically elected Arbenz government in 1954, and in Chile the Allende government in 1973, and in Brazil the military coup in 1964, etc.

3. Conferencia General del Episcopado Latinoamericano, and Louis M. Colonnese, *The Church in the Present-Day Transformation of Latin America in the Light of the Council: Second General Conference of Latin American Bishops, Bogotá, August 24, Medellín, August 26–September 6, Colombia, 1968,* 2 vols. (Bogotá: General Secretariat of CELAM, 1970).

4. However, in no way was this commitment to the "popular church" an attempt by some to create a separate, parallel church. Neither did CEBs members perceive their participation as an expression of faith somehow autonomous or independent from the Roman Catholic Church.

5. The reflections of the Solentiname peasants are recorded by Cardenal in his four volume collection, Ernesto Cardenal, *The Gospel in Solentiname,* 4 vols. (Maryknoll, N.Y.: Orbis Books, 1976). See also the illustrated work by Philip J. Scharper, Sally Scharper, and Ernesto Cardenal, *The Gospel in Art by the Peasants of Solentiname* (Maryknoll, N.Y.: Orbis Books, 1984).

6. Roger N. Lancaster, *Thanks to God and the Revolution: Popular Religion and Class Consciousness in the New Nicaragua* (New York: Columbia University Press, 1988), 56.

7. I have written about Margarida and Frei Damião, whom I discuss below, in my undergraduate thesis, "The Utopic City of Canudos: An Expression of a Religious Ideal," Department of Latin American Studies, University of California–Santa Cruz, 1992.

8.
> Abre a porta, povo
> Que já vem Jesus
> Ele vem cansada
> com o peso da cruz!
>
> De que vale ter
> riqueza amontoada
> Roubada dos pobres
> De sangue manchada?

De que vale poder em todos mandar
Fazer cruz pesada
Pros outros levar?

Pra que ter do mundo a sabedoria
Pra enganar o pobre
Todo santo dia?

Abre a porta, povo
Rasga o coração
Repartee a vida
Com o teu irmão.

9. But it was compelling to scholars as well, both religious and secular, and so it has been much studied, analyzed, and evaluated by intellectuals both within and outside the church. These scholarly portraits emphasize the profound institutional and theological innovation that liberation theology represented, pointing to the ecclesiastic antecedents of the movement and emphasizing the institutional and international forces that gave it birth, all of which makes the clergy central to the movement.

10. "There the bishops of Latin America for the first time in history spent long periods together and, under such inspired leaders as Domo Hélder Câmara (Recife, Brazil), Bishop Manuel Larraín (Talca, Chile), Bishop Sergio Méndez Arceo (Cuernavaca), and Bishop Leónidas Proaño (Riobamba, Ecuador), began to reflect on their problems in a continental framework. The option for the poor as an inescapable element of the Christian commitment emerged as a dominant theme" (Gary MacEoin, *The People's Church: Bishop Samuel Ruiz of Mexico and Why He Matters* [New York: Crossroad, 1996], 23).

11. For a discussion of how it was perceived as bankrupt see Marcos McGrath, "Social Teaching since the Council: A Response from Latin America," in *Vatican II by Those Who Were There*, ed. Alberic Stacpoole (London: G. Chapman, 1986).

12. See the many obituaries written after Câmara's death and Xavier Rynne, *The Second Session: The Debates and Decrees of Vatican Council II, September 29 to December 4, 1963* (New York: Farrar, 1964), 270.

13. Ibid., 111. The bishop of Panama said, "The task of every Christian was to take part in the great work of bringing to perfection the work of creation by getting rid of inequities and eliminating poverty."

14. Carlos Salcedo Palacios, "Participación de don Sergio Méndez Arceo en el Concilio Vaticano II," in *Don Sergio Méndez Arceo, Patriarca de la Solidaridad Liberadora*, ed. Leticia Rentería Chávez and Giulio Girardi (Mexico City: Ediciones Dabar, 2000).

15. For a short but excellent English-language biography see Kenneth Serbin, "Dom Hélder Câmara: The Father of the Church of the Poor," in *The Human Tradition in Brazil*, ed. Peter M. Beattie (Wilmington, Del: Scholastic Resources, 2004), 249–66.

16. For treatments of Catholic Action in indigenous communities in Latin America see Kay B. Warren, *The Symbolism of Subordination: Indian Identity in a Guatemalan Town* (Austin: University of Texas Press, 1978).

17. Serbin, "Dom Hélder Câmara: The Father of the Church of the Poor," 263. Since his death in 1999, Câmara has continued to hold an important place in the popular religious imagination and to be regarded with reverence and affection. In many ways Câmara's stature is not dissimilar to that of other regional folk saints, in a long and distinguished line of itinerant preachers, mystics,

and millennial prophets who populate the religious history of the inhospitable desert backlands of northeast Brazil: Padre Cicero, Antonio Conselheiro, and Frei Damião, among others.

18. See Gebara's many works including Ivone Gebara, *Out of the Depths: Women's Experience of Evil and Salvation* (Minneapolis: Fortress Press, 2002) and Ivone Gebara and Maria Clara Lucchetti Bingemer, *Mary, Mother of God, Mother of the Poor*, Theology and Liberation Series (Maryknoll, N.Y.: Orbis Books, 1989).

19. At his much-regretted retirement, the poor parishes of Morelos declared themselves to be his "living cathedral." At his death in 1993 mourners could not bring themselves to leave their beloved pastor alone through the night and requested permission from the new bishop, Luis Reynoso, to bring the body back to their parish church for further veneration. Reynoso granted their request, saying to his assistant, "Let them take him. If not, these Indians are capable of taking him by force." See Miguel Morayta Mendoza, Catherine Good, Alfredo Paulo, and Cristina Saldaña, "Resolviendo conflictos entre pueblos de tradición nahua de Morelos: Una ruta por la costumbre, lay ley y la diversidad religiosa." Unpublished manuscript.

20. Ruiz was appointed bishop by John XXIII, just one year after he was named pope.

21. For the most compelling and extended treatment of the Indian deacons see Ruth Chojnacki, "Indigenous Apostles: Maya Catholic Catechists Working the Word in Highland Chiapas," Ph.D. dissertation, University of Chicago, 2004.

22. Ginger Thompson, "Vatican Curbing Deacons in Mexico," *New York Times*, March 12, 2002.

23. See John Ross, *Rebellion from the Roots: Indian Uprising in Chiapas* (Monroe, Maine: Common Courage Press, 1995), and Mons. Samuel Ruiz García, *Mi trabajo pastoral en la Diócesis de San Cristóbal de las Casas* (Mexico City: Ediciones Paulinas, 1999).

24. Romero's life and ministry is movingly captured in the film *Romero* (1989). But see also Oscar A. Romero, *Archbishop Oscar Romero: A Shepherd's Diary* (London: CAFOD, 1993).

25. See Paulo Freire, *Pedagogy of the Oppressed*, 30th anniversary ed. (New York: Continuum, 2000).

26. See Warren, *The Symbolism of Subordination*.

27. Several base communities that I visited in the fall of 1989 actually held mock presidential elections in anticipation of Brazil's first democratic elections in decades. But see also Scott Mainwaring and Alexander Wilde, *The Progressive Church in Latin America* (Notre Dame, Ind.: University of Notre Dame Press, 1989).

28. See EGP, "Sebastián Guzmán, principal de principales," *Polémica* 10–11 (1983). See also David Stoll, *Between Two Armies in the Ixil Towns of Guatemala* (New York: Columbia University Press, 1993).

29. See my forthcoming work, *The Biography of a Mexican Crucifix: Lived Religion and Local Faith from the Conquest to the Present* (New York: Oxford University Press).

30. Ruth Chojnacki, "Retrato de un catequista: La religión liberadora y la comunitas en los Altos de Chiapas," *Revista de Ciencias Sociales* 56 (1999).

31. The similarities between liberation theology priests and sixteenth-century missionaries are highlighted in Enrique Dussel's multivolume history of the church in Latin America. That twentieth-century theologians romanticized their colonial predecessors is also evident in Gustavo Gutiérrez's affection for Bartolomé de las Casas, which in part inspired his decision to become a Dominican. See Gustavo Gutiérrez, *Las Casas: In Search of the Poor of Jesus Christ* (Maryknoll, N.Y.: Orbis Books, 1993).

32. Sarah Cline made this comment in the context of a paper she delivered at the University of California Latin American Historian Conference, University of California–Davis, 2001. She observes, "Liberation theology represented the injection of testosterone into the Catholic Church" (personal correspondence).

33. Their experience was in many ways analogous to that of early Peace Corps volunteers sent by the U.S. government to the remote reaches of Latin America to quell the rising tide of socialist-inspired political movements but who were themselves radicalized by their experience of serving poor communities, even, in some cases, to the point of sharply criticizing U.S. foreign policy and allying themselves with local resistance movements.

34. For an excellent collection of theological essays reflecting the full span of thinking see Ignacio Ellacuría and Jon Sobrino, *Mysterium Liberationis: Fundamental Concepts of Liberation Theology* (Maryknoll, N.Y.: Orbis Books, 1993).

35. See Leonardo Boff, *When Theology Listens to the Poor* (San Francisco: Harper & Row, 1988).

36. Argentine lay theologian Enrique Dussel offers the most impressive and sustained engagement with Marx and his many works. Enrique D. Dussel, *La producción téorica de Marx: Un comentario a los Grundrisse*, Biblioteca del pensamiento socialista (Mexico City: Siglo Veintiuno Editores, 1985); Enrique D. Dussel, *Las metáforas teológicas de Marx* (Estella, Navarra: Verbo Divino, 1993); Enrique D. Dussel and Fred Moseley, *Towards an Unknown Marx: A Commentary on the Manuscripts of 1861–63*, Routledge Studies in the History of Economics (New York: Routledge, 2001); and Enrique D. Dussel and Eduardo Mendieta, *Beyond Philosophy: Ethics, History, Marxism, and Liberation Theology*, New Critical Theory (Lanham, Md.: Rowman & Littlefield Publishers, 2003).

37. See Gustavo Gutiérrez, *The Power of the Poor in History: Selected Writings* (London: SCM Press, 1983).

38. See especially Gustavo Gutiérrez, *A Theology of Liberation: History, Politics, and Salvation* (Maryknoll, N.Y.: Orbis Books, 1988).

39. Carol Ann Drogus and Helen Kellogg Institute for International Studies, *Women, Religion, and Social Change in Brazil's Popular Church* (Notre Dame, Ind.: University of Notre Dame Press, 1997). But see also Renny Golden, *The Hour of the Poor, The Hour of Women: Salvadoran Women Speak* (New York: Crossroad, 1991).

40. Lancaster, *Thanks to God and the Revolution*, 32.

41. Frank Graziano, *The Millennial New World* (New York: Oxford University Press, 1999), 126.

42. Euclides da Cunha, *Rebellion in the Backlands* (London: Picador, 1995).

43. Juan Pedro Viqueira Albán, *María de la Candelaria: India natural de Cancuc* (Mexico City: Fondo de Cultura Económica, 1993).

44. Graziano, *The Millennial New World*, 123.

45. See David Sweet and June Nash, eds., *Struggle and Survival in Colonial America* (Berkeley: University of California Press, 1982).

46. See Scharper, Scharper, and Cardenal, *The Gospel in Art by the Peasants of Solentiname*.

47. Lancaster, *Thanks to God and the Revolution*, xv.

48. For a scholarly interpretation of the Italian-born Brazilian Frei Damião de Bozzano, O.F.M. (1898–1997), see Michel de Certeau, "Part V: Ways of Believing," in *The Practice of Everyday Life* (Berkeley: University of California, 2002).

49. This description is based on my own observations, as I was present for these three days of protest. For a brief scholarly treatment of these events see Robin Nagle, *Claiming the Virgin: The Broken Promise of Liberation Theology in Brazil* (New York: Routledge, 1997).

50. Pope John Paul II had long been ambivalent about the movement. He was sympathetic to the sense of regeneration and renewal that it brought but, largely owing to his personal experience with post–World War II Eastern European communism in Poland, he was anxious about Marxist influence on the Latin American Church. For a treatment of criticism of liberation theology, see Arthur F. McGovern, *Liberation Theology and Its Critics: Toward an Assessment* (Maryknoll, N.Y.: Orbis Books, 1989).

51. John Eagleson and Philip J. Scharper, eds., *Puebla and Beyond: Documentation and Commentary* (Maryknoll, N.Y.: Orbis Books, 1979).

52. Harvey Gallagher Cox, *The Silencing of Leonardo Boff: The Vatican and the Future of World Christianity* (Oak Park, Ill.: Meyer-Stone Books, 1988).

53. David Molineux, "Rome Moves to Silence Brazil's Gebara — Controversial Feminist Theologian Sister Ivone Gebara," *National Catholic Reporter,* May 26, 1995.

54. Thompson, "Vatican Curbing Deacons in Mexico."

55. "Deacon Program Suspended," *National Catholic Reporter,* April 21, 2006, 4(1).

56. Larry Rohter, "As Pope Heads to Brazil, a Rival Theology Persists," *New York Times,* May 7, 2007.

57. See for example, Ivan Petrella, ed., *Latin American Liberation Theology: The Next Generation* (Maryknoll, N.Y.: Orbis Books, 2005); María Pilar Aquino et al., eds., *A Reader in Latina Feminist Theology: Religion and Justice* (Austin: University of Texas, 2002); Ada María Isasi-Díaz, *Mujerista Theology: A Theology for the Twenty-First Century* (Maryknoll, N.Y.: Orbis Books, 1996); Orlando Espín, *The Faith of the People: Theological Reflections on Popular Catholicism* (Maryknoll, N.Y.: Orbis Books, 1997); Virgil Elizondo, *Galilean Journey: The Mexican American Promise* (Maryknoll, N.Y.: Orbis Books, 2000).

14

"A Preferential and Evangelizing Option for the Poor"

The Catholic Church from Medellín to Aparecida

ROBERT S. PELTON, C.S.C.

Having participated in the Second Vatican Council of the Roman Catholic Church (1962–65) and, in various roles, in all of the CELAM (*Consejo Episcopal Latino-americano*) Conferences since Vatican II, I was delighted to be again selected, this time as an observer at CELAM V, the Fifth General Conference of the Bishops of Latin America and the Caribbean, held in Aparecida, Brazil, May 13–31, 2007.

Although it would have been unrealistic to expect CELAM V to equal the extraordinary successes of the Medellín Conference in 1968, my hope was that CELAM V would strongly reaffirm the distinctive identity of the Latin American Catholic Church, offer strong encouragement and support for the basic Christian communities (CEBs), and find new creative applications for the spirit and the thrust of the Second Vatican Council in the frenetically changing social, economic, political, cultural, and religious dynamics of twenty-first-century Latin America. Despite excellent work by the 260 delegates leading to many positive results, these hopes were not fully realized. Changes made in the Vatican-approved final document — changes that do not always include the views of a significant number of the bishops — force me to conclude that although Medellín (1968) and Puebla (1979) are alive in the twenty first-century Catholic Church, they continue to be challenged.

Like the watershed conference in Medellín, Colombia, and the two intervening bishops' conferences (Puebla, Santo Domingo), CELAM V conceptualized its proceedings and conclusions relevant to the signs of the times by viewing the rapidly changing dynamics of Latin America in the light of the Gospel. What emerged from Aparecida clearly affirmed that the Catholic Church in Latin America and the Caribbean remains committed to a full and creative expression of the Second Vatican Council (1962–65); that it faces very different but no less daunting challenges in the twenty-first century than it did in the final decades of the twentieth, that it has retained its own distinctive identity, and that it has much to share with the world.

Significantly, the bishops readopted the inductive "see-judge-act" method of discernment that proved so fruitful at Medellín and Puebla, whereas the 1992 Santo Domingo Conference employed a deductive and more theoretical methodology. CELAM V unequivocally endorsed and expanded three key concepts of the Latin American Catholic Church — the preferential option for the poor, ecclesial base communities (CEBs), and opposition to structural sin within the modern context of globalization and neo-liberal economic models — and did so in an enlightened and collegial manner that may diminish the controversy that has sometimes arisen from popular misunderstanding of these principles.

Small ecclesial communities received an endorsement in terms of their relationship with the institutional church that underscores an inclusiveness that already existed in reality but was not universally acknowledged. The "preferential option for the poor" was expanded at Aparecida to become the "preferential and evangelizing option for the poor," making it clearer that the option is not solely a matter of socioeconomics. In a concrete affirmation of the necessity and potential for that preferential and evangelizing option for the poor, the bishops issued a statement to the leaders of the G-8 nations calling for the elimination of extreme poverty from all the world's nations before 2015 and making that goal "one of the most urgent tasks of our time," one that is "inseparably linked with world peace and security." The bishops also criticized "environmental aggression" against the Amazon rainforest, warning that Amazonia — which replenishes much of the world's atmospheric oxygen supply, contains 20 percent of the world's fresh unfrozen water, and nourishes 34 percent of the world's forests — will cease to exist within thirty years if present patterns of corporate, profit-driven destruction continue.

Despite the lack of concrete action in the following areas, many bishops displayed acute concern about the challenges posed by globalization, rapid urbanization, the changing roles of families and youth, and the demand for real dialogue with the indigenous and Afro-American communities. They also recognized the need for greater decision-making roles for women in the church, and for greater clarity regarding the roles of ministry and the laity.

That the bishops are now focusing more attention on these issues than at any other time in CELAM's history suggests their deepening understanding of the full scope of Medellín and Puebla, and a growing commitment to the mandate of promoting social justice as a means of addressing the demands of present realities. Optimism about the full realization of Vatican II was strong in the 1970s, but has gradually receded throughout much of Latin America since Pope John Paul II's episcopal appointments rarely challenged the status quo maintained by the national security states of that era.

Image of the Catholic Church
in the Twenty Latin American Countries

The image of the Catholic Church throughout Latin America is about as diverse as Latin America itself, with little coherence other than that created by Scripture, by CELAM and its declarations, and, to a lesser degree, by communication networks formed by CEBs and other lay groups. The array of parish plans, liturgical forms, and concepts of church that can vary greatly from parish to parish as well as from nation to nation originates from a unique blend of theology, history, necessity, and conscious choice.

Following more than four centuries as an appendage to the Spanish church, the Catholic Church in Latin America finally acquired an identity of its own based on the Second Vatican Council's efforts to transform the Catholic Church into a "World Church" that would integrate its values into the cultures of the various nations. The Latin American Bishops enthusiastically embraced the council's teaching and followed the methodology of the council's *Gaudium et spes* (Pastoral Constitution on the Church in the Modern World) by studying the facts, reflecting upon them, and then taking appropriate action.

It is widely accepted that resulting actions combined to produce a theology and a concept of church that was, in some respects, quite different from that of Europe or North America. Less obvious, however, is the enormous range of cultures and diverse and rapidly changing realities that exist side by side within Latin America, demanding a multiplicity of responses from the church at the most local levels. The bishops realized that the challenge for pastors and bishops alike is to find effective ways to meet the spiritual and temporal needs of parishioners within individual parishes and at the same time maintain close bonds with the universal church, while remaining mindful that a very different pastoral plan may be needed in an adjacent parish.

The Vatican, Centralization, and Subsidiarity

The current Vatican position on decision-making is closer to centralization than to the principle of subsidiarity. It is centralized to a significantly greater degree than was envisioned by the Second Vatican Council or than is favored by many of the bishops of Latin America and the Caribbean. However, there is no indication of Vatican intent to attempt to return to the degree of centralization that existed during the early 1950s, the era that ended the European worker-priest movement and silenced progressive theologians including Yves Congar, Henri de Lubac, and Marie-Dominique Chenu.

The pontificate of Pius XII (1939–58) marked the completion of the near-absolute papal supremacy initiated by Pius IX (1846–78). Over the intervening century, the pope and the Roman Curia, for the first time in history, had come effectively to hold the power of appointment of all the bishops in the church. A neoscholastic orthodoxy was imposed on the church in Leo XIII's 1879 encyclical, *Aeterni patris,* and consolidated by Pius X's intervention and simultaneous condemnation of "Modernism" in *Pascendi gregis* (1907). Although surprising to some, John XXIII (1958–63) who attempted to reassert the importance of the study of Latin (*Veterum sapientiae,* 1962) also convoked the Second Vatican Council (1962–65) which brought the excessive centralization of papal power during the preceding century to a definite end. In the council's central document on the church, *Lumen gentium,* the bishops returned to the early church's emphasis on the significance of the local church and explicitly recognized that the local bishop's office is acquired through his consecration, not through papal delegation. In an obvious attempt to finesse the ancient battle between conciliarism (governance of the church by the body of bishops) and an autocratic papacy, the council fathers proclaimed the ultimate authority of the college of bishops, though never without the presidency of the bishop of Rome.

Joseph Ratzinger (now Pope Benedict XVI), during his tenure as theologian and *peritus* at Vatican II, expressed concern about *Gaudium et spes.* Both before he became cardinal-archbishop of Munich in 1977, and during succeeding decades, while serving as prefect of the Congregation for the Doctrine of the Faith, he expressed displeasure with the manner in which some postconciliar reforms were implemented.

To date, however, there have been no papal reinterpretations of *Gaudium et spes* or other conciliar documents. The early years of Benedict's papacy have been moderate for the most part and have respected both orthopraxis and Catholic social teaching. While attending the World Congress of Families in Valencia, Spain, in July 2006, the pope explained why he had refrained from criticizing Spanish social policies that are strenuously opposed by the Spanish church and had chosen to offer the Catholic vision of family as a positive alternative:

> Christianity, Catholicism isn't a collection of prohibitions; it's a positive option. It's very important that we look at it again because this idea has almost completely disappeared today. We've heard so much about what is not allowed that now it's time to say: we have a positive idea to offer.... The human person must always be respected. But all this is clearer if you say it first in a positive way.[1]

As John L. Allen, Vatican correspondent for the *Tablet* (U.K.), has written, "this effort to phrase the Christian fundamentals in a positive key has become something of a leitmotif. Having been responsible for expressing the 'noes' of the Catholic Church for twenty years, Ratzinger as pope appears determined to articulate what he sees as its much deeper 'yes.' [But] to date [April 2007], expectations of a 'Catholic fundamentalist' papacy have been confounded."[2] In the years since 2007, little if anything has changed to challenge Allen's judgment. One need look no further than Benedict's first two encyclicals, *Deus caritas est* (2005) and *Spe salvi* (2006), where he clearly and carefully expounds a fresh perspective on traditional Catholic teachings that is primarily pastoral and most certainly not fundamentalist.

Promotion of Christian fundamentals without becoming rigidly fundamentalist lies at the core of Pope John XXIII's insistence that the Catholic Church — a diverse and broadly inclusive church, both by choice and necessity — must continuously learn from, and adapt to, the rapidly changing modern world. Since his papacy, progressive churchmen and women have reiterated this concept of church: that it must encourage the free exchange of ideas, not silence that exchange, value orthopraxis over orthodoxy, and never forget that the mission is far more important than the mechanisms. This is the *ecclesia semper reformanda,* that is, a pilgrim church, self-criticizing rather than self-congratulatory, desiring to learn and to grow, constantly striving for better understanding of the great Mystery, all of which Karl Rahner, S.J. (1904–84), and other theologians have been continuously articulating since Vatican II.

The Preferential Option for the Poor Today

Among the vast majority of experienced Latin American priests the preferential option for the poor, which was broadened at Aparecida into the "preferential and evangelizing option for the poor," is regarded not only as a guiding principle but also as one of the most crucial elements of their pastorates. Younger priests, who increasingly come from wealthier families and who grew up under conditions quite different from those experienced by most of their parishioners, often leave the seminaries with more conservative viewpoints, but pastoral realities teach many — perhaps most — of them that the preferential option is essential for the physical, social, and spiritual well-being, and not infrequently, to the very survival of many millions of destitute people.

This reality is clearly reflected in the *Synthesis of Contributions Received for the Fifth General Conference of Latin American bishops* (May 2006):

In many Latin American countries, most of [the] Catholic population is made up of poor people who live excluded from the material, cultural, and social riches present in our countries. The preferential option for the poor distinguished the Church of the region and was influential in other churches. Today, this option faces new challenges that demand its renewal, so that it may manifest the fullness of its evangelical roots, its urgency, and its gospel riches.[3]

The bishops of Latin America and the Caribbean reaffirmed the option for the poor six times during the Fifth General Council, citing it as one of "the pastoral aspects that had the greatest resonance in the life of the Church" (N21); calling for a new integrating synthesis between the option for the poor and care for the middle class (N82); affirming the option as a major Christological criterion for the missionary path of the church (N165); recognizing the evangelization of the poor as the great messianic sign that Christians are called to live as church, see Luke 7:22 (N165); and citing weaknesses in the option as a sin within the individual Christian that must be repented and corrected (N79).

Significantly, the bishops called for further renewal, consolidation, and permanence of the option for the poor:

> In our time, we tend to defend excessively spaces of privacy and enjoyment, and we let ourselves be infected by individualistic consumerism. Hence our option for the poor runs the risk of remaining on a theoretical or merely emotional level, without really affecting our behaviors and our decisions. This generic option must be turned into a permanent attitude that is reflected in concrete options and gestures (cf. *Deus caritas est* [Benedict XVI's first encyclical, 2005], 28, 31). That means first devoting time to the poor, giving them friendly attention, listening to them with interest, accompanying them in the most difficult moments, choosing them for sharing hours, weeks, and years of our lives, and seeking them for the transformation of their situation. Jesus proposed it with how he acted and with his words: "When you hold a banquet, invite the poor, the crippled, the lame, the blind." (Luke 14:13)[4]

In 1968, at the extraordinary conference at Medellín, the bishops of Latin America sought "the presence of the Church in the current transformation of Latin America in the light of Vatican Council II." The preferential option for the poor was only one of many creative applications of conciliar renewal to a continent gripped by poverty, acute social injustice, and institutionalized sin, but it soon became a cornerstone of the Latin American church's new dedication to a Christianity that unites faith with justice, with promotion of people and societies, and with service to the kingdom, all in accord with the teachings of Jesus Christ.

Nearly four decades later, the option continues to serve as a lifeline to countless millions of marginalized people and is a key element of the church's social mission. Once controversial, it has since been almost universally accepted and has been incorporated into canon law, which states: "[The Christian faithful] are also obliged to promote social justice, and mindful of the precept of the Lord, to assist the poor from their own resources."[5] The option has been reaffirmed by the Latin

American Bishops at four consecutive CELAM conferences and by four successive pontiffs, most recently by Pope Benedict, who said in Aparecida on May 11, 2007, "The poor are the privileged audience for the gospel." Clearly, the preferential and evangelizing option for the poor is in place as intended on the continent of its birth and within the church.

The CEBs

Contrary to periodic reports of their impending demise, the *Comunidades Eclesiales de Base* are alive, thriving, and continuing to fulfill a multiplicity of vital roles across Latin America, and on the other continents as well. Some Latin American CEBs exist in forms that would be almost unrecognizable to the pioneering CEB members of the late 1960s and 1970s, and many of these may well transform themselves into still other forms. Conversely, other CEBs have changed little since they were first formed in the immediate aftermath of the Medellín Conference. Both models, and the countless others along the continuum between them, are fulfilling their intended roles as perennial works-in-progress that exist to meet the needs of particular groups of individuals at a specific time and place, and these continue to adapt themselves to new missions as soon as they have fulfilled their original purpose. Thinking "on their feet" and adapting rapidly to the changing needs of their communities is a clear indication of their success, not of failure or disarray.

An excellent summary of contemporary CEBs is contained in *Do Vaticano II a um novo concílio (2004)* by Dom Luiz Alberto Gómez de Souza, former executive director of the Centro de Estatística Religiosa e Investigações Sociais research center in Rio de Janeiro and a former visiting fellow at the University of Notre Dame's Helen Kellogg Institute for International Studies: "The CEBs continue to play an active role in society, from assistential activities to mobilizations and involvement in associations, syndicates, and parties as well as in national campaigns."[6] This study further reports that CEBs in Brazil appear as a consolidated experience. The most successful CEBs make special efforts to attract young people, both to better serve the youth and to revitalize the communities. Women are in the majority (approximately 62 percent of the membership), and this contributes to a certain empowerment for them within the church and in local civic society. Most members come from the middle and lower-middle socioeconomic classes. Most CEBs emphasize the role of the Mass, which also provides a space for communion.[7] Active support from the church hierarchy has waxed and waned over the years, but reports of condemnations of CEBs are unfounded. There have been instructions to the CEBs from the Vatican and from the Latin American bishops, but these have been offered as constructive criticism and guidance, not as efforts to constrain. The *Instrumentum laboris* (1997) for the Synod of America, in Rome in

1997, calls base ecclesial communities "the primary cells of the Church structure" and views them as being "responsible for the richness of faith and its expansion, as well as for the promotion of the person and development."

In his postsynodal exhortation *Ecclesia in America* (1999), Pope John Paul II recognized the CEBs' ability to renew parishes by enabling each to become a community of communities (N41), and their ability to promote interpersonal bonds within the Catholic Church (N73). In *Redemptorio missio* (1990), John Paul II emphasized the evangelizing roles of CEBs (N51) after personally observing some of the results produced by Chilean CEBs, which have remained a pastoral priority of the Chilean Episcopal Conference since 1969.

In May 2006 in Quito, Ecuador, CELAM sponsored a continental meeting, "Small Christian Communities: Schools for the Followers and Missioners of Jesus Christ." Approximately fifty bishops, priests, male and female members of religious orders, and lay members of CEBs from eighteen nations gathered to share detailed information about the successes, failures, and challenges experienced by CEBs across the continent, and to form realistic assessments of the communities' future. Many of the delegates reported difficulties in recruiting members in large cities and among increasingly transient segments of society who would remain committed — a difficulty shared by many urban churches as well — but they concluded that CEBs are doing well overall.

After three days of intensive discussion, the delegates were able to offer specific recommendations to help CEBs overcome challenges and avoid pitfalls:

- reduction of CEB dependence upon individual bishops who might or might not consider them a priority within their dioceses

- recognition that CEBs are, and must remain, works-in-progress and that they must be provided with "missionary space" to take on new forms and to move in new directions, true to their roots

- heightened respect for the works of the Spirit in the grassroots of the church, and for the prophetic role of the CEBs

- greater awareness that CEBs are not merely mass movements, but are the nucleus of the present and future church, as well as its ancestor

- renewed support for CEBs, both as concepts and as fully functional entities flowing from the teachings of the Second Vatican Council and from the Medellín and Puebla Conferences

The participants at the Quito meeting took these recommendations back to their homelands and to the planning sessions of CELAM V. Though the Conference of Latin American Bishops gave strong support to the CEBs in the text they issued before the Fifth General Conference in May 2007, in the Vatican's view that general conference did not actually add its support in its vote on May 30. Cardinal Giovanni Batista Re, the chair of the Pontifical Commission for Latin America, stated that although the text as a whole received a clear majority of the votes cast, not only did the sections concerning CEBs draw only 72 votes of a possible 261, but according to the official procedures of the conference, for a vote to pass a two-thirds vote was needed. Thus, the Vatican-approved document presents a decidedly minimal vision for the CEBs. There is no mention of their prophetic role and no recognition of the need for support from their parishes and their dioceses. Instead the document implies fear of the CEBs and of leadership from below. It respects the Medellín emphasis on CEBs as basic cells of the church, but it mixes them with an array of other ecclesial movements, increasing the risk that the CEBs will lose their specific identity. Despite this setback, the CEBs will continue to function as a model of the church at the service of the poor, contending against structural sin, but there is little question that the alterations made to the final document have made the fulfillment of the CEBs' mission more difficult.

The Church and Social Issues:
Reproductive Rights, Homosexuals, and the Role of Women

Dom Luiz Alberto Gómez de Souza has presented a succinct and accurate overview of these and other issues which, though currently unresolved, cannot be allowed to remain so indefinitely:

> Today, there are many restricted areas of sexuality and reproductive behavior, celibacy of the clergy, and access of women to the various ecclesiastic ministries. In spite of some overtures, such as that of John Paul II at Assisi, the ecumenical and interreligious exchanges are frustrated by many manifestations like the Eucharistic document of the same pope. Some voices have been heard suggesting a new Council but at the moment it seems premature in view of the prevailing ecclesiastic conditions. However, a conciliar process must be prepared. The most important thing is the continuance of an ecclesial and pastoral practice which is experimental and renewing, silent, subversive, and patient, steadily staying ahead of today's institutional politics, and perhaps preparing underground surprises for tomorrow.
>
> In the Church today, there is, therefore, a growing demand to reopen a debate on themes noted above that have remained frozen: sexuality, participation of women in the religious ministries, imposed celibacy of the clergy, inter-religious dialogue, and, especially, shared participation which is nothing other than democratic ecclesial practice.
>
> Who knows, this may form part of a long conciliar process in a future pontificate, while probably not in that of Benedict XVI. If the Church of the

second millennium was a Church with power concentrated in the clergy, a Church may arise with the active and decisive presence of all the faithful.[8]

Although somewhat less controversial than many other issues, the role of women within the church and within secular society is by far the largest issue in terms of the number of persons it directly impacts.

Section 2 of the *Synthesis of Contributions Received for the Fifth General Conference* for CELAM V (2006), entitled "Faces That Question Us," presents a troubling portrait of the realities encountered by all too many Latin American women.

Countless women of every condition have suffered a double exclusion by reason of their socioeconomic situation and their sex. They are not valued in their dignity, they are left alone and abandoned, they are not sufficiently recognized for their selfless sacrifice and every heroic generosity in the care and education of their children or in the transmission of the faith in the family, nor their indispensable and special participation in building a more humane social life and building up the Church in the merging of its Petrine and Marian dimensions sufficiently appreciated or promoted.[9]

Several years ago, Sister Aline Steur, C.S.C., a veteran missioner in Latin America, made similar observations: "Women continue to offer the main support of the Church and to comprise the overwhelming majority of its active members, but the inclusion of women and women's issues does not reflect their numbers, their contributions, or their needs."[10]

CELAM V, which included 25 women among the 267 participants (religious, laity, *periti* [experts], and observers) gave the role of women more attention than any previous General Conference of CELAM.

The Vatican-approved final document praises motherhood as "an excellent mission of women" but also states that motherhood "does not exclude the need for their active participation in the construction of society." A later paragraph calls for women to have decision-making roles in the church, and decries "discrimination against women and their frequent absence in organisms of ecclesial decision."

Pope Benedict has made few statements on the role of women but he has expressed strong opposition to divorce, same-sex marriages, and "the risk of deviations in the area of sexuality," and he has pledged that the church will not compromise on these issues. Many Catholics oppose these practices as threats to traditional family structure but those who cite violations of "natural law" and "universal binding norms" stand on weak foundations. Catholic scholars have responded that "natural law," "absolute truth," and "universal binding norms" are elements of ancient Greek metaphysics — not of Scripture.

It is hardly surprising that complex issues with powerful religious, emotional, and social components are causing divisions within and between the Catholic

Church, churches of other denominations, civil authorities, and secular society— none of which think with one mind or speak with one voice. It is understandable that millions of Catholics, clergy and lay alike, especially those who see merits and shortcomings on both sides of pressing social issues, may prefer to avoid struggling with such challenging issues, or may retreat to familiar, comfortable, but ultimately nonfruitful habits and thought patterns. As the Latin American bishops warn, however, failure to apply the church's social teachings to questions which impact human lives is an abdication both of Christian vocation and civic responsibility. Relying on authority figures to make difficult choices is "one more way of being childishly and massively dependent rather than being involved with creativity and constancy."[11]

How, then, are Catholics to seek conditions in which a healthy politics and consequently solutions to social problems can mature? One possible answer may lie in the CELAM bishops' attempt to translate belief in the possibility of a more just world into a concrete reality, making the defense of life "pro-life" in the much broader sense of promoting better lives for every segment of society.

Deacons and Lay Ministers

"I am the only Bible that most people will ever read," a laywoman said recently, while leading scriptural study at a *casa culto*, a 'house church" in Havana. Her statement may sound overblown and self-aggrandizing to those who hear it with a North American or European mentality, but it accurately reflects the prevailing reality faced by the many millions of Latin Americans who must find ways to cope with shortages of ordained clergy, limited church seating capacities, lack of transportation, ethnic or socioeconomic differences that make church members fear they will be unwelcome in the churches of their "betters," and countless other obstacles. For these and many other members of the faithful, lay catechists and deacons are often the primary source of pastoral care and teaching. Recently, for example, Father José Oscar Beozzo, a leading expert on Brazil's religious vocations and training, pointed out that 80 percent of all the Sunday celebrations in Brazil are led by laity, either because there are not enough priests to celebrate Mass or because the faithful are unable to attend traditional churches.

Working within a multiplicity of initiatives at the grassroots of the church, with different degrees of success, lay ministers have long been essential both to the faithful and to the church, and their role continues to grow. They preach the Word to those who would otherwise rarely hear it or might not understand it in more formal modes of expression. They preside at the celebrations, comfort the ill and the bereaved, and find countless ways both to animate the journey and to contribute decisively to the role of the laity as protagonists within the church. For this reason Edward Cleary, O.P., director of Latin American Studies at Providence

College, cites the 1.1 million lay catechists currently active in Latin America as a basic strength of the Catholic Church there.[12]

The bishops of Latin America and the Caribbean are keenly aware both of the lay ministers' contributions and of the need to promote a still more active laity, as the *Synthesis* of CELAM V makes clear.

> The whole Church is missionary. What is needed for this truth to become reality is that lay people be trained, the Christian and secular character of their vocation be promoted actively without fear, room be made for them in the church, they be respected in their opinions and initiatives, and that room be opened for them to participate in the decisions of the community; in short, that they be treated as adults in a line of communion and participation (cf. p. 11), as is proper to their baptismal vocation, which they subsequently confirmed sacramentally.[13]

Although there is nothing new in the bishops' position, there seems to have been a significant rise in Vatican support for lay involvement in the church's ministries. Rome has long but cautiously endorsed lay ministries. In Aparecida, however, Pope Benedict urged the laity to join with priests and religious in an ambitious program of evangelization, missionary and pastoral outreach, especially at the urban peripheries, and he strongly endorsed the growth of lay ministries while stressing the need for these ministries to remain in alignment with their pastors and in conformity with the orientation of their dioceses.

A Crisis of Vocations?

Father José Oscar Beozzo has repeatedly warned that Brazil has only 18,000 priests to serve a Catholic population of 140 million — a clergy-to-lay ratio of approximately 1 to 8,600.[14] Both the numbers and the ratios vary from diocese to diocese and from country to country, but all twenty Latin American nations are experiencing shortages of priests and nuns so pronounced that they leave gaping holes in the church's pastoral nets.

Edward Cleary, O.P., recently reported that the number of seminarians throughout Latin America has increased approximately 400 percent since 1972, and that there has been a 70 percent increase in the number of Latin American clergy replacing missionaries from other continents — a reversal of the 1960s, when the Vatican was asking that 10 percent of North American clergy go to Latin America to alleviate the critical shortage of priests.[15] Additionally, there are increasing numbers of lay catechists, as well as tens of millions of lay men and women fulfilling Christian vocations within thousands of CEBs and within faith-in-daily-life endeavors in both urban and rural communities throughout every nation of Central and South America. Despite their apparent contradiction of each other, both observations are accurate. Every continent is experiencing a crisis of vocations, but Latin America is responding to this challenge imaginatively and with great success. Certainly, the shortage of priests, sisters, and brothers throughout Latin America is nothing new, nor is it as pronounced as it was throughout most of the past five hundred years. At Medellín in 1968, there was a "crisis of vocations" that was even more profound than it is today. The Latin American church overcame that crisis as it has overcome many daunting obstacles in its long history.

Charismatic Movements

Both the Vatican and the Latin American bishops have expressed concerns about the number of Latin Americans being drawn away from the Catholic Church by the various Pentecostal movements and by evangelical Protestant churches, but those concerns are frequently misunderstood. Declines in church rolls do not threaten the existence of the Catholic Church in Latin America, nor were they the raison d'être for CELAM V, as some media reports have suggested. The Catholic charismatic movement, sometimes blamed for drawing members away from the mainstream church, is actually having the opposite effect.

Nevertheless, the decrease in the per capita percentage of Catholics in Latin America is very real. In Brazil, for example, the national census reveals that 74 percent of Brazilians identified themselves as Catholics in the year 2000, compared to 89 percent in 1980. Those who identified themselves as Pentecostal, evangelical, or fundamentalist Protestants grew from 7 percent to 15 percent during the same period.[16] Similar trends have been documented in three Mexican states and in four Central and South American nations in addition to Brazil, and a 2007 study conducted by the Pew Hispanic Center/Pew Forum on Religion and Public Life found similar trends among Hispanic-Americans in the United States.[17] Despite such declines, South America is home to more Catholics than all other continents combined, and Brazil remains the nation with the greatest number of Catholics, approximately 140 million.[18]

Pope Benedict undoubtedly had both facts in mind at Aparecida when he called for the members of the Latin American religious community to remain "courageous and effective missionaries" in order to uphold Catholicism as the dominant religious force on the continent. The Vatican had already conducted a comprehensive study of what it termed "the expansion of the sects," a terminology that itself is problematic.

The bishops concluded that much of the attraction of the evangelical and Pentecostal churches resulted from proselytizing efforts that are, in some cases, more a matter of marketing than of evangelization. Significantly, however, the bishops identified four specific weaknesses within Catholic parishes: shortage of pastoral agents, inadequate evangelization in the past, deficient pastoral care for the poor and the alienated, and lack of pastoral outreach to those who were baptized but no longer participate. The bishops proclaimed the need for concerted pastoral actions to minister more fully to the underserved and disaffected, as well as campaigns to reassure inactive Catholics that the church will welcome those who wish to recommit themselves.[19]

Although the major part of those who join evangelical or Pentecostal churches come out of the Catholic Church, most researchers agree that the majority of these come from the nonpracticing sector of Catholicism.[20] Their subsequent dropout rate from the new churches is high, probably in the 40 percent range. Some dropouts continue to "church hop" for years, while others give up religious practice altogether.[21]

Except for a need for a more evangelical style of faith and a more animated liturgy than many Catholics are accustomed to, charismatic Catholics seem to share few of the characteristics of those who choose fundamentalist Protestant churches. This is one conclusion reached in the detailed 2007 survey conducted by the Pew Center on Religion and Public Life. As its title implies, "Changing Faiths: Latinos and the Transformation of American Religion" surveyed only U.S. Hispanic Catholics, but the Pew Hispanic Center's analysts are convinced that many of the findings are equally true among charismatic Catholics across the American continents.

The Pew study of 4,016 Hispanic-American adults, conducted between August and October 2006, produced the following findings:

- Despite a decline in the percentage of U.S. Hispanics who self-identify as Catholic — a decline due primarily to those who left to join evangelical or Pentecostal churches — 68 percent of U.S. Hispanics consider themselves Catholics.

- Approximately one-third of all U.S. Catholics are of Latin American origin or ancestry, and that percentage is growing due to immigration and birthrate.

- Hispanics differ little from the general U.S. population in most respects, but "renewal Christianity" has attained much more resonance among Hispanic than non-Hispanic Catholics, only 12 percent of whom consider themselves charismatics. Conversely, the analysts identified 54 percent of Hispanic Catholics as charismatics, based upon "displays of excitement and enthusiasm such as raising hands, shouting, or jumping" during Masses, or participating in prayer groups where participants pray for miraculous healing or deliverance, or speak in tongues.

- Hispanic Protestants were even more likely to join "renewal" churches, with 57 percent in that category: 31 percent Pentecostal and 26 percent charismatic Protestants. In contrast, less than 20 percent of non-Hispanic Protestants are renewalists.

◆ Conversion from Catholicism to other faiths was much more common among second- and third-generation Hispanic-Americans than among recent immigrants. The large majority of those who left Catholicism joined evangelical churches.

◆ Sixty-one percent of former Catholics who became evangelical Protestants said they found the Mass "unexciting," and 36 percent said that was a factor in leaving the church. Forty-six percent disapprove of Catholic restrictions on divorce but only 5 percent claimed this as their reason for leaving.

◆ Among Catholic charismatics, "there's absolutely no evidence that [charismatic religious practices] diminish or undercut their Catholic orthodoxy or their connection to parish life," says Luis Lugo, director of the Pew Forum. To the contrary, involvement in the charismatic style of religious practice strengthens religious identity. "Whether Catholic, Anglican, or mainline Protestant, Latinos who adopt a more charismatic style of practicing their faith remain within their original churches and become stronger in their religious commitment," Lugo reports.

Far from hastening loss of church membership, the rapidly growing Catholic charismatic movement is helping the church to share in the religious renewal that is sweeping across many areas of Latin America. The charismatics also help retain those active Catholics who seek a "high energy" Mass and the practice of charisms, and who might otherwise leave the church to join one of the fundamentalist Protestant denominations. In Brazil and many other nations of Latin America — as in portions of Africa, Europe, and the United States as well — the rapid growth of the Catholic charismatic movement has made charismatics a major constituency in many parishes.

Pope John Paul II regarded the Catholic charismatic movement as integral to the renewal of the Catholic Church. Pope Benedict XVI has cautioned charismatics to remain fully grounded in the universal church but has otherwise acknowledged the many positive elements of the movement.

Concerning those persons who do not follow traditional or charismatic Catholicism, or who turn away from a succession of other churches as well, the Latin American Bishops have stated: "The example of Christ also asks from us a respectful relationship with our brothers and sisters in other Christian communities and with those who follow other religions."[22]

Unfortunately, this degree of ecumenism was not always evident in Aparecida. Although CELAM V welcomed seven observers representing the Anglican, Baptist, Jewish, Lutheran, Methodist, and Presbyterian traditions, many observers —

both Catholic and non-Catholic — have expressed agreement with the *Tablet,* a prominent independent Catholic newspaper published in the United Kingdom, which headlined a recent story "Conference Weak on Ecumenism." Bishop Ricardo Ramírez of Las Cruces, New Mexico, said: "If [CELAM] has any weaknesses from a North American perspective, it is its very limited acknowledgement of ecumenism, which is totally subsumed under the challenge of the 'sects' — the term used in Latin America for proselytizing Christian groups."[23] Although there had been agreement at the Synod for America in 1997 to cease using the word "sects," the disparaging term was used repeatedly during the General Conference.

Despite several clarifications and expressions of respect from prominent members of CELAM, the perception of a general ecumenical weakness — extending beyond semantics — persists in some quarters. "The Rev. Néstor Míguez, an Argentine Methodist observer at Aparecida, agreed with Bishop Ramírez about the lack of ecumenism," the *Tablet* reports. "This was 'not envisaged in the prior agenda and the Pope said not a single word about it. Curial cardinals came from several dicasteries [courts of justice of the Vatican bureaucracy], but no one from the Council for Promoting Christian Unity.... There should always be an ecumenical approach to reading the Bible in Christian communities.' "[24]

Religious Pluralism and the Catholic Church

Although religious pluralism is often perceived as a synonym for ecumenism or religious tolerance, the reform-minded Cardinal Giacomo Lercaro of Bologna (d. 1976) was much more accurate when he defined religious pluralism as "a struggle toward a Church that is truly Catholic yet truly catholic." His point, of course, was that mutual respect and understanding, harmonious coexistence, righteousness without self-righteousness, willingness both to teach and to learn, and ability to disagree without animosity must be fostered within the church as well as between the church and other religions and religious denominations. His use of "yet" instead of "and" reflects the fact that positive goals are all too frequently at odds with each other.

Nearly half a century later, the difficult but vitally important struggle toward catholic Catholicism continues, a fact reflected in Section 4.1 of the *Synthesis of Contributions Received for the Fifth General Conference:*

> The cultural and religious pluralism of contemporary society impacts strongly on the Church. There are other sources of meaning competing with it, relativizing and weakening its social impact and its pastoral action. Not all Catholics were prepared to resist this multiplicity of discourses and practices present in society. Indeed, this fact has been manifested in a certain silent distancing from the Church by many who join other religious beliefs

or institutions with little thought. This situation is aggravated by the ethical and religious relativism of contemporary culture. However, pluralism opens spaces for personal freedom and conscious religious option. All this shows the urgent need for greater Christian formation of the laity, so as to allow it to develop a posture of convinced identification with its Christian vocation and evangelical discernment in the face of this pluralism.

Moreover, the emergence in our time of subjectivity, accompanied by a growing participation of our contemporaries in cultural conquests, also represents a challenge to the Church. A statement is no longer accepted merely because it comes from an authority. An adequate foundation must be offered for doctrinal or ethical discourse, because everyone wants his or her personal autonomy and freedom to be respected; thus as Pope Benedict XVI says, the Church should intervene on the various issues in the life of society "through rational argumentation" (*Deus caritas est,* 28).[25] It should be noted that the weakening of the sources of meaning in society ultimately generates anguish and malaise in those who most seek refuge and distraction in a growing consumerism. The Christian message undoubtedly offers solid frameworks for personal integration and shared social life. It must be announced to our contemporaries with an open and dialogue-oriented posture.

The Catholic Church of Latin America did indeed come into its own with the Second Vatican Council and the CELAM convocations. It continues its mission today, concretely confronting the challenges of Latin American reality and displaying a deep sense of commitment and perseverance in its quest to become *ecclesia semper reformanda.*

Benedict XVI's Episcopal Appointments

Many of the episcopal appointments that Pope Benedict made early in his pontificate had been initiated by Pope John Paul II. Thus, these appointments may or may not accurately reflect the type of churchmen that Pope Benedict sees as models for the church in the twenty-first century. The majority of the more recent appointments into the Holy See and in dioceses throughout Latin America have been ideological moderates who have a strong pastoral orientation. If continued, such appointments bode well for Latin America, but it will take time to see what direction these bishops will take and to what extent they will be influenced by Aparecida.

Benedict has not named an extraordinary number of active or ordinary cardinals. The new prelates include three who head archdioceses in Latin America (Caracas, São Paulo, and Monterrey) and another is Argentinean and a member of the Vatican Curia. The four active cardinals have conservative credentials theologically, pastorally, and politically, but it is too early to conclude that the brutal realities suffered by their urban flocks and the spirit and directives of Aparecida will not inform their eventual outlooks.

John Allen, writing in the *National Catholic Reporter*, believes that the pope's visit to Aparecida may offer some clues regarding the issues he wants addressed by his future appointments as well as about the relationship between the Latin American church and the Vatican:

> Brazil has offered an intriguing mix of what many regard as "the real Ratzinger," with tough talk on abortion, marriage, priestly celibacy, and ecclesiastical discipline, along with the more pastoral Benedict — praising the late Archbishop Oscar Romero of El Salvador; urging work on behalf of the poor, the Amazon rain forest, and in general for "a more just and fraternal society" and, by virtue of his very choice to be here, offering an olive branch to a Brazilian church long seen as estranged from Rome.[26]

In May of 2007, while flying to Brazil to inaugurate CELAM V, reporters reminded the pontiff that Pope John Paul II had designated Archbishop Romero as one of the "new martyrs" of the last millennium.[27] Pope Benedict responded: "I have no doubt he [Romero] will be beatified. I know that the cause is proceeding well at the Congregation for the Cause of the Saints.... He was certainly a great witness for the faith, a man of great Christian virtue who was committed to peace and against dictatorship."[28]

Although definitive conclusions cannot be drawn from a few remarks or from a single papal visit, the pope's esteem for Archbishop Romero — who was, above all, the ultimate pastoral leader — may shed light on Benedict's vision of his own pastorate of the universal church and of the bishops that should lead the Latin American church in this new millennium.

Nor can there be doubt that many Latin American churchmen and millions of Latin American laypersons who revere "St. Romero" would agree that the church needs bishops who strive to model themselves after Oscar Arnulfo Romero y Galdámez, fourth archbishop of San Salvador. Speaking at Notre Dame in 2002, Cardinal Oscar Andrés Rodríguez Maradiaga, S.D.B., of Tegucigalpa, Honduras, said in this regard: "In pastors like Monsignor Romero, we have the figure of the 'Bishop who is a servant of the Gospel of Christ for the hope of the world.' With bishops like him, the Church can truly be the hope for the world."[29]

In closing, I quote a passage from the Conclusion of the Aparecida document that encapsulates much of CELAM's vision of the church's future in Latin America, a vision of "integrating synthesis" that offers "prophetic wisdom" for the world:

In the twentieth century, the life of the Latin American Church was marked by various tendencies, sometimes at odds with one another. We believe that the time has come to create, through a great love for the truth and a fraternal openness and a respectful dialogue, new integrating syntheses. For example: between evangelization and "sacramentalization," between witness and proclamation, between proclamation and denunciation, between ministry among the popular masses and formation of the lay people, between preferential option for the poor and care for the middle class and leadership groups, between ministry and spirituality and social commitment, between traditional values and contemporary searching, between social liberation and developing the faith, between theology and praxis, between worship and life witness, between local and national causes and openness to Latin America and the world, between Catholic identity and openness to dialogue with those who are different. The aim is not to weaken or relativize any of these demands, but rather that the Person of Jesus Christ enlighten all these realities and allow them to be properly interconnected.[30]

Notes

1. John L. Allen, "The Real Ratzinger Revealed," *Tablet,* April 14, 2007.
2. Ibid.
3. *Synthesis of Contributions Received for the Fifth General Conference* (2006), N346.
4. Ibid., N224.
5. 1983 CIC, canon 222 §2.
6. Luiz Alberto Gómez de Souza, S.J., *Do Vaticano II a um novo concílio* (São Paulo: Loyola, 2004).
7. Ibid.
8. Luiz Alberto Gómez de Souza, S.J., *Latin America and the Catholic Church: Points of Convergence and Divergence 1960–2005,* Working Paper 334 (Notre Dame: Helen Kellogg Institute for International Studies, 2007).
9. *Synthesis of Contributions Received for the Fifth General Conference* (2006), N51.
10. Interview of Sr. Aline Steur, C.S.C., November 1, 2005.
11. *Synthesis of Contributions Received for the Fifth General Conference* (2006), N280.
12. "Featured Q&A with Our Board of Advisors," *Inter-American Dialogue,* March 27, 2007.
13. *Synthesis of Contributions Received for the Fifth General Conference* (2006), N349.
14. John L. Allen, "Benedict's Priorities: Feeding Humanity's Spiritual and Material Hunger," *NCRcafe,* May 11, 2007.
15. "Featured Q&A with Our Board of Advisors."
16. "Pope Calls Latin America 'Continent of Hope,'" *Associated Press,* May 13, 2007.
17. Patricia Zapor, "Study Finds U.S. Hispanics Drawn to Charismatic Churches," *Catholic News Service,* April 26, 2007.
18. Allen, "Benedict's Priorities."
19. *Synthesis of Contributions Received for the Fifth General Conference* (2006), N348.
20. "Featured Q&A with Our Board of Advisors."
21. *Synthesis of Contributions Received for the Fifth General Conference* (2006), N347.

22. "Conference Weak on Ecumenism," *Tablet,* June 2, 2007.

23. Ibid.

24. Ibid.

25. Pope Benedict XVI's encyclical *Deus caritas est,* 2005.

26. Allen, "Benedict's Priorities."

27. *Commemorazione ecumenica dei testimoni della fede del XX secolo,* città del Vaticano, 2000, 104.

28. Reported by the Italian news agencies *ANSA* and *APCOM* on May 9, 2007.

29. *Monsignor Romero: A Bishop for the Third Millennium* (Notre Dame, Ind.: University of Notre Dame Press, 2004).

30. *Synthesis of Contributions Received for the Fifth General Conference* (2006), N82.

Index